DICTIONARY OF MATHEMATICS

D0082604

DICTIONARY OF MATHEMATICS

J. A. GLENN
British Campus, University of Evansville

G. H. LITTLER
Derbyshire College of Higher Education

Diagrams drawn by David Parkins

Harper & Row, Publishers
London

Cambridge
Mexico City
New York
Philadelphia

San Francisco
São Paulo
Singapore
Sydney

Copyright © 1984 J. A. Glenn and G. H. Littler

First published 1984
Reprinted 1987

Harper & Row Publishers Ltd
28 Tavistock Street
London WC2E 7PN

British Library Cataloguing in Publication Data

Glenn, John
    Dictionary of mathematics
    1. Mathematics–Dictionaries
    I. Title   II. Littler, Graham
    510'.3'21   QA5

    ISBN 0-06-318292-0

Typeset, printed and bound in Malta by Interprint Limited.

To Joyce and Peggy for their patience and support.

CONTENTS

Advisory Panel

S. Branson, Head of Mathematics, The King's School, Grantham.
T. H. F. Brissenden, Department of Education, University of Wales, Swansea.
F. J. Budden, formerly Head of Mathematics, Royal Grammar School, Newcastle upon Tyne.
F. W. Flisher, Schools Inspector for Mathematics, Nottinghamshire County Council.
K. E. Hirst, Faculty of Mathematical Studies, University of Southampton.
Dr. M. Jackson, Department of Mathematics, University of Nottingham.
J. T. Mathis, William Jewell College, Liberty, Missouri.
W. Middleton, Department of Mathematics and Computer Studies, Sunderland Polytechnic.
N. N. Morris, Head of Mathematics Education, Derbyshire College of Higher Education.
Dr. H. R. Neave, Department of Mathematics, University of Nottingham.
H. Neill, formerly Department of Mathematics, University of Durham.
J. Nuthall, Department of Mathematics, Leicester Polytechnic.
N. Pannell, formerly Headmistress, Kesteven and Grantham Girls' School.
Dr. A. Rothery, Principal Lecturer in Mathematics, Worcester College of Higher Education.
A. Thomas, Department of Mathematics and Statistics, Sheffield Polytechnic.
S. Timperley, Ruston Gas Turbines Ltd., Lincoln.
Dr. D. Woodrow, Department of Mathematics, Manchester Polytechnic.

PREFACE

This dictionary is written for a wide but nevertheless well-defined range of users, from sixth-formers who study mathematics with the intention of continuing it as a main or subsidiary subject, to the first years of institutions of higher education, polytechnic or university mathematicians. It began with a collation of the indexes of some twenty textbooks well known and widely used over this range, together with a few works on the history and philosophy of mathematics from which we made a necessarily limited selection. These last led us to add terms like *primitive root* and *tractrix* unlikely to occur in syllabuses at our chosen level, but which could be met by any interested student who reads around the subject. We added, for special attention, fundamental concepts such as *point* and *theorem* that rarely appear in the textbook indexes and finally included, for brief definition, the ordinary vocabulary of O-level courses.

Together with the standard vocabulary of geometry and analysis, entries are included from statistics, logic, descriptive topology, structural algebra and number theory, with selected entries from areas in which mathematics is applied. As a matter of policy we do not include the vocabulary of modern computing science, apart from a few key words. This vocabulary is now large enough to swamp a dictionary of mathematics and is in rapid transitional development. The exclusion was a joint decision of authors and publisher.

We are fortunate in finding a panel of advisors who between them were or had been active in mathematical education over the entire range or beyond. These very helpfully agreed to send us notes and suggestions for the treatment of entries, aimed at the levels appropriate to their own experience. From these notes we wrote up the entries. We are completely responsible for their final form, and are solely to blame for mistakes, omissions and inelegancies.

We tried to form our text into a set of words closed with respect to mathematical definition, with any term used in an entry checked for its inclusion on the index list, which thus began to expand as writing proceeded. The entries added proved to be among the key concepts of mathematics, words used on every page of the texts but not listed, except in a special context, by their indexers. The student becomes completely familiar with a working vocabulary of words like *plus*, *add* and *divide* from early days at school, at an age when formal discussion of such terms would not make educational sense. We have tried to isolate these words from their everyday uses, and to treat them as part of the foundations of mathematical education.

Unfortunately our first complete draft proved longer than the publishers could accept and we had to cut back. Many of the elementary entries (elementary in the school sense as distinct from logically fundamental) had to go. So, regrettably, did many of the diagrams and, from within the entries, a lot of incidental information included for its interest. We did, however, retain those words, in common use outside mathematics, which are given within it a precision that everyday language does not need. We still have a set of definitions sufficiently closed to make indicated cross-referencing unnecessary. Any term we use in a definition, apart from the language of lower school mathematics (and even here when a word needs a more precise treatment) itself appears as an entry, and we assume that the user can move from term to term without instructions to do so. We sometimes use 'see' or 'see also' to direct attention to related topics, but otherwise hope that we have avoided circularity of definition. Unavoidably, 'elementary' entries such as *multiplication* will refer to more difficult concepts such as *recursive definition*; but in no other way can such words be given their full status within mathematics.

We owe much to our advisors, each of whom took on an allotted set of related terms that reflected a personal interest. We are particularly grateful to Norman Morriss, who undertook to read each batch of manuscript slips as prepared for the first draft, on the principle that if he could understand them anybody could. We also thank the small group of three sixth-formers who as typical users helped to evaluate the first draft sent to the publishers. These were Michael Hughes, Robert Hunt and Jonathan Porter, and we wish them well in their future studies. We are also indebted to the patience and skill of Sheila Harris, who typed the entire text in both first and final draft.

J. A. Glenn
G. H. Littler

A note on the arrangement of entries

Many terms common in mathematics, roughly half of those in this dictionary, consist of two or more words: *partial fractions, vector triple product,* the *mean value theorem* and so on. Since the attributive part of such terms is usually more important than the main noun, as in *linear equation, quadratic equation, Diophantine equation, Laplace's equation* ... we list such terms once only under the first word of the form in which they are usually used. The word *equation* itself has a single entry giving the general definition.

We have, of course, had to make decisions. One commonly hears *Theorem of Pythagoras,* but we have entered it under *Pythagoras' theorem,* like *mean value theorem.* Another example is *point of accumulation* and *accumulation point.* We have chosen the first form, with a cross-reference to *cluster point,* since this is a synonym likely to be seen in a text book. Such cross references are restricted to synonyms or terms where the interrelation is not obvious. Sets of related words such as *pentagon, hexagon* ... , which could be met in isolation, are entered separately but their definitions are grouped under the one entry *polygon,* with a reference to Greek numerical prefixes. The trigonometric ratios are dealt with in a similar way, although the word *haversine,* as a special form, is given its own definition. Throughout, our aim is to use space for the definitions and monographs instead of for repetitive double entries.

Entries in the dictionary are in strict alphabetical order, ignoring spaces, punctuation and any Greek letters.

Russian names are not given in official transliteration, but in the form most commonly found in the texts.

abacus Any device for performing arithmetical calculations using counters, pebbles or beads arranged in grooves or on rods. Common in the ancient world and still in use in Russia, China (*see suan pan*) and Japan (*see soroban*).

Abbott, E. A. Theologian and classicist (1838–1926) whose *jeu d'esprit* of 1884, *Flatland, by A. Square*, imagined societies of geometrical figures in two, three and four dimensions. It is sometimes claimed that this amusing book anticipated the space-time coordinates of Einstein and Minkowsky, but Abbott's fourth dimension was merely a metric coordinate w added to (x, y, z). The very class-conscious triangles and spheres all existed in independent Newtonian time.

Abelian group *See* commutative group.

Abel, Niels Henrik Norwegian mathematician (1802–1829). He gave the first general proof of the binomial theorem, and in 1824 published the first completely satisfactory proof that equations of degree 5 or more cannot be solved by formulae involving their coefficients. A manuscript left with Cauchy in 1826 was only found in 1830 after Abel's death from tuberculosis. This described the elliptical functions of the type sn u.

Abel-Ruffini theorem P. Ruffini had published (1799) a less satisfactory proof of Abel's demonstration that the general quintic cannot be solved in terms of its coefficients. The theorem is now named after them both.

abscissa Specifically the x coordinate of a point (x, y) on a rectangular cartesian graph, the distance of the point from the y axis on a line along or parallel to the x axis. The corresponding y value is the ordinate.

absolute 1. Used of a physical constant that is numerical and hence independent of the units used, such as the ratio between the mass of a proton and an electron.
2. Not relative to and independent of anything else, as absolute space and time in Newtonian kinematics.
3. The phrase 'absolute Newtonian motion' is sometimes used for motion relative to the centre of the sun.

absolute convergence An infinite series $\sum_{n=1}^{\infty} a_n$ is said to be absolutely convergent if the corresponding series of positive terms $\sum_{n=1}^{\infty} |a_n|$ is convergent.

absolute error The actual as distinct from the proportional relative or percentage error in any measurement or calculation, given by $|x' - x|$, where x' is the measured and x the true value.

absolute maximum *See* maximum.

absolute minimum *See* maximum.

absolute space Newton (1687) postulated a single fixed coordinate system for space and a single independent scale of time measurement, against which dynamic problems could be described. The absolute coordinate system transformed to a moving system by the Galilean Transformation which left space and time intervals invariant. Einstein replaced this by a system in which the Lorentz Transformation related space and time coordinates dependently when in relative motion: the invariant was a function of both space and time.

absolute time *See* absolute space.

absolute value Formally defined for a real number x as the positive square root of x^2, and denoted by $|x|$. It can be thought of as the magnitude of a number with its sign ignored.

● $|-4| = |+4| = 4$

The function $f : x \mapsto |x|$ has the cartesian graph

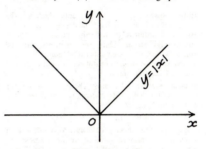

Also called the modulus of x, read as mod x.

absorbing barrier *See* random walk.

abstract 1. Any use of symbols or expressions in mathematics made without reference to specific applications or representations. Thus the distributive law for two binary operations $*$ and O is

$$a * (b \, O \, c) = (a * b) \, O \, (a * c)$$

without specifying the nature either of the operations $*$, O or the elements a, b, c.
2. Used of mathematical systems described by definitions and axioms without direct reference to any physical representation (although such a reference may exist and give importance to the abstract investigations).
3. Also a short description of an article or book, often of value to anyone surveying an area of mathematics for relevant material.

abstract algebra *See* algebraic structure.

abstract geometry The study of abstract spaces using geometrical methods. The points, lines or 'objects' of the space are often left undefined, and relations between them expressed through sets of axioms. Abstract geometry may be metric, as in non-Euclidean geometries, or non-metric, in which case it is usually called point set topology. Theorems are often developed by algebraic or analytic methods, but the general resemblance to the sequences of propositions found in Euclid usually justifies the use of the word geometry. Euclidean theorems appear as special cases.

abstract group A group whose elements consist only of a set of symbols and the structure resulting from combining them. This is usually expressed by a defining relation showing how the group generators combine. For example, an abstract multiplicative group could be given by

$$a^2 = b^2 = c^2 = (ab)^3 = (bc)^3 = (ca)^3 = I$$

A realization of this group is the set of six permutations of three letters taken three at a time.

abstract mathematics Any study in mathematics whose definitions, axioms and theorems do not *necessarily* have a realization either in terms of other mathematical entities or in physical situations. It consists, therefore, in the manipulation of formal symbols according to formal rules. The word 'abstract' does suggest that the concepts originate in the material world (*see*, for example, line, point) although once the abstraction is made mathematics can be generated without further reference to its origins.

abstract space Any set of elements which has the properties of continuity, incidence and order associated intuitively with the points of three-dimensional space. Thus the elements can be functions, vectors or elements called 'points' or 'lines' having assigned properties different from points and lines in Euclidean space.

abundant number Taken by Theon to be a number such that the sum of its divisors is greater than the number itself, as for

● $1 + 2 + 3 + 4 + 6 > 12$

If it is less the number is defective. Also, in the 18th century, any number rounded up for purposes of tabulation, as $\log 5 = 0.699$. Then $\log 3 = 0.477$ was said to be deficient.
See also perfect number.

acceleration The rate of increase of velocity with respect to time, expressed either as $\mathbf{a} = d\mathbf{v}/dt$ or $\mathbf{a} = d^2\mathbf{s}/dt^2$, or commonly as $\mathbf{a} = \dot{\mathbf{v}}$, $\mathbf{a} = \ddot{\mathbf{s}}$. For a general plane position vector $\mathbf{r}$ the acceleration is $\mathbf{a} = \ddot{\mathbf{r}}$.

accuracy The extent to which a numerical result reflects the actual value of a quantity being calculated or measured. It is of importance when the actual value is not known or can only be measured between limits. Thus a length can be given as accurate to two significant figures, to three places of decimals, or to the nearest unit. Accuracy can often be specified as a proportion, as $1:1000$.

Achilles paradox *See* Zeno.

acnode Also called conjugate point. An isolated double point on a real curve at which there are no real tangents, as with $y = (x-2)^2 \sqrt{(x-3)}$ $(x \in \mathbb{R})$

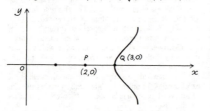

The point $P = (2, 0)$ lies on the curve, but there are no other real points where $x < 3$. From Lat. *acus*, a needle.

Acta Eruditorum The journal founded by Leibnitz in 1684 in which he first published his work in *calculus differentialis* and later replied to accusations that his methods were based on Newton's *analysis per. fluxiones*.

action If the kinetic energy of a body moving from point A at time t_0 to B at t under conservative forces is T, then the action is defined as

$$\int_{t_0}^{t} 2T \, dt.$$

The principle of least action states that for some (but not all) motions, such as trajectories under gravitation, the path taken is such that this integral is a minimum. For zero force this corresponds to Newton's First Law.

acute angle An angle less than one right angle, from Lat. *acutus*, sharpened.
See also obtuse angle.

acute angle hypothesis *See* Saccheri quadrilateral.

addition Any process for combining mathematical entities corresponding to the addition of natural numbers, as defined by counting on (or forming Peano successors), and denoted by the operation symbol +. Read as 'plus' or 'add'.

● $5 + 4 = 5 + 1 + 1 + 1 + 1 = 9$

Definitions of addition for integers and rationals can be constructed using number pairs, and for real numbers according to the adopted definition. The process can also be defined for vectors and matrices. Addition is a binary operation which is commutative, associative and has an identity, denoted 0 (zero) such that for any a

$$a + 0 = 0 + a = a$$

It is conveniently modelled by combining lengths or intervals on the real number line.

addition formulae In elementary trigonometry, formulae of the type $\sin(A \pm B) = \sin A \cos B \pm \cos A \sin B$.

addition law of probability The general addition law states that if A and B are sets of events, then $p(A \cup B) = p(A) + p(B) - p(A \cap B)$. If events A and B are mutually exclusive $p(A \cap B) = 0$ and the law becomes the simple addition law $p(A \cup B) = p(A) + p(B)$.
The law may be extended to any number of mutually exclusive events. It was originally derived intuitively by considering situations arising from events taken to be equiprobable, such as drawing cards from packs; but some modern formulations of probability theory take this law as an axiom.

additive function A function f for which $f(x+y) = f(x) + f(y)$ for all x, y belonging to the domain of f.

additive group Any group for which the binary operation may conveniently be represented by the addition sign +.

additive identity For an operation + (addition) on a set S the additive identity I is a unique element of S such that

$$a + I = I + a = a \text{ for all } a \in S.$$

For the addition of real numbers the identity is zero.
See also multiplicative identity.

additive inverse If a set contains an identity element and has a binary operation of addition, the additive inverse of any element a is usually written as a^{-1}, such that

$$a^{-1} + a = a + a^{-1} = I$$

● -6 is the additive inverse of $+6$ in $\mathbb{Z}$.
2 is the inverse of 4 in the group
$G = \{0, 1, 2, 3, 4, 5\}$ (addition modulo 6).
3 is self-inverse in G.

additive notation The arbitrary representation of a mathematical process by the symbol $+$, when the process is similar in structure to addition as with the addition of vectors $\mathbf{a} + \mathbf{b} = \mathbf{c}$, or the representation of $A \cup B$ as $A + B$. It is sometimes possible to use an alternative (multiplicative) notation for the same process.

● Permutation P_1 followed by P_2 can be written as $P_1 + P_2$ or $P_1 \times P_2$.

adjoint matrix The square matrix whose elements are formed by transposing the cofactors $|A_{ij}|$ of A where A is a square matrix, so that $K_{ij} = (|A_{ji}|)$

● $A = \begin{pmatrix} 1 & 1 & 2 \\ 1 & 2 & 1 \\ 1 & 1 & 1 \end{pmatrix}$ $K = \begin{pmatrix} 1 & 1 & -3 \\ 0 & -1 & 1 \\ -1 & 0 & 1 \end{pmatrix}$

The determinant $|K|$ is the adjoint determinant of A.

adjugate matrix See adjoint matrix.

adjunction A process whereby, given a ring R together with a set S, a new ring R' is produced, which contains both R and S. R' is itself contained in any ring that contains both R and S.

● The set $\{\mathbb{Z} - 1\}$ is a ring.
If the set $\{1\}$ is adjoined to this the set $\mathbb{Z}$ is also a ring.

A similar process applies to any field F.

affine geometry A projective geometry that preserves parallelism and the ratios between linear intervals.
See affine transformation.

affine plane The plane whose points partake of any affine transformation. It can be defined axiomatically, as a set of elements called points and lines related by the property of incidence expressed by 'on', such that

1. There is a unique line on any two distinct points.
2. There are at least three points not on the same line.
3. Given a line l and a point P not on l, there is a unique line m on P such that there is no point both on l and m.

The axioms can be illustrated by Euclidean points and lines.

axiom 1   axiom 2   axiom 3

The Euclidean plane is a special case of the affine plane, with Axiom 3 corresponding to the parallel postulate.

affine transformation A transformation that sets up an 'affinity', or 1:1 correspondence between pairs of points in a plane, first described and named by Euler in 1748. In cartesian coordinates it is given by

$$x' = a_1 x + b_1 y + c_1$$

$$y' = a_2 x + b_2 y + c_2$$

Where (x', y') is the image of the point (x, y) under the transformation. For suitable values of the coefficients the transformation gives all isometry and similarity transformations, and shear or stretch transformations. In general the length of line intervals, areas, angles (and hence shapes) are not preserved. The invariants of any affine transformation A are

1. Straight lines remain straight under A.
2. Parallel lines (and only parallel lines) transform into parallel lines.
3. A line segment divided into any given ratio transforms into one divided in the same ratio.
4. A finite point transforms into a finite point.

affinity See affine transformation.

Agnesi, Maria Italian linguist, theologian and mathematician (1718–1799). She studied the properties of the curve now named after her, the 'Witch of Agnesi', although this was proposed by Fermat.

aleph null | See transfinite cardinal.

algebra Originally from *ḥisāb al-jabr*, part of the title of an Arabic treatise by al-Khuwārizmī, meaning 'calculus (arithmetic) of reduction'. From this work it took its ordinary meaning of 'arithmetic with letters' and its techniques of solving equations. The word is now very general, and applies to any set of non-numerical symbols and the axioms and rules by which they combine or are operated on, as in matrix algebra, non-associative algebras and so on. See also algorithm, abstract algebra.

algebraic dependence Used of the systems of complex numbers $\mathbb{C}$, reals $\mathbb{R}$ and rationals $\mathbb{Q}$ in order of descending generality. Any subset X of $\mathbb{C}$ or $\mathbb{R}$ is algebraically dependent on $\mathbb{R}$ or $\mathbb{Q}$ if its members can appear as the roots of an equation whose coefficients are in $\mathbb{R}$ or $\mathbb{Q}$. Thus, a set of numbers of the form $a + ib$ with a and b in $\mathbb{R}$ will satisfy a polynomial with coefficients in $\mathbb{R}$, and are algebraically dependent on $\mathbb{R}$. Sets of transcendental numbers do not appear as the roots of polynomials with rational coefficients in $\mathbb{Q}$, and these are accordingly algebraically independent of $\mathbb{Q}$.

algebraic expression Used informally for any expression using literal symbols which nominally take the place, or can take the place, of numbers.

algebraic function See function. A function of the general form $F(x, y) = 0$ where F is a polynomial in x and y. This can be extended to further variables.

● $x^2 + y^2 + z^2 = 1$

See also trigonometric functions, exponential function, elliptic functions.

algebraic independence See algebraic dependence.

algebraic integer Any complex or real number which satisfies an algebraic equation with integral coefficients, when the coefficient of the highest power is unity.

algebraic irrationals See irrational number.

algebraic numbers Arise from the solution of polynomial equations with rational coefficients. The set includes the positive and negative numbers arising from $x + a = b$, the rationals arising from $ax = b$, the surds from $x^n = b$ and the complex numbers which

3

arise from the general polynomial

$$a_n x^n + a_{n-1} x^{n-1} + \ldots + a_1 x^1 + a_0 = 0$$

See transcendental number, algebraic integer.

algebraic structure   The complete system of laws obeyed by a set of elements of any kind, as distinct from the properties of the elements themselves. Thus, group theory discusses the properties of closure, commutativity, associativity and the existence of identities and inverses, independently of whether the elements are numbers, geometrical shapes, or whatever. Also called abstract algebra.
See isomorphism.

algebra of propositions   *See* propositional calculus, Boolean algebra.

algorithm (algorism)   A name formed, through Latin translation, from al-Khuwārizmī, the writer of an Arabic treatise on calculation using the Hindu–Arabic numerals. It has two forms:
1. Notational algorithm. A method of numerical calculation which depends on notational devices such as place value, as with the Four Rules of arithmetic.
2. Procedural algorithm. A method described for obtaining a result irrespective of the methods of calculating or recording numbers, as Euclid's algorithm for the greatest common measure.

Alhambra   Arabic *al-ḥambra*, the red (building). A Moorish palace built at Grenada in Spain in 1273. It is claimed that the geometrical patterns on its walls show examples of all seventeen possible plane symmetry patterns.
See wallpaper patterns.

alias transformation   Any transformation of the points on a plane which relabels them without mapping them on other points. Thus the cartesian coordinates of a plane are relabelled to give non-linear coordinates on a Mercator chart. The Pythagorean distance function does not hold for such a transformation unless it is linear. Thus $QP^2 = QN^2 + PN^2$ on the cartesian plane, but this distance measured on a Mercator chart does not give the length of the track QP.

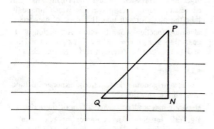

alibi transformation   A transformation of the plane on to itself that in general maps each point on to a different point. Thus

$$T = \begin{pmatrix} 2 & 0 \\ 1 & 3 \end{pmatrix}$$

maps the point $P = (1, 1)$ on to $P' = (2, 4)$.

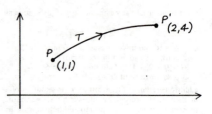

alignment chart   *See* nomogram.

aliquot parts   Exact fractional parts of a number or (more usually) a quantity, that divide it up without remainder. Old arithmetic books contained lists of aliquot parts for compound quantities like pounds, shillings and pence or feet and inches: thus 3s. 4d was an aliquot part of £1. The corresponding divisor is called a proper divisor: thus 8 is a proper divisor of 240.

Al-Khuwārizmī   9th century Persian philosopher, whose treatise on mathematics, which has survived, gave its name to algebra and described Hindu–Arabic positional notation with zero. His own name gave us the word algorithm.

almost lower (upper) bound   A real number x is sometimes called an almost lower (upper) bound of a set A of real numbers if there are only finitely many numbers y in A for which $y \leqslant x$ (or $y \geqslant x$).

alternant   A determinant whose elements are powers of $a, b, c \ldots$ such that the interchange of a, b (or any other pair) is equivalent to interchanging rows or columns and therefore changes the sign of the determinant

$$\begin{vmatrix} 1 & 1 & 1 \\ a & b & c \\ a^2 & b^2 & c^2 \end{vmatrix} = - \begin{vmatrix} 1 & 1 & 1 \\ b & a & c \\ b^2 & a^2 & c^2 \end{vmatrix}$$

alternate segment   The segment of a circle which is the complement of the one first mentioned, as in the theorem: the angle between a chord and a tangent is equal to the angle subtended by the chord at any point in the alternate segment.

alternating group   The set of even permutations, taken alternately from the $n!$ permutations of n symbols taken n at a time. This forms a group under composition of permutations of order $\frac{1}{2}n!$, taking the identity permutation as even. It is usually written as A_n. A_5 is the group of even permutations of five symbols and is of order 60. Its geometrical representation is the cyclic group of the regular dodecahedron or icosahedron.

alternating series   One in which the terms are alternately positive and negative

$$S = 1 - \tfrac{1}{4} + \tfrac{1}{9} - \tfrac{1}{16} + \tfrac{1}{25}$$

Such a series always converges towards a limiting sum if the corresponding series with positive terms converges.

alternative hypothesis   In a significance test this is usually the hypothesis of main practical interest. If, for example, one is examining the correlation of two sets of phenomena, the null hypothesis H_0 is that they are not correlated. Failure to accept H_0 as the result of a significant test implies the tacit acceptance of the alternative hypothesis that the correlation is significant.

altitude   1. Height above a datum line such as sea level.
2. The perpendicular height of any figure such as a triangle above the line chosen as base. The three altitudes of a triangle are concurrent.
3. The angular distance between the horizon and any celestial body measured along a meridian from the zenith to the horizon passing through the body. This is the basic measure in astro-navigation.

amicable numbers   A pair of numbers m, n such that each is the sum of the set of proper divisors of the other, such as 284, 220.

- $284 = 2^2.71$ whose proper divisors are 1, 2, 4, 71, 142 whose sum is 220.
  $220 = 2^2.5.11$ whose proper divisors are 1, 2, 4, 5, 10, 20, 11, 22, 44, 55, 110 whose sum is 284.

amplitude   *See* harmonic motion, argument.

AMS Classification Scheme   Published annually in the last (December) issue of Mathematical Reviews (USA). This breaks down the whole of mathematics into an agreed taxonomy under which the work of the year is recorded. The scheme, devised by the American Mathematical Society, began in 1970 and provides a useful framework into which any mathematical topic can be fitted.

analogue computer   *See* computer.

analogy   An earlier meaning of this word was 'ratio', and in this sense gives us Napier's 'Analogies' for his tables of logarithms, as published.

analysis   That part of mathematics which develops a theory of limiting processes from an axiomatic description of number systems. It includes what was formerly known as infinitesimal calculus but places this on a formally consistent logical basis. In particular, it develops the concepts of convergence of sequences and series, of continuity and differentiability, from a treatment of the completeness of the set of real numbers.
The need for analysis as a discipline arose from the earlier work of Newton and Leibnitz and their successors, and developed mainly in France and Germany during the 19th century.

analysis of variance   Also called factor analysis when the number of variables is larger than two. A method of comparing the variance of one set of independent random observations X, such as the daily outputs of a particular machine, with another Y, such as the outputs of different machines, in order to test the null hypothesis H_0 that they are not significantly different. If they are, it suggests that the machines differ in efficiency. The test statistic is $F = \sigma_1^2/\sigma_2^2$ where the variance σ_1^2 applies to the larger of the X, Y population variables. If the sample sizes are n_1, n_2 and the corresponding sample variances s_1^2, s_2^2 then an estimator for F is

$$\frac{n_1(n_2-1)s_1^2}{n_2(n_1-1)s_2^2}$$

for degrees of freedom (n_1-1), (n_2-1).
Tables of critical values of F are available.

analytic function   Describes a function of a complex variable that can be differentiated. The usual definition of a derivative

$$\lim_{h \to 0} \frac{f(x+h)-f(x)}{h} \quad (x, h \in \mathbb{R})$$

must be modified when x, $h \in \mathbb{C}$ The limit then exists for any $h = \lambda + i\mu$ only where $\lambda \to 0$ and $\mu \to 0$ independently.

analytic geometry   A method of studying geometrical problems by setting up coordinate systems which allow the geometrical elements such as lines and points to be described by the methods of algebra or analysis. Descartes first introduced algebraic methods into geometry. Cartesian coordinates were not introduced by him but were named in his honour. It was Fermat who referred points to number pairs on orthogonal axes and lines to algebraic equations.

The generality of the methods allowed analytic geometry to extend far beyond the properties of polygons and circles as discussed by Euclid. New coordinate system were developed to simplify the description of configurations not easily expressed in cartesians: Bernoulli developed polar coordinates in 1691; Plücker (1829) considered lines and other entities rather than points as fundamental; homogeneous coordinates allowed analytic methods to be applied to projective geometry and Cayley (1843) began to generalize results to more than three dimensions. Riemann (1851) developed, by analytic methods, the intrinsic geometry (differential geometry) of curved surfaces: the application of his methods to actual physical space allowed the general theory of relativity to be formulated.

analytic projective geometry   1. Cartesian coordinates label points with respect to axes on which there is an origin, a unit interval taken as measure and a potential infinity towards which the intervals can increase without limit. Projective (non-homogenous) coordinates label three arbitrary but feasible points on a line A_0, X_1, X_ω not necessarily in that order. These points are the gauge points of the base line, and are also labelled simply 0, 1, ω. Another arbitrary line is similarly drawn with gauge points Y_0, Y_1, Y_ω with Y_0 corresponding to X_0. It is now possible to insert other points on the lines, as X_a, X_b, so that sums and products of these points may be defined. If X_0, X_1, X_ω, X_a, X_b together with the sum or product form an involutory hexad, the sum is the mate of X_0 and the product the mate of X_1. The diagram shows the coordinate system or mesh gauge. Any point P in the field has the coordinates $X_p Y_p$ and lies on the intersection of the lines joining X_p and Y_ω, Y_p and X_ω. It follows that no points can lie on the join of X_ω, Y_ω. The diagram shows the coordinate system. See involutory hexad for diagram of involution. Relationships between P, Q, ... can be defined in terms of sums and products of points on the base lines.

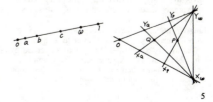

If the mesh diagram is projected so that OY_ω, OX_ω intersect at a right angle and the line $Y_\omega X_\omega$ goes to infinity, the system corresponds to ordinary cartesian coordinates.

2. The system is extended to homogeneous projective coordinates by replacing the a of X_a by $(p, q) = p/q$ where p and q take any values other than $p = q = 0$. Then X_0 corresponds to $(0, k)$, X_1 to (k, k) and X_ω to $(k, 0)$.
See homogeneous coordinates, triangle of reference.

analytic proposition Any proposition whose truth or falsehood is guaranteed by the definition of its terms, e.g. a quadrilateral has four sides.
The negation of a true analytic proposition is self-contradicted.

ancestral relation *See* transitive relation.

anchor ring *See* torus.

AND An operation in Boolean algebra and symbolic logic which is a function of two or more variables having the truth value 1 (or TRUE) when all variables are true, but otherwise 0 (or FALSE). Denoted by &, ∧, ∩, ., or by simple juxtaposition. The truth table defining ∧ is

p	q	$p \wedge q$
1	1	1
1	0	0
0	1	0
0	0	0

AND gate *See* gate.

angle A measure of difference in direction or rotation about a point. The fundamental unit is one complete turn, divided into 360 angular degrees. An alternative measure defines one radian as the angle subtended at the centre of a circle by an arc whose length is equal to the radius, hence

$$2\pi \text{ radians} = 360 \text{ angular degrees.}$$

The second method, which expresses an angle as a ratio, is more convenient mathematically since it relates to the trigonometric ratios of angles. By convention, a positive angle is measured in an anti-clockwise sense.

angle of elevation Using a horizontal line as a datum direction, the angle of elevation is the angle subtended by any object (or frequently the highest point of an object) at a point on the datum. The angle of elevation of an astronomical object, taken for navigational purposes, is usually called its altitude.

angular acceleration *See* angular velocity. For accelerated rotatory motion the angular acceleration is $\ddot{\theta}$ or $d^2\theta/dt^2$ about the centre of rotation.

angular diameter The angle subtended by a diameter of a distant circle or sphere at a point, which gives the actual diameter when distance is known. Commonly used of the objects of astronomical observation.

angular distance This is measured between any two objects or points with respect to a third point taken as a reference, and is the angle subtended by the objects at the reference point, for example the angular distance between the sun and the moon measured at a given moment from Greenwich.

angular measure A measure of difference in direction using the angular degree, denoted °, as unit. One complete turn from the reference direction is divided into 360°, so that a right angle is 90°. Each degree is divided into 60 minutes, denoted ′, and each minute in 60 seconds, denoted ″. Modern angle-measuring instruments such as sextants and theodolites often divide the minute decimally. The measure is very ancient, and dates back to Babylonian mathematics c. 2000 B.C. There are several plausible accounts of the choice of 360 units to a complete turn, but all are conjectural.

angular momentum For a rotating body this corresponds to the linear momentum of Newton's laws, and is the inertial property whereby a massive body continues in its state of rotation unless acted upon by a torque or couple, when the rate of change of momentum is proportional to the torque. For a rigid body angular momentum is given by $I\omega$, where I is the moment of inertia of the rotating body or system of bodies, and ω the angular velocity, about the centre of rotation. Angular momentum is conserved independently of linear momentum on collision or fusion of two bodies, in the absence of external torque. Since moments of inertia are meaningless for sub-atomic particles such as electrons (often considered as point charges) the postulated angular momentum of these is deduced from the total energy, and is usually called *spin*.

angular velocity A measure of rotation per unit time. If a radius vector rotates through an angle θ about an origin, its angular velocity at time t is given by $\omega = d\theta/dt$, often written $\dot{\theta}$. It follows that for constant ω, the total angle through which the radius vector has turned after t seconds is $\theta = \omega t$, corresponding to $s = vt$ for linear motion.
When the motion is circular, any one position of the radius vector will repeat itself after time

$$T = \frac{2\pi}{\omega}$$

T is called the period of the rotation and $\frac{\omega}{2\pi}$ is the frequency. The tangential velocity of a point at a distance r from the centre is $v = \omega r$.

annihilator A name sometimes given to the zero element ν in a set A with a binary operation ο. If, for all $x \in A$

$$x \circ \nu = \nu \circ x = \nu$$

then ν is the annihilator. Note that the operation must be specified for any given ν and A. Zero is the annihilator or zero element for multiplication in ℝ, but is the unit element for addition.

annulus Lat. a ring. The plane area enclosed between two concentric circles.
See also torus.

antecedent Used of the first part of a hypothetical argument, e.g. if a triangle is isosceles (antecedent), then the base angles are equal (consequent).
The Gk. words *protasis* and *apodosis* were also used to name these two parts.

antiderivative Also called the primitive or indefinite integral. The inverse function of a derivative. Thus the derivative of $x^2 + 1$ is $2x$, and the antiderivative of $2x$ is $x^2 + A$, where A is any constant.

More formally, if a function f is continuous in a closed interval $[a, b]$ and F a function in the same interval differentiable over the open interval (a, b), with $F' = f$ on (a, b), then F is called the antiderivative of f.

Antiderivatives illustrate the inverse or reciprocal nature of finding derivatives and integrals.

antidifferentiation The process of finding the antiderivative, and hence a synonym for integration when, but only when, this latter process is not defined independently (e.g. by Riemann integration). All antiderivatives are integrals, but not all integrals are antiderivatives. The process applies to the standard elementary functions, uses the notation $f(x) = \int f'(x)\,dx$ and requires the conditions of continuity discussed under antiderivative. Thus $\int_a^b \frac{dx}{x} = \ln\left|\frac{b}{a}\right|$ only if $[a, b]$ does not contain the origin.

antilogarithm The inverse of logarithm. Thus if $x = b^y$, then x is the antilogarithm of y to the base b.

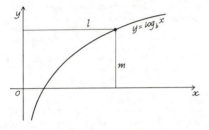

The ordinate m is the logarithm of x to base b, the abscissa l the antilogarithm of y to base b.

antinomy Two or more parallel sets of logical arguments that lead to contradictory conclusions, taken by Kant (1724–1804) as evidence that there are questions that rational discussion cannot answer.

antiparallel Used of two lines which cut any pair of lines to form pairs of equal angles, but in opposite order.

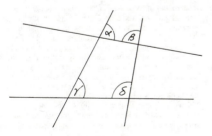

The antiparallel lines are l_1, l_2 if $\alpha = \delta$, $\beta = \gamma$
They would be parallel if $\alpha = \gamma$, $\beta = \delta$

antisymmetric Used of a relation R between a, b such that $a\,\mathrm{R}\,b$ does not imply $b\,\mathrm{R}\,a$. Note that the term asymmetric is not used here.

● R is 'is the square root of', in 3 R 9.

Apollonius of Perga Greek mathematician (fl. 250–220 B.C.) successor to Euclid, and author of a monumental treatise on geometric conics that has come down to us complete.

Apollonius' theorem 1. The extension to the general conic of the theorem of Euclid III. 35, that the two rectangles contained by the segments of two intersecting chords of a circle are equal.

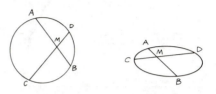

2. The theorem relating the sides of a triangle with the median drawn to any one side.

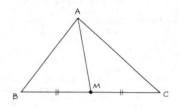

In the diagram shown $AB^2 + AC^2 = BM^2 + AM^2$.

a posteriori (Lat. from that which is after) A form of argument not normally admitted into mathematics, in which an initial cause is argued from an effect or result considered as subsequent. It is likely that many important advances in mathematics are made by *a posteriori* reasoning, afterwards recast as *a priori* arguments from axioms or hypotheses.

applied mathematics Originally a synonym for theoretical mechanics, the term is now used of any application of the methods of pure mathematics to practical problems. The distinction is important in discussing the fundamentals of mathematics. Thus $2 + 3 = 5$ is a proposition of pure mathematics; 2 books + 3 books = 5 books is an application of the proposition.

approach curve A mass moving at constant speed along a curve will experience an acceleration towards the instantaneous centre of curvature at any point. An approach curve, used in designing railway tracks, is such that the rate of increase of the acceleration is constant, so that passengers feel the least discomfort on running into a curve. It is the semicubic parabola given by $27ay^2 = 4(x - 2a)^3$.

approximating polygon A polygon having n sides whose configuration approaches that of a given curve when n increases without limit. Then the sum of the sides of the polygon approximates to the length of the curve, and its area to the area enclosed by it.

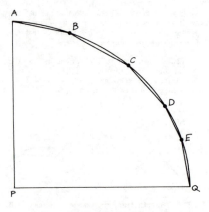

$$AB + BC + CD + DE + EQ \approx \text{arc AQ}$$
$$\text{area PABCDEQ} \approx \text{area PAQ}.$$

approximation 1. A value, more or less reliable according to circumstances, obtained for any physical or statistical quantity, by a process of measurement or sampling procedure. Statistical analysis of the results of repeated measure or sampling can often produce more reliable estimates.

2. A value or sequence of values which approach the true value of a function or root of an equation. Thus for a function expressed as an infinite series

$$f(x) = a_0 + a_1 x + a_2 x^2 + \dots$$

the finite series

$$\sum_{r=0}^{n} a_r x^r$$

is an approximation if $f(x)$ converges.

3. For an equation $f(x) = 0$ there are many methods of finding approximations to the roots, including iterative methods. The value of many common functions thus expressed allow convenient approximations in particular circumstances

- $\sin \theta \approx 0$ (θ small)
  $\cos \theta \approx 1$ (θ small)
  $(1 + x)^n \approx 1 + nx$ (small x)

See also Taylor's theorem.

a priori Used of a deductive as opposed to an inductive argument (Lat. from that which goes before). *A priori* conclusions, given arguments free from logical fallacies, follow necessarily from the premises. In mathematics most arguments are deductive in this way, and follow from initial definitions, axioms or hypotheses. Any inconsistency or error in the conclusions implies inconsistent or erroneous premises. Also used by Kant to describe concepts which he held the mind to form independently of experience.

See also reductio ad absurdum.

a priori **probability** Corresponds to the 'classical' definition given for probability. Thus the *a priori* probability that a coin marked 'head' and 'tail' will land 'head' when spun is $\frac{1}{2}$. This may or may not correspond to the empirical probability expressed as an occurrence ratio.

apse (apsis) The two points in a closed central orbit at which the orbiting body is at its greatest and least distances from the centre of attraction. At these points the tangent to the orbit is at right angles to the radius vector.

Arabic numerals Properly, Hindu–Arabic numerals. The symbols and notation introduced to Europe c. 1000 A.D. by the Arabs, but earlier developed in India. The symbols 1–9 could be as old as 250 B.C. but their use in positional notation with zero as a place holder is not much earlier than 800 A.D. The modern printed symbols were developed and stabilized from the Arabic forms of the original, which are

١٢٣٤٥٦٧٨٩٠

The importance of the system, crucial to the development of arithmetic, was the positional notation whereby each digit became the coefficient of a power of ten. This was later extended to the decimal notation for fractions by allowing negative powers.

arbitrary Any quantity, value or expression which may be chosen, either at random or for a specific purpose, and which is not dictated or made necessary by the process in which it occurs.
Integration involves an arbitrary constant, which may be zero or may depend on initial conditions, but whose value is not given by the process of integration.

arc An interval of any curve taken along the curve, usually with labelled end points which may be free.

arc cos *See* circular functions.

arcosh *See* hyperbolic functions.

Archimedean spiral The curve whose polar equation is $r = a\theta$. It was described by Archimedes but was discovered by an older contemporary, Conon of Samos (322–283 B.C.).

Archimedes' axiom Corresponds to Euclid Book V Def. 5 and states, as an axiom, that any magnitude (or measure of a line) can exceed any other given magnitude if multiplied by a sufficiently large number.

Archimedes of Syracuse Greek mathematician and natural philosopher (287–212 B.C.) He produced a number of mathematical treatises on spirals, conics, etc., and an interesting attempt, in *The Sand Reckoner*, to devise a notation for large numbers. He devised a method for accurately estimating the angular diameter of the sun, as an angle between two measured angles, one too large and the other too small. Although credited with the invention of many mechanical devices connected with levers and screws, his work in mechanics, mainly statics and hydrostatics, lacked empirical foundation. Archimedes produced one of the earliest good approximations to π.

Archimedes' Principle If a non-porous body is wholly or partly immersed in a fluid in equilibrium, the resultant pressure on it is equivalent to a single force equal in magnitude to the weight of the displaced fluid, and acting vertically through the centre of gravity of this fluid. The centre of gravity of the displaced fluid is called the centre of buoyancy of the solid body, and the total upthrust is the buoyancy. The body floats if its weight is less than the buoyancy.

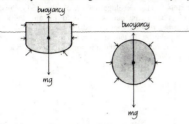

See also metacentre.

arcsin See circular functions.

arctan See circular functions.

area A measure of the surface enclosed by any boundary described on the surface. Originally, in Euclid, the plane area enclosed by a polygon, determined by reducing the figure to an equivalent square. The unit of area, the metre squared, is still defined in this way. Finding the area enclosed by curves, which gave rise to the famous problem of squaring the circle, was not solved directly, but by the method of exhaustions which approximated a polygon to the curve. This in turn gave rise to the modern process of integration. The concept of area can be extended to bounded regions on non-planar surfaces, but apart from special cases such as spheres has had to await modern analysis for a satisfactory treatment.

areal coordinates See homogeneous coordinates and triangle of reference. If XYZ is the triangle of reference its centroid I is taken as the unit point $(1, 1, 1)$.

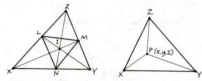

Since LM, MN, NL are parallel to XY, ZY, YZ, these pairs of lines meet on the line at infinity, which has the equation $x + y + z = 0$. If P is any point whose homogeneous coordinates are (a, b, c) it can be shown that $a:b:c = \triangle$PYZ$:\triangle$PZX$:\triangle$PXY; that is, are in the ratio of the areas of the triangles. Moreover, if particles of mass a, b, c are situated at X, Y, Z, P is their centre of mass, and hence these were once called barycentric coordinates.

Argand diagram The complex number $x + iy$ is represented in cartesian coordinates by the point $P = (x, y)$, and makes it clear that the representation of real numbers on a number line can be extended to complex numbers by assigning them to points on a plane.

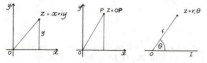

In the first diagram $Q = (x, 0)$ represents the real number x, the line $QP = y$ the second component iy of the complex number $z = x + iy$. The Ox axis is called the real axis, the Oy the 'imaginary' axis. The name is misleading but is given for historical reasons. See Descartes, polar coordinates.

Argand, Jean Robert Swiss mathematician (1768–1822) who published (1806) an account of complex numbers represented on a coordinate system.

argument 1. Is a specific value for x in any function of x. In a table of logarithms, where log $x = 0.3010$, then the argument is $x = 2.0$.
2. The term θ in the expression of a complex number in the form $z = (r, \theta)$ or $z = r$ (cos $\theta + i$ sin θ). If θ is an argument so is $\theta + 2\pi k$ for any integer k. The value $-\pi < \theta \leqslant \pi$ is called the principal argument, usually written arg z. The term argument used in this form is sometimes known as the amplitude. It appears on the Argand diagram as the angle between the line 0P and the real base line 0I.
See modulus.

Aristotle Greek philosopher (384–322 B.C.) credited with laying foundations for many branches of science, literary criticism, philosophy and political theory. Originally a member of Plato's Academy, he later rejected some of Plato's theories, and returned to Athens to found his own school at Lyceius. His work in mathematics was a discussion of foundations rather than exposition. Unlike Plato, he held that mathematical entities had no actual existence, but were abstracted by thought from real objects. He also discussed the structure of logical argument and the art of reasoning from probabilities.

arithmetic From Gk. *arithmos*, a number; originally the study of the nature and properties of number, but now restricted (at least in UK and USA) to a practical knowledge of number facts and the algorithms of calculation that depend on them. The basic processes of arithmetic are algorithms for addition, subtraction, multiplication, division, with raising to powers and the extraction of roots dependent on these four, using number which may possibly be associated with units of measure. Topics studied in arithmetic, such as percentages, fractions, mensuration, ratio, proportion and so on, are all developed from these six processes, of which the first four are called the Four Rules.

arithmetical mean(s) 1. The arithmetic mean of quantities $x_1, x_2, x_3, \ldots x_n$ denoted $\bar{X}$, is

$$\bar{X} = \frac{1}{n} \sum_{i=1}^{n} x_i$$

2. A quantity m (or quantities $m_1, m_2, \ldots$) inserted between two quantities a and l so that a, m, l or a, $m_1, m_2 \ldots, l$ form an arithmetic progression. For 3 means between 3 and 11, since $l = a + (n-1)d$

$$11 = 3 + (5-1)d$$
$$d = 2$$

The required sequence is 3, 5, 7, 9, 11.

arithmetical operations These are binary operations whereby pairs of number are combined to produce a third number, and are to be regarded as distinct from any algorithms or computational procedures which may be needed to perform them if the numbers have more than one digit. The four operations are addition, subtraction, multiplication and division.

arithmetical progression A sequence in which each term differs from its predecessor by a constant quantity, as

$$10, 15, 20, 25, 30, \ldots$$

If a is the first term the last or nth term l is

$$l = a(n-1)d$$

where d is the constant difference. The sum to n terms is

$$S = \frac{n}{2}(a+l) \text{ or } S = \frac{n}{2}[2a+(n-1)d]$$

arithmetico-geometric series A set of terms in geometric progression, but each having coefficients which, taken in order, form an arithmetic progression.

● $1 + 2x + 3x^2 + 4x^3 + \ldots$

array An organized arrangement of numbers or other elements. For example, a matrix of n rows and m columns is an array containing nm elements a_{ij}, where i is the row and j the column locating a_{ij}. Arrays can have more than two dimensions, but cannot then be represented in one double-entry table. There would be a table for each value of the third coordinate or subscript. Four subscripts would require a $k \times l$ array of $n \times m$ tables. Such arrays are used in computer design to store numerical data for easy retrieval.

arrow diagram 1. Used in schools as a synonym for Papygram.

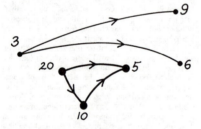

2. A similar diagram in which points are joined in sequence by arrows, and thus a general term for flow charts, critical path diagrams, Markov chains, and network diagrams or trees used in sociology, chemistry, etc. They have in common a need to mark direction. Introduced by Cayley.

arrow paradox *See* Zeno.

arsinh *See* hyperbolic functions.

artan *See* hyperbolic functions.

assertion sign The sign $\vdash$, inserted in propositional calculus before a statement asserted but not yet shown to be true.

● $\vdash (p \rightarrow q) \rightarrow (\sim q \rightarrow \sim p)$
   Assert: 'p implies q' implies 'not-q implies not-p'

associativity A binary operation $*$ on a set S is described as associative if, for all $a, b, c \in S$

$$(a*b)*c = a*(b*c)$$

For real numbers the associative law holds for

addition and multiplication, but not for subtraction and division.

astroid The envelope curve of the rod whose points trace the curves produced by an elliptical trammel. It is the four-cusped hypocycloid produced by a point on the circumference of a circle of radius a when it rolls round the interior of another circle of radius $4a$.

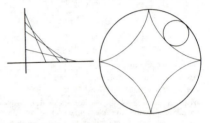

The cartesian equation is

$$x^{2/3} + y^{2/3} = c^{2/3}$$

or $x = b \cos^3 \theta$, $y = b \sin^3 \theta$, $0 \le \theta < 2\pi$

astronomical units Formerly used for comparative studies of planetary motion, taking the gravitational constant G and the earth's distance from the sun both as unity.

asymmetric 1. If R is a relation defined on a set S then R is asymmetric if $a \text{ R } b$ does not imply $b \text{ R } a$, for all $a, b \in S$. The term antisymmetric is preferred.
2. A configuration is asymmetric if it does not contain a point, line or axis of symmetry.

asymptote A straight line, such that a point along the curve is at a distance d from the line, and $\lim d = 0$ as the point moves infinitely far along the line.

● The hyperbola $\dfrac{x^2}{a^2} - \dfrac{y^2}{b^2} = 1$ has two

asymptotes given by $\dfrac{x^2}{a^2} - \dfrac{y^2}{b^2} = 0$

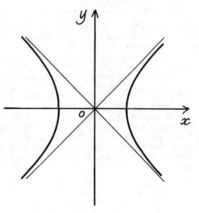

A curve $f(x, y) = 0$ of degree n is cut by the line $y = ax + b$ in points given by substituting x or y

in f and solving for y or x. If the equation has two infinite roots, $y = ax + b$ is an asymptote. This suggests an informal definition: an asymptote is a line which intersects a curve at two coincident points infinitely far from the origin.

atomic statement Any statement that cannot be resolved into other statements, but only into parts which are not themselves statements, either actually or by implication. Such parts are presumably only names, linked by a copula; e.g., Roosevelt is President.

augmented matrix If a set of simultaneous equations is expressed in matrix form by $Ax = h$ the matrix (Ah) which has the elements of h as an extra column, is called the augmented matrix.

aut (Lat.) The exclusive disjunction sometimes denoted $\underline{v}$ for which the English 'or' is ambiguous. For statements p, q it is denoted by the compound statement $(p \vee q)\ \&\ \sim (p\ \&\ q)$ (p or q but not both). It can be defined by the truth table

p	q	$p \underline{\vee} q$
T	T	F
T	F	T
F	T	T
F	F	F

If it relates variables in Boolean algebra the symbol XOR is sometimes used, read ex-or. It is not important in logic but is used in switching algebra.

autocorrelation A measure of the relative uniformity of a sequence of observations of one kind. It is given by the ratio

$$\frac{\text{autocovariance}}{\text{variance}}$$

and lies between -1 and $+1$. Positive values indicate relative smoothness and negative values irregularity or fluctuation. It indicates the reliability of interpolation between the terms of the sequence.

autocovariance Given a time series of values $\{X_t\}$ having a mean value μ, the autocovariance between two terms X_t and X_{t+v} is the value (or mean value for repeated series) of

$$(X_t - \mu)(X_{t+v} - \mu)$$

It is sometimes called the autocovariance of lag v. If this is independent of t for all v the series is said to be stationary, that is, it shows no temporal trend.

automorphism An ismorphism that maps a set on to itself; in effect a rule which preserves its structure, e.g. the mapping $x \mapsto -x$ is an automorphism of the integers under addition, since, if $a + b = c$, $(-a) + (-b) = -c$
Here the image $-c$ of the combination of the two numbers a, b is the combination of the images $-a$, $-b$ of the two numbers.

auxiliary circle 1. The circle drawn with either the major or the minor axis of an ellipse as diameter, from which the ellipse may be constructed by decreasing or increasing parallel half chords in the same ratio.

2. The circle whose diameter is the line joining the vertices of a hyperbola.

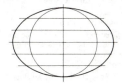

auxiliary equation Sometimes called characteristic equation. For a differential equation such as

$$ay'' + by' + cy = 0$$

a possible solution is $y = e^{mx}$ so that $(am^2 + bm + c)$ $y = 0$ by direct substitution. This equation is satisfied if $am^2 + bm + c = 0$, which is called the auxiliary equation. The complete general solution (*see* complementary function) will then depend on the nature of the roots of this equation.

auxiliary rectangle The rectangle formed by the intersection of the two tangents at the vertices of a hyperbola with the asymptotes, which are then the diagonals of the rectangle.

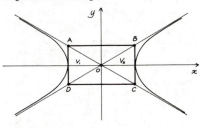

auxiliary variable *See* slack variable.

average This can be any measure of central tendency or indication of a typical value for a set of measures, although it most usually refers to the arithmetic mean.
See arithmetical mean, median, mode.

axial collineation *See* collineation, which is axial if the transformation of the set of points is a reflection in an axis.

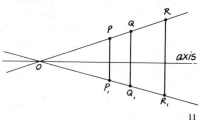

axiom 1. Originally, taken as a self-evident truth or 'common notion' which cannot be demonstrated in terms of simpler concepts.

● Things which are equal to the same thing are equal to one another (Euclid I).

2. In modern mathematics, any statement which is taken as true and used as the starting point for proving a sequence of theorems by logical deduction. The grammatical constituents of an axiom are taken to be undefined symbols, which are normally 'realized' by giving them a physical or other connotation.

● If $a = b$ and $b = c$ then $a = c$.

This is realized by Euclid's first common notion, although it stands by itself as an arbitrary rule for using the $=$ symbol.
See mathematics.

axiomatics Programmes for developing branches of mathematics as logical systems by setting up sets of axioms whose possible realizations are ignored for the purpose of proving sequences of theorems which are both logical and consistent. Normally the mathematical system thus developed is only of interest if it is capable of realization in terms of real objects or other concepts. Hilbert, in *Foundations of Geometry* (1899), developed a sequence of propositions using the undefined terms 'point' and 'line' which is realized as ordinary Euclidean geometry by giving these words their usual everyday meaning as they occur in Euclid.
See formalism.

axiomatic set theory An attempt to put set theory on a logical basis by postulating axioms where naive set theory merely defines its terms. Thus $A \cap B$ is defined on the naive assumption that $A \cap B$ is a set if A and B are sets as defined. Axiomatic set theory, which does not define sets, would make this an axiom. It was developed to avoid paradoxes apparent in set theory.
See heterologisch.

axiom of choice Formulated in 1904 by Ernst Zermolo, and now one of the basic axioms in the foundations of mathematics. If M is any collation of non-empty sets which are pairwise disjoint, then there exists at least one set that has exactly one element in common with each set in M.

$$M = \{\{1, 2, 3\} \quad \{x, y, z, w\} \quad \{4, 5\} \quad \{7\}\}$$
Then a set in the form required is
$$A = \{1, x, 4, 7\}$$
Both M and its elements may be finite or infinite.

axiom of completeness *See* completeness of the reals.

axiom of infinity Peano's axioms of the natural numbers define the successor to a number n as $n + 1$, and thus generate an infinite sequence of numbers. Since, for finite n, a natural number corresponds to the cardinal number of a set or class, the axiom of infinity states that classes having n members exist, and thus enables the process to start.

axioms of incidence Devised by Hilbert (1899) as part of a systematic restatement of Euclidean geometry. Points, lines and planes are not formally defined, but keep their intuitive properties which are expressed as axioms, as

1. Two points are always incident on a line.
2. There are at least three points not incident on one line.
3. There is only one line incident on two points.

The axioms can be realized by diagrams.

In the axioms the word 'line' is taken to have the same sense as 'straight line'.

axioms of order *See* Hilbert's axioms.

axiom systems Any set of axioms used as the starting point for a branch of mathematics developed formally.

● Hilbert's axioms of flat space.
Peano's axioms of the natural numbers.
Kolmogorov's axioms of probability.

What is an axiom in one system may be a theorem in another, deducible from that system's own set of axioms.

axis Lat. an axle.

1. A straight line about which a configuration revolves or may revolve.
2. A line about which a plane figure may revolve to generate a three-dimensional configuration or solid of revolution.
3. A line about which a configuration has symmetries (axis of symmetry).
4. A fixed line from which distances may be measured, as in coordinate axes.

azimuth The angle formed at the zenith by the meridian through a point of observation and the circle of altitude of (usually) a celestial object. It corresponds to the true bearing of a terrestrial object on or above the horizon, and the word may be used in this sense.

B

Babylonian numerals   In use from c. 3000 B.C. to 0 B.C. A mixed-base, part positional, part repetitive notation using the subtraction principle with the sign

$$\text{╋ ╋ ╟} \quad 10+10-1=19$$

$$\text{╋ ╋ ╟╟╟} \quad 10+10+3=23$$

The symbol $\angle$ was also used for ten. The notation is positional to a base 60, each group of symbols representing, from right to left, coefficients of $60°$, 60^1, $60^2 \ldots$ Using the examples given

$$\text{╋ ╋ ╟╟╋╋╋╋╟╟╟}$$

would read $19 \times 60 + 23 = 1140 + 23$
$$= 1163$$

Lack of zero or indication of grouping make these numbers difficult to read. The cuneiform symbols were impressed in clay by a pointed stylus.

The sexagesimal base used in the measure of time is probably of Babylonian origin.

Bachet de Meziriac   (1581–1638) French editor and translator (into Latin) of the *Arithmetica* of Diophantus. He published one of the first collections of numerical tricks and puzzles, the nucleus of most collections published since. Fermat wrote many of his number theoretical results in the margins of his copy of the *Arithmetica*.

back bearing   A check observation used in surveying or navigation. After taking a forward bearing towards an object from an origin or point of departure, a back bearing is taken towards the start-ing point on reaching or approaching the object. The two readings should differ by $\pm 180°$ within the expected margin of error.

ball   The region of space bounded by a spherical surface, as distinct from the surface itself. Thus if $x^2 + y^2 + z^2 = 1$ is a unit sphere centred at the origin, $x^2 + y^2 + z^2 \leqslant 1$ is the set of all points on or contained in the sphere, usually called a *closed ball*. An *open ball* is given by $x^2 + y^2 + z^2 < 1$, a region which does not include its limiting surface. This useful distinction between sphere and ball is not always maintained.

Banach space   A vector space which is also a metric space and is complete (Banach 1922). It is defined by the axioms of a vector space but each element is a vector whose *size*, denoted $\|\mathbf{v}\|$ is defined by

1. $\|\mathbf{v}\|$ is a non-negative real number.
2. $\|\mathbf{v}\| = 0$ if and only if $v = 0$.
3. $\|k\mathbf{v}\| = |k| \, \|\mathbf{v}\|$ for any number k.
4. $\|\mathbf{u} + \mathbf{v}\| = \|\mathbf{u}\| + \|\mathbf{v}\|$

There is also a *distance* $d(\mathbf{u}, \mathbf{v})$ between vectors, defined by

$$d(\mathbf{u}, \mathbf{v}) = \|\mathbf{v} - \mathbf{u}\|$$

In addition, the space must be complete, that is, any contracting sequence of closed regions always con-tains some vector.

● Functions defined for $0 \leqslant x \leqslant \frac{1}{2}$ which are continuous and for which $(f + g)$: $x \mapsto f(x) + g(x)$.
The size $\|f\|$ is defined as the maximum value of $|f(x)|$ so that $d(f, g)$ is the maximum difference bet-ween f and g as shown on the graph.

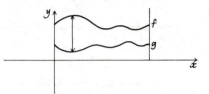

bar   A line placed over a symbol, as $\bar{a}$, $\bar{3}$. Over a letter it can have any assigned meaning, but usually negation. Over a number it is reserved for the characteristic of a logarithm, showing that it is negative when the mantissa is positive.

bar graph   A diagram of parallel horizontal or vertical bars, the lengths of which are proportional to frequencies or other measures in a sample of population.

barycentric coordinates   *See* areal coordinates.

base   As in ordinary speech, anything on which a structure is built. There are many examples in mathematics:

1. The base line, conventionally drawn horizontally at the lowest level, on which a configuration such as a triangle is drawn in descriptive geometry.
2. The base of a number notation is the exchange value chosen in counting by units, as in denary notation.
3. The base a of logarithms chosen so that

$$x = a^b$$

That is, b is the logarithm of x to the base a, or $\log_a x = b$.

base line   1. The half line beginning at an origin 0, used as the reference line for direction in setting up a polar coordinate system.
2. A surveyed line on the earth's surface whose length has been established to the required accuracy, used as the reference line in a survey by triangula-tion.

base (or basis) vectors   Any set of vectors which can be combined by the general rules of vector algebra to generate a set of vectors linearly dependent on them. A commonly used basis in three dimensions is $\mathbf{i} = (1, 0, 0), \mathbf{j} = (0, 1, 0), \mathbf{k} = (0, 0, 1)$.
The vector $\mathbf{a} = (3, 2, 5)$ is expressed as $\mathbf{a} = 3\mathbf{i} + 2\mathbf{j} + 5\mathbf{k}$. The dimensions of a space can be defined as the minimum number of vectors required for a basis.

Bayesian decision procedure   A statistical method whereby prior probability about the values of parameters, based on records, received information, informed opinion, subjective estimates and so on, is combined with analysis of actual data to give pos-terior probability by Bayes' Theorem. From this inferences are made and decisions arrived at.

Bayes' theorem Let n mutually exclusive events $H_1, H_2, H_3 \ldots H_n$ form a partition of a sample space, and have assigned prior probabilities of $p(H_1)$, $p(H_2)$, $p(H_3) \ldots p(H_n)$ and let the probabilities of an event E conditional on $H_1, H_2 \ldots$ be $p(E|H_1)$, $p(E|H_2) \ldots$ Then Bayes' theorem states the posterior probabilities of the H_i given the condition E, to be

$$p(H_i|E) = \frac{p(E|H_i)p(H_i)}{\sum\limits_{j=1}^{n} p(E|H_j)p(H_j)}$$

The denominator is equal to the total probability of E by the addition law. A simpler form of the theorem involving only two events is

$$p(A|B) = \frac{p(B|A)p(A)}{p(B)}$$

This can be derived directly from the definition of conditional probability. The theorem allows the reassessment of probabilities assigned as a result of small-sample testing, by taking into account the prior likelihood.

Bayes, the Rev. Thomas English mathematician and Presbyterian minister (1702–1761). His name is known for a result on probability published posthumously in 1763. The result is given a modern expression as Bayes' theorem.

bearing The angle giving the direction of a distant object or the course of a moving one (such as a ship). It is now always measured in degrees clockwise from the true or the magnetic North, and is expressed in three digits, as $006°T$, $326°M$.

behaviour space A synonym for phase space.

bel *See* decibel.

bending moment If a thin uniform heavy beam QR having a weight w per unit length is cantilevered from a support at R, the forces acting at any point P at a distance x from Q are

1. A sheer due to the weight wx acting downward, balanced by internal forces at P acting upwards.

2. The moment $w \cdot \dfrac{x}{2}$ of the weight of QP, in equilibrium with an internal couple at P in the opposite sense. This couple is known as the bending moment, and tends to deflect the beam at this point.

The bending moment is zero at Q and a maximum at R. Comparable results can be obtained for thick beams or those of various cross-sections.

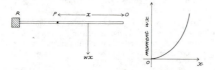

Berkeley, G. Irish bishop (1685–1753) An influential philosopher whose *Theory of Vision* discussed the function of the mind in interpreting sense-data. His criticism of Newton's method of fluxions in the *Analyst* (1735), in which he described the derivative as 'the ghost of a vanished quantity', was not fully answered till the following century.

Bernoulli, Daniel (1700–1782) Second son of Johann.

Contributed to hydrodynamics and the theory of gases and made major advances in probability theory. He gave his name to a key equation in fluid dynamics and a method for finding approximations to roots of algebraic equations by iteration.

Bernoulli distribution *See* binomial distribution.

Bernouilli equation 1. For the steady flow of a uniform fluid where the potential energy per unit mass K is constant, the expression

$$K + \frac{dp}{\rho} + \tfrac{1}{2}q^2$$

is constant, along any streamline where ρ is density, p pressure and q the magnitude of the velocity at any point.
The theorem can be generalized for non-steady flow.
2. The differential equation

$$\frac{dy}{dx} + Ry = Sy^n$$

where R, S are functions of x, given by Jakob Bernoulli.

Bernoulli family This Swiss family produced eight major mathematicians in the 17th century. With Bach, Breughel and other families they often feature in discussions of hereditary abilities (which usually overlook the rarity of the phenomenon).

Bernoulli, Jakob Swiss mathematician (1654–1705) Did early work on polar coordinates and shapes of loaded chains, rods and flexible laminae, and discussed the properties of plane figures of fixed perimeter. He introduced the word 'integral' into the nomenclature of the calculus.

Bernoulli, Johann Swiss mathematician (1676–1748) Brother to Jakob and father of the later Bernoullis. He did much early work on the calculus and its applications using series, trigonometric and exponential functions. He defined the brachystochrone and determined its shape.

Bernoulli theorem Usually the name given to the result that, for Bernoulli trials, the probability for r successes in n trials, each with constant probability p is

$$p(r) = \binom{n}{r} p^r q^{n-r}$$

where $q + p = 1$.

Bernoulli trial A random experiment or event with two possible outcomes, success or failure, whose probability remains constant throughout any repetition of the experiment, as in spinning coins. If p is probability of success and q is probability of failure

$$p + q = 1$$

The binomial distribution arises from a sequence of independent Bernoulli trials.

Bertrand's paradox What is the probability p that a chord drawn at random in a circle Γ is greater than the side of the inscribed equilateral triangle ABC? This question gives three possible answers and is an example of an antinomy arising from insufficiently defined premises.

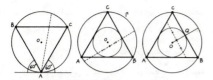

The criteria are satisfied by:

1. Chords from A lying in the angle CAB, giving $p = \frac{1}{3}$.
2. Chords whose centres lie in the inscribed circle of ABC of area $\pi r^2/4$, giving $p = \frac{1}{4}$.
3. Chords whose distances OP from the centre O are less than $OQ = \frac{1}{2} OR$, giving $p = \frac{1}{2}$.

Bessel functions Non-elementary integrals, denoted $J_n(x)$, that arise from the solution of differential equations of the form

$$x^2 y'' + xy' + (x^2 - n^2) y = 0$$

For example, if $n = 0$, the solution of $xy'' + y' + xy = 0$ is, for $y(0) = 1$, $y'(0) = 0$, given by the function

$$J_0(x) = \frac{1}{\pi} \int_{-1}^{+1} \frac{\cos xt}{\sqrt{(1 - t^2)}} \, dt$$

This may be checked by direct substitution. Tables of numerical values and lists of series expansions, addition and recurrence formulae are available.

beta function Also called Euler's beta function. For all positive non-zero values of s, t it is the function given by

$$B(s, t) = \int_0^1 x^{s-1} (1 - x)^{t-1} \, dx$$

It is also expressible in terms of the gamma function

$$B(s, t) = \frac{\Gamma(s)\Gamma(t)}{\Gamma(s + t)}$$

The beta function can be used to express the binomial coefficients and the integrals of powers of the circular functions.

biased *See* unbiased.

bicimals An unfortunate coinage by false analogy with decimal.
See binary notation.

biconditional *See* iff.

bijection *See* one-one mapping, one-one correspondence.

bilateral symmetry Symmetry about a fixed line in a plane (the line of symmetry). Each point P of the symmetrical configuration has an image point P' such that the line of symmetry is the perpendicular bisector of PP'. Points on the line transform into themselves. In three dimensions bilateral symmetry can exist about a fixed plane.

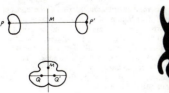

bilinear Describes an expression of the form $azw + bz + cw + d$ ($a \neq 0$). This is linear in z if w is constant and in w if z is constant.

bilinear transformation The transformation $azw + bz + cw + d = 0$ ($ad \neq bc$), also written $w = \dfrac{az + b}{cz + d}$, which sets up a unique 1:1 correspondence between a set of numbers $(z_1 z_2 z_3 \ldots)$ and a set of $(w_1 w_2 w_3 \ldots)$, is bilinear in z and w. The numbers can be complex and may then represent configurations of points on lines or planes.

billion The British billion was 10^{12}, but the US billion, 10^9, is commonly used in journalism and politics.

bimodal distribution One whose probability density or distribution function has two local maxima. The word is also applied to histograms or frequency polygons that show a similar effect.

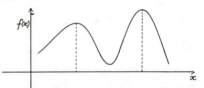

A bimodal distribution may arise if two separate distributions, each normal but having different means, are combined additively, for example shoe sizes worn by men and women. The bimodality can then appear merely as a flattening (sometimes called platykurtosis) of the normal curve.

binary code Any representation of an item of data, usually alphabetic or numerical, by a unique sequence of binary digits.

binary fractions *See* binary notation.

binary notation Representation of numbers using the base or radix two. For any N, $N = d_n 2^n + d_{n-1} 2^{n-1} + \ldots + d_1 2^1 + d_0$ and may be written using place value notation, as $d_n d_{n-1} \ldots d_1 d_0$ where $N \in \mathbb{N}$ and $d_i \in \{0, 1\}$. It is usual to show the base as a suffix unless this is understood in context, $6_{(10)} = 110_{(2)}$. Each binary digit is sometimes called a *bit*, and a string of m bits can represent 2^m distinct numbers. A binary point can be inserted after d_0 and the notation extended to binary fractions of the form

$$0 . d_1 2^{-1} + d_2 2^{-2} + \ldots$$

binary operation A mapping from ordered pairs (a, b) of a set S into a set S'. A general operation is usually denoted by $*$ or o, and is also called a law of composition

$$a * b = c \text{ where } a, b \in S, \ c \in S'$$

If the operation on S is such that for all $a, b \in S$, $c = a * b$ is also in S, then $S' = S$ and S is said to be closed with respect to $*$.

1. If S is the set of vectors and $+$ represents vector addition

$$\mathbf{a} + \mathbf{b} = \mathbf{c} \ (\mathbf{a}, \mathbf{b}, \mathbf{c} \in S)$$

the operation is closed.
2. If . represents formation of vector scalar products

$$\mathbf{a} . \mathbf{b} = x \ (\mathbf{a}, \mathbf{b} \in S, x \notin S)$$

15

the operation is not closed.

A few writers use the term binary of an operation on a set only when it is closed (*but see* gruppoid).

binary quadratic form   An expression of the type $ax^2 + 2hxy + by^2$. The quantity $ab - h^2$ is an invariant of this expression under linear transformation.

binary relation   Any relationship in mathematics fully defined for two entities, as $x < y$, x is the square of y or x maps on to y. It should be distinguished from a binary operation, which involves a third quantity as the result of the operation, as in $x + y = c$. *See also* binary operation.

binomial coefficients   The coefficients that appear in the expansion of $(a + b)^n$ for positive integral n. The coefficient of the $(r + 1)$th term is

$$\frac{n!}{r!(n - r)!} = \frac{n(n - 1)\ldots(n - r + 1)}{r(r - 1)(r - 2)\ldots 2.1}$$

also written as $\binom{n}{r}$, ^nC_r, nCr. It also expresses the number of combinations of n different objects taken r at a time.

binomial distribution   The discrete probability distribution of successful outcomes in n independent Bernoulli trials with constant probability of success p and of failure $q = 1 - p$. The probability of x successful outcomes in n trials is given by

$$\frac{n!}{x!(n - x)!} p^x q^{n - x}$$

which is the $(x + 1)$th term in the binomial expansion of $(q + p)^n$. The mean and variance of the distribution are np and npq.

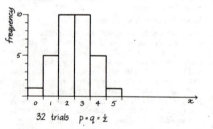

32 trials $p = q = \frac{1}{2}$

binomial theorem   Gives the expansion of $(x + a)^n$ for all permissible values of x, a, n. For all x, a and integral n the expansion is

$$(x + a)^n = x^n + nax^{n-1} + \frac{n(n - 1)}{2^1} a^2 x^{n-2} + \ldots + a^n$$

The $(r + 1)$th term is

$$\frac{n(n - 1)\ldots(n - r + 1)a^r x^{n-r}}{r!}$$

which can be written, for integral n, as

$$\frac{n!}{r!(n - r)!} a^r x^{n-r} \text{ or } \binom{n}{r} a^r x^{n-r}$$

In 1676 Newton, using a notation that expressed each term as a compound of all previous terms, showed that $(x + a)^n$ could be expanded for

16

rational powers of the form $\frac{p}{q}$. Abel (1802–1829) showed that the expansion held for all complex n, and hence for all real n.

See also Pascal's triangle.

bipolar coordinates   A system in which any point is located by means of its distances from two fixed points. It is equivalent to triangulation from a base line. The bipolar equation of an ellipse is $r_1 + r_2 = k$.

biquadratic   An expression containing terms to the fourth power, as $x^4 + 3x^3 + x + 1$. Also called quartic.

birthday problem   A standard problem in probability theory, often discussed because the result confounds naive intuition. It asks the probability that in any group of persons two or more should have the same birthday. If leap years are ignored and the monthly birthrate is taken as constant the probability p that all n persons have *different* birthdays is

$$p = \frac{365.364.\ldots.(365 - n + 1)}{365^n}$$

An approximation to this is given by

$$\log p = \frac{n(n - 1)}{730}$$

so that $p \approx \frac{1}{2}$ for a group of 23 persons. With 50 people the probability that two have the same birthday is about 0.97.

bisection   The process of dividing into two equal parts, usually in a geometrical context, as the bisection of a line or an angle. In Euclid bisection is subject to the Platonic restriction, since measurement is not permitted as a process.

bistable   Any device which has two and only two positions or states, each of which is stable and can be maintained indefinitely unless changed by an external force or input, as a switch in a circuit which can be either ON or OFF.

bit   Short for *bi*nary dig*it*, and thus having one of the two values 0, 1. It can thus be readily represented by a mechanical or electrical system with two states such as ON/OFF.

bivariate distribution   The distribution of a two-component vector whose elements are variates (or random variables), that is, of pairs of scalar variates. The individual variates may or may not be independent. Multivariate distribution extends the concept. *See also* discrete probability distribution.

bivariate normal distribution   Extends the concept of normal distribution of a random variate to two variates which are correlated. If X and Y are normally distributed quantities (X, Y) will have a bivariate normal distribution if but only if all linear combinations $aX + bY$ have normal distributions. The distribution is represented by the surface $z = f(x, y)$ whose sections by planes perpendicular to $0x$, $0y$ are normal distribution curves.

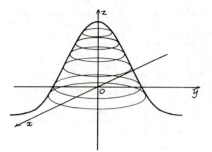

bivariate populations Each recorded numerical feature or non-numerical attribute of the elements of a population is called a variate. If two variates are recorded for each element the population is called bivariate. For a group of people we have a bivariate population if their heights and weights are recorded.

block graph A pictorial representation of information in which vertical blocks have heights which correspond to the frequency of data, such as rainfall in successive months. The graph is discontinuous, and interpolation is not meaningful. Distinguish from the visually similar histogram. The blocks may also be drawn as bars.

Bolyai, Janos Hungarian mathematician (1802–1860) who in 1832 published, as an appendix to another work, consistent theorems based on the denial of Playfair's axiom. He assumed that more than one line parallel to a given line could pass through a given point. He was, like other early workers in non-Euclidean geometries, probably hoping to prove the parallel axiom by establishing a contradiction, but concluded that the axiom was not deducible from the other axioms of Euclid.
See also proof by contradiction.

Bolzano–Weierstrass theorem If A is an infinite set of points contained in a closed interval, then at least one point of the interval is a cluster point (limit point, accumulation point) of A. It is equivalent to the statement that every bounded infinite sequence of terms contains at least one convergent subsequence.

- The interval $1 \leqslant x \leqslant 2$ contains the sequence of partial terms 1, 1.4, 1.41, 1.414, ... which converge to the limit $\sqrt{2}$.

Bonnycastle, John English teacher of mathematics (1750–1821). He wrote many mathematical works, of which the *Scholar's Guide to Arithmetic* (1780) was kept in print for over 70 years. It contained (in the year of the Gordon Riots) the notorious question: If a cardinal can pray a soul out of purgatory, by himself, in an hour, a bishop in 3 hours, a priest in 5 and a friar in 7, in what time can they pray out 3 souls, all praying together?
The answer, to an accuracy that would not seem justified by the data, is given as 1 hour 47 min. $23\frac{2}{11}$ secs.

Boolean algebra Originally developed as a form of symbolic logic or propositional calculus. Its variables x, y, z ... stood for statements, its operations $+$, $.$ and $'$ corresponded to the connectives OR, AND and negation, the symbols 0, 1 for false and true.

$x.y = 1$ reads x and y is true
$x + y = 0$ reads x or y is false

It is now regarded as an abstract structure defined by postulates for any set $B = \{a, b, c, \dots\}$ with operations $+$ and $.$, such that

1. The operations $+$ and $.$ are commutative.
2. There are identity elements 0 with respect to $+$ and 1 with respect to $..$
3. Each of the operations $+$ and $.$ is distributive over the other.
4. For each $a \in B$ there is an inverse element a' such that

$$a + a' = 1 \quad a.a' = 0$$

The structure of this algebra corresponds to that of the propositional calculus and also to set algebra if $+, ., 0, 1$ are replaced by $\cup, \cap, \emptyset, U$ and the elements $a, b, c, \dots$ by sets. Boolean algebra may be extended to multivalued logic by allowing values other than 0 and 1, e.g. $\frac{1}{2}$ to denote 'undecided'.

Boolean duality The principle that any valid theorem in Boolean algebra generates another valid theorem if the symbols $+$ and $.$ and the symbols 0 and 1 are interchanged throughout. The Boolean dual of $x + 1 = 1$ is $x.0 = 0$. The duality also applies to propositional calculus and set algebra, which have the same structure as Boolean algebra.

Boolean function Any permissible expression containing the elements $x, y, z, \dots$ of a Boolean algebra taking the values 0 and 1 and combined by the operations denoted $+, .$ and $'$. Other symbols are often used in logic or set theory

$+$ corresponds to $\cup, \vee,$ or
$.$ corresponds to $\cap, \wedge, \&,$ and
$'$ corresponds to $\sim, \neg,$ not

Boolean polynomial Any Boolean function constructed from the union of distinct intersections, denoted by $+, .$ or $\cup, \cap$.

$x.y$ is a mononomial
$x + y.z$ is a polynomial

Boole, George English mathematician (1815–64). He did work on differential equations and the calculus of finite differences, but is best known for his *Laws of Thought* (1854), which laid the foundations for mathematical or symbolic logic and led to the development of Boolean algebra.
See switching algebra.

Borda mouthpiece An idealized system in hydrodynamics. A tubular mouthpiece of circular section is inserted in an incompressible fluid so that the effect of the walls of the container are negligible.

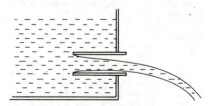

It can be shown that the resulting jet of fluid contracts to a diameter of half that of the tube. This

coefficient of contraction is modified if the walls are close to the orifice *A*.

bound Any number which, relative to a given set, is greater than, less than or equal to all the numbers in the set. All finite sets are bounded, so the term is usually applied to infinite sets of numbers which are in this way restricted.

- 1 is a bound for $1, 1, 1, \ldots$
  -2 is a bound for $0, 1, 2, \ldots$
  4 is a bound for $1, \frac{1}{2}, \frac{1}{4}, \frac{1}{8}, \ldots$
  $\ldots -3, -2, -1, 0, 1, 2, 3, \ldots$ is unbounded.

See also greatest lower bound, least upper bound.

boundary conditions (or values) In a situation described by differential equations the general solution may involve $1, 2 \ldots n$ arbitrary constants. If numerical values can be given at $1, 2 \ldots n$ points or states of the system these constants can be determined and values between these states can be calculated. Such previously assigned values are called boundary conditions. If the general solution is $f(t)$ the value at $t = 0$ is usually called an initial condition. For example, Newton's law of cooling is expressed by

$$\frac{d\theta}{dt} = -k\theta$$

which has the solution $\theta = Ce^{-kt}$, where θ is the excess over the ambient temperature. Given the values of θ at $t = 0$ and $t = t_1$, both C and k can be found. A boundary value problem is a differential equation whose required solution must satisfy conditions specified at more than one value of the independent variable

- $$\frac{d^2x}{dt^2} + \frac{3dx}{dt} - 4 = 0$$

satisfying $x = 1$ when $t = 0$ and $x = 3$ when $t = 1$.

bounded sequences A sequence $\{u_n\}$ is said to be bounded above or to have an upper bound K if there is a fixed real number K such that

$$u_n \leqslant K \text{ for all } n$$

Similarly for bounded below.

bounded set A set S of real numbers which is bounded both above and below. If the lower bound is L and the upper bound is U then for

$$x \in S \quad L \leqslant x \leqslant U$$
$$\text{or } S = \{x \mid L \leqslant x \leqslant U\}$$

bound vector Also localized vector. A geometrical vector, representing a displacement originating at a fixed point in space.
See free vector.

Bourbaki, Nicholas A name for which there is no corresponding mathematician. It appears on the title pages of the volumes of *Elements de Mathématiques*, a major survey of all worthwhile mathematics based on a strict axiomatic approach and abstract general form. The volumes are produced by a group of mainly French mathematicians, and began appearing in 1939. The work of Bourbaki has been very influential, but is sometimes considered to hinder mathematical education by too great an insistence on logical form.

Bow's notation A method based on reciprocal diagrams, introduced by R. H. Bow in 1873, for representing the internal and external forces in a system of girders or ties so that thrusts and tensions may be calculated. The system is modelled in light rods so that forces act only at the joints. The spaces between the lines of the diagram are lettered: the lines of the reciprocal diagram (or dual) are labelled to correspond to the regions by going anticlockwise round the joints. This reciprocal diagram is then a vector polygon representing the forces acting at the joints, that is, the reactions at supports and the thrusts at tensions along the framework.

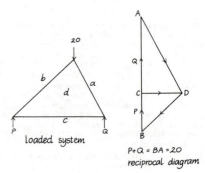

loaded system

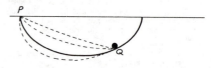

$P + Q = BA = 20$
reciprocal diagram

Starting from BC, direction of $P = BC$ is known, hence by continuing round triangle BCD, CD is a tension on frame and BD is a thrust.

brachystochrone A mass slides under gravity without friction down a path from P to a lower point not immediately below it. For what path is the time of descent least? The required curve was named *brachystochrone* (Gk. shortest time) by John Bernoulli (1696).

The curve is a cycloid described below the horizontal line PX, passing through Q with a cusp at P.
See also tautochrone, calculus of variations.

Brahe, Tycho Swedish astronomer (1546–1601). From 1576 to 1596 he had an observatory endowed by Frederick II of Denmark, where he obtained positional data of great accuracy, which after his death were used by Kepler. He held that the five known planets revolved round the sun, while the entire system revolved round the fixed earth.
See also Kepler.

branch 1. Each of the parts of a curve meeting at a cusp.
2. Each of the parts into which a multivalued expression such as $y = \sqrt{x}$ is divided to ensure compliance with the criteria for a function.

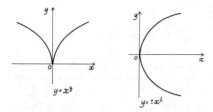

$y = x^{\frac{2}{3}}$

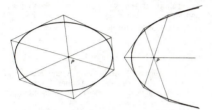

$y = \pm x^{\frac{1}{2}}$

Brianchon's theorem If any hexagon is circumscribed to a closed conic, then the joins of opposite pairs of vertices are concurrent. This is the dual of Pascal's theorem and may be generalized.

By projecting the configuration for a closed conic so that the one point goes towards infinity it can be shown that the theorem holds for any conic.

Briggs, Henry (1561–1631) The first Savilian professor of astronomy at Oxford, who in 1615 proposed a system of logarithms to base 10, with the use of the words characteristic and mantissa (Lat. a makeweight) for the integral and decimal parts of a logarithm. He calculated logarithms for numbers 1–20,000 and 90,000–100,000: the gap was filled by Vlacq (1600–1660).
See also Napier, natural logarithms.

Briggsian logarithms *See* Briggs.

Brocard's point Named by Henri Brocard (1845–1922). A point within a triangle ABC where three circles $\Gamma_1, \Gamma_2, \Gamma_3$ intersect.

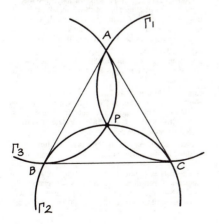

Γ_1 touches at A and C, having BA and BC as tangents.
Γ_2 touches at C and B, having AC and AB as tangents.
Γ_3 touches at B and A, having CB and CA as tangents.
The construction must be taken either clockwise or anticlockwise round the triangle.
P is the Brocard point.

Brouwer, L. E. J. Dutch mathematician (1882–1966). One of the leading topologists of his time, but mainly remembered as one of the leaders of the 'intuitionist' view of the foundations of mathematics, as opposed to the formalist logical school. Brouwer argued that formal logic was abstracted from mathematics in the first place, and so could not serve as a basis for its subsequent development.

Buffon's needle An experiment in geometrical probability conducted by the Comte de Buffon (1707–1788). A plane surface is ruled with parallel lines a units apart, and a needle of length c, where $c < a$, is repeatedly dropped on it at random. He found that the probability of the needle lying on one of the lines, as an experimental occurrence ratio, is approximately $\dfrac{2c}{\pi a}$ The result, equivalent to a Monte Carlo method for determining π, approximates to the value of

$$\frac{c \displaystyle\int_0^{\pi} \sin\theta \, d\theta}{a \displaystyle\int_0^{\pi} d\theta}$$

which arises by considering possible orientations of the needle.

bulk modulus *See* modulus of elasticity. If the deforming force is an external pressure compressing a solid body which returns to its original volume when the pressure is removed, the constant of elasticity is called the bulk modulus, K. Then

$$K = \frac{\text{stress}}{\text{strain}} = F / \frac{\delta v}{v}$$

where stress is force per unit of surface area and strain is ratio between the change of volume and the original volume.

C

calculation Originally the work of the calculator. It now refers to a routine process for performing the operations of arithmetic using a knowledge of number facts and standard or *ad hoc* algorithmic methods. Calculation often follows algebraic or analytic processes to reduce them to a numerical answer and is now frequently performed by mechanical or electronic devices. *See also* numerical methods.

calculator 1. Originally a person who performed number operations with a pile of small pebbles (Lat. *calculus*, a little pebble). Now a term for a machine, usually small, portable and electronic, which performs and displays the results of arithmetic and other operations on numerical data.
2. Programmable calculator. An electronic device which will accept external programs and can encode and store them internally.
3. Desk calculator. Any calculator too large to be hand-held or conveniently portable, frequently displaying numerical results in printed form on paper.

calculus (Lat. a little pebble, as used by the *calculator*, one who reckoned by using pebbles as counters). A word used generally for any method of calculation for dealing with specific problems, as calculus of errors, calculus of variations and infinitesimal calculus (now called analysis).

calculus of errors If a physical quantity depends on a number of measured variables each of which is subject to error, the final calculation of the quantity will be subject to error. The calculus of errors discusses the limits between which the 'true' (or indeterminable) value may be expected to lie, and thus allows physical quantities to be given with suitable tolerances.

calculus of variations Investigates the total behaviour of a function f, and in particular whether the function has maximum or minimum values between given limits. Its use is best seen by examples:
1. If a particle slides down a smooth arc of the curve between points A, B, how does the total time vary with the parameters and what is the shape of this curve so that the total time is a minimum? This path is the brachystochrone.

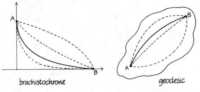

brachistochrone   geodesic

2. Of all paths between A and B on any surface given by $\int_A^B ds$ which is the shortest?

See geodesic.

cancellation law 1. Rule for removing common factors in the numerator and denominator of fractions

by dividing through by the factor, as in

$$\frac{yx}{zx} = \frac{y}{z}$$

It is an unsatisfactory term, and its verbal equivalent 'cancel x' leads to mistakes in elementary arithmetic.
2. Used specifically for a set of related theorems involving additive or multiplicative operations. In each case a repeated symbol may be deleted without affecting the result.

If $a+c = b+c$ then $a = b$ for all a, b, c.
If $a.c = b.c$ then $a = b$ for all a, b and $c \neq 0$.

canonical Used generally of an expression that is standard, typical or representative, as in 'canonical form', a form chosen as in some respects the simplest and most illuminating representative of its class.

1. The canonical form for the equation of an ellipse is

$$\frac{x^2}{a^2} + \frac{y^2}{b^2} = 1$$

2 If an absorbing Markov chain is represented by the matrix of its possible set of states $a, b, c \ldots$ the matrix is canonical if the elements are arranged so that the absorbing states come first.
3. A Boolean function in n variables becomes canonical if it is rewritten so that each of the n variables occurs in each term:
$X' \cup (X \cap Y') = (X' \cap \mathcal{E}) \cup (X \cap Y')$ where $\mathcal{E}$ is the universal set
$$= (X' \cap (Y \cup Y')) \cup (X \cap Y')$$
$$= (X' \cap Y) \cup (X' \cap Y') \cup (X \cap Y')$$

Cantor, Georg German mathematician (1845–1918). After early work in number theory and trigonometrical functions he became interested in the foundations of mathematics. He defined real numbers as convergent sequences of rationals, introduced the concept of set by definition, and developed a theory of transfinite numbers. The validity of his later arguments is still a matter of controversy.

Cantor, Moritz (1829–1920) Writer of a standard history of mathematics up to end of the 18th century.

Cantor's paradox A paradox of naive set theory. Since the cardinal number of the set of all subsets of any set S is greater than that of S itself, it follows that if U is the set of all sets (which includes all subsets) then cardinal U is greater than itself.

cap 1. *See* cup.
2. A spherical segment smaller than a hemisphere, cut off by a plane not passing through the centre of the sphere.

capacity Not a defined term in mathematics. It is equivalent to volume, but is used of a three-dimensional region acting as a container or boundary, usually for fluids. It gives the measure of such a region without reference to shape.

cardinal arithmetic Has the same structure as the arithmetic of natural numbers. Each of the symbols $0, 1, 2, 3 \ldots$ is associated with equinumerous (or equipotent) sets and is arrived at by counting the elements. Operations of addition etc. between the cardinals then corresponds to operations on the sets. Thus if card $A = a$, card $B = b$ then $a+b =$ card $(A \cup B)$, if but only if $A \cap B = \emptyset$.

20

cardinal number A word describing how many elements are contained in a given set without reference to their order. Sets are said to be 'numerically equivalent' or to 'have the same cardinal number' if the elements of one set can be put into one to one correspondence with the elements of the other. The null set is then given the cardinal number *zero*, the set of all null sets is given cardinal *one*. The set A defined as follows has cardinal two:

If $x, y, z \in A$ then either $z = x$ or $z = y$.

The union of disjoint sets of cardinalities one and two has cardinality three, and thus a sequence of cardinal numbers is generated in order of magnitude. They are sometimes denoted by $\bar{0}, \bar{1}, \bar{2}, \bar{3}, \ldots$ The natural numbers $0, 1, 2, 3, \ldots$ are mathematical entities, which correspond to the cardinals, and which form a realization of Peano's axioms, although some accounts do not recognize 0 as a natural number. Ordinary usage in arithmetic does not distinguish between the symbols, and cardinals are written $0, 1, 2, 3, \ldots$ The cardinality of a set can then be established by putting its elements into 1:1 correspondence with the set of natural numbers.
See finite cardinal, transfinite cardinal.

cardinal of the continuum *See* transfinite cardinal.

cardioid A heart-shaped closed curve whose polar equation is of the form $r = a(1 + \cos\theta)$ having a cusp at the origin or pole.

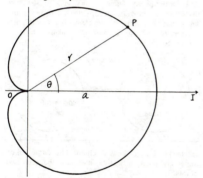

Rotation about the pole through angles $\pi, \pi/2, 3\pi/2$ gives the alternative forms $r = a(1 - \cos\theta)$, $r = a(1 + \sin\theta)$, $r = a(1 - \sin\theta)$. This curve is a special case of the limaçon.

cartesian coordinates A system for representing vectors or fixing points by reference to a set of intersecting linear axes. The point of intersection is the origin and the coordinates are the intercepts on the axes, formed *either* by dropping perpendiculars *or* by drawing lines parallel to the axes.
The two constructions give the same result for rectangular coordinates, but gave rise to different coordinate systems for oblique axes. (*See* covariant and contravariant.)

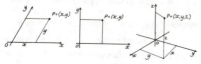

The axes can be constructed in two or three dimensions, and extended by analogy to n.

cartesian graph Any set of points, usually representing a line or any given configuration, plotted as number pairs on a cartesian coordinate system.

cartesian oval The set of all points in a plane whose distances r_1, r_2 from the two fixed points of the plane are related linearly, that is $lr_1 + mr_2 = P$. If $l = m$ the oval is an ellipse, as drawn with a loop of string around two fixed pins.

cartesian product If A and B are sets, the set of all ordered pairs (a, b), where $a \in A$ and $b \in B$, is called the cartesian or cross-product of A and B, written $A \times B$. The product $A \times A$ is often written A^2. The operation is not in general commutative.

- $A = \{a, b\}$
  $B = \{1, 2, 3\}$
$A \times B = \{(a, 1), (a, 2), (a, 3), (b, 1), (b, 2), (b, 3)\}$
$B \times A = \{(1, a), (1, b), (2, a), (2, b), (3, a), (3, b)\}$

The operation can be extended to more than two sets.
See also product.

Cassini ovals The set of plane curves produced by considering points P such that the distances r_1, r_2 from fixed points S and S' are related by

$$r_1 r_2 = b^2$$

where b is a constant. They were originally suggested by Cassini as the shapes of planetary orbits, as an alternative to the Newtonian ellipses.
The cartesian equation is

$$[(x - a)^2 + y^2][(x + a)^2 + y^2] = b^4$$

where $SS' = 2a$.

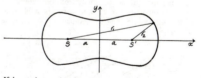

If $b < a$ the oval reduces to two ovals.

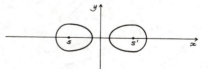

If $b = a$ the oval becomes the lemniscate of Bernoulli, of which the polar equation is

$$r^2 = c^2 \cos 2\theta \text{ where } c = \sqrt{2}b$$

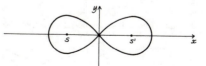

Cassini projection A modified cylindrical projection formerly used for the Ordnance Survey of Great Britain (up to about 1938). It is only used for small countries or land areas.

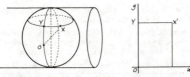

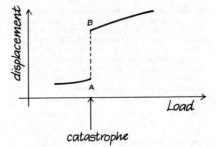

catastrophe

The cylinder is tangent to the standard meridian chosen, and O is the point on the earth chosen as the origin of the projection. If X is any point on the earth, XY is the great circle distance from X to the meridian. The distances OY, YX are calculated as the sides of spherical triangles, and these are transferred as rectangular cartesian coordinates to the graticule, so that the position of X is given as X′ on the map. The projection distorts directions as it moves away from the central meridian. Devised by the Cassinis (father and son) 1625–1712, 1677–1756.

catastrophe Originally a technical term for the final action in Greek drama, the word now applies to a sudden disastrous event, but in mathematics is used for any discontinuous change in the values of a function which may model a physical system. Based on work done by René Thom in 1972 on the classification of functional discontinuities, it aroused interest because the mathematical models seemed to apply not only to physical systems, such as the bursting of a bubble or the collapse of a stressed framework, but, at least qualitatively, to changes of mood and the outbreak of quarrels. For $1, 2 \ldots n$ variables the expressions relating them split into a number of functional branches separated by cusps and/or discontinuities of which there are only a finite (and small) number of distinct types. At the cusp the variables move discontinuously from one branch of the function to the other, and hence in a physical system move from one to another of two possible states.

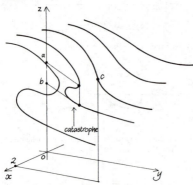

A simple example is the vertical displacement of a loaded spring strip as shown in the diagram.

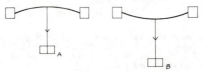

As the load increases continuously the spring snaps into a second equilibrium position and the graph jumps from A to B. Note that it is the mathematical model that shows discontinuities: the physical phenomena are merely in rapid chaotic (q.v) change, as a high-speed camera would show with the steel spring.

category 1. According to the philosopher Immanuel Kant (1724–1804) mathematical (and other knowledge) is founded on the primary concepts of unity, multiplicity, continuity and so on, which he called 'categories': these are the essential and necessary bases of all thinking.
2. An attempt to define a very general structure involving sets, function, groups etc. A category is any set or class of entities whose elements taken in pairs are related by a set of homomorphisms subject to certain conditions.

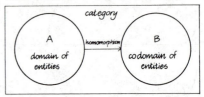

catenary Lat. *catenus* a chain. The curve taken under gravity by a flexible chain hung between two points.

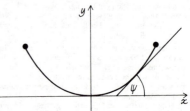

It is given by $y = a \cosh \dfrac{x}{a}$. Its intrinsic equation is $s = a \tan \psi$. The involute to the catenary is the tractrix.

catenoid The surface of revolution formed by rotating the catenary $y = a \cosh \dfrac{x}{a} + c$ about $y = 0$. It is the minimal plateau surface joining two circles, and can be demonstrated by supporting a soap bubble between two parallel loops, pricking the film within the circles.

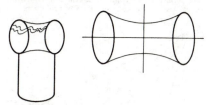

Cauchy, Baron August Louis French mathematician (1789–1857). One of the founders of modern analysis who published a *Cours d'analyse* in 1821. He also studied the functions of complex numbers.

Cauchy mean value theorem *See* mean value theorem.

Cauchy sequence A sequence provided with a metric or distance function with the property that the distance or difference between two successive terms becomes arbitrarily small after a certain term. Then $|u_{n+1} - u_n| < \epsilon$ for all $n > N(\epsilon)$ where ϵ is chosen arbitrarily and $N(\epsilon)$ is the number of a term that depends on the value of ϵ chosen. The modulus sign denotes the distance function. The result is also written $|\lim u_{n+1} - u_n| = 0$ in which case $\lim_{n \to \infty} u_n$ is called the limit of the sequence. The existence of this limit may be postulated as an axiom. When this limit is irrational, as with the sequence $\{u_n\} = 1, 1.4, 1.41, 1.414, 1.4142\ldots$, which arises in calculating $\sqrt{2}$, the sequence can be held to define a real number. This is the number assigned to the set of all sequences equal to $\{u_n\}$.
See also Dedekind section, completeness.

Cauchy's tests Tests for the convergence of the infinite series $\sum\limits_{n=1}^{\alpha} a_n$

1. Condensation test: The series $\sum\limits_{n=1}^{\infty} a_n$ such that $a_{n+1} \leqslant a_n$ converges if and only if $\sum\limits_{k=0}^{\infty} 2^k a_{2^k}$ converges. The test holds for divergence.
2. Root test: If $a_n \geqslant 0$ and the nth root of a_n tends to a limit as n increases indefinitely, then $\sum\limits_{n=1}^{\infty} a_n$ converges if $L < 1$ and diverges if $L > 1$. The test gives no information for a series such as $\sum \dfrac{1}{n(n+1)}$ where $L = 1$.

caustic curve *See* hypocycloid.

Cayley, Arthur English lawyer and mathematician (1821–95), who became the first Sadlerian professor at Cambridge in 1863. He did important work on matrices, groups, elliptic functions and projective geometry.

Cayley's theorem Every finite group G is isomorphic with a permutation group P.
● The additive group $G = \{0, 1, 2\}$ of residues mod 3 and the group of permutations $\{ABC, BCA, CAB\}$ with respect to combination.

c.d.f. *See* cumulative distribution function.

Celsius, Anders Swedish astronomer (1701–1744). Took part in French expedition of 1736 to measure the arc of a meridian, and described his thermometer scale to the Swedish Academy in 1742. The scale of degrees Celsius is named after him.
See also centigrade.

centigrade 1. A measure of angle (*see* grad), now rarely used.
2. The anomalous English usage for the Celsius temperature scale, still commonly found.

central conic Any conic section symmetrical about a point.

central force Any force directed towards a pole or centre, as the gravitational attraction by the sun on a planet in Newton's hypothesis.

central inversion The mapping of a configuration on to itself relative to an origin about which it is symmetrical. Each point is transformed into its reflection in the origin. It is one of the total symmetries of the configuration.

central limit theorem This states that the means of successive sufficiently large random samples drawn from any population will be normally distributed, irrespective of the distribution of the population. That is, if $x_1, x_2 \ldots x_n$ is a random sample of size n from any probability distribution whatsoever having a mean μ and variance σ^2 then the distribution of the sample means is normal, having mean μ and variance σ^2/n.

central moments *See* moment.

central orbit The path of a body moving freely in space under the action of a centripetal force. If the force is due to an inverse square gravitational attraction of a mass large compared with that of the moving body, the central orbits are conics.

central projection A mapping relating one configuration to another so that the lines joining corresponding points are concurrent.
See also perspectivity.

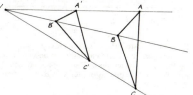

Note that the configurations are not necessarily similar, but *see also* homothetic.

central quadric *See* quadric surface.

central symmetry *See* point of symmetry.

central tendency A measure (also called measure of location) which indicates the average or typical value in a sample or population. The most usual measures are the mean (or arithmetic mean) the median and the mode.

centre (Gk. *kentron*, a sharp point). In Euclid, the point around which a circle is drawn, and hence considered by him to be part of the circle. Also, of conics or other configurations, the centre of symmetry, from which any point P and its image are equidistant.

centre of buoyancy For a body wholly or partly submerged in a liquid, the point through which the resultant upthrust acts is called the centre of buoyancy. It corresponds to the centre of mass of the liquid displaced.
See also metacentre.

centre of curvature *See* radius of curvature.

centre of gravity Every rigid body, considered as a system of mass elements, has a unique point, not necessarily within it, at which the total moment on the mass elements due to a uniform gravitational field is zero. This point is the centre of gravity. For a system of discrete point masses on an axis at distances $x_1, x_2 \ldots x_n$ from the origin, having weights $w_1, w_2 \ldots w_n$ the distance $\bar{x}$ of the centre of gravity is given by

$$\bar{x} = \frac{\sum\limits_{i=1}^{n} w_i x_i}{\sum\limits_{i=1}^{n} w_i}$$

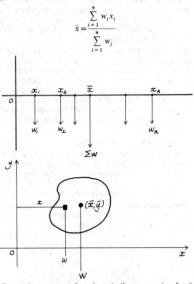

For a plane system there is a similar expression for $\bar{y}$ and for continuous laminae the position of $\bar{x}, \bar{y}$ can be found by integration. The summation can be extended to three dimensions for a solid.
See centroid.

centre of inversion *See* inversion.

centre of mass If a mass m_1, at x_1, y_1 is considered to have a moment about the y axis of $m_1 x_1$ and about the x axis of $m_1 y_1$, then the centre of mass of a system of such masses is given by $\bar{x}, \bar{y}$, where

$$\bar{x} = \frac{\sum\limits_{i=1}^{n} m_i x_i}{\sum\limits_{i=1}^{n} m_i}$$

with a similar expression for $\bar{y}$. The point corresponds to the centre of gravity if the system is in a uniform gravitational field. The centre of mass of a plane region considered as a set of elements whose masses are proportional to their areas corresponds to the centroid.

centre of oscillation *See* compound pendulum.

centre of perspective The point at which lines joining corresponding points in a central perspectivity meet. Also called centre or vertex of projection.

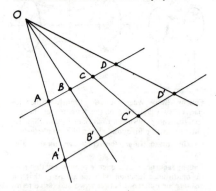

centre of pressure The point on a surface subject to hydrostatic pressure through which the resultant thrust acts.

centre of similitude *See* homothetic transformation, where it is called the centre of enlargement or dilatation. It is commonly used of the dilatation of coplanar circles, in which case the general enlargement has two centres of similitude.

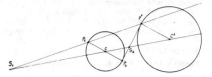

These are S_1 and S_2 and lie on the line joining the centres of the circles, and are such that $S_1 P_1 P'$, $S_2 P_2 P'$ are straight lines, where CP_1, CP_2 are parallel to $C'P'$. Concentric or equal circles have only one centre of similitude on the Euclidean plane.

centrifugal force A virtual force arising as the reaction to an actual centripetal force. Thus a string exerts a tension to deflect a mass from a straight line path into a circle described about one end of the string: the reaction to this tension is a force directed away from the centre, and is the so-called centrifugal force. A hypothetical observer moving with the mass would experience the force as a tendency to move away radially from the centre, but this force would disappear should the string snap, allowing the mass to continue in a straight line.
See also Coriolis force.

centripetal force Any force acting on a moving body and directed towards a centre so that the motion becomes a curve concave towards the centre. Examples are the gravitational force postulated by Newton to explain planetary orbits or the tension in a string constraining a mass to revolve in a circular arc.

centroid *See* centre of gravity. Sometimes used for centre of gravity of a plane area.

Ceva's theorem   1. If three points divide the three sides of a triangle, internally or externally, into three ratios whose product is unity, then the joins of the points to opposite vertices are concurrent.

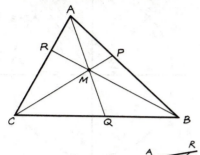

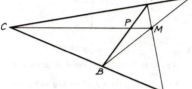

In each diagram, for triangle ABC

$$\frac{AP}{PB} \times \frac{BQ}{QC} \times \frac{CR}{RA} = 1$$

A corollary of this theorem is that the medians of a triangle are concurrent.
2. The corresponding theorem in projective geometry for triangle ABC and a point O.

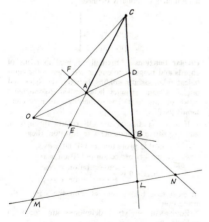

If $AO \cap BC = D$, $BO \cap CA = E$, $CO \cap BA = F$, and if BC, CA, AB meet an arbitrary line in L, M, N then the product of cross ratios (BCDL).(CAEM). (ABFN) = −1. AO, BO, CO, are the Cevian lines of the configuration.

Ceva, Tomasso   (1648–1746) An Italian Jesuit who taught mathematics in Milan. The theorem named after him was published in 1678.

c.g.s.   An earlier system of physical units taking the centimetre, the gram and the second as fundamental. It proved to be inconvenient in electrotechnology, and was eventually replaced by the MKSA system, using the metre, kilogram, second and ampere. This, subject to internationally agreed definitions and conventions, became the Système International d'Unités or SI.
See Appendix 1.

chain rule   1. Commonly given in the Leibnitz notation, for $y = f(u)$, $u = f(v) = f(w) \dots$ as

$$\frac{dy}{dx} = \frac{dy}{du} \cdot \frac{du}{dv} \cdot \frac{dv}{dw} \dots$$

The notation makes this result look more obvious than actually it is. It is avoided in analysis but is of general use in applied mathematics.
2. If a function g has a derivative at a and a function f has a derivative at $g(a)$, then $f \circ g$, read 'f of g', has a derivative at a, given by the chain rule as $(f \circ g)'(a) = f'[g(a)].g'(a)$ and so on for $(f \circ g)oh$. A similar rule is stated for partial derivatives.
For g, f in three dimensions

$$\frac{\partial g}{\partial v} = \frac{\partial f}{\partial x} \cdot \frac{\partial x}{\partial v} + \frac{\partial f}{\partial y} \cdot \frac{\partial y}{\partial v} + \frac{\partial f}{\partial z} \cdot \frac{\partial z}{\partial v}$$

where $f(x, y, z)$ is transformed to $g(u, v, w)$ using the transformations $x = x(u, v, w)$, $y = y(u, v, w)$ and $z = z(u, v, w)$.

chance   *See* random.

chaotic   In its technical use describes a physical system governed over any small region by a large number of ill-conditioned equations whose coefficients vary from point to point within the region whose boundaries are also unstable. The system is indeterminate at any one point and tends to develop quasi-stable regional sub-systems, although the mean parameters over the system as a whole are determined. An example is a turbulent air stream with vortices.

characteristic   1. The integral part of a logarithm.

● $\log 33 = 1.5185 \dots$ Here the characteristic is 1.

2. The word is also sometimes used for the determinant of a set of simultaneous equations whose terms form a square array.

$$\begin{vmatrix} a_1 & b_1 & c_1 \\ a_2 & b_2 & c_2 \\ a_3 & b_3 & c_3 \end{vmatrix}$$

is the characteristic of

$$a_1 x + b_1 y + c_1 = 0$$
$$a_2 x + b_2 y + c_2 = 0$$
$$a_3 x + b_3 y + c_3 = 0$$

characteristic equation   For a difference equation

$$a_k u_{n+k} + a_{k-1} u_{n+k-1} + \dots + a_0 u_0 = 0$$

the characteristic equation is

$$a_k r^k + a_{k-1} r^{k-1} + \dots a_0 = 0$$

The roots of this equation determine the general solution of the difference equation.
See also eigenequation.

characteristic function If x is a variate, its characteristic function is the expected value $E(e^{ixt})$. This can be expanded as a power series and is hence a moment-generating function.

chi-squared (χ^2) distribution This is a gamma distribution with parameters $\alpha = \dfrac{v}{2}$ and $\lambda = \dfrac{1}{2}$ where v is the degrees of freedom of the systems investigated. The probability density function is

$$f_\chi(x) = \frac{1}{2^{v/2}\Gamma(\frac{v}{2})} \cdot x^{v/2-1} e^{-x/2} \quad \text{for } x \geqslant 0$$
$$= 0 \text{ for } x < 0$$

chi-squared (χ^2) test A test used on frequency data, where each observation falls into one set of classes. The test statistic of the form $\chi^2 = \sum\limits_{j=1}^{n} \dfrac{(O_j - E_j)^2}{E_j}$ ($j = 1 \dots n$) has the χ^2 distribution, with $v = n - 1$ for degrees of freedom. For a $k \times r$ contingency table

$$\chi^2 = \sum_{i=1}^{k} \sum_{j=1}^{r} \frac{(O_{ij} - E_{ij})^2}{E_{ij}} \quad \text{with } v = (k-1)(r-1)$$

There is a special case for a 2×2 table, where $v = 1$, and the numerator then becomes $(|O_{ij} - E_{ij}| - \frac{1}{2})^2$.

chord tables Give the length of the chords for arcs of a unit circle subtending given angles, at the centre, and formerly used for marking out angles. A scale of chords was often given on sectors, using the arms as a unit radius.

circle The set of coplanar points equidistant from a fixed point, given by the equation $(x-h)^2 + (y-k)^2 = a^2$ for a circle of radius a and centre (h, k). Euclid (Book I Def. 15) considers the circle to be the region contained by the circumference but the modern view distinguishes the circle from the disc.

circle of Apollonius The set of all coplanar points, whose distances from fixed points A, B in the plane are in a constant ratio $r \neq 1$, lie on the circle so named.

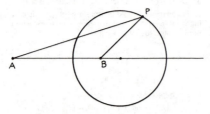

As PA/PB$\to$1 the radius of the circle increases without limit. Its arc then approaches the perpendicular bisector of AB.

circle of convergence If a power series $\Sigma a_n z^n$ ($z \in \mathbb{C}$) is absolutely convergent for all values of z within the circle $|z| = r$ but divergent outside the circle then $|z| = r$ is the circle of convergence of radius r. The series is not necessarily convergent when $|z| = r$, and diverges if $|z| > r$.

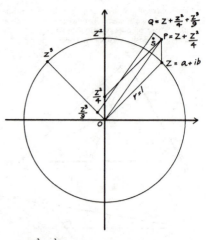

- $\dfrac{z}{1^2} + \dfrac{z^2}{2^2} + \dfrac{z^3}{3^2} + \dots$ converges if $|z| \leqslant 1$

The first three terms are plotted on an Argand diagram.

The parallelogram sum of the first two is represented by P, and of the first three by Q, and it is clear that the successive partial sums spiral inwards to a point S very close to Q, which itself need not be within the circle.

circle of curvature *See* radius of curvature.

circle of inversion *See* inversion.

circulant A determinant of order n whose rows (or columns) are successive cyclic permutations of the n elements in the first row (or column). A circulant $n \times n$ matrix is similarly defined:

$$\begin{vmatrix} a_1 & a_2 & a_3 \\ a_2 & a_3 & a_1 \\ a_3 & a_1 & a_2 \end{vmatrix}$$

circular functions Originally defined in terms of chords and tangents to circles and later as the equivalent relationships holding between the sides and angles of right triangles, hence called trigonometric ratios or functions. Two definitions are now commonly used:

1. If a unit radius vector OP rotates through an angle (positive in anticlockwise direction) then,

sine θ is projection of OP on y axis.
cosine θ is projection of OP on x axis.
tangent θ is $\dfrac{\text{projection on } y \text{ axis}}{\text{projection on } x \text{ axis}}$

in each case taking into account the sign of the projection.

2. Equivalent analytical definitions are, for θ in radians

$$\sin \theta = \theta - \theta^3/3! + \theta^5/5! - \theta^7/7! + \dots$$
$$\cos \theta = 1 - \theta^2/2! + \theta^4/4! - \theta^6/6! + \dots$$
$$\tan \theta = \sin \theta / \cos \theta \ (\cos \theta \neq 0)$$

The reciprocals of the circular functions when these

are non-zero are:

$$1/\sin\theta = \text{cosecant }\theta \text{ or csc }\theta$$
$$1/\cos\theta = \text{secant }\theta \text{ or sec }\theta$$
$$1/\tan\theta = \text{cotangent }\theta \text{ or cot }\theta$$

(*See also* hyperbolic functions).
The inverses of the circular functions, that is, the angles corresponding to any values of the function, are denoted by arc sin θ, arc cos θ, arc tan θ. An older notation uses $\sin^{-1}\theta$, $\cos^{-1}\theta$, $\tan^{-1}\theta$.

circular measure Measures angle as a pure number, the ratio between the length of arc of a circle subtending the angle at its centre, and the radius of the circle. Hence one complete turn is given by $2\pi r/r = 2\pi$. The unit is taken as the angle subtended by an arc of length equal to the radius and is called the radian (rad). Hence

$$2\pi \text{ rad} = 360°$$
$$1 \text{ rad} \approx 57.29°$$

The measure is taken as positive in the anticlockwise sense. Sometimes 2π rad is denoted by $2\pi^c$.
The radian is a supplementary unit of SI.

circular points (at infinity) In general, any two conics intersect in four points, given by the four roots of the quartic equation which arises when the two quadratic equations in x and y representing the conics are solved simultaneously. If the two conics are circles, coefficients of the terms in x^4 and x^3 are zero, and hence the quartic has two infinite roots. Alternatively the circles of the form

$$(x+g)^2 + (y+h)^2 = a^2$$

may be written in homogeneous coordinates which reduce to $x^2 + y^2 = 0$ when $z = 0$. These have the solution $y = +ix$, hence all circles contain the points whose homogeneous coordinates are $(1, i, 0)$ and $(1, -i, 0)$. These are the so-called circular points at infinity.

circulating decimal *See* recurring decimal.

circulation The product of the tangential velocity and the perimeter when an element of fluid moves at a constant velocity round a closed loop in the fluid (as with vortex motion). If the velocity is not uniform the circulation is given by

$$\oint v dl, \text{ or, with vectors } \oint v \mathbf{dr}$$

that is, by the integral round the closed loop or contour.
See also reducible loop.

circumference *See* perimeter.

cis θ An abbreviation sometimes used for $(\cos\theta + i\sin\theta)$.

Cissoid of Diocles Curve constructed by Diocles (c. 180 B.C.).

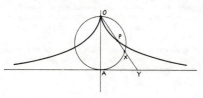

A tangent is drawn at A to a circle of diameter OA. Lines OXY are drawn cutting the circle in X and the tangent in Y. Points P are taken on OX so that OP = XY. The set of all points P forms the cissoid, whose pole is at O.
The cartesian equation of the cissoid with O as origin and OA = 2a as the positive x axis is

$$y^2 = \frac{x^3}{2a - x}$$

The cissoid solves the Delian problem of duplicating the cube.

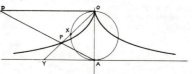

Draw a parallel tangent at O and take D on this tangent so that OD = 2OA. Let DA cut the cissoid at P and OP produced cut the tangent at Y. Then, from the equation,

$$AY^3 = 2OA^3$$

Hence AY is the side of the cube which duplicates a cube of side OA.

Clairaut, Alexis French mathematician (1713–65) remembered for his computation of the return of Halley's comet in 1759, his discussion of the shape of the earth as an oblate spheroid, and the differential equation given in modern notation by

$$y = y'x + f(y')$$

class 1. Any convenient subdivision of a set or range of data into subsets for the purposes of statistical analysis. (*See also* class boundaries).
2. A synonym of set which is normally used only when the members are closely related. Thus one speaks of the set of integers, but of the class of residues modulo *n*.
3. In discussions of the foundation of mathematics, the word is sometimes used as a wider term than set, so that one speaks of the 'class of all sets' rather than 'set of all sets'.

class boundaries When a data-range is divided into subranges or classes for the purposes of statistical analysis, each class must be mutually exclusive.
For discrete values of the data the class boundaries should be non-observable quantities to avoid ambiguity, for example the data set $\{1, 2, 3, 4, 5, 6\}$ is divided unambiguously into two classes by the boundaries $\frac{1}{2}, 3\frac{1}{2}, 6\frac{1}{2}$.
See also class limits.

class interval When extensive data are to be analysed it is usual to group the data into a convenient number of classes to give a clearer impression of the overall distribution. Such groups are usually equal and mutually exclusive, although within them the data may be discrete or continuous. The class interval then defines or gives the range of each class.

class limits The smallest and largest observable values in a class or subrange of data.
See also class boundaries.

class midpoint If a set of data or observations is

grouped or divided into classes for the purposes of statistical analysis, the central value of each class interval is the class midpoint.

closed ball *See* ball.

closed curve A continuous curve with coincident end points. If the curve is $x=f(t)$, $y=g(t)$, then for $t_1 \leqslant t \leqslant t_2$ a closed curve will have the property

$$f(t_1)=f(t_2)$$
$$g(t_1)=g(t_2)$$

Similarly for a three-dimensional curve defined by

$$x=f(t),\ y=g(t),\ z=h(t)$$

over the interval.
A *simple* closed curve such as the ellipse is one that does not intersect itself. The lemniscate is not simple.

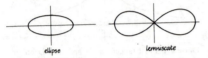

ellipse   lemniscate

closed disc *See* disc.

closed interval A subset of the set $\mathbb{R}$ of real numbers. If $a,\ b \in \mathbb{R}$ then the set of all real numbers x such that $a \leqslant x \leqslant b$ is called a closed interval and denoted $[a,b]$. Such an interval may be represented by a finite section of the real number line between a and b, including these two end points. Closed intervals are often associated with continuous functions and are thus important in analysis. They are sometimes shown in diagrams as intervals between heavy dots, as $1 \leqslant x \leqslant 3$ below:

0   1   2   3   4

Since a and b are limit points a closed interval may be defined as one that contains all its limit points.

closed set 1. Any closed interval, closed disc or closed ball such as $x^2+y^2+z^2 \leqslant 1$ is a closed set of points, corresponding to subsets of numbers in $\mathbb{R}$, $\mathbb{R}^2$ or $\mathbb{R}^3$.
2. In topology, where there is no meaning to the symbols $\leqslant$ or $\geqslant$ a closed set is defined as the complement of an open set.

closure When two elements of a set A are combined by a binary operation the result may or may not be an element of the set A. If the result does lie in the set A for all possible choices of pairs of elements the set is said to be closed for that operation. For a set S with operation $*$, this means that $\forall x$, $y \in S \Rightarrow x*y \in S$.

● The set $\mathbb{Z}$ is closed under multiplication but not division.
  The set of plane vectors is closed for vector addition, but not for scalar product.

Note that some writers use the term binary operation only when the closure condition is satisfied.

cluster point Consider a set of points S, or of real or complex numbers which may be represented by points, and a suitable metric that defines distance or difference d between members of the set. If there is a point or number x, not necessarily an element of S, such that for any $d>0$, however small, there is a member of S whose distance from x is less than d,

then x is a cluster point of S. Also called limit point or point of accumulation. That is, the interval $(x-d)$ to $(x+d)$ always contains at least one point $x_1 \in S$. The concept is linked to the idea of the boundary of a region or the limit of a sequence.

● The set $\mathbb{Z}$ has no cluster points.
  The set $S=\{1,\frac{1}{2},\frac{1}{3},\frac{1}{4}\dots\}$ has a cluster point at the origin, not in S.
  In the set $\mathbb{Q}$ every point is a cluster point.

coaxial circles There are two formulations

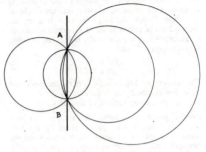

1. The set Γ of all coplanar circles passing through points A, B on a line PQ, called the *radical axis*, which is the line of symmetry for the configuration.

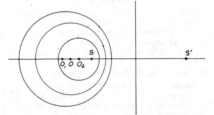

2. A point S is inverted into a point S' with respect to a circle centre O radius r so that $OS.OS'=r^2$. A second circle centre O_1 radius r_1 is drawn so that $O_1S.O_1S'=r^2$, and similarly for circles centre O_2, $O_3 \dots$, with respect to which S, S' are mates in the inversion. By inverting S' to S the configuration is seen to be symmetrical about PQ, the perpendicular bisector of S S', which is the radical axis of the coaxial set of circles Γ_2. S and S' are the limit points of the system. If O initially coincides with S the radical axis is at infinity and Γ becomes a set of concentric circles.

cobasal range If the range R of all points on a given line is put into correspondence with itself, so that for every $A \in R$ there is an $A' \in R$, then the ranges $A,\ B,\ C \dots,\ A',\ B',\ C',\dots$ (which could be sub-ranges of R) are said to be cobasal.

cobweb curve If an equation $f(x)=0$ is written as $F(x)-x=0$ then a root $x=\alpha$ is given by the simultaneous solution of

$$y=x$$
$$y=F(x)$$

This is shown graphically below

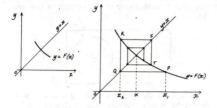

If an approximate root x_1 for $f(x) = 0$ is taken on $F(x)$ at P then $F(x_1) = y$, which corresponds to the points Q on $y = x$. The abscissa of Q is x_2, say. Then R is the point (x_2, y_2) where $y_2 = F(x_2)$ and so on for successive points R, S, T ... If the mean slope M in an interval of α containing x_1 is given by

$$|M| < 1$$

the successive lines will converge to α, otherwise they will diverge. The name cobweb curve describes the shape of the configuration. It is used in economics, where it is found that arbitrary values of production, later modified to meet actual demand, tend to spiral in to a theoretical value at which demand and supply coincide. It also shows a possible iterative process for solving $f(x) = 0$.

co-domain Synonym for range of a function, avoiding confusion with 'range' in statistics.

coefficient 1. A general term for any quantity which is jointly effective with another in determining the total value of some function of the other. For example, if y depends on x^2 and is given by $y = ax^2$, a is the coefficient of x^2, and would either be a constant as x varies or would give rise to a family of expressions if it took a set of values.
2. Any specific constant which appears in a formula involving a physical variable, as coefficient of friction or coefficient of expansion.
3. Differential coefficient—*see* derivative.

coefficient of contraction *See* Borda mouthpiece.

cofactor The signed minor of an element in a determinant.

colatitude *See* latitude.

collapse A collapse is the one-by-one removal of the arcs of a network.

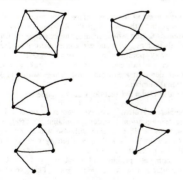

Isolated nodes are not part of the network and are ignored if left.

collection The non-mathematical word usually used in defining the word 'set'. Although set and collection are related words in ordinary language, a set is a collection subject to certain restrictions which make it a precise concept.

collinear Used of a set of points all of which lie on the same straight line.

collineation Any transformation of the plane in which a set of collinear points are transformed into another set of collinear points.

collocation polynomial A polynomial $P(x)$ of degree n which takes the same values as any given function $f(x)$ at $(n + 1)$ points. $P(x)$ can often be used to calculate approximate numerical values for the function.

column transformation *See* row transformation.

column vector *See* row vector.

combination A possible arrangement of objects or elements, which may or may not be distinct, taken r at a time, when no account is taken of order within any one arrangement, e.g. ABC, CAB, BCA are regarded as the same combination from the letters ABCD taken three at a time. The number of combinations of distinct elements is

$$\frac{n!}{r! \, (n-r)!}$$

and is usually denoted by ^nC_r, nCr or $\binom{n}{r}$.
See also permutation.

combinatorial methods A strategy for solving problems, for example in probability, by considering the possible ways in which the elements of sets can be combined or permuted. The methods were developed by Leibniz and Euler, and provide a calculus that parallels, for discrete quantities, the role of analysis with continuous functions.

commensurable Any two quantities are commensurable if both can be expressed or measured in terms of the same arbitrary unit. The concept arises in Euclid, where the unit is a line interval or area. Thus 4.23 and 5.76214 are both expressible as a whole number of units each 0.00001, but 4.23 and $\sqrt{2}$ cannot both be expressed as a whole number of the same units.
See incommensurable.

common denominator Any number divisible by the denominators of a set of fractions, all of which are then expressed in terms of this number. For fractions a/b, c/d ... a common denominator is bd ... since

$$\frac{a}{b} = \frac{ad}{bd}, \frac{c}{d} = \frac{bc}{bd} \cdots$$

The least common denominator (or multiple) is the smallest integer having this property.

common factor An element which is common by multiplication to two or more numbers or algebraic expressions.

- 12, 18, 96 have the common factors 2, 3, 6 since each is a multiple of each of these.
  abc and abd have the common factors a and b.

Note that a multiplicative process is always implied, so that $a+b+c$ and $a+b+d$ do not, in general, have common factors.

common logarithms The system of logarithms to base ten devised by Henry Briggs (1561–1631), who decided to compute the table after a meeting with Napier who devised the original system. *See* Briggsian logarithms. Their use as an aid in computing has been largely supplanted by pocket calculators.

common multiple An integer m is a common multiple of a set of two or more integers a, b, c ... if m can be obtained by multiplying each element of the set by some integer

- 24 is a common multiple of 2, 3, 4, 6, 8, 12 but not of 2, 5 since it is not a multiple of 5.

common tangent A single straight line that is tangent to two or more separate curves. Common tangents to two circles are said to be direct or external if they do not intersect between the circles.

communication theory *See* information theory.

commutative group A group for which the defining binary operation is commutative. Also called Abelian group.
All cyclic groups are commutative.

commutative ring A ring R which for all a, $b \in R$, has the property $ab = ba$. E.g. the set of all continuous functions in the closed interval [0, 1], together with operations of addition and multiplication. The zero of this ring is $f_0(x) = 0$, the unit element $f_1(x) = 1$.

commutativity The property, usually referring to any binary operation $\circ$, of being interchangeable or symmetric.
That is for any x, y $x \circ y = y \circ x$
Thus addition of positive integers is commutative, but not subtraction.

commutator *See* cross product.

compact Any metric space X is compact if, and only if, for any infinite sequence x_n in X, some subsequence x_p of x_n converges to a limit in X, that is, it has a cluster point.

comparison test If, for a sequence $\{a_n\}$, $0 \leqslant a_n \leqslant b_n$ for all n then the series

$$\sum_{n=1}^{\infty} a_n$$

will converge if the test series

$$\sum_{n=1}^{\infty} b_n$$

converges. If $0 \leqslant b_n \leqslant a_n$ then the first series diverges if the test series diverges.

complement That which fills up or makes complete.
1. Of acute angles, the angle which when added makes a right angle. The two angles are then said to be complementary.

2. Of sets. Given a set A, its complement written A' is such that $A \cup A' = \mathscr{E}$ and $A \cap A' = \phi$; that is, it contains all elements under considerations that are not A.

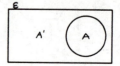

3. Of two sets. Given A and B, the complement of A in B is the set of all elements in B which are not in A, sometimes called B difference A and written $B \backslash A$ (note $B \backslash A \neq A \backslash B$).

4. Of numbers, the complement of a relative to b is the number which when added to a gives b.

complementary *See* complement.

complementary addition The process of obtaining the difference between two numbers by writing down the complement of the smaller with respect to the larger.

complementary function (C.F.) Term used for the solution u of the differential equation $au'' + bu' + cu = 0$ which with the particular integral v of $av'' + bv' + cv = p(x)$ gives the general solution of the equation $ay'' + by' + cy = p(x)$ where $y = u + v$. It can be applied to equations of any order in this form.

completeness A set of numbers S is said to be complete when every Cauchy sequence in S has a limit which is also a member of S.
1. Any convergent sequence of real numbers converges to a real number, and the set $\mathbf{R}$ is complete.
2. The sequence of rationals given by $\left(1 + \dfrac{1}{n}\right)^n$, $n \in \mathbf{N}$ converges to the irrational e, hence the set $\mathbf{Q}$ is incomplete.
For the completeness of formal systems *see* Gödel's theorem.

completeness of the reals This is the property that distinguishes the set of reals $\mathbf{R}$ from the set of rationals $\mathbf{Q}$ and which ensures the existence of irrationals such as $\sqrt{2}$, π and e. Geometrically, it ensures that every point on a line corresponds to some number, the existence of which can be taken as an axiom demonstrated from constructions with sets of rational numbers.
See also Dedekind section, Cauchy sequence.

complete primitive The complete solution of a differential equation of order n containing n arbitrary constants A, B, C... Any solution which contains only specific or less than n arbitrary constants is called a particular solution.
The complete primitive of $y'' = 0$ is $y = Ax + b$ but particular solutions are $y = x$, $y = 2x + 1$ and so on.

complete quadrangle The configuration of six lines and four points formed by taking the joins in pairs of the points of a complete four-point (any set of four points of which no three are collinear).

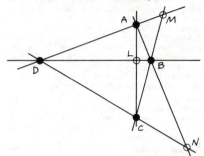

The points L, M, N of the four-point ABCD are the three diagonal points (or diagonal triangle) of the quadrangle. The dual of this configuration is the complete quadrilateral.

complete quadrilateral The configuration of six points and four lines formed by taking the intersection in pairs of the lines of a complete four-line (any set of four lines of which no three are concurrent).

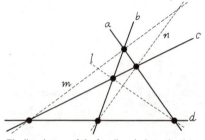

The lines l, m, n of the four-line abcd are the three diagonal lines (or diagonal trilateral) of the quadrilateral. The dual of this configuration is the complete quadrangle.

completing the square The process of adding terms to any expression so that it becomes a perfect square, usually applied to expressions of one variable and degree two. Since $x^2 + 2bx + b^2 = (x+b)^2$ an expression such as $x^2 + px$ becomes a perfect square if $(p/2)^2$ is added

$$x^2 + px + \left(\frac{p}{2}\right)^2 = \left(x + \frac{p}{2}\right)^2$$

The method allows the general solution of the quadratic $ax^2 + bx + c = 0$ ($a, b, c \in \mathbb{R}$) to give the familiar formula

$$x = \frac{-b \pm \sqrt{(b^2 - 4ac)}}{2a}$$

complex analysis Extension of the methods of analysis (or differential and integral calculus) from real to complex variables. Thus a power series $\Sigma a x^n$ ($a \in \mathbb{R}$) may converge to a unique value, but the corresponding complex series $\Sigma a z^n$ may have a circle of convergence or converge to a unique value. An exponential $y = e^x$ corresponds to a function as defined, but $e^z = e^{z+2\pi i}$ so its inverse is many valued. It is, however, possible to develop a satisfactory theory by suitable restrictions. The set of all complex functions satisfying required conditions for integrability is called a Hilbert space.

complex conjugate (number) The conjugate of a complex number $z = x + iy$ ($x, y \in \mathbb{R}$) is defined as $x - iy$. This conjugate $\bar{z}$ or z^* is thus the reflection of z in the real axis of the Argand diagram.

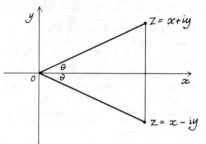

complex function An ambiguous term for either
1. A complex-valued function, or
2. A function of a complex variable.

complex number 1. An earlier formulation, emerging from a long period of mathematical history from Cardan (c. 1550) to Gauss et al. (c. 1800) defined a complex number z as $a + ib$ where $i^2 = -1$. Here a was said to be the 'real' part, ib the 'imaginary' (see Descartes for the origin of these terms). The complex number was given a graphical representation by Gauss, Wessel and Argand, and complex functions became accepted mathematical entities. The set of complex numbers is denoted by $\mathbb{C}$. Since a single complex number z has two independent components a and b, it can carry more information than a real number, and proved to be of value in discussing, for example, the flow of fluids where both pressure and velocity vary from point to point. Complex numbers always have square roots, and are more general than real numbers which only have roots when non-negative. This permitted the Gauss theorem that any polynomial in z had at least one root.
2. A modern formulation due to Hamilton (1837) defined a complex number as an ordered pair (a, b) of real numbers with an appropriate algebra.
$(a, b) = (c, d)$ if and only if $a = c$ and $b = d$
$(a, b) + (c, d) = (a + c, b + d)$
$(a, b) \times (c, d) = (ac - bd, ad + bc)$
This definition in terms of real numbers is equivalent to the one already given. In particular the pair $(0, 1)$, as may be seen by calculating $(0, 1) \times (0, 1)$, is an alternative formulation of i. Complex algebra does not define an ordering relation using $>$ or $<$ so that the field is not ordered. The symbol j is also used instead of i.
See Argand diagram.

complex valued function Any function of a real number whose value is complex; that is, its domain is

31

R or a subset of **R**, its range or co-domain **C** or a subset of **C**, e.g. e^{ix} ($x \in$ **R**). It should be distinguished from the function of a complex variable.

complex variable   Used of expressions or functions the domain of whose variable is **C** or a sub-set of **C**. Thus z^2, $\cos z$, e^{iz} are all functions of the complex variable $z \in$ **C**. It should be distinguished from a complex valued function.

component   Term used as the inverse of resolute when applied to vectors or vector quantities. A vector can be represented by its resolutes in two given directions, or appears as the resultant of two or more vectors which are then called its components.

composite   A whole number which is not prime. That is, it has factors other than itself and one.

composite function   The composition of two functions f and g is denoted usually by $\circ$ or $*$ and defined as
$$(f \circ g)(x) = f\{g(x)\}$$
In general, composition is non-commutative, and
$$(f \circ g)(x) \neq (g \circ f)(x)$$

composition   The process, usually denoted $\circ$ and read 'circle', by which a function g becomes the argument of a function f.
Then $(f \circ g)(x) = f\{g(x)\}$
● If $f: x \mapsto \sin x$, $g: x \mapsto 3x + 2$
$(f \circ g)(x) = \sin(3x + 2)$
Note that $(g \circ f)(x) = 3 \sin x + 2$
The operation is not in general commutative, but is associative and can extend to more than two functions.

compounded permutation   The result of one permutation of n elements followed by another, often described as addition or multiplication of permutations. If $P_0 = (ABC)$; $P_1 = (CAB)$; $P_2 = (BCA)$, then $P_2 (P_1) = (ABC) = P_0$.

compound harmonic motion   See harmonic motion.

compound pendulum   A rigid body swinging in a vertical plane about a fixed horizontal axis under the action of gravity. If the centre O is on the axis and G is the centre of gravity with $OG = l$, and if k is the radius of gyration, the time of swing t for small amplitude is approximately
$$t = 2\pi \sqrt{\frac{k^2 + l^2}{lg}}$$
The point O is a centre of oscillation for the pendulum. For any pendulum and any chosen O, there is another point O′, the reciprocal centre of oscillation, for which the period is the same. If O and O′ are the centres for which t is the minimum, OO′ is the length of an equivalent simple pendulum.

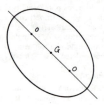

See also Kater's pendulum.

computer   1. Digital computer. This operates on numerical, alphabetic, graphic or other data by transforming its input into sequences of binary digits, which are then operated on by digital algorithms controlled by programs. The final output can be printed or displayed graphically on a screen.
2. Analogue computer. A device, mechanical or more usually electrical, which produced immediate numerical answers to problems such as the solution of equations, by measuring the output of a physical system set up to be described by the equations. It is now superseded by the digital computer.

concave   Lat. concavus, hollow. Curved inwards, as a concave lens. Term often used to designate one side of a given curve, the other being then convex. Also used of a polygon having a re-entrant angle, as concave quadrilateral.

conchoid   Devised by Nicomedes (c. 240 B.C.) who is said to have constructed it by a mechanical linkage. It is the curve
$$x^2 y^2 = (a + y)^2 (b^2 - y^2)$$

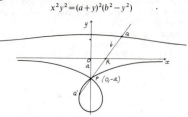

A line PR through $(O, -a)$ cuts the x axis in R. Points Q, Q′ on PR are such that $QR = Q'R = b$. The two branches of the conchoid are the loci of these points. The loop shown develops if $a < b$. If $a = b$ there is a cusp at P. If $a > b$ the cusp disappears but there is an acnode at P.
In polar coordinates, but with P as the pole, the equation becomes $r = a \csc \theta \pm b$ for the two branches.

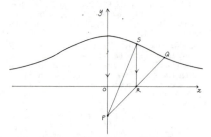

If PRQ is drawn so that $RQ = b = 2$ PR, and the ordinate RS to the upper branch of the conchoid is drawn, then SP will trisect the angle RPQ.
See also trisectrix.

concurrent   Used of two or more lines that have a point in common, as the medians of a triangle.

concyclic   Used of any set of points, such as the vertices of a polygon, that lie on the circumference of a given circle.

condensation *See* Gaussian condensation.

conditional In logic the relation between statements p, q denoted by $p \rightarrow q$ or formerly $p \supset q$, read as 'if p then q'. There are numerous equivalent formulations: p implies q, p is sufficient for q, q is necessary for p, p is true only if q is true. The relation is defined by the truth table

p	q	$p \rightarrow q$
T	T	T
T	F	F
F	T	T
F	F	T

The last line of this definition corresponds to the statement that a false proposition implies any proposition whatsoever, e.g. if this theorem is true then pigs can fly. *See* biconditional.

conditional convergence Used of an infinite series which is convergent but not absolutely convergent.

● The alternating series $1 - \frac{1}{2} + \frac{1}{3} - \frac{1}{4} + \frac{1}{5} - \dots$

conditional inequality An inequality which is not true for all values of the variable, as $(x - 2) \geqslant 0$ true only for $x \geqslant 2$ compared with $(x - 2)^2 \geqslant 0$ true for all real x.

conditional probability The probability that an event A will occur, subject to the condition that B has occurred, written $p(A|B)$.

$$p(A|B) = p\frac{(A \cap B)}{p(B)} \quad (p(B) > 0)$$

If A and B are mutually exclusive events $A \cap B = \emptyset$, $p(A \cap B) = 0$, and hence $p(A|B) = 0$. If A and B are independent, then $p(A|B) = p(A)$ and $p(A \cap B) = p(A) \cdot p(B)$

● Scores from rolling a die are $A = \{1, 2, 3, 4, 5, 6\}$
Odd scores are $B = \{1, 3, 5\}$
Even scores are $C = \{2, 4, 6\}$
Then $p(6) = \frac{1}{6}$ (unconditional)
$p(6|C) = \frac{1}{3}$ (conditional on C having occurred)
$p(6|B) = 0$ (conditional on B having occurred)

cone 1. The solid or surface generated by rotating an isosceles triangle about its axis of symmetry.
2. The set of all straight lines passing through the points of a circle or ellipse and a fixed point not in the plane of the circle.

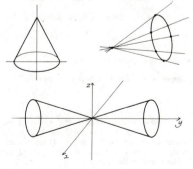

The second, more general definition, generates a double cone (cone of two nappes).
3. The surface given by $x^2 + z^2 - ay^2 = 0$.

confidence interval An interval within whose limits a population parameter such as a mean will lie with a probability p. This is usually expressed as a percentage of the long term proportion of such intervals, which in repeated observations would in fact contain the parameter.

confidence limits The boundaries of the confidence interval.

configuration Any assemblage of lines, points or curves in two or three dimensions, which illustrates or presents itself as a topic for mathematical study. Note that in Euclid a 'figure' is usually contained within a boundary or made up from finite line intervals.

confocal Having the same foci, as confocal ellipses.

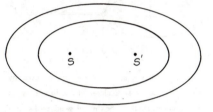

conformable matrices Two matrices A and B (in that order) are conformable if the product AB exists, that is if A is $m \times n$ and B is $n \times p$ for any m, n, p.

conformal transformation Any transformation which preserves the angles between tangents at the points of intersection of curves (and hence the angles between straight lines). For example, inversion with respect to a fixed point O, where $OX \cdot OX'$ is constant for all corresponding points X, X' on the two configurations Γ, Γ'.

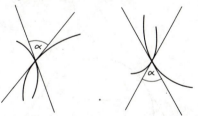

congruence 1. The term expresses Euclid's Common Notion 4, that 'things which coincide' are equal, and is based on the intuitive procedure of superimposing one plane configuration over another. The logical implications of regarding geometrical figures as rigid bodies have often been discussed. Hilbert (1903) treats congruence between line segments and angles, denoted $\equiv$, as a primary undefined concept whose properties are governed by axioms (e.g. $A \equiv B \Rightarrow B \equiv A$). Euclidean congruence excludes configurations which are mirror images of one another, and is replaced in transformation geometry by the concept of isometry.
2. *See also* modular arithmetic.

conical pendulum   A mass suspended by a string of length l from a point and projected so as to move in a horizontal circle around the point with angular velocity ω, so that the string generates a cone.

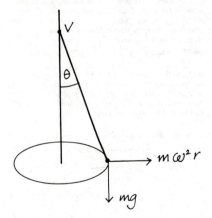

If ω is small the period of rotation is given by $t = 2\pi \sqrt{\dfrac{l}{g}}$ where g is acceleration due to gravity, so that it corresponds to the time of swing of a simple pendulum.

conical projection   In cartography, a method for projecting part of the surface of a sphere (specifically that of the earth) on to a cone. The tangent circle to the cone is usually a parallel of latitude, called the standard parallel, and the projection is useful for areas not far north or south of this latitude. If the cone cuts the sphere the two circles of intersection form standard parallels. Such a projection gives minimum distortion over a wider range of latitude.

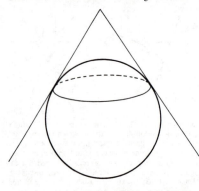

conicoid   Synonym for quadric surface. A plane section of any conicoid is a conic.

conic sections   General name given to the ellipse, hyperbola and parabola, with the circle and a pair of straight lines as limiting cases. The name comes from the very detailed treatment by Apollonius of Perga, who derived and discussed them geometrically, as produced by a plane cutting a double cone. If the slant height of the cone makes an angle θ with the base and the plane makes an angle α, then if

> $\alpha < \theta$ the section is an ellipse
> $\alpha = \theta$ the section is a parabola
> $\alpha > \theta$ the section is a two-branched hyperbola

The three names come from the Greek geometric equivalents for the symbols $<$, $=$ and $>$, *elleipsis* a defect, *parabole* a placing alongside, *hyperbole* an excess or overshoot.

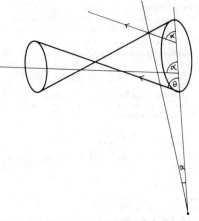

Their properties are now studied analytically using coordinates.

conjugate   An all-purpose term (Lat. *conjugare*, yoke together) which describes pairs of elements which are related in some way.
1. $(x + iy)$, $(x - iy)$ are conjugate complex numbers.
2. Conjugate diameters of a conic are formed when each contains the set of midpoints of chords drawn parallel to the other.
3. Conjugate hyperbolas are those of the form

$$\frac{x^2}{a^2} - \frac{y^2}{b^2} = 1 \qquad \frac{x^2}{b^2} - \frac{y^2}{a^2} = 1$$

which share the same asymptotes.

conjugate axis   The hyperbola given by

$$\frac{x^2}{a^2} - \frac{y^2}{b^2} = 1$$

has a transverse axis which is the x axis of the coordinates. If $x = 0$, $y^2 = -b^2$, which has the complex conjugate roots $y = (0 \pm ib)$. Hence the line joining the points $(0, b)$ and $(0, -b)$ is called the conjugate axis of the hyperbola.

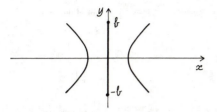

conjunction The linking of statements by the propositional function 'and' symbolized by $., \wedge, \&$, or in Boolean algebra by juxtaposition. The written forms $p.q$, $p \wedge q$, $p \& q$, pq are equivalent, and can be defined by the truth table

p	q	$p.q$
T	T	T
T	F	F
F	T	F
F	F	F

connected 1. In descriptive topology a region is connected if its points cannot be partitioned into two disjoint open sets, e.g. the interval $1 \leqslant x \leqslant 3$ on a line can be divided into $1 \leqslant x \leqslant 2$ and $2 < x \leqslant 3$. Of these, the first interval is closed and the total interval must be connected. If $1 \leqslant x < 2$ and $2 < x \leqslant 3$ both intervals are open at one end and the point $x = 2$ has been omitted so the interval now becomes disconnected. Connectedness corresponds to continuity in a function.
2. A region is arc-wise connected if a path or arc, wholly within the region, may be drawn between any two points.
3. A region is simply connected if every closed curve within it can be reduced to a point in the region.

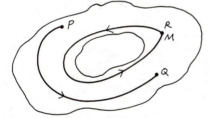

R is arc-wise connected but not simply connected.

connective In logic, a connective is a symbol uniting two or more statements p, q, ..., although the symbol signifying negation of any one proposition is included. Connectives are best defined by truth tables

p	q	$p \leftrightarrow q$	$\sim p$	$p \& q$	$p \vee q$	$p \underline{\vee} q$	$p \rightarrow q$	$p \mid q$
T	T	T	F	T	T	F	T	F
T	F	F	—	F	T	T	F	T
F	T	F	T	F	T	T	T	T
F	F	T	—	F	F	F	T	T

The usual readings and names of the connectives are as follows:

$p \leftrightarrow q$ p if but only if q (biconditional implication)
$\sim p$ not p (negation)
$p \& q$ p and q (conjunction)
$p \vee q$ p or q (inclusive disjunction = vel)
$p \underline{\vee} q$ p or q but not both (exclusive disjunction = aut)
$p \rightarrow q$ p implies q (conditional implication); if p then q.
$p \mid q$ not both p and q (p, q incompatible)

There are alternative forms of the symbols:

$$\text{not } p \quad \rightarrow p, p', \bar{p}$$
$$p \text{ and } q \quad p \cap q, p \wedge q, p.q$$
$$p \text{ implies } q \quad p \Rightarrow q \; p \supset q$$

See also implication

conormal points The points from which normals may be drawn from any conic to pass through a given point.

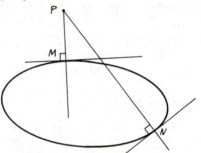

consequent *See* antecedent.

conservative field A physical field of force in which the work done in taking a particle round a closed path against the force is zero, that is $\oint F.ds = 0$.
Thus gravitational and electromagnetic forces give conservative fields, friction does not.

consistent 1. A set of equations is consistent if there is a solution set which satisfies all equations simultaneously. $2x - 1 = 1$, $x + y = 2$ is consistent with $x = 1$, $y = 1$, but $4x - 2y = 3$, $2x - y = 1$ is inconsistent since no pair (x, y) satisfying the first will satisfy the second.
2. Any set of axioms defining a system is said to be consistent if the system contains no contradictory theorems. Since all possible theorems generated by an axiom set need not be known, it follows that axiomatic consistency is logically provisional. If the known theorems form a consistent system, the axioms are consistent.
3. Used of any system of symbolic notation in which there are established conventions. Although these are initially arbitrary (as, for example, positive angles described anticlockwise) departure from the convention leads to contradictions and ambiguity.

constant 1. Any quantity, usually denoted by an agreed conventional symbol, which has a fixed numerical value, either in mathematics or in physical measurement, as G the gravitational constant, c the speed of light,

2. Any quantity specific to a given substance or situation, as melting points or coefficients of expansion, usually called physical constants.

3. A convention in algebra by which certain variables are given values from their domain in the expressions containing them and are then regarded as fixed, the other variables then being assigned any value, not necessarily from the same domain.

Given $y = mx + c$, then if m, c are constants, the equation represents a straight line where x takes any value. Then y takes a set of corresponding values expressed by the equality. The convention, established by Descartes, uses the later letters of the alphabet as 'variables', the earlier as 'constants'.

4. In particular, the constant of integration which arises if an integral is taken as an antiderivative.

- $f(x) = x^3 + 4$
  $f'(x) = 3x^2$
  $f'(x)dx = x^3 + C$
  where C is a constant depending on initial conditions.

constructible Capable of being constructed using the Platonic restriction to straight edge and compasses.

- A square equal in area to any polygon.
  A number of the form $a + b$ where a, b, are rational line segments.

constructive Used of a theory that is not developed from an axiomatic basis but from intuition or empirical observation, as naive set theory or the properties of lines and points as discussed by Euclid. Usually applied to physical theories.

contain A set A is said to contain a set B if all elements of B are also in A. Denoted $A \supset B$, and usually written $B \subset A$, B is contained in A, or is a subset of A. If $A \supset B$ and $B \supset A$, then $A = B$.

contingency table A cross-classification table recording the frequencies of two classification schemes of a sample, usually analysed by a chi-squared or other test to investigate the null hypothesis that there is no connection between the two. A contingency table will in general have r rows and k columns, as in the example with $r = k = 2$

- Applicants for a job

Age	Men	Women	Totals
under 40	13	10	23
40+	17	12	29
Totals	30	22	52

contingent (noun, contingency) 1. Used of a conclusion that does not *necessarily* follow from a premise, but depends on one or more other conditions which may or may not hold good.

2. Used of events (or numerical values) that tend to occur together without a necessary connection, as correlated attributes.

3. Events that happen to occur together by chance (not used in mathematics or logic).

The range of meanings arises from Lat. *contingo* — (a) to touch, (b) to happen.

continued fractions Fractions of the form

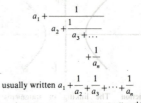

$$a_1 + \cfrac{1}{a_2 + \cfrac{1}{a_3 + \cdots}}$$

usually written $a_1 + \dfrac{1}{a_2} + \dfrac{1}{a_3} + \cdots + \dfrac{1}{a_n}$

The denominators a_2, $a_3 \ldots$ are usually taken as positive integers. The first 1, 2, 3 $\ldots$ r terms taken together is the rth convergent of the fractions, and these convergents form a sequence, whose values are alternately less than and greater than the value of the fraction for a given n. As $n \to \infty$ the sequence converges to a limit.

- $1 + \dfrac{1}{1} + \dfrac{1}{1} + \dfrac{1}{1} + \cdots$ gives the sequence

  1, 2, 3/2, 5/3, $\ldots$, the value of whose limit is the golden ratio.

Continued fractions were used at one time to calculate ratios in the gear trains of screw-cutting lathes.

continued product *See* infinite product.

continuous Continuity is an intuitive concept formalized for mathematical purposes using the concept of limit. A function f of a real variable is said to be continuous at any point a if

$$\lim_{x \to a} f(x) = f(a)$$

The force of this definition is best seen by considering functions discontinuous at a

1. $f : x \mapsto \dfrac{1}{x}$ at $x = 0$ where f is not defined at $x = 0$

2. $f(x) = \begin{cases} |x| & \text{if } x \neq 0 \\ 1 & \text{if } x = 0 \end{cases}$

In this example $f(0) = 1$ but $\lim_{x \to 0} |x| = 0$

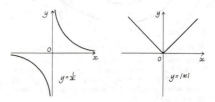

The discontinuity is not always apparent from a diagram

$$f : x \mapsto x \sin \dfrac{1}{x}$$

Here $\lim_{x \to 0} \left(x \sin \dfrac{1}{x} \right) = 0$ although f is not defined at 0

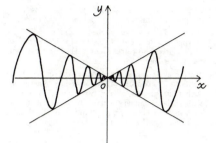

The diagram as sketched appears continuous.

continuum A set forms a continuum if it is infinite and everywhere continuous, as the set of reals or the set of points on a line interval.

continuum hypothesis If $\aleph_0$ is taken as the cardinal of the set $\mathbf{N}$, that is of a denumerably infinite set, the hypothesis states that the cardinal c of $\mathbf{R}$ or any non-denumerable infinite set, is $2_0^{\aleph}$, given by Cantor (1895) as greater than $\aleph_0$. None of the claims to have settled the question is accepted by all mathematicians.

contour Originally an outline (Italian), then used of a line joining points of equal height above sea level on a map. In mathematics it is a general term for a line joining equivalent points plotted on a coordinate system. In physics, geography etc., it tends to be replaced by specific terms having the prefix iso- as isobars, isotherms, isoclines, which plot pressure, temperature, magnetic dip and so on.

contour integration A non-elementary method for evaluating integrals of complex valued functions by using contours. The integration is no longer over an interval (a,b) on the x axis as in

$$\int_a^b f(x)\,\mathrm{d}x$$

but around a plane contour enclosing in general, a region of the complex plane of z. The limits of integration are now points in the plane on the contour. Integration round a closed contour is denoted by $\int_c$ or $\oint$ and a theorem due to Cauchy states that, for an analytic complex function integrated round a closed contour,

$$\int_c f(z)\,\mathrm{d}z = 0$$

The corresponding integrals for real functions of two variables are usually called line integrals.

contradictory Statements are contradictory (or give a contradiction) if the falsehood of one logically implies the truth of the other, or vice versa.

● p = All triangles are isosceles.
q = Some triangles are non-isosceles.

Note that the falsehood of p does not imply

r = No triangles are isosceles, or
s = All triangles are non-isosceles.

The propositions r and s are said to be the *contraries* of p.

contrapositive A form of proposition whose subject is the negative of the predicate of some other positive proposition, and usually the predicate is the negative of the original subject.

● Positive: All triangles are figures with three sides.
Contrapositive: All figures not with three sides are not triangles.

The contrapositive is equivalent to the original positive and may be easier to prove, for example the theorem for natural numbers *if x^2 is odd, x is odd* is easily proved by demonstrating its contrapositive: *If x is even, x^2 is even.*

contrary *See* contradictory, from which it must be distinguished.

contravariant Used of the coordinates of a point or the components of a vector referred to either oblique or orthogonal cartesian axes, with intercepts defined by lines parallel to the axes.

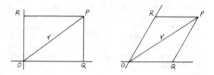

Thus, for $\mathbf{r} = \mathrm{OP}$, the contravariant components are OQ, OR. A general set of three axes used in this way is denoted x^1, x^2, x^3 where the context shows that x^i is written as a superscript and not a power. The contravariant components are then usually written as a^1, a^2, a^3. Ordinary use of rectangular coordinate assumes contravariance but the term and its superscript notation are only used in contexts when covariant components are also being considered on oblique coordinates.

control chart Also quality control chart. A chart used for plotting periodic returns from the routine inspection of a production process. It usually has a central line representing the expected reading (of dimensions, defective items and so on) and a line or lines above or below showing the limits beyond which the reading must not be allowed to pass. The lines mark the 'action' limits. Some charts have intermediate lines indicating 'warning' limits, which may call for action such as further sampling or inspection.

In practice, the interpretation of the charts is a matter of experience, and successive readings may suggest a trend which if continued may result in failure of the process.

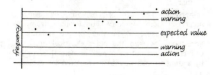

convention Any well-established and universally accepted rule for the use of mathematical symbols, without which they would be ambiguous.
- A positive angle is described anticlockwise. A row suffix precedes a column suffix in specifying matrix elements. A negative value is shown to the left of the origin on a number line.

convergence A term used to describe the behaviour of a Cauchy sequence (see both sequence and Cauchy sequence), that is, a sequence $\{a_n\}$ converges if for all $n > n_0(\epsilon)$

$$|a_n - L| < \epsilon$$

where ϵ is any arbitrarily small non-zero number, $n_0(\epsilon)$ is an integer calculated after ϵ is assigned, and L is the quantity known as the limit of the sequence. For example, if $\{a_n\} = 1/2^n$ $L = 1$. Then for $\epsilon = \frac{1}{32}$, $n_0(\epsilon) = 5$ and $|a_n - L| < \frac{1}{32}$ if $n > 5$. If $\{f_n\}$ is a sequence of functions defined for x in a closed interval (a,b) the required condition describes uniform convergence with respect to x since it is possible to define functions which have a limit but for which the $n_0(\epsilon)$ criterion does not apply.
See also absolute convergence.

convergent series An infinite series is said to be convergent if the sequence of partial sums obtained by taking its terms 1, 2, 3 ... n ... at a time are convergent. Where the sum to n terms can be expressed explicitly, it is often possible to establish convergence by letting n increase without limit in the expression.
Thus

$$s_n = \frac{1}{1.2} + \frac{1}{2.3} + \ldots + \frac{1}{n(n+1)}$$

$$= (1 - \tfrac{1}{2}) + (\tfrac{1}{2} - \tfrac{1}{3}) + \ldots + \left(\frac{1}{n} - \frac{1}{n+1}\right)$$

$$= 1 - \frac{1}{n+1}$$

from which it is clear that $\sum_{r=1}^{r=\infty} \frac{1}{r(r+1)} = 1$ and the series converges to 1.

converse If a statement p implies a statement q, the converse of this implication is that q implies p. This implication may or may not be true. If the first implication is a theorem of mathematics, the second is the converse theorem.
- If ABCD is a cyclic quadrilateral then its opposite angles are supplementary. The converse, which is true, is: If the opposite angles of a quadrilateral ABCD are supplementary then ABCD is cyclic.
If n is a prime number greater than 2, then n is odd. The converse, which is not true, is: If n is odd, then it is a prime number greater than 2.

conversion The act of changing, by using a numerical factor or conversion formula, from one unit of measure to another of the same kind. Sometimes, as with the older electrical units, the conversion was not by a pure numerical factor but by a dimensioned quantity. The need for extensive lists of factors and conversion tables has now disappeared with the general adoption of SI.

convex Lat. *convexus*, arched or vaulted. Having a curve like the *outside* or top of an arch or vault. Curved outwards. A curve which is convex on one side is concave on the other.

convex set Any set of points lying in a region bounded by a convex polygon or in the closed region such that the join of any two points lies wholly within the boundary curve. Any set of linear equations whose representation in cartesian coordinates encloses such a polygonal region.

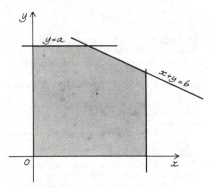

convolution Term used for the multiplicative composition of two finite sequences or series of numbers having the same number of terms.
If

$$a_n = a_0, a_1, a_2 \ldots a_n$$
$$b_n = b_0, b_1, b_2 \ldots b_n$$

then their convolution is

$$C_n = a_0 b_n, a_1 b_{(n-1)}, a_2 b_{n-2} \ldots a_n b_0.$$

It may be denoted

$$C_n = a_n b_n$$

Convolution is a commutative composition.

coordinates The sets of numbers used in coordinate systems. The word is usually used in context, but must otherwise be specifically described, as cartesian, polar, etc.

coordinate system Any specified mapping from a set of points to a set of numbers, usually ordered pairs, triplets or n-tuples, which are called coordinates (see specific systems under areal, cartesian, cylindrical, homogeneous, oblique, polar etc.).
See also mesh system.

coplanar Belonging to or lying in the same plane, as coplanar points, coplanar vectors.

coprime Two or more numbers are coprime when they have no common factor other than unity. Clearly, any set of prime numbers is coprime, but so for example is (8, 15, 49).

Coriolis force A virtual force related to centrifugal force. Consider a body of mass m moving with velocity v along a radius AO marked on a disc rotating in a plane with angular velocity ω.

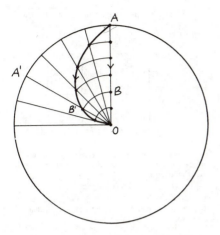

When the body has reached B on this path ABO will have rotated to A'B'O relative to the plane. The path of the body relative to the disc is along AB; relative to the stationary coordinate system it is along the curve AB', and is thus accelerated away from AB. To keep it on AB a lateral force $2m\omega v$ must be applied to the body, and the reaction to this force is experienced at the body as the Coriolis force tending to throw it off the marked path. It is this virtual force, acting on air masses moving to or from the poles, that sets up circulating wind systems. A better term would be Coriolis effect. It is, of course, felt simultaneously with the virtual centrifugal force acting along the radius.

corollary A theorem whose truth follows directly from that of another which has already been proved. Often a corollary is a special case of a general theorem.

● Ceva's theorem about three points on the sides of a triangle has the corollary that the medians of a triangle are concurrent.

correlation The degree of association between two variates.
See correlation coefficient, linear correlation coefficient, rank order correlation.

correlation coefficient
See linear correlation coefficient.

correspondence 1. Two sets X, Y and a relation R which links some or all of the elements of X with one or more of the elements of Y form together a correspondence from X to Y.
2. If G is a subset of the cartesian product $X \times Y$ the triple (G, X, Y) is a correspondence from X to Y.

The two definitions are equivalent. An important special case is one-to-one correspondence. Each element of X is associated with exactly one element of Y, and each element of Y with exactly one of X. For functional correspondence each element of X is associated with one and one only of Y. The inverse relation need not be functional.
(*See also* function).

cosecant *See* circular functions.

cosech *See* hyperbolic functions.

coset If H is a subgroup of order m of a finite group G of order n, and a is any member of G, then the left coset aH of H is the set $\{ah : h \in H\}$. The right coset Ha is similarly defined. The process partitions the group G into precisely r left or right cosets relative to H, where $r = n/m$. Cosets may also be generated within infinite groups. If a group is commutative the left and right cosets coincide.
(*See also* Lagrange's theorem.)

cosh *See* hyperbolic functions.

cosine *See* circular functions.

cosine formula 1. Name given in spherical trigonometry to the formula

$$\cos a = \cos b \cos c + \sin b \sin c \cos A.$$

This applies to a spherical triangle ABC whose sides subtend angles a, b, c at the centre of the sphere, with A the angle included between c and b.

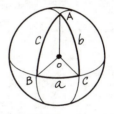

See also haversine formula.

2. Name given to the formula

$$a^2 = b^2 + c^2 - 2bc \cos A$$

for a plane triangle ABC.
See extensions to Pythagoras' theorem.

cotangent *See* circular functions.

coth *See* hyperbolic functions.

counter example An example, devised or discovered, which disproves a supposition or a conjecture advanced as a general theorem.

1. Supposition: a point of inflexion occurs on a curve where the second derivative is zero. Counter example: consider $y = x^4$.
2. Goldbach's conjecture would be conclusively disproved if, as a counter example, an even number greater than 2 were discovered which is not the sum of two primes.

counting The physical process of putting a set of distinct entities of any kind into one-one correspondence with the reference set of number words *one, two, three* ... By a necessary linguistic convention the sequence of number words must

1. be capable of indefinite extension without repetition of any term;
2. have a unique ordering so that all users of ·the sequence make the same count for any given set of objects;
3. be capable of being put into one-to-one correspondence with any other number-word sequence, used for example by speakers of a different language.

counting board Also checkerboard. A kind of abacus resembling a chess-board, a board marked in squares on which counters were placed in reckoning.

couple The combination of two equal and opposite parallel forces not acting through the same point. The sum of the moments of the two forces about any point of the plane is constant and is called the moment or torque of the couple. A couple cannot be replaced by any system of forces other than an equal couple, and two couples are equivalent to a single couple whose torque is the sum of their torques.

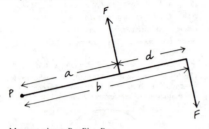

Moment about $P = Fb - Fa$
$$= F(b - a)$$
$$= F d$$

for all P in the plane.

course The direction, usually given as a magnetic or true bearing, of a moving ship or aircraft, relative to its own axis.

covariant 1. Used of coordinates or components of a vector referred to oblique cartesian systems, defined by perpendiculars dropped to the axes and thus distinct from contravariant systems.

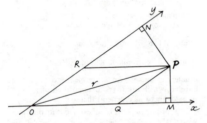

The covariant components of $\mathbf{r} = OP$ are given by OM, ON. In a general oblique system of three dimensions the coordinates are usually written as x_1, x_2, x_3 and the corresponding components as a_1, a_2, a_3. If, but only if, the axes are orthogonal, the covariant components are equivalent to the ordinary contravariant components.
2. A covariant transformation expresses a set of covariant components relative to one coordinate system S in terms of an equivalent set in another system S'.

covering *See* index. If $\{A_1, A_2, A_3 \ldots\}$ form an indexed set of subsets of some set X, then any subset B of X is said to be covered by the indexed set if

$$B \subset A_1 \cup A_2 \cup A_3 \cup \ldots$$

Cramer's rule A method for solving a set of n simultaneous equations in n variables. If the system is $A\mathbf{x} = \mathbf{k}$, the solutions are given as

$$x_i = \frac{|A^{(i)}|}{|A|} \quad i = 1, 2 \ldots n$$

Where $|A|$ is the determinant of the matrix A and $|A^{(i)}|$ is $|A|$ with the ith column replaced with the column vector $\mathbf{k}$

- $2x_1 + 3x_2 = 7$
  $4x_1 - 5x_2 = 6$

$$x_1 = \frac{\begin{vmatrix} 7 & 3 \\ 6 & -5 \end{vmatrix}}{\begin{vmatrix} 2 & 3 \\ 4 & -5 \end{vmatrix}} \qquad x_2 = \frac{\begin{vmatrix} 2 & 7 \\ 4 & 6 \end{vmatrix}}{\begin{vmatrix} 2 & 3 \\ 4 & -5 \end{vmatrix}}$$

It is of little practicable value for $n > 2$.

critical point On a curve representing a function a critical point (x, y) corresponds to a number x such that the derivative

$$f'(x) = 0$$

The value of $f(x)$ at this point is the critical value. The terms stationary point and stationary value are also used.
See turning point.

critical region The range of values of the test statistic in a significance test for which the null hypothesis H_0 is to be rejected in favour of the alternative hypothesis H_1. The boundaries of the critical region are the critical values.

critical value The value taken by a function at a critical point. The term is used in applied mathematics for any value of a quantity above or below which new phenomena appear in any system, such as the resonance frequency at which the effect of a periodic disturbance or forcing function on the system increases suddenly. It is particularly important in the statistics of hypothesis testing, since it is the point at which, for a given level of significance, the assumption that the null hypothesis is true is considered to be false.
See critical point.

cross cap A topological structure. If a cap is removed from a sphere and replaced with a Möbius band the attached band is said to form a cross cap. If the band is represented as a rectangle (*see* Möbius strip) the connections are shown in the diagram, where the circle represents the section of the sphere.

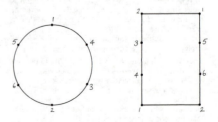

A paper model showing the coincidence of the six points marked can be made by constructing the Möbius band from a skeletal rectangle.

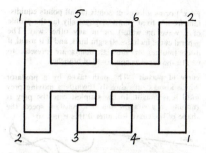

It is not possible to model continuous coincidence with material surfaces having physical thickness.

cross multiplication   1. The process of multiplying the numerator and denominator of one fraction, in that order, by the denominator and numerator of another, a process that preserves the relationship expressed by $=$, $>$ or $<$.

● · $(a/b = c/d) \Rightarrow (ad = cb)$
$(2/3 < 5/6) \Rightarrow (12 < 15)$

2. (Obsolete) A name formerly given to multiplication of duodecimal fractions.

cross product   1. If A and B are two $n \times n$ matrices whose elements are a_{ij}, b_{ij} the cross product of the matrices is defined as

$$A \times B = AB - BA$$

This is sometimes known as the Lie product or commutation of two given matrices.
2. If a and b are two non-parallel vectors in a plane, the cross product of these two vectors determines a vector which is perpendicular to the plane in which they lie, so that $\mathbf{a}$, $\mathbf{b}$, $\mathbf{a} \times \mathbf{b}$ form a right-handed triad.

If $\mathbf{a}$ is the vector (a_1, a_2, a_3)
If $\mathbf{b}$ is the vector (b_1, b_2, b_3)
Then

$$\mathbf{a} \times \mathbf{b} = (a_2 b_3 - a_3 b_2, a_3 b_1 - a_1 b_3, a_1 b_2 - a_2 b_1)$$

Also called the vector product.
3. The cross product of two sets is another term for Cartesian product.

cross ratio   If four points A, B, C, D are in that order on a straight line the line interval AC is divided internally and externally into the ratios AB/BC, AD/DC, where DC is negative. The cross ratio (ABCD) or (AC, BD) of the points is the ratio of these ratios

$$(ABCD) = \frac{AB/BC}{AD/DC}$$

This is usually rearranged as

$$(ABCD) = \frac{AB \cdot CD}{AD \cdot CB}$$

and then agrees with the diagrammatic scheme.

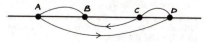

This form is easily remembered but masks the derivation. Other arrangements may be found. The cross ratio is important in projective geometry since it is invariant under central projection.

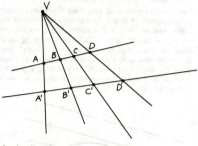

In the diagram

$$(ABCD) = (A' B' C' D')$$

The concept is generalized for any four coplanar points by assigning complex numbers z_1, z_2, z_3, z_4. Then

$$(z_1 z_2 z_3 z_4) = \frac{(z_1 - z_2)(z_3 - z_4)}{(z_1 - z_4)(z_3 - z_2)}$$

which is invariant under any bilinear transformation. *See also* harmonic range.

crunode   The simplest form of node, a point at which there are two real branches of a curve having two distinct tangents.

cube roots of unity   *See* nth roots of unity.

cubic equation   A polynomial equation of the form $ax^3 + bx^2 + cx + d = 0$ in which the highest power of the variable is three. Nicolo of Brescia, called Tartaglia, produced a general solution to equations of the form $ax^3 + bx^2 + c = 0$ and $ax^3 + bx + c = 0$ in 1535. There is some controversy about the early history of these equations.

cuboid   A special case of the parallelepiped, in which all six faces are rectangles.

cumulative   Of sums or frequencies, applied to the process of adding each new value to the sum of all previous values from x_1 to x_n so that the ith entry is

$$\sum_{j=1}^{i} x_j.$$

cumulative distribution function   Also c.d.f. *See* distribution function.

cumulative frequency curve *See* frequency polygon.

cup and cap Words sometimes used to read the symbols ∪ and ∩. Since they merely describe the shape of the symbols, the significant readings union and intersection are to be preferred.

curl Also rotation or rot., since it applies to rotational aspects of fluids. An expression involving the differential operator ∇. If a vector field is not conservative, as in the velocity field of a rotating fluid, then the line integral round a closed loop or area δA is not zero unless the loop is normal to the flow lines. The maximum value of this line integral per unit area as the plane of loop is rotated and as $\delta A \to 0$ is called the curl of the vector field.

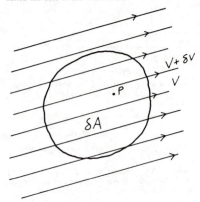

It is given by the vector product of the differential operator ∇ and the vector $\mathbf{V}$ at the point of which δA is the neighbourhood. That is,

curl $\mathbf{V} = \nabla \times \mathbf{V}$

$$= \left(\mathbf{i}\frac{\partial}{\partial x} + \mathbf{j}\frac{\partial}{\partial y} + \mathbf{k}\frac{\partial}{\partial z} \right) \times (v_x\mathbf{i} + v_y\mathbf{j} + v_z\mathbf{k})$$

or curl $\mathbf{V} = \begin{vmatrix} \mathbf{i} & \mathbf{j} & \mathbf{k} \\ \dfrac{\partial}{\partial x} & \dfrac{\partial}{\partial y} & \dfrac{\partial}{\partial z} \\ v_x & v_y & v_z \end{vmatrix}$

curtate cycloid *See* cycloid. Curve described by a point P on a fixed radius a of a circle rolling along a fixed line, a distance $b < a$ from the centre. The equations are

$$x = a\theta + b\sin\theta$$
$$y = a - b\cos\theta.$$

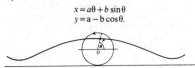

In the diagram the circle rolls to the left so that θ is positive.

curvature *See* radius of curvature.

curve From Lat. *curvus*, bent. Not precisely defined in mathematics, but used as convenient, usually for a continuous set of points with some law for generating them, either analytically (as the curve

$y = x^2$) or as a locus of points (as all points equidistant from a fixed point) or physically (as the profile of a wave on water), or in any other way. The general curve includes straight lines, and it is usual, if discontinuities or singular points are present, to regard the curve as composed of branches.

curve of pursuit The path taken by a predator which always runs directly towards a moving prey until it is caught. In the simplest case the prey is running in a straight line at a constant speed: the shape of the curve will alter if this is not so.

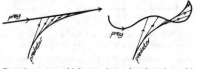

Pursuit curves, which can always be plotted graphically, can be found by considering the differential equations of the motions, called predator-prey equations.

curvilinear regression *See* regression line. If a scatter diagram shows that a straight line will not fit a set of points satisfactorily, it may be possible to find a suitable curve. This can, as with a linear regression line, be used to estimate the value of one variate given the other.

cusp A 'double point' on a curve (an example of a singularity) where the two tangents that can be drawn coincide. A Type 1 cusp has a branch of the curve on each side of the tangent, a Type 2 has both branches on the same side.

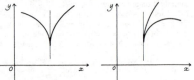

cusum analysis An abbreviation for cumulative sum analysis. A method for monitoring the performance of a process or machine. For an automobile, the cusum of the distance run between each filling of the tank is divided by the cusum of the fuel added. Any upward trend in the cusum average thus obtained indicates a deteriorating performance. In effect, an overall estimate is obtained by considering repeated small samples, so that non-significant fluctuations are smoothed out.

cybernetics Originally the study, not always in mathematical and quantitative terms, of control systems using feedback to automate the process, as in the governor invented by James Watt for steam engines, the characteristics of which (*see* hunting) introduced the study. (Both words come from Gk. *kubernan* to steer.) Since cybernetics was developed by the mathematician Wiener in 1947, it has been extended by analogy to social organization, biological functioning and so on, which, it is argued, are controlled in similar ways.

cycle Any sequence of events that repeats regularly, also the time for completion of such a sequence (usually called the period).

cyclic group A group, every element of which may be expressed in terms of a single generator. The abstract cyclic group of order n, generator g may be expressed as $(I, g, g^2 \ldots g^{n-1})$ where $g^n = I$.

- The integers $1, 2, 3 \ldots (n-1)$ under addition modulo n
  The rotation group of a regular $n-gon$
  The infinite group $(Z, +)$

Cyclic groups are commutative.

cyclic subgroup Although any subgroup of a cyclic group is cyclic, there may be cyclic subgroups of non-cyclic groups, if one element of these will generate a group.

- The group P_3 of all compounded permutations of 3 symbols ABC (order 6) has a cyclic subgroup $\{(ABC), (CAB), (BCA)\}$ generated by (CAB) or (BCA).

cycloid The locus of a point on the circumference of a generating circle that rolls without stopping along a straight line, given, as the circle rotates through an angle θ, by the parametric equations

$$x = a(\theta + \sin \theta)$$
$$y = a(1 - \cos \theta)$$

or by the intrinsic equation $S = 4a \sin \psi$ where $\tan \psi$ is the slope of the tangent at P.

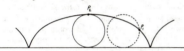

The curve was named by Galileo, who proposed it as a form for the arch of a bridge. The evolute of a cycloid is another cycloid, and the area beneath one arch is three times that of the generating circle.
See also epicycloid, hypocycloid.

cycloidal pendulum Since the evolute of a cycloid is a cycloid, a string held between cycloidal cheek pieces will unwrap from each in turn as it swings and the bob will describe a cycloid. Such a pendulum was shown by Huygens to be exactly isochronous; that is, it has a time of swing independent of the amplitude.

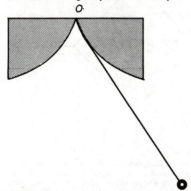

cyclotomic equation *See* nth roots of unity.

cylinder In general, a surface generated by a set of lines passing through a plane curve and parallel to a fixed line (the axis) not in the plane of the curve.

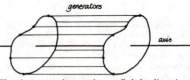

The plane curve is sometimes called the directrix of the cylinder. In particular, the directrix is a circle and the generators are perpendicular to its plane. (From Gk. *kylindros*, that which rolls).

cylindrical coordinates Ordered triples (r, θ, z) which transform to cartesians by the equations

$$x = r \cos \theta$$
$$y = r \sin \theta$$
$$z = z$$

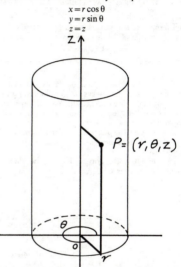

In effect they replace the $x - y$ plane of cartesian coordinates (x, y, z) by polar coordinates.

cylindrical projection A general term for the class of projections in which the surface of a sphere is mapped on to the surface of a cylinder, as the central cylindrical projection shown in the diagram.

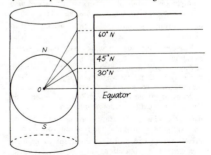

Several types of cylindrical projection are used in practice for map making.
See Mercator projection, equal area projection, Cassini projection.

D

d'Alembert, Jean le Rond French mathematician and encyclopaedist (1717–1783) who first clarified the concept of limit in analysis. His *Traité de Dynamique* was published in 1743.

d'Alembert's principle This was derived from Newton's third law and published in 1743. It is a general method for reducing dynamical problems to static ones by superimposing additional forces corresponding to accelerations.

d'Alembert's test *See* ratio test.

damped harmonic motion Harmonic motion is described by the differential equation

$$\ddot{x} + n^2 x = 0$$

If a term is added which gives a resisting force as a linear function of the velocity, as in

$$x + k\dot{x} + n^2 x = 0$$

the subsequent motion depends on the value of $k^2 - 4n^2$.

1. If $k^2 - 4n^2 > 0$ the period is suppressed and the moving particle approaches the equilibrium position asymptotically or at most after one passage. Such motion is called 'dead beat' and has practical use in measuring instruments.

2. $k^2 - 4n^2 < 0$. The particle oscillates harmonically but the amplitude decreases continually towards a limit zero.

3. $k^2 - 4n^2 = 0$. At this critical value the motion is not oscillatory and resembles case 1.

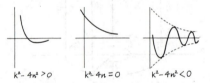

$k^2 - 4n^2 > 0$ $k^2 - 4n = 0$ $k^2 - 4n^2 < 0$

Other functions of x may be considered.

Dase, Zacharias German 'lightning calculator' (1824–1861). For any discussion of the processes of thought, his most interesting feats were not his impressive lightning calculations, but mental algorithms taking several hours. He did, for example, multiply two 100-digit numbers in just under nine hours, without recording intermediate steps.

data From Lat. *datum*, something given. Used in plural.

1. Numerical information which is given for statistical analysis.

2. Any information which is to be processed, generally by computer systems, as input data. Data may consist of numbers, names, words, letters, symbols or graphical constructions and are usually encoded in binary form for storage and processing.

data processing The transformation of data and the extraction of required information from data.

deceleration This word is equivalent to negative acceleration or retardation.

decibel A relative (not an absolute) measure of intensity, usually of sound level, giving the gain or loss of the level I over an initial level I_0. The measure in decibels (db) is defined as

$$10 \log \frac{I}{I_0}$$

I for sound is measured in watts per metre squared. The standard level used in reporting sound intensity is $I_0 = 1 \text{ pWm}^{-2}$, which corresponds approximately to the least sound detectable by a keen ear. The basic unit bel $= 10$ db is rarely used.

deciles These are defined as for quartiles, but the total range is divided into ten equal parts. They are of value for a discrete distribution only if the number of observations is large. *See also* percentiles.

decimal *See* Latin numerical prefixes. Relating to tenths (*decimus*) and hence used of decimal fractions in the denary notation.

decimal fraction A proper fraction whose denominator is a positive integral power of ten. The theory derives from Stevin. The original British form, with a raised point, 0·123 for 123/1000, is no longer used by printers. Most other countries use a comma (0,123) but the form 0.123 as used in Britain and the USA is gaining international acceptance. Since $0.123\ldots = 1 \times 10^{-1} + 2 \times 10^{-2} + 3 \times 10^{-3} \quad \ldots$ a decimal fraction is equivalent to the sum of a series.

decimal point The point as a separator or a mark showing that the preceding digit represents units and the following digits fractions. The notation did not become general till the 18th century.

decimal system Any system of measures or numbers whose place values are expressed in powers of ten, as decimal currency.

decision box Part of a flowchart diagram usually drawn as a diamond shape.

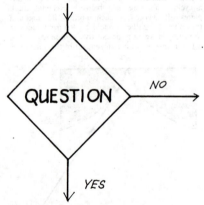

Used in analysing problems as a first stage in programming them for calculation. Generally has one input branch; the output follows one of two output branches corresponding to YES and NO answers to the decision to be made.

declination 1. *See* variation, which is the preferred term.

2. The angle between the celestial equator and a celestial body, measured along a celestial meridian. The declination of a star córresponds to its celestial latitude.

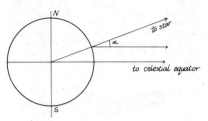

Distinguish from altitude.

decreasing function One whose value decreases as the numerical value of the variable increases, hence one whose derivative is always negative.

decrement A measure of the successive values of a periodic decreasing quantity, such as the amplitude of a pendulum swinging in a resisting medium, or of damped oscillations generally. For damped simple harmonic motion given by

$$y = ae^{-kt} \sin \omega t$$

the ratio of successive maxima is given by $e^{k\pi}$ whose logarithm $k\pi$ is called the logarithmic decrement.

Dedekind section Or 'cut'. Given by Dedekind (1831–1871) as a definition of real numbers. Let the set $\mathbb{Q}$ of rationals be partitioned into two sets L, U so that

$$L \cup U = \mathbb{Q}$$
$$L \neq \emptyset$$
$$U \neq \emptyset$$
$$L \cap U = \emptyset$$

and $a \in L$ & $b \in U \Rightarrow a < b$ for all $a, b, \in \mathbb{Q}$

It follows that in $\mathbb{Q}$ either L has a greatest number, l say, or U has a least, u say. These conditions cannot occur together, or else $\frac{1}{2}(l+u)$ is neither in L or U, which contradicts hypothesis $L \cap U = \emptyset$. There are now three possibilities to consider

1. L has a greatest member, so that U has no least member (see above).
2. U has a least member so that L has no greatest member.
3. L has no greatest member and U has no least member.

In the first and second cases we say that $\mathbb{Q}$ has been cut by a real number l, a number (i.e. the cutting number) corresponding to the rationals l or u respectively.

In the second case we say that $\mathbb{Q}$ has been cut by a real number which is irrational and does not correspond to a member of L or U. Consider for example a cut by a number r where $r^2 = 2$. Then either $p/q < r$ or $p/q > r$ where p/q is any rational, so that r belongs to neither set since r cannot be of the form p/q.

See incommensurable, irrational number.

Dedekind's postulate Formulated (1872) for a line segment, and used by him in defining a real number by a section of the rationals, intuitively represented by points on the line. If a line AB is divided into two parts so that every point in one part is to the left of every point in the other part, then there is exactly one point C on the line which produces this division. In discussing sets of rationals $\{a, b, c \dots\}$ the relation 'to the left of' is replaced by 'less than'. Several of Euclid's early theorems assume this postulate.

deduction The ordinary use of this word as equivalent to subtraction (as in deduction of tax from wages) is better avoided in mathematical contexts. An argument by deduction is one that proceeds from the general to the particular, from given premises to a necessary conclusion.

● We deduce that a triangle whose sides are 3456, 3367, 4825 units is right angled, by showing that the Pythagorean relationship applies to these values.

defective number Taken by Theon to be a number such that the sum of its divisors is less than the number itself, as

$$1 + 2 + 4 < 8 \text{ or } 1 + 2 + 7 < 14.$$

See perfect number.

deficient number See abundant number.

defining relation A relation on the elements of a set which identifies a particular subset.

● A relation 'is a multiple of 3' on the set $\mathbb{N}$ defines the subset of $\mathbb{N}$ given by $\{3, 6, 9, 12 \dots\}$

definite integral This is a real number, associated with a function $f(x)$ and a closed interval $a \leqslant x \leqslant b$. It can arise from an indefinite integral by taking limits, as the limit of a Riemann sum, or (at a very abstract level) from the work of Lebesque. It is written

$$\int_a^b f(x) dx$$ and is used to calculate areas, volumes,

centres of mass and many other quantities that depend on totalling continuously varying quantities, such as the total area of the region containing the strip of area δA in the diagram.

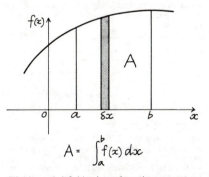

$$A = \int_a^b f(x)\, dx$$

definition A definition in mathematics, except at an elementary level, frequently summarizes an earlier discursive treatment.

1. A ring is defined as an additive abelian group together with a binary multiplicative operation that

satisfies the associative law and distributes over addition.

2. Addition between natural numbers a and b, denoted $+$, is defined by
$$\left.\begin{array}{l} a+0=a \\ a+(b+1)=(a+b)+1 \end{array}\right\}$$
In each case, the formal definition needs expansion to become instructive.

degenerate conic   Also reducible conic.

1. The section of the cone, consisting of two straight lines, when the plane of intersection passes through the vertex.

2. The general equation of the second degree
$$Ax^2 + Bxy + Cy^2 + Dx + Ey + F = 0$$
will represent a conic in cartesian coordinates. If the expression factorizes into two linear factors it becomes equivalent to the geometric case above.

- $2x^2 - 5xy + 27^2 + 7x - 5y + 3 = 0$
  factorizes into
  $(x - 2y + 3)(2x - y + 1) = 0$
  This corresponds to the two lines given by the linear factors, a degenerate conic whose vertex is at $V = (1/3, 5/3)$.

In a limiting case the two factors are the same and the lines coincide.

degree   1. Unit of angular measurement, 1/360th part of a complete turn
See also angular measure.

2. Various other units, e.g. of temperature, alcoholic strength.

3. The degree of a polynomial $P(x)$ is the highest power of x that appears in $P(x) = a_0 + a_1 x + a_2 x^2 \dots + a_n x^x$. When $a_n \neq 0$ $P(x)$ has degree n.

4. The degree of a differential equation (compare order) is the power of the derivative of highest order that appears in the equation.
$$x \frac{d^2 y}{dx^2} + y = \frac{dy^2}{dx} \quad \text{is of degree 1.}$$
$$x \left(\frac{d^2 y}{dx^2}\right)^2 + y = \left(\frac{dy}{dx}\right)^3 \quad \text{is of degree 2.}$$

degree of a polynomial   The highest power of the variable present with a non-zero coefficient in any polynomial.

- $p(x) = 2x^5 - 3x^2 + 2x - 2$ has degree 5.

A polynomial in two variables x, y would have a degree in each of them.

- $p(x, y) = 3x^2 y - 4xy^3 + y^2 - 2$ is of degree 2 in x and 3 in y.

It is, however, more usual to add the powers of each term, so that $p(x, y)$ above would be of degree 5.
See also homogeneous.

degrees of freedom   1. The number of coordinates or independent elements in the vector that specifies any one state of a physical system. Thus a moving aircraft can have component accelerations in the x, y, z directions, and angular accelerations about the x, y, z axes, any one of which can vary independently of the five others.

2. In statistics it is the number of independent items of information given by the data; that is, the total number of items less the number of relevant summary statistics or restraints. Thus a set of independent results $x_1, x_2, \dots x_n$ has n degrees of freedom, but $n - 1$ if the mean $\bar{x}$ is known, since any one of the x_i is now dependent on the sum of others. Note that a sample of size n retains n degrees of freedom if the population mean μ is known, since this does not determine x_i for $i = 1 \dots n$ if the $(n - 1)$ values are known. The concept is of importance in statistical inference since it defines the effective size of a sample.

del   *See* differential operator, divergence.

deleted neighbourhood   If the set of points N is a neighbourhood of the point x, the deleted neighbourhood of x is $N \setminus \{x\}$ that is, the set N without x itself.

Delian problem   The oracle at Delos is said to have required the volume of Apollo's cubical altar to be doubled, and thus launched the problem of the duplication of the cube. As studied by the Greeks, it was subject at first to the Platonic restriction, and is hence insoluble. It was later solved by other methods.

delta notation   The use of δ or Δ to denote difference or increment. It occurs in two forms

1. *See* difference operator.

2. As δx or Δx, denoting an increment (positive or negative) in the value of x, which thus becomes $x + \delta x$. In most applications δx is small, but is always finite.
See also derivative, differentials.

Demoivre's theorem   The analytical equivalent of the Argand diagram given as
$$(\cos \theta + j \sin \theta)^n = \cos n\theta + j \sin n\theta$$
It is also written with i instead of j and sometimes as
$$(\text{cis } \theta)^n = \text{cis } n\theta$$
For integral n it can be shown to hold good by formal expansion using the binomial theorem and substituting $-1 = j^2$.

De Morgan, A.   English mathematician and logician (1806–1871). He discussed the structure of algebra in terms of its laws, and formulated equivalent laws governing logical propositions.

De Morgan's laws   Originally given for compound propositions using AND, OR, and negation
$$\text{NOT (A AND B)} \Leftrightarrow \text{NOT (A) OR NOT (B)}$$
$$\text{NOT (A OR B)} \Leftrightarrow \text{NOT (A) AND NOT (B)}$$
In propositional calculus this becomes
$$\sim(p . q) = \sim p \vee \sim q$$
$$\sim(p \vee q) = \sim p . \sim q$$
The corresponding expression for set algebra is
$$(A \cap B)' = A' \cup B'$$
$$(A \cup B)' = A' \cap B'$$
The laws hold good for any Boolean algebra.

denary   From Lat. *deni*, ten by ten. Pertaining to ten. A counting notation or any system based on tens, in which the number is written as one-zero or 10, using the Hindu–Arabic place value system.

- The number $(3 \times 10^3) + (4 \times 10^2) + (5 \times 10) + 6$, written as 3456 in denary notation.

denominate number   Formerly, but now rarely, used of a number associated with a unit, as distinct from a pure number. Thus £7 is denominate, but 7 is not.

denominator Fron Lat. *denominare*, to name. The second number in a fraction expressed as a/b, which names the parts into which the unit is divided, as 'thirds' in 2/3.
See numerator.

dense A totally ordered set S is dense if for any pair of distinct elements a, $b \in S$, there is a third element c lying between a and b.

● The set **Q** of rational numbers is everywhere dense since for any pair of fractions $p/q < r/s$ there is a fraction x/y such that

$$\frac{p}{q} < \frac{x}{y} < \frac{r}{s}$$

where $\dfrac{x}{y} = \tfrac{1}{2}\left(\dfrac{p}{q} + \dfrac{r}{s}\right)$

Note that 'dense' does not imply 'continuous': $\sqrt{2}$ lies between 1.41 and 1.42 but does not belong to **Q** since the set **Q** has no member a/b such that $a^2/b^2 = 2$.

density function *See* probability density function.

denumerable infinity Also countable infinity. Used of an infinite set whose members can be put into one-to-one correspondence with the set of natural numbers and subjected to a continued counting procedure. For example, if the rationals are arranged in order as a Farey series, then all rationals occurring before a given rational may be counted.

$$1\ 2\ 3\ 4\ 5\ 6\ 7 \ldots$$
$$\tfrac{1}{1}\ \tfrac{2}{1}\ \tfrac{1}{2}\ \tfrac{3}{1}\ \tfrac{1}{3}\ \tfrac{4}{1}\ \tfrac{3}{2} \ldots$$

Such a procedure cannot be devised for the real numbers which thus appear to form a non-denumerable infinite set. Cantor constructed a proof that the reals are non-denumerable, but Wittgenstein and others have queried the logic of his construction.

dependent *See* independent.

dependent events Two random events A and B are dependent if the outcome of the second depends on the outcome of the first; that is, the probability of A conditional on B, denoted $P(A|B)$, is not the probability of A.

● If A is the event 'scoring a six on the throw of a die', $p(A) = \tfrac{1}{6}$
If B is the event 'throwing an even score', $p(B) = \tfrac{1}{2}$
Then $p(A|B) = \tfrac{1}{3}$

derivative Also called differential coefficient. The basic concept of the differential calculus. Given a function f mapping **R** on **R** there is a function S, for two values $x, (x+h)$ of its argument, given by

$$S(x) = \frac{f(x+h) - f(x)}{h}$$

This is sometimes called the chord or secant function and will give the slope of the chord joining the two points concerned in cartesians.

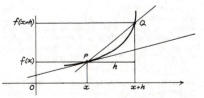

In the diagram this is the average slope of the curve between P and Q, and hence the average change in $f(x)$ as x changes. By considering the behaviour of $S(x)$ as $h \to 0$, that is, as $Q \to P$ and the chord PQ approaches the tangent at P, we obtain the expression called the *derivative* of f at the point x, written variously as $f'(x)$, $Df(x)$ or $\dfrac{df(x)}{dx}$ This is given by

$$f'(x) = \lim_{h \to 0} \frac{f(x+h) - f(x)}{h}$$

The theory of differentiation discusses whether and under what conditions this limit exists for positive or negative h and investigates methods for determining it. Geometrically, the derivative is the slope of the tangent to the curve at any point (if such a tangent exists) and expresses, for x changing at a known rate, the rate at which $f(x)$ is changing at the point.

derived curve The curve plotting the derivative or gradient of a function against its argument, that is, for any $f(x)$ the derived curve is that of $f'(x)$, also plotted against x.

Desargues' theorem Due to Desargues (1593–1662). If the joins of corresponding pairs of vertices of two triangles are concurrent, then the joins of corresponding sides produced are collinear. That is, if two triangles are perspective to a vertex they are perspective to an axis.

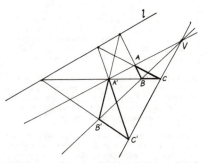

This theorem becomes intuitively obvious if the triangles ABC, A′ B′ C′ are drawn in different planes intersecting in the line l and V is a point not in either plane. Projection of this three-dimensional construction into any convenient plane demonstrates the theorem.

Descartes, René French philosopher and mathematician (1596–1650). His work on geometry was published as a long appendix to a longer work

(*A Discourse on Method*). In it he represented the square of a quantity, in his notation, not as a geometrical square in the Greek manner, but as a longer line segment. He was thus able to extend to higher powers of x, for which he introduced the notation x^3, x^4,... by considering the ratios

$$1:x = x:xx = xx:x^3 = x^3:x^4 = ...$$

and then using a construction for the fourth proportional. He was also able, by constructing lines as secants and tangents to circles, to solve quadratic equations. He found that, for certain values of the coefficients, the lines did not intersect the circles and spoke of solutions as 'imaginary'. This name remained in use to describe what are now called complex roots, and has given the topic an almost metaphysical status outside mathematics. Descartes did in fact represent two numbers x, y as segments of two lines at an angle to one another, but the modern construction of Cartesian coordinates is due to Leibnitz, and only later named in Descartes' honour.

Descartes' rule of signs A rule about the roots of a polynomial equation $f(x) = 0$ with real coefficients, based intuitively on the form of the representational graph. If the coefficients are arranged in descending powers of x the number of positive roots is either equal to the number of changes of sign of the coefficients or is less than this number by a positive even number. Similarly the number of negative roots is given by the coefficients of $f(-x) = 0$.

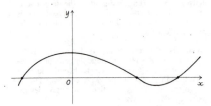

● Consider the polynomial $y = 4x^5 + 5x^3 - 30x + 8 = 0$
This has two variations of sign and hence has two or no positive roots. If $-x$ is substituted we get $-4x^5 - 5x^3 + 30x + 8 = 0$ which has one.

detached coefficients Calculation and manipulation of algebraic expressions and equations can often be abbreviated by the use of coefficients alone, the variables and the powers being indicated by position. *See* synthetic division, tableau, matrix.

determinant An array of n^2 elements, written as an $n \times n$ square. It is denoted by vertical lines enclosing the array. The elements are often written with a double suffix giving the row and column occupied by each element.
Thus the 2×2 determinant

$$\begin{vmatrix} a_{11} & a_{12} \\ a_{21} & a_{22} \end{vmatrix} = a_{11}a_{22} - a_{21}a_{12}$$

is of order 2 and has this value *by definition*. Determinants of order $n(n > 2)$ can be defined in terms of determinants of order $n - 1$. Thus, for $n = 3$

$$\begin{vmatrix} a_{11} & a_{12} & a_{13} \\ a_{21} & a_{22} & a_{23} \\ a_{31} & a_{32} & a_{33} \end{vmatrix} = a_{11}\begin{vmatrix} a_{22} & a_{23} \\ a_{32} & a_{33} \end{vmatrix} - a_{12}\begin{vmatrix} a_{21} & a_{23} \\ a_{31} & a_{33} \end{vmatrix} + a_{13}\begin{vmatrix} a_{21} & a_{22} \\ a_{31} & a_{32} \end{vmatrix}$$

In general, a determinant of order n is the sum of $n!$ terms.

deviation 1. *See* variance, standard deviation, mean deviation.
2. The angular difference between magnetic north and that shown by a magnetic compass on a ship, caused by the ship's own magnetic field. Also used for difference between true north and that shown by a gyrocompass, due to various errors.

diagonal matrix One whose elements are zero except for those in the leading diagonal. Any element $a_{ij} = 0$ if $i \neq j$.

diagram Any picture, plan, sketch or configuration intended for explanation or exposition rather than accurate pictorial or dimensional representation.

diameter (Gk. *diametron*, measure through or across). A line drawn across a figure (usually a circle, sphere, central conic or conicoid) and passing through the centre.

diametral plane A plane that bisects and is perpendicular to any system of parallel chords drawn to a curve.

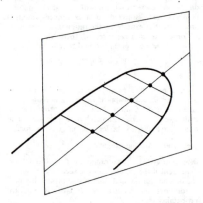

The diametral plane of a circle contains the diameter.

dichotomy The partition of a set into two disjoint subsets, used as a method of classification. The rule for partition must assign each element unambiguously into one of the subsets, e.g. numbers are negative or non-negative, not negative or positive, since the status of zero is ambiguous. Repeated dichotomy (the 'tree' of Porphyry) classifies a set into subsets in binary stages, as in Proclus' classification of quadrilaterals

		quadrilaterals				
	parallelograms				non-parallelograms	
rectangular		non-rectangular		trapezium		trapezoid
square	oblong	rhombus	rhomboid	isosceles		scalene

The law of dichotomy is a synonym for the law of excluded middle.

difference   The difference between two quantities is the quantity to be added to the lesser to make it equal to the greater. Thus the difference between 5 and 13 is 8. For quantities expressed algebraically the term is sometimes ambiguous because of sign. Thus $a \sim b$ denotes difference as above, but $a - b$ is also called difference and is negative if $b > a$. The absolute value $|a - b|$ is often used as equivalent to $a \sim b$.

difference equations   *See* recurrence relation.

difference operator   Used in numerical analysis, particularly for problems of interpolation and with functions given numerically at equally spaced intervals, as with tables of experimental data. There are three operators in common use

1. Forward difference operator, Δ defined by $\Delta f(x) = f(x + h) - f(x)$
2. Backward difference operator ∇, defined by $\nabla f(x) = f(x) - f(x - h)$
3. Central difference operator δ, defined by $\delta f(x) = f(x + \frac{1}{2}h) - f(x - \frac{1}{2}h)$

Higher order operators are defined, using a power notation

$$\Delta^2 f(x) = \Delta(\Delta f(x))$$
$$\Delta^{n+1} f(x) = \Delta(\Delta^n f(x))$$

Differences are usually tabulated as below

x	$f(x)$	$\Delta f(x)$	$\Delta^2 f(x)$	$\Delta^3 f(x)$
1	1			
		3		
2	4		2	
		5		0
3	9.		2	
		7		0
4	16		2	
		9		0
5	25		2	
		11		
6	36			

Other arrangements for the table are possible.

difference quotient   For a function $f(x)$, with values $f(a)$ and $f(b)$ at $x = a$, $x = b$, the difference quotient is given by

$$\frac{f(a) - f(b)}{a - b}$$

This becomes the derivative of $f(x)$ at $x = a$ in the limit as $b \to a$, providing that this limit exists.

difference ring   The ring of cosets $r + N$ in a ring R, where $r \in \mathbb{R}$ is a difference ring if N is an ideal in R. Also called residue class ring of R modulo N, and denoted by $R|N$. Synonyms: factor ring, quotient ring.

differentiable   A real valued function of a real variable $f(x)$ is differentiable at a point a if the derivative $f'(a)$ exists. The definition extends to complex functions.
Alternative definition. The function f is differentiable at a if there is a linear transformation T such that

$$f(a + x) - f(a) = T(x) + g(x)$$

for all x in some neighbourhood of zero, and if $\frac{g(x)}{|x|}$ approaches 0 as x approaches 0.
It follows that $f(a) + T(x)$ is a linear approximation to $f(a + x)$ near $x = 0$.

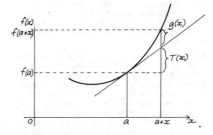

See also differentials.

differential analyser   An instrument used to solve differential equations, introduced by Bush in 1920. In effect it set up differential gearboxes and disc mechanisms governed by the equations to be solved, and recorded numerical values of the solutions. It has now been made obsolete by the greater speed and capacity of digital computers.

differential calculus   A branch of analysis concerned with the derivatives of functions and their applications. A few typical applications are:
1. Study of rates of change and concepts such as acceleration or force that depend on them.
2. Approximations, including polynomial approximations and Taylor's theorem.
3. Determining the existence and nature of stationary points in functions.

differential coefficient   A term once commonly used for the derivative. It arose from Leibnitz' treatment of the quantities dy, dx which (working before the concept of limits was established) he regarded as actual infinitesimals or differentials, representing the changes in x, y for a function at a given point. The ratio R between these was needed, so that, in the Leibnitz notation, $\mathrm{d}y = \left(\frac{\mathrm{d}y}{\mathrm{d}x}\right) \mathrm{d}x$ where $\frac{\mathrm{d}y}{\mathrm{d}x}$ is the single symbol which becomes a numerical value for a given function at a given point. The name arises because the ratio is one of the coefficients of h in the expansion of $f(x + h)^n$ in terms of h.
● The 'differential coefficient' of h is $3x^2$, the second coefficient in
  $(x + h)^3 = (x^3) + (3x^2)h + (3x)h^2 + h^3$
See also differentials, derivative.

differential equation   Any equation relating to the derivatives of a set of variables. The equations may

49

include the variables themselves

1. $\dfrac{dy}{dx} + ay + b = 0$

2. $\left(\dfrac{dy}{dx}\right)^2 = 9$

3. $x\dfrac{d^2y}{dx^2} + \dfrac{dy}{dx} + 1 = 0$

The order of the equation is the highest derivative that occurs, the degree of the equation is the highest power of the highest derivative that occurs.
See also differential operator. Most physical laws are expressible in terms of differential equations, and possible physical states are described in terms of their solutions.

differential geometry   Applies the methods of analysis to geometry. As developed originally by Monge, Riemann and others, it considered curves and surfaces in Euclidean space, but was later generalized to spaces of n dimensions. The line intervals and distance functions of synthetic plane geometry are replaced by differentials, so that the Pythagoras relation becomes $ds^2 = dx^2 + dy^2$. It becomes possible to describe vanishingly small distances between points on a surface by rewriting the Pythagorean distance function. Thus for the surface of an ellipsoid $ds^2 = f.dx^2 + 2g dx.dy + h dy^2$, where f, g, h are constants. Extended to four coordinates x, y, z, t the methods have proved of value in general relativity theory.

differential operator   The Hamilton–Tait operator denoted by ∇ read *del* or *nabla*, given by

$$\mathbf{i}\frac{\partial}{\partial x} + \mathbf{j}\frac{\partial}{\partial y} + \mathbf{k}\frac{\partial}{\partial z}$$

See divergence and gradient for examples of use.

differentials   A construction by Cauchy to replace the undefined quantities called 'infinitesimals' by the early analysts. If $y = f(x)$ we can define a finite change from x to $(x+h)$ as the differential of x, written dx. This, of course, corresponds to the ordinary finite difference δx. We now *define* the differential dy of y as $dx.f'(x)$ for any x, and it follows that $f'(x)$ is now the actual quotient dy/dx. This quotient, which must not be confused with the Leibnitz notation for the derivative, is given (as is the derivative) by the slope of the tangent to $f(x)$ at x. The differential of a function f at a is sometimes written $d_a f$ and is the quantity $T(x)$ discussed under the entry for differentiable.

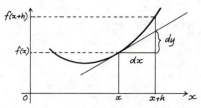

The diagram shows that this is the linear part of the increment in $f(x)$ due to the finite increment h of x.

For any finite h, however small, differentials may be treated as any other real quantities.
See differentiable, infinitesimals.

differentiation   The process, applied to any function, of finding the derivative.

digit   Any one of the set of Hindu–Arabic numerals 0–9, from Lat. *digitus* finger. Often generalized to numeric symbols in other bases, as hexadecimal digit, binary digit.

digital computer   *See* computer.

digital root   Formed by repeated addition of the digits of a number until only a single digit remains, as in

$$8489 \rightarrow 29 \rightarrow 11 \rightarrow 2$$

This final number is the digital root.

dihedral angle   The angle between two intersecting planes.

dihedral groups   One of the classifications of symmetry groups which considers both sides of a plane configuration (a dihedron) as distinct. It therefore consists of the rotational symmetry positions of the configuration together with the axes of reflectional symmetry, which can be realized in cut-out shapes by turning them over.
For a regular n-gon the corresponding group would be of order $2n$.

dihedron   *See* polyhedron.

dilatation   *See* enlargement.

dimension   1. A measure of distance (or length) taken along a single line or axis from an origin or reference point.
2. Plural, the number of measures of distance that need to be taken to specify the position of a point with respect to an origin. Thus a line has one, a plane surface two and a region of space three dimensions.

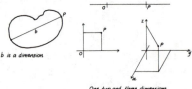

One, two and three dimensions

3. In general the number of coordinates required to specify any one state of a phase space. Thus position and time require 4; position, time, pressure and temperature require 6, and so on. Written as an ordered set, as (x, y, z, t, T, p) this would form a vector of dimension 6, and the phase space would have this number of dimensions.
4. A set of fundamental physical units chosen to express other physical units as derived units. In certain circumstances these are called dimensions. Thus density is mass per unit volume, but volume is the product of three measures of length. Hence taking mass (**M**) and length (**L**) as fundamental, the *dimensions* of density are given as $\mathbf{ML}^{-3}$. For dynamics, time (**T**) is also taken as fundamental, and for electromagnetics the measure of current **I**. Examples of physical dimensions (which are independent of

any constants of proportionality or actual units chosen) are

velocity	$\mathbf{LT^{-1}}$
moment of inertia	$\mathbf{ML^2}$
force	$\mathbf{MLT^{-2}}$
permeability	$\mathbf{MLT^{-2}I^{-2}}$

(*See* next entry)
Dimensions have the important property of *homogeneity*; that is, if two physical quantities are related by an equation, the two sides must have the same dimensions as defined.

dimensional analysis   A method of checking the form of proposed relationships between physical quantities by establishing that they are dimensionally homogeneous (see above). Thus, if we write an *incorrect* relation for velocity, distance and time

$$v = as \quad (a = \text{acceleration}, \ s = \text{distance})$$

dimensional analysis gives

$$\mathbf{LT^{-1} = LT^{-2}.L}$$

This is obviously a false statement, but it is corrected dimensionally by writing

$$v^2 = as$$

The true relation is $v^2 = 2as$, but any numerical constant cannot be found by this method. Sometimes a constant can be shown to have dimensions. Thus Newton's Law of attraction, for point masses m_1, m_2 at a distance d is

$$F = G\frac{m_1 . m_2}{d^2}$$

Inserting dimensions $\mathbf{MLT^{-2}} \equiv G(\mathbf{M^2 L^{-2}})$.
Hence G, the gravitational constant, has dimensions $\mathbf{M^{-1}L^3T^{-2}}$.
See also SI.

dimensionless variable   Any variable in a physical system (such as the number of particles in the system) which does not have dimensions associated with it, and is therefore a pure number.

Diophantine equations   *See* indeterminate equations.

Dirac δ function   A non-realizable function $\delta(u-v)$ postulated for use in the quantum theory, which becomes infinite if $u=v$ and has the value zero if $u=v$. It is also to be taken as a probability distribution of zero dispersion so that it requires $\int\delta(u-v)du = 1$ for suitable limits. An approximate realization, omitting the last requirement, is a curve which is, for a given small positive ε, large near the origin and small elsewhere. An example is the derived curve

$$y' = \frac{\epsilon}{t^2 + \epsilon^2}$$

The primitive of this curve approximates to the Heaviside step function H(t), which itself has no finite derivative at $t=0$ and a zero derivative elsewhere.

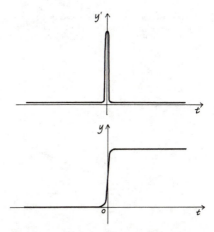

direct common tangent   *See* common tangent.

direct congruence   Used of two configurations one of which can be superimposed on the other by translation or rotation in the plane, as distinct from reflection.
See isometry.

directed graph   Usually equivalent to an arrow diagram, a set of points or nodes connected by lines or arcs, each of which is associated with a given direction.

directed line segment   A geometrical representation of a vector. If **v** is the vector (x_1, y_1) and we then let V be the point (x_1, y_1) then OV is a directed line segment, where O is the origin of the coordinates.

directed numbers   Signed integers in which the sign is interpreted as indicating direction. For displacements, a positive sign is taken to represent a direction to the right of or above an origin, a negative to the left or below. For rotations, positive is usually taken as anticlockwise.

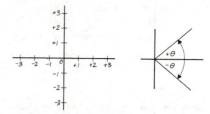

A useful but not yet established convention writes directed numbers as ^+a, ^-a to avoid confusion with the signs for addition and subtraction. Then $^+a + ^-a = 0$.

directed set   An ordered set of numbers whose every finite subset is bounded from above.

directional angles   The angles made by a line with the coordinates axes x, y and z, corresponding to the direction cosines.

direction cosines Also called direction ratios. A point P has a position vector r, so that in cartesian coordinates OP makes angles α, β, γ with the axes Ox, Oy, Oz.

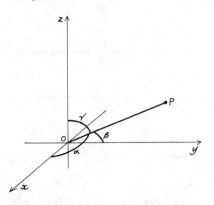

Then $\cos\alpha$, $\cos\beta$, $\cos\gamma$, usually denoted λ, μ, ν, are the direction cosines of OP and $\lambda^2+\mu^2+\nu^2=1$. The direction cosines are not independent in this expression. As a vector, OP is $k\hat{r}$, where $\hat{r}$ is the unit vector given by $\hat{r}=\lambda\mathbf{i}+\mu\mathbf{j}+\nu\mathbf{k}$ and the dot product $\hat{r}.\hat{r}$ gives $\lambda^2+\mu^2+\nu^2=1$ as before.

direction of correspondence If any one-to-one correspondence R is not symmetric, so that $a\,R\,b$ does not imply $b\,R\,a$, then the correspondence goes in the direction from a to b only.

director circle The circle which is the set of all points of intersection of pairs of perpendicular tangents to a conic.

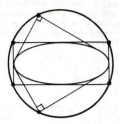

See auxiliary circle.

direct proof A result or theorem whose logical structure is in the form $p\Rightarrow q$, read as 'if p then q' where the assertion of p can be shown to entail the truth of q. It is regarded as the most satisfactory form of mathematical proof.
See indirect proof.

directrix A fixed line associated with a conic. In the focus-directrix definition, the conic is the set of all points whose distance from a fixed point S, the focus, is in a constant ratio with its perpendicular distance from the directrix.

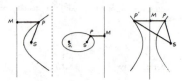

Three cases arise, as in the diagrams.

PS/PM $=1$ gives a parabola
PS/PM <1 gives an ellipse
PS/PM >1 gives a hyperbola

The third curve has two branches since there is another set of points P′ for which P′S/P′M $=$ PS/PM. Also used for the circle through which pass the generating lines of a cylinder.

Dirichlet, P. G. Lejeune French mathematician (1805–1859), who did work on prime numbers and was responsible for the definition of a function in terms of dependent and independent variables, the precursor of the modern set theoretic definition.

Dirichlet's test A test for the convergence of a series, which depends on writing the general term u_n as the product of two factors a_n, v_n. If Σa_n converges or oscillates finitely, and if $\{v_n\}$ converges uniformly to zero as $n\to\infty$ then $\Sigma a_n v_n=\Sigma u_n$ converges uniformly.
It is often applied to trigonometrical series such as $a\cos\theta+b\cos 2\theta+c\cos 3\theta+\ldots$

disc 1. The region defined by all the points on or within the circumference of a circle, $x^2+y^2\leqslant a^2$. It is useful to distinguish this from the circle $x^2+y^2=a^2$.
2. In the complex plane, $|z-c|\leqslant r$ represents all points in or on a circle centre c and radius r if z, $c\in\mathbb{C}$.
3. The disc is open if points on the circumference are not included, otherwise it is closed, $x^2+y^2<a^2$ as distinct from $x^2+y^2\leqslant a^2$.

disconnected *See* connected. If the criteria for connectedness do not apply a set or region is disconnected. Thus a line whose points are labelled with the rational numbers only can be divided into two open intervals defined by $x<\sqrt{2}$, $x>\sqrt{2}$, and hence the set of labelled points is disconnected at $\sqrt{2}$. The term corresponds to discontinuous as used in analysis.

discontinuity 1. A point at which a function is defined but fails to meet the conditions for continuity.
2. A point at which a function is not defined. $\dfrac{1}{x}$ is not defined if $x=0$. There are several types of discontinuity, not mutually exclusive. Some common examples are:
1. Removable discontinuity. A point at which the function can be made continuous by redefining it at the point of discontinuity

$$f(x)=\begin{cases} x\sin\dfrac{1}{x} & x\neq 0 \\ 0 & x=0 \end{cases}$$

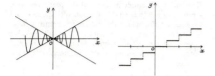

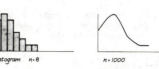

histogram n=8   n=1000

2. Jump discontinuity. Here the limits of the function from the right and from the left both exist but are different, as $y = [\![x]\!]$ where $[\![x]\!]$ denotes the greatest integer not greater than x.

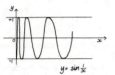

$y = \sin \frac{1}{x}$

At $x = 1$ the limit approaching x from the left is 0, from the right is 1.

3. Finite discontinuity. There is an interval about the point in which the function values are bounded.

$f(x) = \sin \dfrac{1}{x}$ at $x = 0$ is wholly contained in

$$-1 \leqslant f(x) \leqslant 1$$

4. Infinite discontinuity. Here $f(x)$ becomes arbitrarily large in any interval, however small, about a point.

$$y = 1/(x-1) \text{ as } x \rightarrow 1$$

$y = \frac{1}{x-1}$

A discontinuity is an example of a singularity.

discontinuous function A function having discontinuities, which may be at a point, in an interval or even at all points of its domain; as examples:

● $f(x) = \begin{cases} x \text{ at } x \neq 0 \\ 1 \text{ at } x = 0 \end{cases}$ is discontinuous at $x = 0$

$f(x) = \begin{cases} 0 & x \text{ is rational} \\ 1 & x \text{ is irrational} \end{cases}$

is everywhere discontinuous

$f(x) = \begin{cases} 0 & x < 1 \\ 1 & 1 \leqslant x \leqslant 2 \\ 0 & x > 2 \end{cases}$

is discontinuous at $x = 1$ and $x = 2$.

discrete probability distribution Any non-continuous probability distribution, which can take at most a denumerably infinite set of values. Thus a distribution of integers or rational values would be discrete, as distinct from all real values in an interval. A finite discrete distribution is properly represented by a histogram, but is conventionally shown by a continuous curve when the intervals are small.

discrete variable A variable that takes a finite set of values $a_1, a_2 \ldots a_n$, or an infinite set of values $a_1, a_2, a_3 \ldots$ that may be put into a simple sequence. That is, it does not contain intermediate values such as $(a_1 + a_2)/2$ or $\sqrt{a_1 a_2}$. An interval corresponding to a discrete variable does not contain cluster points.

discriminant If $x_1, x_2 \ldots x_n$ are the n roots of a polynomial equation $ax^n + bx^{n-1} + \ldots + k = 0$ where $a = 0$, then the discriminant Δ whose value discriminates between the roots, is defined as the continued product

$$\Delta = a^{2n-2} \, \Pi(a_i - a_j)^2 \quad i \neq j$$

For a quadratic $ax^2 + bx + c = 0$ whose roots are α, β

$$\Delta = a^2(\alpha - \beta)^2$$
$$= a^2\{(\alpha + \beta)^2 - 4\alpha\beta\}$$

Hence $\Delta = 4(b^2 - 4ac)$ since $(\alpha + \beta) = \dfrac{-b}{a}, \ \alpha\beta = \dfrac{c}{a}$.

If Δ or $b^2 - 4ac$ is positive, the equation has two distinct real roots; if zero, two equal roots; if negative, no real but two complex roots.

disjoint Two sets A and B are disjoint if their intersection is empty, that is, if $A \cap B = 0$. This means that A and B have no elements in common. The phrase 'mutually exclusive' is also used.

disjunction The ambiguous propositional relation denoted by the word 'or'.
See both aut and vel.

disjunctive normal form The same as canonical form for a Boolean function.

dispersion A measure of the spread of a population. Dispersions from the arithmetic mean are measured by mean deviation, standard deviation, interquartile or interpercentile ranges, and approximately by the range itself.

dissection The cutting of a plane or solid region into parts, often with the intention to rearrange them to produce a different configuration. A dissection is a partition of the set of points defining the region.

● The square on the hypotenuse of a right angled triangle may be dissected to cover the squares on the other two sides.
A tangram is a seven-part dissection of a square.

distance 1. An intuitive concept related to the time or physical effort required to pass from one point to another, or the length of a rod required to bridge the gap between the points. It is given precision by the operation of measurement, which compares the distance with that between the extremities of an arbitrary but standard unit.
2. Elementary mathematics adopts the concept of distance as defined by measurement, although it tacitly assumes the concept of exact distance, ignoring the tolerances always implied by physical measurement.
3. Distance, in mathematics, is an undefined quantity that satisfies a suitable axiom set. Given a set

53

$X = \{x, y, z, \ldots\}$ which may but need not correspond to points in real space, any binary relation $D(x, y)$ between them is a distance function, if:

1. $D(x, y) \geqslant 0$
2. $D(x, y) = D(y, x)$
3. $D(x, y) = 0$ iff $x = y$
4. $D(x, z) \leqslant D(x, y) + D(y, z)$

The set X together with the function D together form a general metric space. In addition a metric space is said to have a *metric* which defines the actual form of the relation $D(x, y)$. For example, a space has a Euclidean metric if for points p, q whose cartesian coordinates are the pairs of real numbers (x_1, y_1) (x_2, y_2)

$$[D(p, q)]^2 = [D(x_1, x_2)]^2 + [D(y_1, y_2)]^2$$

This corresponds to the Pythagoras theorem for Euclidean space.

4. A plane perspective projection as of a picture or photograph has an intrinsic distance function which is Pythagorean. This can be related to the actual spatial distance between points represented by the geometry of the projection. The relation is important for interpreting the results of aerial photography. *See* vanishing point.

distinct factors Those which are not repeated.

$$x^3 + 4x^2 + x - 6 = (x + 3)(x + 2)(x - 1)$$
$$x^3 + 3x^2 - 4 = (x + 2)(x + 2)(x - 1)$$

The second cubic gives only two distinct factors.

distribution 1. A key concept of statistical analysis. Instead of the 1:1 correspondence characteristic of algebraic relationships, a range of values, either discrete or continuous, arises for any statistical measure or for any random variable X. Values within this range will occur with frequencies whose pattern describes the distribution, as with normal, exponential or rectangular distributions.

2. In traditional logic, an affirmative or a negative is said to distribute the subject p or predicate q of a statement of the form 'p is q', if it applies to all or none of the p, q, but not if it applies only to some.

● 'All triangles are polygons' distributes 'triangles' but not 'polygons' since there are polygons other than triangles.

3. Also used of pairs of binary operations. *See* distributive law.

distribution free A term applied to data about which no assumptions such as normality are assumed. The recently developed field of hypothesis testing using non-parametric methods is applicable to distribution-free data.

distribution function The function $F(x)$ that represents the probability $(X \leqslant x)$; i.e., that the value of a random observation X from the distribution is at most x. It describes both discrete and continuous distribution for all x.

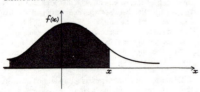

distribution of sample means If the measures X of a population P, have a distribution with mean μ and variance σ^2 (for which the moment generating function exists) then the distribution of all possible samples of size n taken from P tends to a normal distribution with mean μ and variance σ^2/n as n increases.

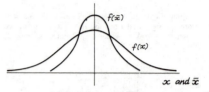

The diagram shows the curves for X and $\bar{X}$ superimposed when $n = 9$.

distributive law If there are two binary operations $*$ and $\circ$ defined on any set S, we say that $*$ distributes over $\circ$ if, for all a, b, $c \in S$

$$a * (b \circ c) = (a * b) \circ (a * c)$$
and
$$(b \circ c) * a = (b * a) \circ (c * a)$$

Note that multiplication distributes over addition, but addition does not distribute over multiplication.

divergence 1. Usually equivalent to non-convergence. The term proper divergence is sometimes used to distinguish from a non-convergent sequence or series which oscillates. Criteria for divergence are given by contradicting those for convergence. Thus, a series diverges if the Cauchy criteria do not hold, as in the following:

$$S_n = 1 + \tfrac{1}{2} + \tfrac{1}{3} + \ldots + \frac{1}{n}$$

$$S_{2n} = 1 + \tfrac{1}{2} + \tfrac{1}{3} + \ldots + \frac{1}{n} + \frac{1}{n+1} + \ldots + \frac{1}{2n}$$

then

$$S_{2n} - S_n = \frac{1}{n+1} + \frac{1}{n+2} + \ldots + \frac{1}{2n}$$

$$> \frac{n}{2n}$$

$$> \tfrac{1}{2}$$

Hence if $\epsilon = \tfrac{1}{4}$, say,

$$S_m - S_n \not< \epsilon \text{ for some } m > n(\epsilon)$$

This contradicts the criteria for a Cauchy sequence and therefore $\sum \frac{1}{n}$ diverges.

2. Given any vector function $\mathbf{F}(x, y, z)$ which defines a vector field, the divergence of $\mathbf{F}$, written div $\mathbf{F}$, is given by the scalar or inner product $\nabla . \mathbf{F}$, where ∇ is the Hamilton–Tait differential operator

$$\mathbf{i} \frac{\partial}{\partial x} + \mathbf{j} \frac{\partial}{\partial y} + \mathbf{k} \frac{\partial}{\partial z}$$

Hence

$$\text{div } \mathbf{F} = \nabla . \mathbf{F} = \left(\mathbf{i} \frac{\partial}{\partial x} + \mathbf{j} \frac{\partial}{\partial y} + \mathbf{k} \frac{\partial}{\partial z} \right) \cdot (\mathbf{i}F_x + \mathbf{j}F_y + \mathbf{k}F_z)$$

$$= \frac{\partial F_x}{\partial x} + \frac{\partial F_y}{\partial y} + \frac{\partial F_z}{\partial z}$$

For example if **F** is a velocity field at $P(x, y, z)$ given by volume units per second through any vanishingly small area, than $\nabla . \mathbf{F}$ or div **F** is the rate of change of volume per unit volume over any small volume δV as $\delta V \to 0$. P is, for example, a source or sink of fluid, or a point in a region of expansion or contraction. Distinguish between $\nabla . \mathbf{F}$ the divergence of a vector field and ∇S the gradient of a scalar field. ∇ is often read *nabla* or *del*.

divergent integral   If f is any function integrable in the closed interval $[a, X]$ where X is any arbitrarily large number, the integral $\displaystyle\int_a^\infty f(x)\,dx$ is said to be divergent if $\displaystyle\int_a^X f(x)\,dx$ does not tend to a finite limit as $X \to \infty$. For example $\displaystyle\int_1^X \frac{dx}{x} = \ln X$ and $\ln X \to \infty$ as $X \to \infty$. Hence $\displaystyle\int_1^X \frac{dx}{x}$ is a divergent integral and the area to the right of the ordinate $x = 1$ is unbounded.

divergent series   A divergent series is one whose partial sums form a divergent sequence.

- $S_n = 1 + 2 + 3 + \ldots + n + \ldots$
  gives the sequence $= 1, 3, 6, 10, \ldots \dfrac{n(n+1)}{2} \ldots$
  which is divergent.

The criterion for convergence is that the nth partial sum tends to a limit as $n \to \infty$. If this criterion does not hold the series diverges, as, e.g. $\sum \dfrac{1}{n}$.

See divergence.

dividend   The number which is divided. In a/b a is the dividend, b the divisor. Also used of profits distributed among shareholders, in which case the term usually refers to a percentage of the nominal or face value of the shares.

divisibility tests   These establish whether one number can be divided by another, without actually completing the process of division. Common examples are

Any number ending in 0 or 5 is divisible by 5.
Any number such that the sum of its digits (or its digital root) is 3 or 9 is divisible by 3 or 9, respectively.
If the number formed by the last two digits of a number is divisible by 4 the number is divisible by 4.
Any even number, the sum of whose digits is divisible by 3 is divisible by 6.

Many of these tests were devised by Arab mathematicians before written algorithms were generally available.

division   One of the Four Rules of elementary arithmetic, which arises by repeated subtraction as the inverse of multiplication, which is repeated addition. The result has two distinct concrete realizations (with apples, say).

1. Partition. 17 apples are shared equally among 5 people. How many does each get, and how many remain? Without knowledge of arithmetic this could be done by giving one apple to each person repeatedly till less than five were left.

2. Quotition. How many persons could be given five apples each? Without arithmetic, this could be done by handing out clutches of five apples till less than five remained.
In one case the quotient represents apples, in the other persons.

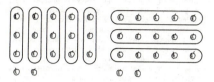

These are both written

$$17/5 = 3 \text{ rem. } 2$$

Where 17 is the dividend, 5 the divisor, 3 the quotient (Lat. *quotiens*, how many times) and 2 the remainder.
Division can also be defined as a binary operation on the real numbers denoted by /, which defines a/b as $a \times 1/b$, where $1/b(b \neq 0)$ is separately defined as the reciprocal of b. The operation is neither commutative nor associative.
See also rational, real, reciprocal.

divisor   *See* dividend.

divisors of zero   When a set has additive and multiplicative operations and an identity for addition (that is, $+$, $-$ and 0 for the set of real numbers $\mathbb{R}$), there may exist non-zero elements x, y with the property that $X \times y = 0$. Such elements are known as divisors of zero.

- The ring Z_6 with $+$, x modulo 6.
  Here $3 \times 2 = 0$ $(3 \times 2 = 0 \bmod 6)$ and 3 and 2 are divisors of zero.

d notation   The Leibnitz notation $\dfrac{dy}{dx}$ for the derivative.
See also dot notations, differential coefficient.

dodecagon   *See* polygon.

dodecahedron   *See* polyhedron.

domain   Of a function. The set of values for which the function is defined. This should be given explicitly, but is often understood from context.

$$f : x \mapsto x^2 (x \in \mathbb{N})$$

The domain of the function $f = \{(0, 1), (2, 1)\}$ is the set $\{0, 2\}$.

domino   *See* polyomino. In the usual context of a mathematical activity a domino is merely the one possible arrangement of two equal squares joined edge to edge, although the name comes from the game in which the squares bear patterns of dots.

Doppler effect   The alteration in the frequency of a wave such as light, sound or surface wave of liquid, caused by the motion of either source or observer. For sound in still air the motions of source S or observer O relative to the air give different results, but for light the only factor is the relative velocity of S and O.

dot notations   Apart from its use in punctuation the dot, (also called stop, period or point according to context) has several uses in mathematics.

1. In English-speaking countries as the decimal separator. The point is now (B.S. 5261) always written or printed on the line, thus 6.3, read as 'six point three' or 'six decimal three'. A comma is used in most countries, as 6,3.
2. To show multiplication, when it can be placed either on or above the line. The multiplication sign, ×, should be used for the product of two numbers except where confusion with the decimal point is unlikely. Thus $6 = 3.2$ is acceptable, if factors are being discussed, but $x = 3.2$ is not unless it is clear from context that a decimal is not intended.
3. As a sign to denote any operations which behave in some ways like arithmetical multiplication. It is better to use an alternative notation if available.
Examples $p.q$ for $p\&q$ or $p \wedge q$ (logical product)
$A.B$ for $A \cap B$ (intersection of sets)
(Note that here × cannot be used, since $A \times B$ denotes the cross product.) The standard notation for scalar product of vectors **a**, **b** is **a**.**b**.
4. The notation developed by Newton for his 'fluxions' (or derivatives), which corresponded to what Leibnitz independently called 'differences'. Newton wrote $\dot{y}$ for the 'fluxion' of the 'fluent' y, and $\ddot{y}$ for the fluxion of the fluxion which would now be called the first and second derivatives. The notation is still used conveniently in applied mathematics for derivatives with respect to time t, as $\ddot{\theta}$ for angular acceleration.
See also Newton–Leibnitz controversy, Lagrange notation.

dot product *See* scalar product (of vectors).

double arrow notation *See* iff.

double false position Lat. *regula duorum falsorum.* An early trial and error method for solving an equation by taking two trial values, one too big and one too small, and then interpolating. The process could be repeated as often as needed.
See also false position.

double integral *See* multiple integral.

double negation Expresses the logical axiom that $\sim(\sim p) = p$, where p is a proposition. Note that double negatives may be idiomatic in some languages and do not then cancel.

double point A node at which a curve intersects itself once, as with the limaçon $r = 1 + 2\cos\theta$. There are, in general two tangents at such a point. Multiple points are possible, as with the 'rose-petal' curve $r = a\sin 2\theta$.

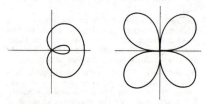

double roots *See* multiple roots.

double sampling The simplest case of multistage sampling in statistics. In testing an hypothesis, an initial sample is taken, and a decision to accept or reject is made if the data prove sufficiently informative. If they do not, a second sample is taken and the decision is then made on the basis of the combined samples. This is a more efficient procedure than working with a single larger sample.

doubly periodic function Describes a function of a complex variable which has two distinct periods of different argument. An example is the elliptic function $sn\, x$.
See also periodic function.

dragon curve A curve of order $n = 1, 2, 3\ldots$ having no derivative at $2^n - 1$ points. As n increases the curve develops a resemblance to an animal form with head, legs and tail which is just detectable at $n = 5$. The curve is modelled by folding a long strip of paper in half once, repeating the folding $2, 3, \ldots$ times, and opening out so that the angle formed at each fold is $90°$.

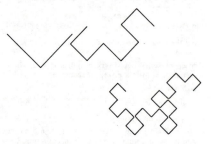

duality Shown by any mathematical statement which is true when two of its terms are interchanged.
● $A \cap (B \cup C) = (A \cap B) \cup (A \cap C)$ gives the dual statement $A \cup (B \cap C) = (A \cup B) \cap (A \cup C)$.
'Two lines define a point' gives the dual
'two points define a line'
Most geometrical statements of duality can be represented diagrammatically, and give rise to dual diagrams even if no statement is made.

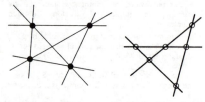

See also self dual.

Dubrovnik programme An early programme for reforming the content of mathematics teaching in the light of modern developments within mathematics. Issued by the Organisation of Economic Co-operation and Development in 1961 from Dubrovnik in Yugoslavia.

dummy variable A symbol, having the usual form of a variable such as x, y or θ, but used merely as a place holder or 'container' into which a true variable can be inserted. It is used to specify operational rules in the most compact way as in $\int x^2 dx = \frac{1}{3}x^3 + C$ which gives the instruction 'multiply the variable by $\frac{1}{3}$, increase power to 3, add a constant'. This is distinct from

$$\int_0^1 x^2\,dx = 1/3$$

in which the function is evaluated over the interval $0 \leqslant x \leqslant 1$. Another example is

$$\begin{pmatrix} 2 & 1 \\ 1 & 3 \end{pmatrix}\begin{pmatrix} x \\ y \end{pmatrix} = \begin{pmatrix} 2x+y \\ x+3y \end{pmatrix}$$

In so far as this defines multiplication by the given 2×2 matrix the x, y are only place holders or dummies, although they could become true variables if all x, y satisfying a function $f(x, y) = 0$ were taken.

duodecimal   Having twelve as a base of notation for natural numbers.

duodecimal fractions   A notation, expressing whole numbers in base ten and their fractional parts in base 12, read as primes, seconds, thirds ... and denoted by $'$, $''$, $'''$, ...

$$3\ 6'\ 2'' = 3 + \tfrac{6}{12} + \tfrac{2}{144}$$

Calculation with duodecimals is not now practised, but was used, for example, in calculating areas from linear measure in feet, inches and parts (12 parts = 1 inch). The above example would read 3 feet 6 inches and 2 parts.

duodenary   A number system, using twelve as its base, that expresses integers in the form $a + 12b + 144c + \ldots$ where the digits a, b, $c \leqslant 11$. Such numbers would be written $\ldots c\,b\,a$ and would accordingly need symbols for the words 'ten' and 'eleven'. Twelve would be written 10.

duplication of cube   *See* Cissoid of Diocles.

Durand's rule   An approximate integration, now rarely used, that gives values intermediate between the trapezoidal rule and the more accurate Simpson's rule.

dyadic   *See* differential operator. In forming the quantity $\nabla.\mathbf{v}$, the divergence of the vector $\mathbf{v}$, by taking resolutes and unit vectors i, j, k in the three coordinate directions, we get

$$\nabla.\mathbf{v} = \left(\mathbf{i}\frac{\partial}{\partial x} + \mathbf{j}\frac{\partial}{\partial y} + \mathbf{k}\frac{\partial}{\partial z} \right) \cdot (\mathbf{v}_x i + \mathbf{v}_y j + \mathbf{v}_z k)$$

If the two bracketed expressions on the R.H.S. are formally multiplied this gives 9 terms each containing products such as $\mathbf{i}.\mathbf{i}$, $\mathbf{i}.\mathbf{j}$.
These products are called dyads, and the entire expression is called a dyadic.

dynamic programming   A method for finding the optimum solution to a problem, as in production engineering or constructional processes, which is dependent on many variables. The problem is reduced to a set of sub-problems each of which is optimized with respect to one variable only.

dynamics   The general study of matter in motion. From Gk. *dynamis*, power, a name that preserves the Greek belief that in all cases force is needed to sustain motion. It includes kinematics, kinetics, hydrodynamics and, by analogy with the latter, electrodynamics.

eccentric angle If the ordinate through any point P on an ellipse, centre O, meets the x axis at N and the auxiliary circle at Q, the angle NOQ is the eccentric angle θ. The parametric equations of the ellipse

$$\frac{x^2}{a^2}+\frac{y^2}{b^2}=1$$

are then

$$x=a\cos\theta$$
$$y=b\sin\theta$$

The angle is, less commonly, referred to a hyperbola. Here the tangent at P meets the x axis at T and Q is the point where the perpendicular to the line joining the foci at T meets the auxiliary circle.
Angle TOQ = θ. The parameters for the hyberbola

$$\frac{x^2}{n^2}-\frac{y^2}{b^2}=1$$

are then

$$x=a\sec\theta$$
$$y=b\tan\theta$$

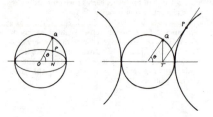

eccentricity See focus-directrix definition. The eccentricity of any central conic referred to a focus on the x axis is given by

$$e^2=1-b^2/a^2 \text{ for ellipse}$$
$$e^2=1+b^2/a^2 \text{ for hyperbola}$$

echelon matrix One having all the elements zero either above (lower echelon) or below (upper echelon) the leading diagonal.

$$\begin{pmatrix} a_{11} & a_{12} & a_{13} \\ 0 & a_{22} & a_{23} \\ 0 & 0 & a_{33} \end{pmatrix}$$

For the lower echelon $a_{ij}=0$, $i<j$.
For the upper echelon $a_{ij}=0$, $i>j$.
Echelon matrices can be obtained from other matrices by suitable row transformations, and it is sometimes specified that the first non-zero element in each row of the final echelon should be unity. A set of simultaneous equations may be solved by reducing its matrix to echelon form: the process corresponds to Gaussian condensation.

ecliptic The great circle on the notional celestial sphere that marks the apparent path of the sun as seen from the earth (or earth relative to the sun). It is inclined at $23°\,27'$ to the plane of the equator.

Egyptian fractions A special symbol for $\frac{2}{3}$ was used, but all other fractions in the notation had unit numerators. Fractions with other numerators were represented as sums of these, but it is not known with certainty how the sum was obtained; in any case there was no symbol corresponding to the total fraction. The fraction symbol represented a unit divided into parts.

Egyptian numerals In use from c. 3000 B.C. until Graeco-Roman era. Each power of 10 had a different symbol, repeated as often as necessary in any convenient pattern, often set by the space available.

Egyptian arithmetic was essentially additive and did not arrive at convenient calculating processes.

Egyptian ropestretchers The Greek equivalent of 'surveyor' was 'ropestretcher', and there is in the British Museum a papyrus showing ancient Egyptian surveyors with a coil of rope marked by evenly spaced knots. There is, however, no evidence whatever that they used the 3:4:5 triangle to mark right angles.

eigen German word meaning own, peculiar to, characteristic of, singular.
(See eigenvalue and then refer to other eigen- words.) The word 'characteristic' is sometimes used as a synonym, but this already has other uses in mathematics and lacks resonance.

eigenequation Any equation whose solutions depend on the existence of eigenvalues.

● For any $n \times n$ matrix A and column vector $\mathbf{x}$ such that $A\mathbf{x}=\lambda\mathbf{x}$ the eigenequation is $(A-\lambda I)\mathbf{x}=0$, where I is the $n \times n$ unit matrix. This will in general have n roots $\lambda_1, \lambda_2 \ldots \lambda_n$ which are the eigenvalues.

eigensolution Or eigenfunction. Any solution of an eigenequation obtained by assigning to it one of its eigenvalues.

eigenvalue Also called latent root. Certain equations have a characteristic property. An example is the differential equation

$$\frac{\partial^2 y}{\partial t^2}=c^2\frac{\partial^2 y}{\partial x^2}$$

for the transverse displacement y of a plucked string fixed at both ends, at any point x from one end. They all involve, either explicitly or implicitly, a quantity λ and only have solutions when λ takes one of a number of values. These are called the eigenvalues or latent roots of the equation. For the plucked string the eigenvalues are $\lambda=1, 2, 3, \ldots$ and the corresponding solutions give the harmonic modes in which the string can vibrate.

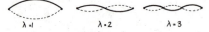

eigenvector An eigensolution in the form of a vector. If a column vector $\mathbf{x}$ of dimension 2, say, undergoes a matrix transformation A such that its direction does not change then $A\mathbf{x}=\lambda\mathbf{x}$ where λ is a scalar multiplier. This equation has solutions, if at all, for two values of λ, and the two vectors $\mathbf{x}_1$ and $\mathbf{x}_2$ thus obtained are the eigenvectors of A.

- $$\begin{pmatrix} 4 & -2 \\ 1 & 1 \end{pmatrix}\begin{pmatrix} x \\ y \end{pmatrix}=\lambda\begin{pmatrix} x \\ y \end{pmatrix}$$

has eigenvalues $\lambda=2, 3$, giving the eigenvectors

$$\mathbf{x}_1=\begin{pmatrix} 1 \\ 1 \end{pmatrix} \mathbf{x}_2=\begin{pmatrix} 2 \\ 1 \end{pmatrix}$$

These solutions correspond to the lines $y=x$, $2y=x$ which are invariant under the transformation, any point P moving to P' on the same line.

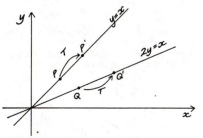

eightfold way Name given to a Pythagorean number pattern which matches the properties of eight known subnuclear particles, the mesons. These all have a comparable mass and zero angular momentum but differ in electric charge and in a further quantity called hypercharge. Both charge and hypercharge can take the values $\{0, +1, -1\}$ although hypercharge is not observable in bulk matter. If the values for the eight mesons are plotted in covariant oblique coordinates of angle $60°$, the corresponding points show a regular hexagon with two points at the origin. In the diagram Q is the charge and Y the hypercharge.

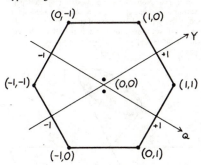

This pattern, although produced merely by the coordinate system chosen, aroused great interest because two other sets of particles gave a similar result. Then a set of nine known particles, whose Y, Q values were in the set $\{0, \pm1, \pm2\}$, when so plotted gave an equilateral triangle with its vertex missing. A

hypothetical particle was described to fit the vacant space, at $Y=-2$, $Q=-1$. This was eventually discovered and named omega minus.

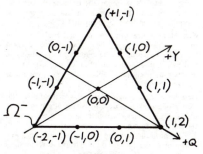

See also unitary group.

Einstein, Albert German, Swiss and eventually American mathematical physicist (1879–1955). In 1905 he published three papers, the first postulating the existence of photons in accounting for certain photo-electric effects, the second explaining Brownian movement quantitatively in terms of diffusive molecular movement and the third introducing the theory later known as Special (or restricted) Relativity. His paper on General Relativity followed in 1916. His work is of great interest of mathematicians, since it develops the logical consequences of initially very simple physical postulates. The two theories of relativity, for example, can be interpreted as the consequences of a single initial postulate, that physical laws take a form that is independent of the coordinate system in which they are expressed. Subsequent experiments have tended to confirm these theories.

either...or *See* connective.

elasticity The ratio of imposed stress to the deformation or strain produced when forces act on a solid object gives rise to several distinct moduli of elasticity.

1. For a body under tensional stress only, Young's modulus is

$$\frac{\text{force per unit area of cross-section}}{\text{increase in length per unit length}}$$

2. For a body compressed or dilated the bulk modulus is

$$\frac{\text{force per unit area of surface}}{\text{change of volume per unit volume}}$$

3. For a shearing force the modulus of rigidity is

$$\frac{\text{force per unit area in plane of area}}{\text{angular deformation}}$$

The various moduli are interrelated.

element One of any collection of distinguishable entities that go to make up a set or configuration

a is an element of the set $\{a, b, c\}$

a_{22} is an element of the determinant $\begin{vmatrix} a_{11} & a_{12} \\ a_{21} & a_{22} \end{vmatrix}$

elementary function A term usually taken to be restricted to polynomials, circular and hyperbolic functions, logarithmic and exponential functions in real variables. It is important because, in analysis, expressions such as integrals cannot in general be expressed in terms of these functions.

elementary operations A conventional term for those operations in mathematical systems derived from or analogous to the numerical operations of addition, subtraction, multiplication and division, as matrix multiplication or solution of linear equations by elimination.

elevation 1. An angle made above the horizontal from a point taken as datum, usually at ground level, as the angle of elevation of the top of a tower or of the barrel of a gun.
2. The projection of an object or configuration, drawn on a plane perpendicular to the horizontal, as end elevation, side elevation, etc.

eliminant An older name for determinant, since it arose when a variable was eliminated from a set of equations

- $a_1 x + b_1 y = c_1$
  $a_2 x + b_2 y = c_2$
  $(a_1 b_2 - a_2 b_1) x = (c_1 b_2 - b_1 c_2)$
  Here $a_1 b_2 - a_2 b_1$ is the eliminant.

elimination The process whereby the number of variables in any set of equations is reduced as a step in their solution

- $2x + y = 3$
  $4x - y = 2$
  Here y is eliminated by adding the two equations.

ellipse One of the conic sections. It can arise or be formulated in different ways, any one of which serves to define it. Four examples follow:

1. The section of a cone (or cylinder) made by a plane whose angle with its axis is greater than that made by a generator of the cone.

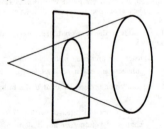

2. The set of all points whose distance from a fixed point, the focus, is a constant multiple, less than unity, of its distance from a fixed line, the directrix. The multiple $e < 1$ is called the eccentricity.
3. The set of all points such that the sums of their distances from two fixed points is constant.

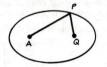

4. The curve $\dfrac{x^2}{a^2} + \dfrac{y^2}{b^2} = 1$, $(a \neq b)$

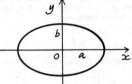

as represented on cartesian coordinates.
See also major axis.

ellipsoid A central quadric surface whose equation has the form

$$\frac{x^2}{a^2} + \frac{y^2}{b^2} + \frac{z^2}{c^2} = 1 \quad (a, b, c \neq 0).$$

The constants a, b, c give its semi-axes. The spheroids are special cases of the ellipsoid.

elliptical cylinder A cylinder whose directrix is an ellipse, having, for suitable axes, the equation

$$\frac{x^2}{a^2} + \frac{y^2}{b^2} = 1 \text{ for all } z$$

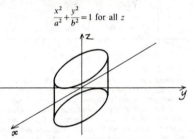

elliptical projection *See* Mollweide's projection.

elliptic cone The central quadric and ruled surface given by

$$\frac{x^2}{a^2} + \frac{y^2}{b^2} + \frac{z^2}{c^2} = 0 \quad (a, b, c \neq 0)$$

The cross-sections in the z planes are ellipses degenerating to a point at the origin, the cross-sections in the x and y planes are pairs of straight lines at $x = 0$ and $y = 0$, otherwise they are hyperbolas. The circular cone is a special case where $a = b$.

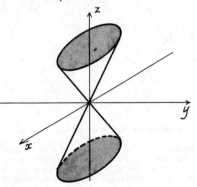

elliptic functions Defined by Abel and independently by Jacobi on the analogy of circular functions considered as inverses of the inverse circular functions. Thus if we begin with a function

$$\int \frac{dx}{\sqrt{(1-x^2)}} \, dx = \arcsin x$$

we could define a function

$$y = \sin x$$

as its inverse. The typical elliptic integral

$$\int_0^y \frac{dx}{\sqrt{\{(1-x^2)(1-e^2 x^2)\}}}$$

is thus taken as the inverse of a function $y = \operatorname{sn} x$ otherwise left undefined, so that $\operatorname{sn} x$ is the inverse of the integral. Jacobi (1829) gave an addition theorem for $\operatorname{sn}(\theta + \phi)$ corresponding to $\sin(\theta + \phi)$ The elliptic functions in a complex domain have two periods, of which at least one is complex.

elliptic geometry The geometry of elliptic space developed by Riemann, in which Euclid's Fifth Postulate, that only one straight line can be drawn that does not meet a given straight line when it passes through a point not on the line, is replaced by the axiom that there is no such line. The name was given by Klein to describe this 'defective' structure (Gk. *elleipsis*, a defect) and corresponds to the second possibility in Saccheri's quadrilateral. The geometry is realized by geodesic lines on a sphere or ellipsoid. Although it cannot be detected by local measurement, the actual space of the universe may, on an astronomical scale, be elliptic.

elliptic hyperboloid of one sheet The central quadric and ruled surface given by

$$\frac{x^2}{a^2} + \frac{y^2}{b^2} - \frac{z^2}{c^2} = 1 \quad (a, b, c \neq 0)$$

The cross-section in any plane parallel to $z = 0$ is an ellipse, the sections in the x and y planes hyperbolas.

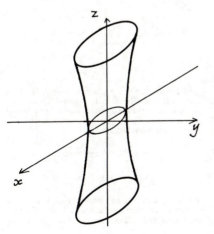

elliptic hyperboloid of two sheets The central quadric surface given by

$$-\frac{x^2}{a^2} - \frac{y^2}{b^2} + \frac{z^2}{c^2} = 1 \quad (a, b, c \neq 0)$$

The cross-sections in the x and y planes are hyperbolas, but the elliptical sections parallel to the plane $z = 0$ only exist for real variables when $-c > z > c$ and reduce to points at $z = \pm c$.

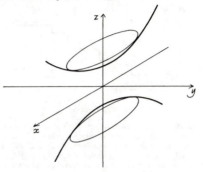

elliptic paraboloid A non-central quadric given by

$$\frac{x^2}{a^2} + \frac{y^2}{b^2} - \frac{z}{c} = 0 \quad (a, b, c \neq 0)$$

Its cross-sections in the x and y planes are parabolas, and are ellipses in the planes parallel to $z = 0$, for $z > 0$.

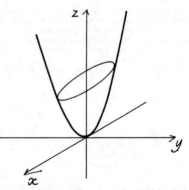

elliptic integrals A class of integrals which cannot be evaluated by standard methods in terms of elementary functions, so called because they first arose in the attempt to find the length of an arc of an ellipse from the usual expression

$$S = \int_a^b \sqrt{\left\{ 1 + \left(\frac{dy}{dx} \right)^2 \right\}} \, dx$$

This cannot be integrated if $\frac{x^2}{a^2} + \frac{y^2}{b^2} = 1 \ (a \neq b)$.

The integrals have been extensively tabulated using numerical methods.

61

empirical Used in mathematics of results or conjectures that appear to be true from observation or trial, but are not offered with a formal proof, e.g. Goldbach's conjecture.

empirical distribution function For a sample of size n the function $F_n(x)$, which represents the proportion of the n observations less than or equal to x. It is thus a step function initially zero, rising by discrete steps to a value 1 at maximum x.

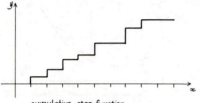

cumulative step function

empty set, the Also null set. The set containing no elements, and hence of cardinal number zero. It is the complement of the universal set U or $\mathcal{E}$ and is usually symbolised $\emptyset$ (a modified zero, not *phi*). It is the identity element for the set operations union and symmetric difference

$$A \cup \emptyset = A \quad A \triangle \emptyset = A$$

The symbol is sometimes read as 'lero' from 'logical zero'. Note that one always speaks of *the* empty set. A set of no integers is not distinct from a set of no elephants, and 'empty set' is therefore a proper name unique by definition.
See also set, zero.

enlargement Any transformation of a configuration that increases or decreases all linear dimensions in the same ratio but leaves angles unchanged, i.e., that alters size but not shape. Also called dilatation. The constant ratio between corresponding dimension is the scale factor m and the term 'enlargement' is used even if $m < 1$. All similar figures are enlargements of one another. A negative scale factor transforms by central inversion.
See homothetic transformation.

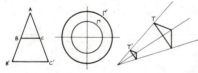

enlargement matrix or dilatation matrix. Any matrix that transforms a configuration into an enlarged similar configuration, such as

$$A = \begin{pmatrix} k & 0 \\ 0 & k \end{pmatrix} \quad k \neq 1$$

entire function Sometimes called integral function. A complex-valued function such as e^z which is an analytic function for all finite values of its domain.

entire series If $f(z)$ can be expended into a series

$$f(z) = a_0 + a_1 z + a_2 z^2 + \dots$$

then the series is entire if $f(z)$ is an entire function.

enumerated Used of a set defined by enumerating its elements, as the set $\{a, b, c, d\}$.

enunciation The general preliminary statement of a proposition (particularly in Euclid), setting out what is to be demonstrated. Also called *protasis*.

envelope A curve or curved surface touching every member of some system of lines or planes, curves or surfaces, often modelled physically by moving rigid bodies.

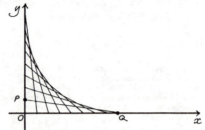

A rigid rod P slides down axes OY OX, to give the astroid. If a set of curves is given by $f(x, y, t) = 0$ where t is a parametric constant defining the family taking the values t_0, $t_0 + \delta t$, $t_0 + 2\delta t \dots$ then the envelope is the limiting set of intersection points of the members as $\delta t \to 0$.

epicycloid The locus described by a point P on the circumference of a circle that rolls without slipping on the exterior of another circle. If the radius of the inner circle is a and that of the generating circle b, the epicycloid will have n cusps if $b = na(n = 1, 2, 3, \dots)$.

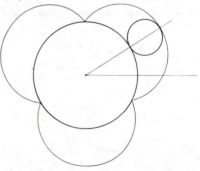

The diagram shows $n = 3$. If n is rational the set of cusps will eventually close and repeat themselves. If θ is the angle of the radius vector joining the centre of the generating circle to that of its motion, the equations of the epicycloid are

$$x = (a + b) \cos \theta - b \cos \frac{a + b}{b} \theta$$

$$y = (a + b) \sin \theta - b \sin \frac{a + b}{b} \theta$$

epoch The time of an event or configuration of a system as measured from a standard arbitrary zero, as distinct from a time interval between two events or the modular time shown by a clock. The date measures epoch time.

equal area projection Any map projection in which the area between meridians and parallels is proportional to the area on the globe, so that the areas of land masses or oceans can be measured directly from the map.

equality 1. Used of entities having the same numerical values or measures, but otherwise necessarily distinct in order to give meaning to a statement of equality denoted by $=$, as

$$\text{area ACB} = \text{area DEF}$$
$$x^2 + y^2 = 1$$

2. Also used to show that one expression is equivalent to another, as

$$\begin{vmatrix} a & b \\ c & d \end{vmatrix} = ad - bc$$

$$\mathbf{x} = (x_1, x_2, x_3 \ldots)$$

equally likely events The undefined intuitive basis of the classical formulation of probability.

equation 1. A statement of the equality of two expressions involving quantities or variables, which may be true for some but not necessarily all values of the variables. The roots of an equation are the values for which the statement is true, and a process for finding these roots is called solving the equation. The set of roots is sometimes called the solution set. The domain of the variables must be given for any equation proposed for solution.

- $3x + 2 = 0$ $(x \in \mathbb{Z})$ has no roots
  $x - 2y = 0$ $(x, y \in \mathbb{R})$ has an infinite number of pairs of roots.
  $x^2 + 10 = 2x$ $(x \in \mathbb{R})$ has no roots.
  $x^2 + 10 = 2x$ $(x \in \mathbb{C})$ has two roots.

2. Equations may be represented in Cartesian form, by referring to x, y axes the pairs of values (x, y) that satisfy the equation, and hence defining a set of points that lie on the curve

- $y = mx + c$, the equation of a straight line
  $x^2 + y^2 = 1$, the equation of a unit circle

Equations can be given in other forms, as in polar · coordinates.

3. An equation true for all values of the variables in a given domain is sometimes called an identity, denoted by $\equiv$.

- $(x + y)^2 \equiv x^2 + 2xy + y^2$ for all x, $y \in \mathbb{R}$

equations of constraint These express any limits imposed on the numerical values of variables by physical or other factors, and often occur in linear programming. Values which satisfy these equations are termed feasible values; any others lie outside the region (*see* convex set) determined by the lines representing them.

equator The great circle whose plane is at right angles to the N–S axis of the earth. The corresponding circle on any rotating heavenly body.

equiangular spiral A curve such that the angle α between the tangent and the radius vector describing the curve is constant.

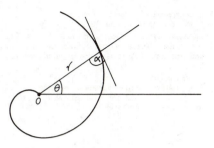

If $\alpha = 90°$ the curve becomes a circle
The polar equation is $\log r = k\theta$ and hence the curve is also called the logarithmic spiral. It is common in natural forms such as shells.

equiconjugate diameters Conjugate diameters having the same length. For the ellipse

$$\frac{x^2}{a^2} + \frac{y^2}{b^2} = 1$$

they are along the lines $y = \pm \frac{b}{a} x$; that is, the diagonals of the rectangle formed by the tangents at the ends of the two axes.

equinumerous Also equipotent or numerically equivalent. This translates the German *gleichzahlig* coined by Frege to describe sets whose members could be put into complete one-to-one correspondence. His account stresses that both 'sets' (a word he avoids by using 'concept' in the same sense) and the notion of correspondence are entirely conceptual and independent of any selected sets or entities, so that numerical equivalence is a logical relation independent of actual counting. Equinumerous sets have the same cardinal number.

equipotential surface Any surface in which any point is at the same potential, commonly used of electrical or gravitational fields, as on the surface of a sphere surrounding a point electrical charge situated at its centre.

equipotent sets *See* equinumerous.

equivalence class An equivalence relation on a set S partitions it into subsets called equivalence classes.

- The set C of all triangles congruent to a given triangle ABC is an equivalence class contained in the set S of all triangles.

Any one member of an equivalence class can be selected as a representative of that class. This is often done in geometry, in which a proof referring to a given configuration such as 'parallelogram ABCD' is taken as valid for all parallelograms.

equivalence relation A relation R on a set S with the following properties

1. It is reflexive: $x \in S \Rightarrow x \, \text{R} \, x$
2. It is symmetric: x, $y \in S$ and $x \, \text{R} \, y \Rightarrow y \, \text{R} \, x$
3. It is transitive: y, $z \in S$ and $x \, \text{R} \, y$, $y \, \text{R} \, z \Rightarrow x \, \text{R} \, z$

There are many examples throughout mathematics

- numerical equality
  similarity of geometrical figures
  parallelism of lines in three-dimensional space

congruence of integers to some modulo
membership of the same left or right coset.

equivalent matrices Used of matrices A, B of the same order where B can be obtained from A by a finite sequence of elementary row operations, that is, by

1. interchanging two rows;
2. multiplying any row by a non-zero scalar;
3 adding a scalar multiple of the elements of one row to the elements of another; as

$$A=\begin{pmatrix}1 & 2 & 0\\ 3 & 1 & 0\\ 1 & 1 & 1\end{pmatrix} \quad B=\begin{pmatrix}2 & 4 & 0\\ 1 & 1 & 1\\ 6 & 4 & 3\end{pmatrix}$$

The rows of B are formed by multiplying R_1 by 2, interchanging R_2 and R_3, adding R_2 to three times R_3.

Eratosthenes of Cyrene Alexandrian geographer and mathematician (275–194 B.C.) who estimated the circumference of the earth by taking the sun's altitude at Syene in Upper Egypt and Alexandria, places a known distance apart on approximately the same longitude, at noon on the day of the summer solstice. His result made it possible to determine latitude by sundial and hence find geographical distances along meridians.

Eratosthenes' Sieve A method for obtaining the prime numbers less than or equal to any given N. Ring 2 from a list of whole numbers $2 \ldots N$, then strike out all multiples of 2. Ring the smallest remaining number and delete all its remaining multiples. Repeat the process indefinitely. The ringed numbers undeleted are therefore without smallers factors and hence the process generates the set of primes.

	②	③	4	⑤	6	⑦	8	9	10
⑪	12	⑬	14	15	16	⑰	18	⑲	20
21	22	㉓	24	25	26	27	28	㉙	30
㉛	32	33	34	35	36	㊲	38	㊴	40

ergodic Markov chain *See* Markov chain.

Erlanger Programme Formulated by Klein (1872) in a lecture at Erlangen University, Germany. It described a programme for the future development of geometry by means of group theory. Each geometry, e.g. Euclidean, projective or topological, is to be described in terms of the properties it has which are invariant under groups of transformation. Thus the groups of translations and rotations characterize Euclidean geometry and the Lie group of continuous transformations characterizes topology.

error Should be distinguished from *mistake*. An error, particularly in applied mathematics, is a term representing the uncertainty of measurement or the degree of imprecision in a calculation, resulting from numerical approximation, rounding off digits or the neglect of given terms. The calculus of errors analyses the range within which true results lie. The distinction between error and mistake is not always maintained.

error function A function sometimes used in statistical analysis, given by

$$2G\,(x\sqrt{2})-1$$

where $G(x)$ is the Gaussian or normal distribution with mean 0, variance $\sigma^2=1$.

error term *See* truncation error.

escape velocity The minimum velocity a body must have in a direction opposite to the gravitational attraction of a massive body, in order that it should 'escape' from its gravitation field, that is, not fall back towards its surface. The kinetic energy possessed by the body having this velocity is equal to the potential energy it would have if removed a distance d from the massive body, as $d \to \infty$. For a light body on the surface of a planet of radius r and mass M the escape velocity is given by $\sqrt{\frac{2GM}{r}}$ where G is the gravitational constant, or $\sqrt{2gr}$ where g is the gravitational acceleration near the surface. Escape velocity for the earth is (neglecting air resistance) about 11 kms^{-1}.

estimate 1. A working value taken for any quantity in lieu of an exact value which may not be known or may be in principle unobtainable.
2. In statistics, a value taken for an estimator by calculating from the data available.

estimator A function of sampled observations used to investigate a population parameter: its value is an estimate of this.

- The sample mean $\bar{x}$ is an unbiased estimator of the population mean μ.

estis Gk. verbal form, '*is*'. Its initial letter $\in$ is read 'is a member of'. Then $x \in \mathbb{R}$ is read 'x is a member of the set of all real numbers', abbreviated to 'x is real'.

Euclid Greek mathematician (fl. 300 B.C.). Little is known of his life except that he lived in Alexandria. He compiled the famous 'Elements', a systematic presentation of the geometry and number theory of his day. This is the world's oldest textbook and was in general use up to the beginning of the 20th century, when it began to be replaced by equivalent texts written in a form more suitable for schools and students. Euclid begins his elements with a set of definitions and axioms that has been the model for mathematics ever since: the analysis and criticism of these has been the starting point for modern geometrical developments.

Euclidean geometry The general name for all geometry, including post-Euclidean results or theorems, that rests on four postulates that were implied by, although not explicitly stated in, the methods of Euclid's Elements.

1. Space is continuous and infinitely divisible.
2. Space is everywhere 'flat'; that is, the distance between points referred to cartesian coordinates is given by the Pythagoras' relationship.
3. Space is isotropic, so that any body or configuration can be moved anywhere without altering its size or shape.
4. That any configuration may be enlarged without altering its shape; that is, that similar figures may be drawn by a suitable linear transformation.

The last condition implies the existence of parallel lines.

Euclid's algorithm Usually given as an arithmetical algorithm for determining the highest common factor of two integers. The smaller is divided into the larger, the quotient is discarded and the remainder is then divided into the smaller. The process is continued until a zero remainder is obtained. The HCF is then the final divisor. For example the HCF of 224, 768.

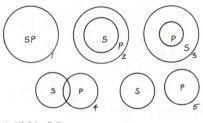

The process is the arithmetical equivalent of the method for finding the greatest common measure of two commensurable line intervals given in Euclid X, 3. The geometrical process does not terminate if the lines are incommensurable.

Euler circle 1. *See* nine-point circle.
2. Plural. A method of representing propositions in traditional logic diagrammatically, propounded by Euler.

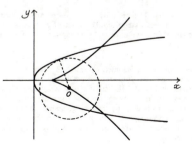

1. All S is all P
2. All S is P
3. All P is S
4. Some S is P
5. No S is P

These were later modified by Venn, and in recent years became adapted to diagrams in elementary set theory.

Euler function $\phi(n)$ *See* primitive roots.

Euler, Leonhard Swiss mathematician (1707–1783). His published works were mainly written in Latin and a large number of them remained unpublished till after his death. There are many important results first due to him. He discussed Newtonian mechanics, the calculus, algebra, number theory and indeed most mathematical topics current in his lifetime. He was in early life a pupil of Johann Bernoulli. In later life he suffered from blindness.

Euler line In any triangle, the line formed by the centroid, the circumcentre and the orthocentre (which are collinear).

Euler points The midpoints of the lines joining the orthocentre of a triangle to its vertices. They are three of the points of the nine-point circle.

Euler's constant The function $F(n)$ defined as

$$F(n) = 1 + \tfrac{1}{2} + \tfrac{1}{3} + \ldots + \frac{1}{n} - \ln n$$

has the limiting value γ as $n \to \infty$ where $\gamma = 0.577215\ldots$
This constant is also given by

$$\gamma = -\int_0^\infty e^{-x} \ln x \, dx$$

It is not yet known whether γ is rational or irrational.

Euler's formula 1. The relation $V - E + F = 2$ for the vertices V, edges E and faces F of a simple closed polyhedron.
2. The formula $e^{ix} = \cos x + i \sin x$ which reduces to $e^{i\pi} + 1 = 0$ if $x = \pi$.
3. The difference formula given by $y_{r+1} = y_r + h f(x_r, y_r)$ for solving numerically a differential equation

$$\frac{dy}{dx} = f(x, y)$$

where h is the interval between x values given by $x_{r+1} - x_r$. The successive numerical values for y thus produced are not accurate, but their existence shows when a solution is possible.

Euler's theorem Although Euler formulated many theorems the one usually so named is

$$p^{\phi(n)} - 1 \equiv 0 \bmod n$$

where $\phi(n)$ is the totient function and p is a positive integer relatively prime to n.

evaluation The process of finding the numerical value of any mathematical expression or of reaching such a value by means of numerical algorithms.

even function *See* odd function.

even number *See* odd number.

even permutation *See* permutation.

event Any element of an event space.

event space This is a sample space, whose elements are the total possible events from which any trial procedure or experiment selects a subset.

● The event space for rolling a die is $\{1, 2, 3, 4, 5, 6\}$

evolute The locus of the centres of curvature taken along any curve. Thus the evolute of a parabola is the semicubic parabola. The evolute is also the envelope of all normals drawn to the curve.

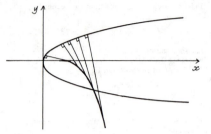

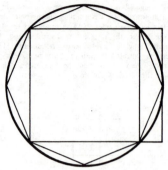

evolution   The extraction of roots, the inverse of involution.

exact differential   If M and N are functions of x, y an expression of the form $M\,dy + N\,dx$, where dy, dx are differentials, is called an exact differential if

$$M\,dy + N\,dx = du$$

for a function $u(x, y)$. This will be true if $\partial M/\partial y = \partial N/\partial x$. An example is $u = xy$ which gives $du = x\,dy + y\,dx$.

exact equation   *See* integrating factor.

exactly one   Synonymous with one and one only. For an example see Dedekind's postulate.

exchange value   In any form of notation for number, other than one-to-one tally symbols, the exchange value (on the analogy of coinage) is either the value of one symbol in terms of another (as $X = \text{ten I's in Roman numerals}$) or, in a place value system, the values of symbols according to the column in which they are entered.
See denary.

excluded middle   The postulation of a binary choice in logic or mathematics, equivalent in some circumstances to yes–no, either–or, odd–even, positive–negative, true–false and so on, is held necessarily to exclude a third possibility (or *tertium quid*). This gives the Law of Excluded Middle, which may be expressed as *A is either B or not B*, or as *two contradictories cannot both be false together*. Put in this form its status is clear. The distinction is not, for example, between positive and negative, but positive and non-positive, between an attribute and its contradictory, not merely contrary.
Modern logic based on this law and investigating the relations obtained from p and not-p is called two-term logic.
See also three term logic, for which this principle does not hold.

exclusion   The opposite of inclusion. Any process that ensures that an entity or set of entities is *not* counted in forming or enumerating a set with given properties.

exclusive   *See* aut.

exhaustion   A geometrical method attributed by Archimedes to Eudoxus, usually illustrated by the proof in Euclid XII, 2 that the areas of circles are proportional to the squares of their diameters. In Euclid this is done by inscribing squares, then octagons, hexadecagons ... in the circle and then adding a rectangle to the side of the square as in the diagram.

A more modern version alternately inscribes and escribes the successive polygons, showing at each step that the circle is greater than the one but less than the other.
It corresponds to the process of integration, deriving the area of the circle as the limit of successive approximations.
See also proof by exhaustion.

exhaustive   A form of argument, verification or proof which aims to list all possible alternatives in a problem and consider each in turn. It is, of course, fallacious if alternatives are incompletely given or incorrectly formulated.

existence theorem   A proof that a given set is not empty, which often initiates or encourages a search for the solution to a problem. Similarly, a proof that a concept is empty can terminate a search, for the greatest prime, say.

expansion   The writing of an expression in full.
- $(x + a)^3 = x^3 + 3x^2 a + 3xa^2 + a^3$

expected value   A formulation of the intuitive expectation of a given result. The expectation of a function $g(x)$ is denoted $E[g(x)]$ and given by

$$\int_{-\infty}^{\infty} g(x)\,f(x)\,dx$$

for continuous data with a p.d.f. $f(x)$, and by

$$\sum_{i=1}^{n} g(x_i)\,P(x_i)$$

for discrete data with probability function $P(x)$.

experimental design   An area of statistical investigation dealing with situations where observations and effects may be influenced by various empirical factors and interactions between them.
See also analysis of variance.

explicit function   A function defined in the form $y = f(x)$ or more generally $y = f(x, z, w \ldots)$
- $y = x^2 + 2x$
  $y = x^2 + z^2$

Not all functions involving y and one or more other variables can be made explicit. Thus $e^{xy} - x = 0$ becomes $y = \dfrac{1}{x}\ln x$ but if $x^3 + 6xy + y^3 = 8$, y cannot be expressed explicitly in terms of x.
See implicit function, implicit differentiation.

explicit relation Any relation, not necessarily functional, that gives one variable y explicitly in terms of other variables.

● $y = \arcsin x$.

See implicit.

exponent *See* index.

exponential Generally, an expression in terms of powers or exponents. It is usually taken that exponential functions and series involve the quantity e, and the function written $\exp(x)$ or exponential x is specifically e^x.

exponential constant The constant $2.71828\ldots$ which can be defined by

$$e = \sum_{n=0}^{\infty} \frac{1}{n!}$$

or by the exponential function $e = \exp(1)$. Named in honour of Euler, it was shown to be a transcendental number by Hermite in 1873.

exponential curve A curve representing a function whose variable appears as a power or exponent, usually written in the form

$$y = A e^{Bx}$$

It is the inverse of the logarithmic curve.

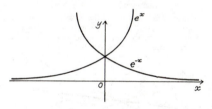

exponential distribution More properly, the negative exponential distribution, a continuous distribution with p.d.f.

$$f(t) = \begin{cases} \mu e^{-\mu t} & (t \geqslant 0) \\ 0 & (t < 0) \end{cases}$$

whose mean and standard deviation both equal μ. It applies for example to the probable time between successive events or the probable distance travelled by gas molecules between collisions. If μ events occur in a unit of time, then in any small interval δt the probability of the event is $\mu \delta t$. Since μ is constant the distribution describes a Poisson process.

exponential function One of the basic functions of mathematics, written as e^x or $\exp x$. Within the domain of $\mathbb{R}$ it has five equivalent definitions:

1. The solution of the differential equation

$$\frac{dx}{dt} = x \quad (x = 1 \text{ if } t = 0)$$

That is, $\exp x$ is the function whose slope at any point is equal to the value of the ordinate.

2. The limiting sum of the infinite series

$$1 + x + \frac{x^2}{2!} + \frac{x^3}{3!} + \ldots + \frac{x^n}{n!} + \ldots$$

If $x = 1$ this gives the numerical value

$$= 1 + 1 + \frac{1}{2!} + \frac{1}{3!} + \ldots + \frac{1}{n!} + \ldots$$
$$= 2.71828\ldots$$

3. The solution of the functional equation $f(x + y) = f(x)f(y)$ such that $f(1) = e$.

4. The inverse of the logarithmic function. If $f(x) = \log_e x$ (or $\ln x$) where $x > 0$ then $f^{-1}(x) = e^x$

5. $e^x = \underset{n \to \infty}{\mathrm{Lt}} \left(1 + \frac{x}{n}\right)^n$

The function $\exp(-x)$ is similarly defined, and the domain of the function may be extended to $\mathbb{C}$ by replacing $x \in \mathbb{R}$ by $z \in \mathbb{C}$. The function is related to the circular and hyperbolic functions by the formulae:

$$e^{i\theta} = \cos\theta + i\sin\theta$$
$$e^{\theta} = \cosh\theta + \sinh\theta$$

(Note that if $\theta = \pi$ the first formula above becomes Euler's formula $e^{i\pi} + 1 = 0$). The exponential function is generalized by

$$a^x = e^{x \ln a} (x \in \mathbb{R}, a > 0).$$

exponential growth The type of increase (or decrease) found throughout quantitative science or technology, obeying a law of the form

$$y = a e^{kt}$$

where a, k are constants and t is elapsed time.

Differentiation gives $\dfrac{dy}{dt} = ky$.

That is, the rate of change of the quantity y at any time is proportional to its value at that time. This statement is sometimes used to define exponential growth, as with the initial reproduction of bacteria. If k is negative y is decreasing and the expression defines exponential decay. Examples are radioactive decay, or rates of cooling.

exponential matrix For any square matrix A this is defined as

$$e^A = I + \frac{A}{1!} + \frac{A^2}{2!} + \frac{A^3}{3!} + \ldots$$

where $A^n = A.A.A.\ldots A$ n times and I is the corresponding identity matrix.

expression A term used loosely in mathematics for any string of symbols under consideration, or used to express one quantity in terms of another. Typical sentences are

● Is the expression $\sqrt{x}$ a function of x?

The expression $\int^2 + - x$ is meaningless.

If $x^2 + y^2 = a^2$, express y in terms of x.
$x^2 + 5x + 6$ is a quadratic expression.

See also function.

extended number system 1. Any set of numbers that allows operations which are restricted in the systems of which they are the extension. Thus subtraction is not always possible in the set $\mathbb{N}$ but is unrestricted in $\mathbb{Z}$. Originally such numbers as negative integers were thought of as actually extending or being added to natural numbers, but extended systems such as $\mathbb{Z}$, $\mathbb{Q}$, $\mathbb{R}$ and $\mathbb{C}$ are now regarded as independent constructions defined in terms of ℕ, having subsets whose elements correspond to one another, as $\{1\} \subset \mathbb{N}$ and $\{1\} \subset \mathbb{Z}$, in the form $a + ib$ where $a = 1$, $b = 0$.

2. In some branches of analysis it is convenient to allow functions to take positive or negative infinite values. An extended number system is thus formed, with rules governing how those values combine with real numbers.

3. The addition of defined infinitesimals to ℝ gives an actually extended number system used in non-standard analysis.
See also transfinite numbers.

extension 1. Often used of theorems which are modified to extend them to more general cases, as the extension to Pythagoras' theorem for a general triangle.

2. Any finite set defined by listing its members (compare intension).

3. In algebra an extension field is one formed by adjoining a new element or set of elements to an existing field.

- The real number field $\{\mathbb{R}, x, +\}$ extends to the complex number field by the addition of element i to give complex elements of the form $a + ib$ $(a, b \in \mathbb{R})$, where $i^2 = -1$.

extensions to Pythagoras The corresponding theorems for a triangle which is not right angled.

1. The square of the side opposite an obtuse angle is equal to the sum of the squares on the remaining two sides, together with twice the product of one of these sides and the projection upon it of the other.

2. For an acute angle the sum is *less* twice the above product.

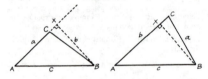

The theorem becomes the cosine rule when expressed trigonometrically

$$c^2 = a^2 + b^2 - 2\,ab \cos C.$$

external division In Euclid, the external divisor of a line interval is given as a point on the line produced. A modern formulation would be that P divides AB externally (or internally) as P falls outside (or inside) the line of which AB is an interval.
See line.

extraction The process of finding a root or roots, as in extracting the cube root of 7.

extrapolation The assignment of values to a sequence of results, beyond the range of those actually given or determined. Compare interpolation. Unless there is a known functional relation between the results (in which case extrapolation is merely the calculation of additional values), any process of extrapolation assumes that a relation is maintained beyond the range and domain for which it is actually established.

extreme value A general term including absolute or relative maximum or minimum values of functions, and the values determined by the calculus of variations. An important current use is the solution of the 'minimax' problem — the values obtained by a variable subject to linear constraints, whose domain is a bounded convex set in a vector space.
See linear programming.

extreme value theorem If the domain of a function is a convex polyhedral set C on a vector space x_n, then the extreme values of the function are reached at the vertices or extreme points of C.
See linear programming.

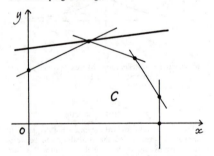

F

factor An integer is a factor of another integer if it can be divided into the second integer without remainder, so that x is a factor of y if $y \equiv 0 \pmod{x}$. The term is extended to algebraic expressions, so that $(a+b)$ is a factor of $a^2 - b^2$ but not of $a^2 + b^2$. *See also* remainder theorem, unique factorization.

factor analysis *See* experimental design.

factor group Also called quotient group. If H is a normal subgroup of G with x, $y \in G$, the set of all cosets Hx, Hy of H will form a group under the operation $Hx * Hy = Hxy$. If G is finite of order n with a subgroup of order m ($n = rm$ by Lagrange's theorem), there will be r cosets and the factor group will have order r. It is written as G/H, and the value $|G/H| = r$ is called the index of H in G. The cosets may be left or right.

factorial Factorial n, denoted by $n!$, is defined, for positive integral n, as

$$\left. \begin{array}{l} n! = n(n-1)(n-2) \ldots 1 \\ 0! = 1 \end{array} \right\}$$

See also gamma function and Jordan factorial.

factorial design The design of experiments, usually in statistical contexts or operational research, to enable the influence of various factors on the results to be investigated or at least detected.

factorial function *See* gamma function.

factor ring *See* difference ring.

factor set Also called quotient set. The set of all right cosets of a subgroup H of a group G is called the right factor set. The left quotient or factor set is similarly defined. *See also* factor group.

factor theorem A special case of the remainder theorem, when the remainder is zero.

fair Unbiased, as in a fair sample, a fair die.

fallacy The word is commonly used for a false conclusion, but is better restricted to formal adjectival use. An argument is fallacious if

(a) it is validly derived from false premises, or
(b) its alleged conclusions do not follow from its premises within a consistent logic.

false 1. Used of a meaningful statement or conclusion that does not correspond to the facts, as, all triangles are congruent.
2. One of the two truth values assigned to a statement or proposition in two term logic, and denoted by F. False is the negation of 'true'. *See* truth table, truth.

false position Translates Lat. *regula falsorum*. An early method for solving a problem equivalent to solving a linear equation by taking a trial value.

● A number and half a number come to thirty-three. What is the number? Try 2, then $2 + 1 = 3$ which is only one-eleventh of the required sum. Hence true value is $2 \times 11 = 22$.

See also double false position.

family Any set of curves, expressions or configurations in mathematics which have the same general form but differ in taking successive values of a coefficient or parameter. A family of concentric circles of the form $x^2 + y^2 = c^2$ is generated by taking successive real values for c.

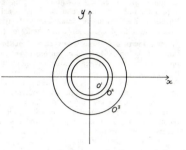

Farey sequence A sequence of order n consisting of all distinct positive rationals p/q subject to the conditions

1. $0 \leqslant p/q \leqslant 1$
2. $0 < q \leqslant n$ (n is a positive integer)
3. $0 \leqslant p \leqslant q$
4. The fractions p/q are arranged in increasing order of magnitude

● $n = 3$ $F_3 = 0/1, 1/3, 1/2, 2/3, 1$
   $n = 4$ $F_4 = 0/1, 1/4, 1/3, 1/2, 2/3, 3/4, 1$
   $n = 5$ $F_5 = 0/1, 1/5, 1/4, 1/3, 2/5, 1/2, 3/5, 2/3, 3/4, 4/5, 1$

Farey stated (and Cauchy proved) that if three consecutive terms are a/b, c/d, e/f then $bc - ad = 1$ and $c/d = (a+e)/(b+f)$.

F-distribution Fisher's distribution, a name given by G. W. Snedecor in honour of R. A. Fisher·who first studied it in a different form. The distribution of the ratio of two independent variates, each of which is a chi-squared distribution, when each is divided by the number of degrees of freedom. The p.d.f. gives the null distribution of the statistic of the F-test in analysis of variance. Tabulated values are available, entered for the degrees of freedom of the two sets of variates.

feasible points In linear programming feasible points P are those whose values are within those set by the equations of constraint. In a plane graphical representation they fall within the convex polygonal set.

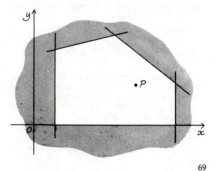

Fermat numbers These are generated by the expressions

$$f(n) = 2^{2^n} + 1 \text{ for } n = 0, 1, 2, \ldots$$

Fermat incorrectly conjectured that $f(n)$ is prime for all non-negative integral n. A regular polygon having a prime number of sides can be constructed by Euclidean methods using compasses and straight edge if, but only if, the number has the form $f(n)$.

Fermat, Pierre de French lawyer and mathematician (1601–1665). Made contributions to the developing study of analytical geometry, much of it in correspondence published after his death. His fame rests mainly on many contributions to number theory, some recorded as unproved theorems in the margins of his copy of a translation of the *Arithmetica* of Diophantos. These include the theorem named after him and also the notorious Fermat's Last Theorem.
See also Bachet de Meziriac.

Fermat's last theorem Also 'great' theorem. The equation $x^n + y^n = z^n$ where x, y, z, $n \in \mathbb{N}$ has no solutions if $n > 2$. The statement is known to be true (1983) for $n \leqslant 125\,000$ but no general proof exists so that it is a conjecture rather than a theorem. It is said that more incorrect 'proofs' of this conjecture have been published than proposed Euclidean constructions for squaring the circle.

Fermat's theorem Also called Fermat's 'little' theorem, first stated by him in a letter to a correspondent. If p is prime and a is not divisible by p, then $a^{p-1} - 1$ is divisible by p, that is

$$a^{p-1} \equiv 1 \pmod{p}$$

The first proof was supplied by Euler in 1736, nearly a century later.

Feuerbach circle *See* nine-point circle.

Feuerbach's theorem Stated, in 1822, that the nine-point circle has common tangents with the inscribed and the three escribed circles of its triangle. That is, it touches all four circles.

Fibonacci sequence The sequence generated by the recurrence relation

$$u_n = u_{n-1} + u_{n-2}$$

For $u_1 = u_2 = 1$ the sequence is

$$1, 1, 2, 3, 5, 8, 13, 21 \ldots$$

It has many interesting properties. For example, the ratios of successive terms u_{n-1}/u_n as n increases approach the value of the ratio of the golden section $0.618 \ldots$, for any initial values u_1, u_2. The general term u_n for $u_1 = u_2 = 1$, found by solving the recurrence equation, is $u_n = \dfrac{\alpha^n - \beta^n}{\sqrt{5}}$, $\alpha > \beta$, where α, β are the roots of the equation of the golden section

$$x^2 - x - 1 = 0$$

Fibonacci (1175–1250) derived the earlier members of the sequence to express the population of rabbits subject to a remarkably disciplined programme of breeding, but the recurrence pattern was not discovered till the 16th century.

fiducial inference R. A. Fisher in 1930 discussed the making of probabilistic statements about unknown parameters, basing them on intuition,

experience or logical arguments. He took the name from Lat. *fiducia*, trust or confidence.

field A commutative division ring. A set of elements forming an abelian additive group (or module) under the operation $+$ and also an abelian group under $\times$ when zero (or any element without inverse) is omitted. The operation $\times$ must also distribute over the operation $+$

- The set $\mathbb{Q}$ of rationals
  The set $\mathbb{R}$ of reals
  The set $\mathbb{C}$ of complex numbers
  The set $\mathbb{Z}_p$ of integers where both $+$ and $\times$ are performed modulo prime p. This is a finite field.

2. Any region of space, which may or may not be occupied by matter, in which there is a physical quantity which is described by a continuous function. There are two elementary types:

(a) Scalar field. The value of the function is given by a scalar, or non-directional quantity, as temperature or electric potential. It has contour lines or surfaces of constant value.

(b) Vector field. The value at any point is given in magnitude and direction by a vector quantity. The direction at any point is normal to a line or surface, as velocity in fluid flow or electrostatic field strength.

See gradient.

field extensions A field extension E of an initial field F is one that includes F as a sub-field. Thus the field $\mathbb{R}$ of real numbers is an extension of the field $\mathbb{Q}$ of rationals. A *simple* field extension is one generated by a single additional element. Thus the field $\mathbb{C}$ of complex numbers is a simple extension of $\mathbb{R}$ generated by the additional element i where $i^2 = -1$.

fifth postulate *See* parallel postulate.

figurate numbers *See* polygonal numbers.

figure *See* configuration.

figures of the syllogism The four possible arrangements of a syllogistic argument in traditional logic, as given by the position of the middle term in the major and minor premises. The first figure is

- (primes greater than 2) are odd.
  P is a (prime greater than two).
  Therefore P is odd.

The middle term is in brackets. These arrangements are no longer of importance.

finite From Lat. *finere*, end or finish. Any quantity, number or region which is bounded and does not exceed or extend beyond an arbitrary quantity, which may or may not be specifically assigned.

finite affine plane A plane configuration given by the affine transformation of a finite set of points.

finite algebra Any algebra over a field F that is itself of finite dimensions, for example a vector space of dimension 3.

finite arithmetic *See* modular arithmetic.

finite cardinal The cardinal number of a finite set, in which the process of putting its elements into one-to-one correspondence with the set $\mathbb{N} = \{1, 2, 3, \ldots\}$ terminates at n, the required cardinality.
See transfinite cardinal.

finite difference   *See* difference operator.

finite field   Any field with a finite number of elements, such as $F = \{a, b\}$ with operations $\oplus$ and $\odot$ defined by

$\oplus$	a	b		$\odot$	a	b
a	a	b		a	a	a
b	b	a		b	a	b

finite geometry   The geometry (as in Euclid's Elements) of line segments, bounded surfaces and finite regions of three-dimensional space (i.e. solids).

finite group   Any group having a finite number of elements, such as $G = \{1, 3, 5, 9, 11, 13\}$ under multiplication modulo 14, which has order 6. An infinite group may contain finite subgroups, for example $\{-1, 1\}$ is a subgroup of the group of all integers under multiplication.

finite number   Any real number x for which the modulus $|x|$ has an upper bound or for which x does not exceed an arbitrary value. A finite whole number (or cardinal of a countable set) is one that cannot be put into one-to-one correspondence with a proper subset of itself (Cantor).

finite set   A set containing a finite number of elements. Note that this number may be large, unknown or even indeterminate.
See also infinite set, denumerable infinity.

first integral   A term used in discussing second order differential equations, such as those that arise in considering accelerations in dynamics. The first integral is a partial solution involving first order equations, and gives information about the velocities involved.

first moment   Also first moment about the origin or first central moment. In statistics this corresponds to the mean, and is given by $\mu'_1 = E(x) = \mu$ the population mean.
See moment.

first order differential equation   An equation containing only first derivatives, although its terms may be raised to any power.

$\bullet$
$$y' = f(x)g(y)$$
$$y' + P(x)y = Q(x)$$
$$x(y')^2 + y = a$$

Fisher, R. A.   Statistician (1890–1962) responsible for much of the early development of mathematical statistics, the discussion of parametric inference and the design of experiments subject to statistical interpretation.

Fisher's z   An earlier version of Snedecor's F statistic used in the analysis of variance. It uses standard deviation to test the null hypotheses that the two samples come from populations having the same variance, and is given by

$$z = \ln \sigma_1, \; -\ln \sigma_2$$

where σ_1, is the larger estimate of the population standard deviation. Reference to F (*see* analysis of variance) shows that

$$z = \tfrac{1}{2} \ln F$$

This z is not related to the z score used in describing normal distributions.

fixed point theorems   A class of theorems which relate topology to other branches of mathematics. There are many specific forms, such as Brouwer's fixed-point theorem:

For any continuous transformation of a disc into itself, there is at least one point which is mapped to itself.

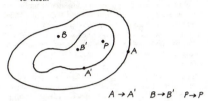

$$A \to A' \qquad B \to B' \qquad P \to P$$

floating point decimals   *See* scientific notation.

flowchart   A diagram representing the stages in which a task is performed, reduced to a sequence of

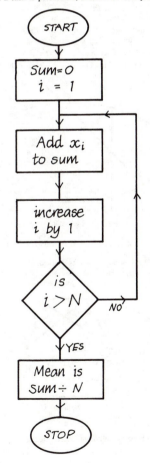

steps that can be easily visualized. Each step is shown by a box in which is written a brief description of its action. Its shape may indicate the type of operation involved (such as a binary choice). Boxes are linked by arrows showing the sequence, with closed loops taking the process back to an earlier stage.

Commonly used for planning computer programs or manufacturing operations. The level of detail included in the boxes is variable: it is usually higher for purposes of demonstration.

The example shown is a flowchart for the stages in calculating the mean of N numbers $\{x_1, x_2 \ldots x_n\}$ $N \geqslant 1$.

fluent Newton thought of a line as produced by the 'flow' (Lat. *fluo*) of a point, and hence an algebraic expression given by $y = E(x)$ as the result of the 'flowing' of the x and y values, which he called fluents. He then called the rates at which x and y flowed the 'fluxions' of x and y, denoted by $\dot{x}$, $\dot{y}$. The relation between $\dot{x}$ and $\dot{y}$ gave Newton his Method of Fluxions, later the Differential Calculus.
See also Newton–Leibnitz controversy.

fluid mechanics Synonym for hydrostatics and hydrodynamics when studied together.

fluxion *See* fluent.

focal chord Any chord in a conic that passes through a focus.

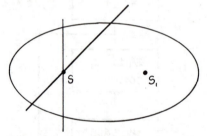

focus 1. In physics, a point to which rays of light converge (or from which they appear to diverge) after reflection in a curved mirror or refraction by a lens (Lat. a hearth).
2. A fixed point or points associated with a conic. *See* directrix. The points are so called because they can act as reflective foci, as in the example below.

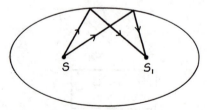

Light rays emanating from one focus S of an elliptical mirror are reflected to pass through the other.

focus-directrix definition *See* directrix.

folium of Descartes The curve representing the implicit equation $x^3 + y^3 - 3axy = 0$ in rectangular coordinates.

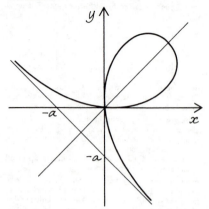

The line through $(-a, 0)$ and $(0), (-a)$ is an asymptote and the curve is symmetrical about $y = x$. It is conveniently drawn by taking the parametric form

$$x = \frac{3at}{1+t^3} \quad y = \frac{3at^2}{1+t^3}$$

for suitable values of t.

force Newton postulated that a massive body continues indefinitely in a state of rest or uniform rectilinear motion unless acted on by a force; hence a force can be defined as any cause that alters or tends to alter this state. Forces may be pushes or pulls transmitted through rigid bodies or, like the Newtonian force of gravity, be themselves hypothesized to explain departure from rest or uniform rectilinear motion.
See also virtual force.

force diagram A diagram showing the forces acting on an object, by lines showing the directions of the forces, whose lengths represent their magnitude. If the forces are in equilibrium, the reciprocal diagram is closed.

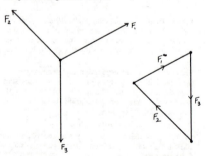

forced oscillation Vibration or oscillation of a system at a frequency not necessarily equal to its natural frequency, produced by an external oscillating or periodic force. If a naturally oscillating system is described by a differential equation $F(D)x=0$ where $F(D)$ is a polynomial involving the differential operator D, then $F(D)x=f(t)$ is a system with a forcing function $f(t)$. The amplitude of a forced oscillation usually increases if the frequency of the external forcing function approaches the natural frequency of the system, as with a tuned radio circuit on receiving a signal input.

force of gravity The force postulated by Newton to exist between bodies having mass, given by

$$F = G\frac{m_1 m_2}{d^2}$$

where d is the distance between particles of mass m_1, m_2. The gravitational constant G takes the value of $6.67 \times 10^{-11} \, \mathrm{m^3\,kg^{-1}\,s^{-2}}$. The masses may be determined either by balancing against known masses in a gravitational field, or by measuring acceleration under a known force. In Newton's theory, it is the gravitational force that deflects satellites or planets from the straight line postulated by the First Law of Motion and constrains them into orbits.

formal implication *See* implication.

formalism Beginning from any set of axioms, a formal system of mathematics is any internally consistent set of theorems logically dependent on the axioms. That is, it is not possible to deduce two theorems T_1, T_2 where T_2 contradicts T_1. It is not necessary, according to formalism, to be able to realize the axioms or theorems in concrete terms (as with Euclidean line intervals) although this realization may occur. In practice, the formal systems employ the ordinary entities of points, lines, numbers, etc., but these are not given material definition.

Thus the theorem $2+3=5$, which follows from Peano's axioms, can be realized with counters, but any theorem involving infinite quantities cannot be realized. Gödel, in an ingenious and difficult proof, showed that theorems whose truth was not decidable could be generated within formal systems so that the sets of theorems could *not* be shown to be consistent. *See also* intuitionism, Hilbert, Russell.

formula A term used generally in mathematics or its applications for any expression that relates two or more quantities, either implicitly or explicitly, empirically or as a theorem. The existence of a formula does not imply a functional relationship (although this may exist) but is taken as a convenient quantitative statement.

foundations of mathematics General name for studies of the logical basis and epistemological status of any branch of mathematics.
See also Plato, formalism, intuitionism, axiomatics and any reference there given.

four-bar linkage Any closed linkage of four rigid bars joined by free pivots. The kinematic geometry of any one configuration depends on the relative lengths and angles of the quadrilateral linkages, which are then incorporated in various mechanisms. One bar is commonly fixed, and may then be represented by the framework of the machine: such notional bars are shown by dotted lines in the examples.

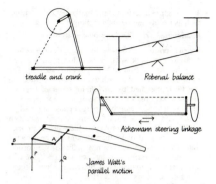

treadle and crank   Roberval balance

Ackermann steering linkage

James Watt's parallel motion

In the Watt motion points P and Q are jointed to parallel acting piston and pump rods, the point A is constrained to move in a circular arc by the arm AB, with B a fixed pivot. The Ackermann linkage allows an inner wheel to roll around a smaller circle than the outer, and is used in steering mechanisms.
See also Peaucellier's linkage.

four colour problem One of the famous former conjectures of mathematics. Any map or partition of the surface of a plane or sphere requires at the most four colours to define regions, so that no two countries or areas having a common boundary will have the same colour.

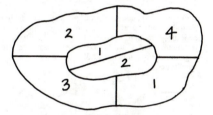

No one had constructed a map (however improbable topographically) which needed more than four colours, but no valid proof had been found, although for some years in the 19th century an invalid one was accepted by many mathematicians. It was finally proved in 1976 by classifying all maps into a large but finite number of possible types of network and testing each type with a computer program.

four-group Translates the German *Viergruppe*, a name given by Klein to the group which may be defined by the operation table

1	x	y	z
x	1	z	y
y	z	1	x
z	y	x	1

It contains the sub group defined by the table

1	x
x	1

The structure describes many mathematical relations, such as the symmetries of a rectangle.

Fourier analysis *See* harmonic analysis.

Fourier series Introduced by J. B. J. Fourier (1768–1830) as a result of work on heat flow problems, and now the basis of Fourier (or harmonic) analysis. The Fourier theorem states that any periodic function can be represented by an infinite series of trigonometric functions, or, more strongly, that *any* continuous function can be approximated by such a series $S(x)$ with $-\pi \leqslant x \leqslant \pi$, an interval in which $S(x)$ converges. For many years the work of Fourier was not accepted by mathematicians on the grounds that his derivations were not sufficiently rigorous, but his successful results were later given a satisfactory theoretical basis by Dirichlet and others. The Fourier series is

$$S(x) = a_0 + \sum_{n=1}^{\infty} (a_n \cos nx + b_n \sin nx)$$

An example of an expansion, valid for $-\pi \leqslant x \leqslant \pi$, is

$$x^2 = \frac{\pi^3}{3} - 4\left(\frac{\cos x}{1^2} - \frac{\cos 2x}{2^2} + \frac{\cos 3x}{3^2} - \dots\right)$$

The part of the curve between $\pm\pi$ is a good approximation for x^2.

Fourier transform The Fourier transform of a function $f(t)$ is proportional to

$$\int_0^{\infty} f(t) \cos ut \, dt$$

or the corresponding expression with $\sin ut$. In Fourier analysis, the transform permits a non-periodic function, representing say a single rectangular pulse, to be expressed as a sum of trigonometrical functions of vanishingly small amplitudes.

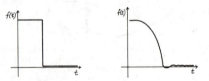

(*Compare* Laplace transform)

four-line *See* complete quadrilateral.

four-point *See* complete quadrangle.

Four Rules *See* arithmetic.

fourth dimension In mathematics this is simply the addition of a fourth coordinate to a vector that needs more than three to specify completely any event of an event or phase space, as (p, v, T, t) which specifies the pressure, volume and temperature of a gas at time t, or (x, y, z, t) which locates the position and epoch time of any event. Although such a vector cannot be represented on a graph with four independent axes in space, formal relations (such as Pythagoras' theorem for cartesian coordinates) can be extended to four or more variables, and a number of mathematical generalizations can be obtained to dimensions n. Many of these can be applied to physical situations involving n variables.

(*See* E. A. Abbott for 'Fourth Dimension' as in science fiction.)

fourth proportional Originally a problem expressed geometrically as in Euclid VI. 12. Given three line segments l_1, l_2, l_3, to find a line segment l_4 such that $l_1 : l_2 = l_3 : l_4$. Later given as the numerical equivalent: if a, b, c are known quantities, find d such that $a/b = c/d$.

fraction Any numerical quantity not an integer, which can be expressed as the ratio between two integers. A proper fraction has the form a/b where $a < b$, as $2/3$; an improper fraction has the form a/b where $a > b$, as $7/5$. A mixed fraction has the form $a + b/c$ where a is an integer and b/c is proper, as $1 + \frac{2}{3} = 1\frac{2}{3}$. The denominator b of the fraction a/b can be taken as the number of parts into which the unit is subdivided, or alternatively, as in Euclid, as the number of arbitrary units that make up the whole quantity. The numerator a is then the number of parts or units taken.

two thirds of interval

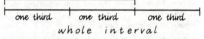

one third | *one third* | *one third*
w h o l e   i n t e r v a l

The Greeks thought of a fraction geometrically, as any part of a whole measure taken as unity (Lat. *fractio*, a breaking). The rational number $a/b (b \neq 0)$ is a formal mathematical structure based on the original intuitive concept.

frame of reference Any mesh or coordinate system defined with reference to any origin taken as fixed, with respect to which angular and linear velocities and accelerations may be specified. Their values are only significant relative to the given frame. Inertial frames of reference are frames without acceleration relative to one another.

free variable Any one of a set of variables which is not subject to constraints and is able to take any value within the domain.

● If $F = x + y + z$ and $x + y \leqslant 20$, z is a free variable but x, y are subject to an equation of constraint.

free vector A vector specified by magnitude and direction only, and not by an ordered pair with reference to an origin. The latter is sometimes called a localized or bound vector. The diagram shows equal free vectors.

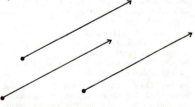

See also vector.

Frege, Gottlob German mathematician and logician (1848–1925). Author of the influential *Die Grundlagen der Arithmetik* (1893/1903). This investigated the concept of natural number, which he considered to be an analytical construction of pure logic independent of all experience. Frege also devised a symbolism for propositional calculus which, although completely unambiguous, is diagrammatic and difficult to read or print. Only the assertion sign ⊢ is still in use.

frequency 1. Of an oscillating or vibrating system, the number of complete cycles in a unit of time.
2. The number of occurrences of any event or observation.

frequency curve A smooth curve fitted to the discrete points of a frequency polygon. This is done for convenience when the number of ordinates is large. It then shows the general form of the polygon, but it must not be allowed to suggest continuity or the possibility of interpolation.

frequency density The quantity represented by the vertical scale on a frequency histogram or distribution. For a histogram the total frequency of a variable X in a class interval is the frequency density multiplied by the interval, that is, the area of the representative rectangle.

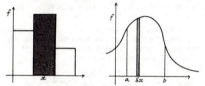

For a continuous distribution the total frequency over the interval (a,b) is given by $\int_a^b f(x)\,dx$ where $f(x)$ is the frequency density function.

frequency distribution function This corresponds to a probability density function, except that the ordinates give actual or relative frequencies of events instead of probabilities.

frequency polygon A pictorial representation of grouped data obtained by joining the midpoints of the tops of the rectangles of the corresponding histogram. Two empty classes are often added, one at each end, to complete the diagram.

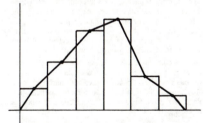

frequency ratio The same as occurrence ratio. *See* under probability.

frequency surface *See* joint frequency function.

frequency table A summary of data obtained by dividing the data-range into disjoint classes and counting the number of occurrences in each class. The frequencies may be given for each class recorded as a cumulative frequency, or both.

Friedmann's test A nonparametric equivalent of the analysis of variance for two variates, applicable

when there are k values which can be ranked within each of n blocks (for example n tasters arrange k wines in order of merit):

Taster number	Type of wine			
	A	B	C	D
1	2	1	3	4
2	2	1	4	3
3	1	3	2	4
R	5	5	9	11
R^2	25	25	81	121

The test statistic has the chi-squared distribution and is given by $\chi^2 = \dfrac{12S}{nk(k+1)} - 3n(k+1)$ with $(k-1)(n-1)$ degrees of freedom. Here S is the sum of the squares of the rank order totals $R_1, R_2 \ldots R_k$ for each of the k. Specially computed tables are available for $3 \leqslant k \leqslant 6$, and for $n \leqslant 25$. (Neave, H. R. *Statistical Tables*, London 1978.)
See Kruskal-Wallis test.

frieze pattern *See* strip pattern.

frustum (Lat. a piece) Originally a truncated cone, sometimes used for any part of a solid intercepted between two parallel planes.

full adder *See* half adder. A device, usually of electronic gates, which carries out one complete stage in binary addition. It adds *three* binary digits, one from each of the two numbers being added, and one carry digit from the previous stage (or column) in the addition process, thus producing a sum digit and a carry digit to the next stage. Its action is shown by the operation table

Carry from previous stage	a	b	sum	Carry to next stage
0	0	0	0	0
1	0	0	1	0
0	0	1	1	0
1	0	1	0	1
0	1	0	1	0
1	1	0	0	1
0	1	1	0	1
1	1	1	1	1

function 1. Formerly defined as any mathematical expression whose values depended on some other given values. Its form gave the rule for calculating the output values given any input values

$y = x^2$ gives an output of $y = 9$ if the input is $x = \pm 3$
$y = \sin x$ gives $y = 0$ if $x = 0$

Then y was said to be a function of x and the relation in general was written

$$y = f(x)$$

2. A modern formulation revises this definition by considering a function as associating a real number x with another given by the function, but with two

important provisions:

Each one input value shall correspond to one but not more than one output value; and

the function need not give the general form of the rule as in $y=x^2$ above, but can merely list or otherwise specify the pairs of values which are to be associated.

Subject to the convention that the input value is taken first, the output value second, we now have the definitions:

A function f is a set of ordered pair of numbers $(x, f(x))$ of which no two pairs can have the same first element.

Pairs can, however, have the same second element. The value taken by the function when the input is x, may be expressible by a rule (e.g. square x and add three times x, written $f(x) = x^2 + 3x$. This rule then generates the second number in each pair.
Another type of function is given by the example

$$f(x) = \begin{cases} 0 \text{ if } x < 1 \\ 1 \text{ if } x \geq 1 \end{cases}$$

This function, which has only two outputs (or image points) requires more than one statement to define it. If in any function x takes successive values $0, 1, 2 \ldots$ the values of the function can be written as

$$f(0), f(1), f(2) \ldots$$

for example if $f(x) = x^2 + 3x$, $f(2) = 10$.
The symbol $f(x)$ is read 'f of x' and is taken to mean the value of the function f at point x.
A function in general is written f, and the function that associates each x with the value of $x^2 + 3x$ is usually written

$$f: x \mapsto x^2 + 3x$$

Similarly, for a numerically defined function

$$f: x \mapsto 0 \text{ if } x < 1$$
$$f: x \mapsto 10 \text{ if } x \geq 1$$

A function can also consist merely of listed values, such as

$$f = \{(0, 1), (2, 3), (3, 1)\}$$

The formal definition excludes such expressions as $y = \sqrt{(1 + x^2)}$ where the root gives positive and negative values. This is taken to be a double function having two branches

$$f: x \mapsto + \sqrt{(1 + x^2)} \text{ and}$$
$$f: x \mapsto - \sqrt{(1 + x^2)}$$

Similarly $y = \arcsin x$ is many-valued. If only the principal values are taken this defines a function. As in real algebra generally, an unsigned expression such as x is always taken to be positive, so that $f: x \mapsto \sqrt{(1 + x^2)}$ would normally define a function unless otherwise stated.

functional Used of any relationship that has the formal properties of a function.

functional determinant *See* Jacobian determinant.

functional equation Synonym for recursive formula, used where x is continuous, as for the gamma function where $\Gamma(x + 1) = x\Gamma(x)$.

function box or machine A teaching device used to illustrate the structure of a function, which transforms a numerical input into a corresponding numerical output.

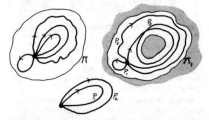

function space Given two sets X, Y the set F of all functions, which map X into Y forms the 'points' of a function space F. We can also consider subsets of F having certain properties such as continuity, differentiability and so on as spaces F_c, F_d, etc. If f, g are functions they form a space if

$$(f + g)x = f(x) + g(x)$$
$$(af)x = af(x)$$

where a is a scalar multiplier. It follows that a function space is a form of linear space or vector space.
See space.

fundamental 1. Describes any concept or theorem held to be basic in developing a mathematical topic, as in the fundamental theorem of calculus.
2. The fundamental is the lowest frequency with which a system naturally oscillates. Harmonics have frequencies which are integral multiples of the fundamental.

fundamental group The group usually so named was first defined by Poincaré and used in discussing topological spaces. Its elements are the set of all homotopic loops in the given space.

For a simply connected plane region Π all simple loops are homotopic and the group contains one element only, the identity I such that I o $I = I$ where the group operation o traces the paths one after the other. For the region Π_1 which is not simply connected, the paths p_1, p_2, p_3, are not homotopic: there is in fact an infinity of homotopic classes of loops and the fundamental group is infinite.

fundamental theorems These are the theorems which may be taken as the *logical* starting points of various branches of mathematics, although they were only formulated late in the history of mathematics. Three are given for algebra, arithmetic and calculus
1. Algebra

Every polynomial $\sum_{r=0}^{n} a_r z^r$ $(a_r, z \in \mathbb{C})$ which is not merely a constant has at least one zero in $\mathbb{C}$, that is, every non-constant polynomial $f(z) = 0 (z \in \mathbb{C})$, has at least one root. Theorem proved by Gauss at the age of 20.
2. Arithmetic
Any composite number can be expressed as a product of primes in one way only (apart from rearrangement). This is called the Unique Factor Theorem. The theorem is equivalent to Euclid IX, 14

3. Calculus (usually of Integral Calculus)

The theorem relates integrals and derivatives, formalizing the concept of an integral as an antiderivative. If a function $f(x)$ can be integrated over a closed interval $[a, b]$ and $f(x) = g'(x)$ for some other function $g(x)$ then

$$\int_a^b f(x)\mathrm{d}x = g(b) - g(a)$$

- If $g(x) = \frac{1}{3}x^3$, $g'(x) = x^2$
  Then

$$\int_2^3 x^2\mathrm{d}x = \frac{1}{3}(3)^3 - \frac{1}{3}(2)^3$$

fundamental units   *See* S.I. in Appendix 1.

funicular polygon   From Lat. *funis*, a cord. The form taken by a light cord between two points when loaded with a number of weights or other forces.

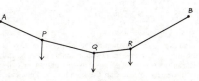

fuzzy set   A concept first formalized at a US–Japanese seminar in 1974, which relaxes the two criteria given by Cantor for the definition of set. That is, in a fuzzy set there is a continuum of set membership in which the rules for inclusion and distinguishability may prove ambiguous. An example could be 'the set of all behavioural characteristics genetically transmitted'. The study of fuzzy sets is put forward as a systematic approach to approximate reasoning, and could give results in psychology, legal discussion and the design of computers which model intelligent behaviour. It avoids the paradoxes that have emerged from the Cantor definition of set.

G

Galilean transformation Let a point occupy a position x at time t in any coordinate system S, and let another system g' move with uniform velocity with respect to S so that the x and x' axes coincide. Then if time is measured from 0 when the origins of S and S' coincide

$$x' = x \pm ut$$
$$t' = t$$

This is a fundamental principle of Newtonian mechanics, and can be written as

$$\begin{pmatrix} 1 \pm u \\ 0 \quad 1 \end{pmatrix}\begin{pmatrix} x \\ t \end{pmatrix} = \begin{pmatrix} x' \\ t' \end{pmatrix}$$

The matrix given, which may be extended to uniform rectilinear motion in a plane or in space, describes the so-called Galilean transformation from S to S'. The name was not given until an alternative transformation was postulated by Lorentz and Einstein, who thus queried the tacit assumption of its physical validity.

Galois, Evariste French mathematician (1811–32). Pioneer of group theory and modern algebra. He was killed in a duel, leaving a letter detailing his work and asking for its publication in the *Revue Encyclopedique*.

Galois theory The application of group theory, finite fields and field extensions to the theory of the solution of equations. One notable result is that although polynomial equations up to degree 4 can be solved generally by the use of algebraic formulae including radicals, this is impossible for the general equation of degree 5. The proof depends on the fact that the alternating group A_5 has no normal subgroups.

gambler's ruin Any game of chance between two players that is governed by an absorbing Markov chain. It exemplifies the theorem that an absorbing Markov chain always absorbs.

A and B have n coins each and take turns to spin. The loser of each throw gives a coin to the other. After a sufficiently large number of throws, either A or B will have no coins left and the game terminates.

games theory A branch of statistics related to decision theory, concerned with problems which can be described as strategic contests between two or more players, defined by strict rules and conditions. It is claimed that games theory gives an insight into strategic decisions in commerce and politics.

gamma distribution Continuous positive valued distribution of which one form is

$$f(x) = \frac{1}{\Gamma(\alpha)} x^{\alpha - 1} e^{-x} \quad (x \geqslant 0)$$

where $\Gamma(\alpha)$ is the gamma function.

gamma function One of the Eulerian integrals, defined by

$$\Gamma(x) = \int_0^\infty e^{-t} t^{x-1} \, dt \quad (x > 0)$$

This converges uniformly for any $x > 0$ and is therefore continuous. Integration by parts gives the recursive formula

$$\Gamma(x+1) = x\Gamma(x) \quad (x > 0)$$

Since $\Gamma(1) = 1$, then for integers $n = 2, 3 \ldots$ this gives

$$\Gamma(n) = (n-1)(n-2) \ldots 2.1$$
$$= (n-1)!$$

Hence $\Gamma(n+1) = n!$
which is true for all non-negative n since $0! = 1$. It follows that $\Gamma(x)$ is a continuous function that takes integral values x whenever x is an integer. $\Gamma(x)$ is not defined at $x = 0$, although $0! = 1$ by definition.

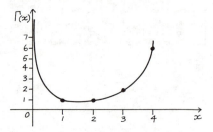

The gamma function can be used to express other integrals, beta functions and expressions involving factorials.

gate A mechanical or, more usually, an electronic device which transforms one or more digital input signals into an output signal. It is in general a two-state device equivalent to some Boolean function in two-term logic, operating on signals which represent data on a binary code. Its operation corresponds to the truth table of the required Boolean function. Thus an AND gate has the operation table

a	b	a AND b
0	0	0
0	1	0
1	0	0
1	1	1

The gate can be shown as

Electronic data processing and computing is achieved by the passage of binary signals through sequences of gates.

gauge points *See* analytical projective geometry.

Gaussian condensation A method used by Gauss, but developed by Chio (1853) for calculating the value of determinants, reducing them from order n to $(n-1)$. Also called pivotal condensation, from the element or 'pivot' chosen to start the process. Applied to the coefficients of a set of simultaneous linear equations it is called Gaussian elimination. It is readily programmed for a computer.

Gaussian curve of error *See* normal distribution curve.

Gaussian distribution *See* normal distribution curve.

Gaussian elimination *See* Gaussian condensation.

Gaussian integer A complex number of the form $a+ib$ where a, b are integers, frequently used in number theory. Products of them may often express real integers, such as sums of two squares.

$$a^2+b^2=(a+ib)(a-ib)$$
$$5=(3+2i)(3-2i)$$

Gauss, J.K.F. German mathematician (1777–1855) He did important work in deducing the orbits of asteroids from relatively few observations, using what later became the Gaussian distribution or normal curve of errors and the method of least squares. He also worked on surveying, terrestrial magnetism, electrostatics and the development of units for electrical measurement. He proved the fundamental theorem of algebra and published many results in number theory and geometry. He wrote that 'mathematics is the queen of the sciences, and number theory the queen of mathematics'.

Gaussian prime A prime number which cannot be factorized into two Gaussian integers, that is, cannot be put into the form $p=(a+ib)(c+id)$ where p is prime and $p,a,b,c,d \in \mathbb{Z}$. 7 is a Gaussian prime, but 5 is not, since $5=(3+2i)(3-2i)$.

gelosia method From Italian, jealousy, and hence a lattice-work screen for a window. An earlier method for multiplying numbers, in which the partial products are set in a grid resembling a lattice and added diagonally.

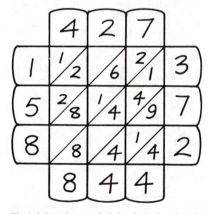

'Napier's bones' are a calculating device based on the pattern.

general quadratic form In two variables this is the expression $ax^2+2hxy+by^2$, or, in matrix notation

$$(x\ y)\begin{pmatrix} a & h \\ h & b \end{pmatrix}\begin{pmatrix} x \\ y \end{pmatrix}$$

In three variables it becomes

$$(x\ y\ z)\begin{pmatrix} a & h & g \\ h & b & f \\ g & f & c \end{pmatrix}\begin{pmatrix} x \\ y \\ z \end{pmatrix}$$

This pattern can be extended to n dimensions.

general relativity The theory of relativity was first developed to relate physical laws established for one frame of reference S to another S' moving uniformly in a straight line relative to S. This was later extended to frames accelerated with respect to one another as in gravitational effects, and postulates that all physical laws take the same form in any coordinate systems, however moving. *See* relativity.

general solution Also called complete primitive. The most general solution of an ordinary differential equation of the nth order contains n arbitrary constants. Thus the full solution of

$$\frac{d^3y}{dx^3}=\frac{dy}{dx}$$

is $y=A_0+A_1\sinh x+A_2\cosh x$.
It follows that $y=\sinh x$ is a solution but not the general solution.

generating function A function whose coefficients provide, after expansion as a series, moments or probabilities of a distribution.
See under characteristic function, moment generating function, probability generating function.
Such functions have the property that the generating function of the sum of independent random variates is given by the product of the individual generating functions.

generator 1. One of a system of straight lines each of which lies wholly within a surface, so that they serve to develop or generate the surface. Intuitively, it is a straight line that sweeps out the surface as it moves. A surface so generated is called a ruled surface and can be modelled physically by a set of rods or threads.
The cone $x^2+z^2-y^2=0$ has a set of generators, two of which, in the y, z plane, are given by $y=\pm z$

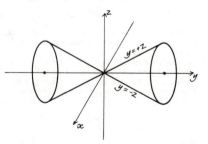

2. Also used of a set of curves which similarly generate a surface, as a set of semicircles around a fixed diameter. The sphere can be thought of as generated by the rotation of one of the semicircles.
3. In group theory, the generator of a cyclic group is any element g such that the powers g, g^2, g^3 ... together form all the elements of the group.

● $\{G,x\}=\{1,\omega,\omega^2,\omega^3\}$
where $\omega^2=-1$
Here ω and ω^3 are generators.

In general if $A=\{a_1,a_2,a_3\ldots\}$ is a subset (not necessarily a subgroup) of a group $\{G,o\}$, such that any element of G can arise from a combination of the a_i under the operation o, then A is the generator set of G.
4. A term sometimes used for the basis of a vector space, which is then said to be spanned by this basis.

genus of a surface The largest number of non-intersecting closed curves that can be drawn on a surface without dividing it into two distinct regions.

A sphere is of genus 0

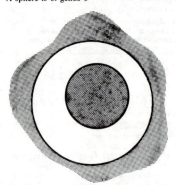

An anchor chain link is of genus 2

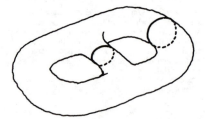

geodesic The minimum path between two points on a surface which lies wholly within the surface. On a convex surface it is the line taken by a stretched string between the two points. It is the straight line joining two points on an Euclidean plane.
If there is any path between two points P, Q and δs is an element of distance along it the length of the path will be

$$\int_Q^P ds$$

Then the geodesic is that path for which this expression is a minimum. The word is used in relativity theory for a function in x, y, z, t expressing the path of a body moving freely in a gravitational field.
See calculus of variations.

geoid A shape having the mean configuration of the earth (i.e. with all land masses shifted to the sea bed). A prolate spheroid of equatorial diameter

12756 km and polar diameter 12714 km approximately, of ellipticity 1/297.

geometric distribution A special case of the negative binomial distribution when $r=1$; that is, the discrete distribution $p(X=x)=pq^x$ $(p+q=1)$, where x is number of trials before the first success. It becomes an exponential distribution if X is continuous, as with the waiting time before the arrival of a customer at a service point. The mean of the distribution is q/p.

geometric mean Given two numbers a and b, the geometric mean m is given by $m^2=ab$, so that a, m, b form a geometric progression. In general, any number of geometric means can be inserted.
● m, n are means between a and b if
$m^3=a^2b$, $n^3=ab^2$

geometric progression (G.P.) A sequence or, more usually, a series in which each term is a constant multiple of the previous term. Thus the series

$$a+ar+ar^2+\ldots+ar^{n-1}+ar^n$$

is a G.P. with common ratio r.
The sum of the series converges to $\dfrac{a}{1-r}$ if $-1<r<1$ as n increases without limit.
See also arithmetical progression.

geometry The etymology of the word (Gk. *geometres*, earth measure) suggests a practical origin, but from the earliest records available it has been an abstract study. For the Greeks, ideal geometrical configurations and their properties were realized by points and lines as intuitively conceived. During the 19th century, geometry began to be interpreted as a set of theorems arising from axioms which assigned properties to undefined elements called points and lines. These properties could (but need not) correspond to realizable finite structures, and numerous geometries were developed according to the axioms chosen.
See also elliptical, hyperbolic, parabolic, projective geometries.

glide reflection One of the isometries of transformation geometry, given by a reflection M in a line m followed by a translation T parallel to the line.

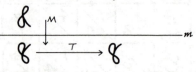

Successive reflections in three non-parallel or non-concurrent mirror lines m_1,m_2,m_3 ... produce a glide reflection.

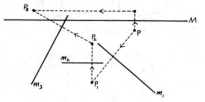

glissette Any curve produced by sliding a curve, supposed rigid, along another curve or set of curves or lines. The point tracing the glissette need not be on the curve, but on the plane containing it. For example *see* astroid.

gnomon Originally the index of a sundial (Gk. *gnomon*, one who knows). From its shape it was applied to the configuration which when added to a square produced another square, and hence to the configuration that preserved similarity for any figure.

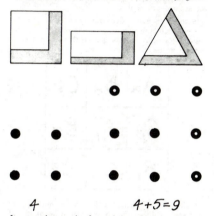

$$4 \qquad\qquad 4+5=9$$

It was also used of numbers added to figurate numbers to produce the sequence, as with square numbers.

Gödel number The number produced by assigning a unique integer to each and every symbol in closed mathematical systems such as the theory of numbers or elementary arithmetic, in such a way that every string of symbols has a unique numerical code. Thus, if

$$a = 121$$
$$b = 122$$
$$c = 123$$
$$> \,= 001$$
$$\Rightarrow \,= 002$$
$$\& = 432$$

the theorem $a > b \,\&\, \cdot b > c \Rightarrow a > c$ then has the code number 121 001 122 432 122 001 123 002 121 001 123. The example merely illustrates a principle that could be employed to assign numbers to theorems. Gödel showed how theorems could be arranged systematically so that their numbers could be calculated in principle by recursive methods, and used the numbers thus generated in his theorem.

Gödel's theorem Also called Gödel's incompleteness theorem (1931). It was originally derived for the system of Russell and Whitehead's *Principia Mathematica* which purports to deduce all mathematics from a foundation of pure logic, but it applies to any consistent axiomatic formalization of a theory of natural numbers and their properties. The theorem states that any such system S contains a logically derived formula A such that neither A nor its negation $\sim A$ can be proved within the theorems of the system. These are the ordinary theorems of arithmetic and logic such as 'there is no largest prime', 7

is odd, or $\sim (\sim p) \rightarrow p$. Just as one can assign coordinates to all points in Euclidean space and represent configurations numerically, Gödel assigned a unique Gödel number to each theorem in the system. To each set or class of expressions in S there corresponds a set of Gödel numbers. If T is the set of all theorems in S, then G will be the set of all corresponding Gödel numbers. Gödel then argued that if $x \in G$, then this is a property of the integer x and is therefore a theorem of T. If we now consider any y such that $y \notin G$, then this exclusion is also a property of y and ought to be a theorem of T. It follows that it has a Gödel number and $y \in G$, which contradicts the original assumption that y is not in G. Gödel was able to describe a process for calculating his numbers in principle (using recursive functions, q.v.) and hence constructing in principle a theorem not provable in S.

Goldbach's conjecture In a letter to Euler dated 1742 Goldbach noted that all even integers greater than 2 and tested by him were the sum of two primes, and suggested this as an unproved theorem. No complete proof has been found; but no counter example is known. It can be shown, from the known distribution of primes, that the probability of finding a counter example, is less than 10^{-2911} (Clarke and Shannon, 1983).

golden number No connection with the golden section. It is the remainder R when the date year increased by one is divided by 19, as $(1981 + 1)/19$ gives $R = 6$. The Greek astronomer Meton (432 B.C.) calculated that 19 years equalled 125 lunar months, so that on New Year's day from a suitable zero year $R/19$ of a lunar month has elapsed. This allowed, in the days before almanacs, the calculation of the first full moon after the spring equinox, and hence the date of religious festivals dependent on it. The added year is a cumulative correction.

golden ratio Also golden section. A name given by M. Ohm in 1835 to the result of Euclid II, 11, in which a given straight line is cut so that the rectangle contained by the whole line and one of the segments, is equal to the square on the other segment.

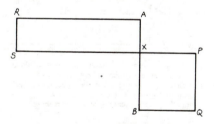

In the diagram $AB = AR$ and AB is cut at X so that AXSR, BXPQ have the same area. AXSR is called the golden rectangle.
Euclid merely gives a construction for this problem, but later writers, from the Renaissance onwards, following Plato, have given the ratio AX:XB as an aesthetic absolute, as the proportions of a rectangle that is most pleasing to the eye.
It follows from the definition of the golden rectangle that if a square is drawn on its longest side the resulting rectangle is also golden.

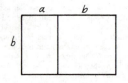

Then $\dfrac{a}{b}=\dfrac{b}{a+b}$. If $a=1$ the resulting quadratic $b^2-b-1=0$ gives the numerical result $(1+\sqrt{5})/2$ or $1.618\ldots$, often denoted ϕ. In the Fibonacci sequence, where $a_{n+2}=a_n+a_{n+1}$ (as in 1, 1, 2, 3, 5, 8 $\ldots$) the ratio L between a large term and its successor is approximately constant. If x is a large term the next two terms are approximately Lx and L^2x. Since $L^2x=x+Lx$ it follows that $L=\phi$ as before. This ratio appears in other geometrical or algebraic contexts.
See also Modulor.

goodness of fit The agreement between a set of observations and a set of values based wholly or partly on a hypothetical model. Agreement between the data and a proposed 'line of best fit' constructed for data plotted on coordinates is a special case.

Gossett, W. S. *See* 'Student'.

grad *See* angular measure.

gradient 1. The measure of the steepness of a slope, expressed in the cartesian plane as the ratio between differences of ordinates and abscissae. Thus the gradient of the line PQ joining $P(x_1,y_1)$ to $Q(x_2,y_2)$ is given by

$$\frac{y_2-y_1}{x_2-x_1}$$

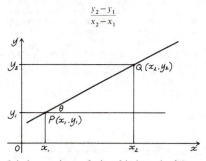

It is then equal to $\tan\theta$ where θ is the angle of slope.
2. In surveying, a gradient is the ratio between height and distance measured along the slope, and is thus equivalent to $\sin\theta$, not $\tan\theta$. It is now, by international convention, expressed as a percentage

$$\text{gradient}=\frac{100h}{d}$$

3. The gradient of a curve at a point is defined as the gradient of the tangent to the curve at that point if it exists.
See derivative for fuller details.

gradient of a field A scalar quantity such as temperature can vary from point to point in space continuously. If points of equal temperature are mapped as surfaces in the region, the gradient measures the greatest rate of increase in the direction

of this increase as one moves away from the surface. The values of the gradient are independent of the coordinate system chosen and hence are invariant under transformations. In rectangular cartesian coordinates x, y, z the gradient of S is given by

$$\frac{\partial S}{\partial x}\mathbf{i}+\frac{\partial S}{\partial y}\mathbf{j}+\frac{\partial S}{\partial z}\mathbf{k}$$

where $\mathbf{i}$, $\mathbf{j}$, $\mathbf{k}$ are unit vectors. This quantity is written ∇S, read grad S. The symbol ∇ is the differential operator del or nabla.

graeco-latin square *See* latin square of order n. An $n\times n$ graeco-latin square is a composite of two latin squares of order n, arranged so that no two pairs appear in the same row or column.

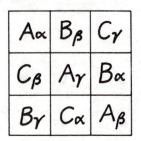

graph 1. A diagrammatic representation of numerical values, either those taken by functions and other expressions, or of statistical records and data. For typical graphs *see* histogram, block graph, cartesian coordinates, polar coordinates.
2. More recently, as synonym for network, any set of points and arcs or paths joining them. The points and arcs may, but need not, represent the vertices and edges of solid figures, a set of physical interconnections as with electrical circuits, or relations between any sets of entities. Graph theory has been used in enumerating isomers of chemical compounds.
See network.

graph theory Also called network theory. A branch of topology discussing the possible interconnections of two sets of elements, represented by points, lines and regions enclosed by them. Euler's formula

$$F+V-E=2$$

is an example of a result in graph theory.

Grassmann, H. German mathematician (1809–1877) In 1844 he published an account of abstract algebras, one of which corresponded to modern vector algebra. He also considered spaces as coordinate sets of more than three dimensions.

graticule 1. The grid or network formed by the projection of the lines of latitude and longitude (parallels and meridians) on to a plane surface. The form of the graticule defines the properties of any given type of geographical map, such as Mercator or conical.
2. Also used of any coordinate network of discrete lines.

grating method *See* gelosia method.

gravitational potential *See* potential.

great circle A circle drawn on a sphere, having the same centre as the sphere. Specifically applied to the figure of the earth, as great circle route in navigation. A great circle is formed when a plane which intersects a sphere passes through its centre. This circle is a surface geodesic between any two points on its circumference.
See small circle.

greater than *See* inequality.

greatest common divisor *See* highest common factor.

greatest common measure (GCM) *See* highest common factor.

greatest integer function For any real number x the function given by $[x]$ or $[\![x]\!]$, denoting the greatest integer n such that $n \leqslant x$.

$$[\![3.2]\!] = 3 \quad [\![\pi]\!] = 3 \quad [\![3]\!] = 3 \quad [\![-3.2]\!] = -4$$

greatest lower bound *See* least upper bound.

Greek mathematics Developed over a period of about 1000 years, from the collection of results attributed (by later writers) to Pythagoras c. 550 B.C. up to the fall of the Graeco–Roman empire. Little original work was achieved during the last three centuries or so, but much useful compilation and commentary emerged. Although they produced many results which are now subsumed under number theory and algebra, the Greeks used geometrical methods. A number, for instance, was considered to be the measure of one line interval by another, arbitrarily taken as the unit, or to have a structure (*see* polygonal numbers) derived from spatial arrangement of unit elements. It is probable that their mathematics took this direction because the Greeks lacked an efficient notation for number. *See also* Euclid.

Greek numerals 1. Early Greeks used the initial letters of number names in a repetitive notation

$$\Delta = 10, \text{ from } deka, \text{ ten}$$
$$\Delta\Delta\Delta = 30$$

2. From c. 500 B.C. alphabetic symbols were used, the first ten letters for 1–10, the next ten for 20, 30 . . . 100, 200. It was a clumsy system which blocked the development of numerical mathematics. There was no symbol for zero, which the Greeks did not recognize as a number.

Greek numerical prefixes Commonly used to specify polygons, polyhedra and so on. The convention is that a Greek word takes a Greek prefix, a Latin word a Latin, as tetrahedron but quadrilateral. The prefixes are the adverbial forms of the numerals, omitting the final -s or -kis

2 di-	8 octa-
3 tri-	9 nona-
4 tetra-	10 deca-
5 penta-	11 hendeca-
6 hexa-	12 dodeca-
7 hepta-	20 icosa-

Those not listed are rarely used (*but see* SI).

Green's theorem Expresses the double integral over the plane area of a normal closed region in terms of the line integral round its boundary, or vice versa. If $F(r) = f(x, y)$

$$\oint F(r)\,dr = \int_R \int f(x, y)\,dx\,dy$$

A similar formulation applies to a closed convex region in three dimensions.

Greenwich hour angle Since the celestial sphere rotates in 24 hours relative to the earth, the right ascension of any celestial meridian can be expressed as an elapsed time relative to Greenwich Mean Time, at the Greenwich meridian. The relation between the known position of a star relative to Greenwich and its apparent position enables longitude to be found using a chronometer keeping Greenwich time.

Greenwich Mean Time The 'mean sun' is a fictitious approximation to the real sun, and is taken to complete a circuit of the celestial equator in one year at a *uniform* rate (unlike the real sun). The time between successive transits of the mean sun over the Greenwich meridian defines the mean solar day, which gives the units of G.M.T. when divided in hours, minutes and seconds.

Gregory's series Essentially a series of arctan x, but more usually given as a series for determining π. Discovered independently by J. Gregory (1671) and Leibnitz. The series gives

$$\arctan x = x - \frac{x^3}{3} + \frac{x^5}{5} - \frac{x^7}{7} \ldots (-1 < x \leqslant 1)$$

Since it is true for $x = 1$ it gives, for arctan 1 which is $\pi/4$

$$\frac{\pi}{4} = 1 - 1/3 + 1/5 - 1/7 + \ldots$$

The series converges very slowly and is of no practical use.

group A set G, finite or infinite, whose elements can be combined by a binary operation subject to four conditions:

1. The operation is associative

$$(a * b) * c = a * (b * c) \text{ where } a, b, c, \in G$$

2. The set is closed under the operation

$$a * b = x \Rightarrow x \in G$$

3. There is an identity element $I \in G$ such that

$$a * I = I * a = a$$

4. Each element a has an inverse element a^{-1} such that

$$a * a^{-1} = a^{-1} * a = I$$

For any $a, b, \in G$ there are solutions $x, y, \in G$ of the equations $a * x = b$ and $y * a = b$.
See also abstract group and entries for exemplary groups.

group table The representation of a finite group by tabulating the results of the group operation on its elements.

● The cyclic additive group $G = \{1, a, b\}$ is represented by

+	1	a	b
1	1	a	b
a	a	b	1
b	b	1	a

group theory The study of the structure, representations and applications of the group concept.

gruppoid Also groupoid. A set X, together with a binary operation on X for which the set is closed, denoted $(X, *)$. For example, the set of integers with respect to addition.

Gudermannian The function arctan $(\sinh \theta)$ or gd θ, whose values were originally used to calculate hyperbolic functions from tables of circular functions. If $\phi = \text{gd } \theta$, all the hyperbolic functions are expressible in terms of ϕ, e.g. $\cosh \theta = \sec \phi$. Of historical interest only.

Guldin's (or Guldinius') theorem Due to P. Guldin (1577–1642).
1. If a plane region is rotated about a line in the plane which does not intersect the region, then the volume of the solid of revolution so formed is the product of the area of the region and the circumference of the circle traced by its centroid.

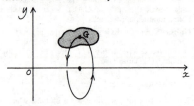

2. The corresponding theorem about the revolution of a plane arc. The area of the surface swept out is the length of the arc multiplied by the circumference of the circle traced by the centroid of the arc.

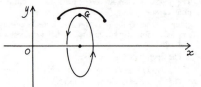

See Pappus' theorem.

Gunter scale A single logarithmic scale devised by Gunter (1620) on which calculations could be performed with the aid of dividers. The precursor to the slide rule.

gyroscope A rotating body free to rotate about three mutually perpendicular axes, often in the form of a rotating heavy wheel on an axle freely pivoted at one end, on a support as at O.

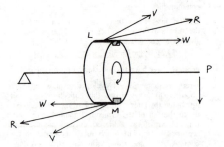

Suppose the wheel rotates rapidly and is also supported at P. The elements of the wheel shaded at L, M, have (high) velocity v in opposite directions as shown. If support is removed at P the axle begins to move downwards under gravity, and L, M now have equal and opposite velocities w. The resultants of v and w are the velocities R, making an angle θ to OP. The system therefore rotates (precesses) about the fixed pivot O with a constant angular velocity (which increases if the wheel slows down). In general, a force applied about an axis does not rotate it about that axis but about a perpendicular axis. Gyroscopic forces are produced when the axis of any rotating body is changed, and are of importance in powered aircraft.

hairy ball theorem Name given to the fixed point theorem for a sphere or its topological equivalent. If a function f maps the surface S of a sphere on to itself then there is always a point $X \in S$ which maps on to itself. (If the nap of a tennis ball, considered as a fibre at every point, were brushed flat so that each fibre linked two points on its surface, then there would be, given an infinitude of fibres, one point unlinked.)

half The word half and the underlying concept is part of ordinary speech and predates mathematics. The notation $1/2$ or 0.5 brings the concept into the formal arithmetic of fractions.

half adder Any device, usually electronic, that adds two but only two binary digits, according to the rules of binary arithmetic, to produce their sum and carry digit. Its operation is thus governed by the table

a	b	sum	carry
0	0	0	0
0	1	1	0
1	0	1	0
1	1	0	1

It will be seen that the sum column corresponds to a XOR b, (the exclusive or), the carry column to a AND b, so that the electronic device will respond to inputs of 0 or 1 as an AND gate and XOR gate in parallel.

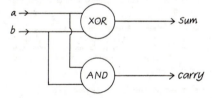

half angle formula Any one of set of formulae involving the trigonometric ratios of half-angles

$$\sin A = \frac{2t}{1 - t^2}$$

where $t = \tan\left(\frac{A}{2}\right)$

half closed interval The set of all points $x \in \mathbb{R}$ such that $a \leqslant x < b$ denoted $[a, b)$ or $[a, b[$, or $a < x \leqslant b$, denoted $(a, b]$ or $]a, b]$. If $a \leqslant x < b$ then b is a limit point of the set and also a greatest upper bound, but it is not contained in the set which itself has a minimum a but no maximum. Half open intervals are important in analysis. For example, $1/x$ is defined in the interval $]0, 1]$ but not in $[0, 1]$ since it is undefined at $x = 0$.

half line Any straight line extending to infinity in one direction from a given origin, as the positive half of the real number line, the region for which $x \geqslant 0$.

half plane That part of a plane lying on one side of a line drawn in the plane, or the set of all points satisfying the linear function $f(x, y) \leqslant 0$ or $f(x, y) \geqslant 0$.

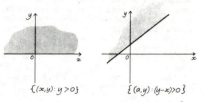

$\{(x, y) : y > 0\}$ $\{(a, y) : (y - x) > 0\}$

half space The concept of half plane extended to three or more dimensions. In particular a partition of three-dimensional space by a plane.

half turn Rotation of 180° about a given point, or the transformation of any configuration equivalent to such a rotation.

Two half turns $P \rightarrow P_1$, $P_1 \rightarrow P_2$ about different centres A, B are equivalent to a translation $P \rightarrow P_2$ equal to $2AB$. Any one half turn is equivalent to successive reflections in two mirrors at right angles to one another.

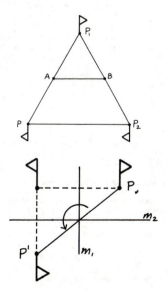

Hamiltonian In Newtonian mechanics this can be taken as the expression $H = T + V$, giving the sum of the kinetic and potential energies of a system at any time.

Hamilton, Sir William Rowan Dublin-born mathematician and astronomer (1805–1865). In 1837 he gave the modern definition of a complex number $(a + ib)$ as an ordered pair (a, b) with an appropriate algebra. He later extended this work to quaternions, a system of ordered quadruples (a, b, c, d), which in effect treated three-dimensional mechanics as an exercise in four-dimensional geometry. The applications of quaternions were developed by Tait (1867 and later) but modern vector methods have proved easier and more convenient.

Hardy, G. H. Cambridge mathematician (1877–1947). He worked extensively on number theory, and introduced the modern rigorous treatment of analysis into English mathematical education. The Hardy–Weinberg theorem gives a mathematical model for distribution of recessive genes in breeding experiments.

harmonic 1. A general term in mathematics applied to numbers, proportions and relations which resemble those of musical concords.
2. Specifically the superimposed modes of simple harmonic oscillation that make up many vibrating systems, particularly those that produce musical sounds, investigated by Sauveur in 1701. The modes are shown diagrammatically for a vibrating string.

fundamental   first   second

(In physics the musician's 'fundamental' is often called the first harmonic, and so on.)

harmonic analyser An instrument, originally devised by Kelvin for analysing tidal ranges and hence predicting tides, for demonstrating a compound harmonic motion as the sum of its constituent SHMs. The receptors of the ear act as harmonic analysers for the sound wave pressure function and can become very efficient on training.

harmonic analysis Also called Fourier analysis. A technique for expressing any periodic motion whatsoever as the sum of simple harmonic motions. Also, more generally, the expression of a continuous function over a finite interval as a finite or infinite trigonometric series.

harmonic conjugate *See* harmonic range.

harmonic functions The functions appearing in harmonic analysis. Often used specifically of the solutions to Laplace's equation.

harmonic mean The number H defined by

$$\frac{n}{H} = \frac{1}{a_1} + \frac{1}{a_2} + \ldots + \frac{1}{a_n} \text{ or } H = n \bigg/ \sum_{i=1}^{n} \frac{1}{a_i}$$

for a set of positive numbers $a_1, a_2 \ldots a_n$

It is used for calculating the value of resistances in parallel or the focal lengths of combinations of lenses. It is always less than or equal to the geometric mean.

harmonic motion 1. Simple. The motion of a point which moves in a straight line with an acceleration directed towards a fixed origin on the line, proportional to its distance from the origin. Also, the parallel projection on a straight line of a point moving with uniform circular motion. The displacement is represented by a sine curve if plotted against time. SHM is an oscillatory motion; for example that of a mass supported by an elastic string subject to Hooke's Law.

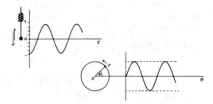

The maximum displacement is called the amplitude of the motion, the time of each complete cycle of motion the period, the number of complete oscillations in one unit of time the frequency, the angle corresponding to any point in the motion (second diagram) is the phase.
2. Compound. Two or more simple harmonic motions of different amplitudes, periods and initial phase may be combined into a single accelerated motion. *See* harmonic analysis, wave equation, wave motion.

harmonic range A set of four points $\{A, B, C, D\}$ on a line whose cross ratio $(ABCD) = -1$. The sets $\{A, B\}$, $\{C, D\}$ are said to be harmonic conjugates with respect to one another. $\{A, B, C, D\}$ is also called a harmonic tetrad.

harmonic sequence The sequence $1, \frac{1}{2}, \frac{1}{3}, \frac{1}{4}, \ldots \frac{1}{n} \ldots$ The sum of these terms gives the harmonic series.

harmonic tetrad *See* harmonic range.

haversine The function $\frac{1}{2}(1 - \cos\theta)$, used in one method of finding position from astronomical observation, and having the advantage for navigational calculation of being non-negative for all θ. Tables are available.

haversine formula The cosine formula for a spherical triangle ABC expressed in terms of haversines, hav $a = $ hav $(b \sim c) + \sin b \, \sin c \,$ hav A. Since b, $c < 180°$ all terms are always positive.

Heath, Sir Thomas L. Cambridge historian and interpreter of Greek mathematics (1861–1940), famous for his edition of Euclid's Elements in three volumes.

Heaviside, Oliver British electrical engineer (1850–1925) who, as a telegraph clerk without formal training, initiated the operational calculus and derived many theoretical results which explained the behaviour of alternating currents and telephone transmission lines. His calculation (1889) of the field of an electric charge moving at velocity v showed a discontinuity when $v=c$, a result of importance in the later theory of relativity. He was one of the earliest advocates of rationalized units, the modern SI.

Heaviside operator The symbol D^n which represents the operation of finding the nth derivative, is used to write differential equations as polynomials in D. Working with this notation, Heaviside solved equations with known boundary or initial conditions, using the equivalent of the Laplace transform.

Heaviside step function Denoted by $H(t)$ this is a theoretical input function to a system governed by a differential equation. It is defined as

$$H(t) = \begin{cases} 1 \text{ if } t>0 \\ 0 \text{ if } t<0 \end{cases}$$

Sometimes $H(t)$ is taken as $\frac{1}{2}$ if $t=0$, but is usually left undefined.

The output is then the theoretical response of the system. Heaviside himself ignored mathematical difficulties associated with discontinuity at $t=0$, but was able to show that the response of an electrical circuit when a switch is initially closed (as $t=0$ becomes $t>0$) is a transient surge of current, which can reach a high peak value.
See Dirac δ function.

height 1. Has its ordinary use in elementary mathematics, as in 'base × height'.
2. The height $H(x)$ of a polynomial of degree n with integral coefficients. If $P(x)=a_n x^n + a_{n-1} x^{n-1} + \dots + a$ then $H(x)=n+|a_n|+|a_{n-1}|+\dots|a_0|$. Since to any value h of $H(x)$ there corresponds only a finite number of polynomials, then the corresponding polynomial equations will have a finite number of roots.

- $h=3$ gives the polynomials
  x^2, $2x$, $x+1$, $x-1$, 3
  The corresponding equations have the roots $+1$, -1, 0.
  It follows that for $h=0, 1, 2, 3, \dots$ the roots can be completely enumerated, and hence are only denumerably infinite.

Heine-Borel theorem An abstract formulation of value in discussing periodic or oscillating functions. Given a set of intervals I_1, I_2, I_3... which may be open or closed sets and may or may not overlap, and which lie wholly within an interval or closed set L and

1. $L=I_1 \cup I_2 \cup I_3 \cup \dots \cup I_n \cup \dots$
2. Any $x \in L$ other than its end points lies also within at least one of the I_n for all n.

Then the theorem states that x is contained within the union of only a finite number of the I_n.

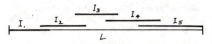

helix A curve in three dimensions, which cuts the generators of a cylinder or cone $f(x, y, z)$ at an angle which is constant or functionally dependent on z.

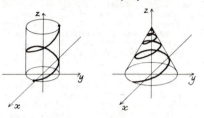

hemigroup Also semigroup. Any gruppoid $(X, *)$ for which the operation is associative; for example, the set of natural numbers with respect to addition.

heptagon *See* polygon.

hereditary property A property possessed by any entity or set of entities by virtue of its being a subset of a set that possesses those properties. Thus if S is the class of all number systems $\{\mathbb{N}, \mathbb{Z}, \mathbb{Q}, \dots\}$ then $\mathbb{Z} \in S$ and $\mathbb{Z}^+ \in \mathbb{Z} \Rightarrow \mathbb{Z}^+ \in S$.
Hence $\mathbb{Z}^+$ will possess properties which it has because it belongs to a subset $\mathbb{Z}$ of S.

Hermitian matrix A square matrix that remains unchanged if its elements are transposed and replaced by their complex conjugates, so that $A = \overline{A}^T$

$$A = \begin{pmatrix} a & b+\text{i}c \\ b-\text{i}c & d \end{pmatrix} \quad \overline{A}^T = \begin{pmatrix} a & b+\text{i}c \\ b-\text{i}c & d \end{pmatrix}$$

If $A = -\overline{A}^T$ the matrix is skew Hermitian.

$$A = \begin{pmatrix} a\text{i} & -b+\text{i}c \\ b+\text{i}c & d\text{i} \end{pmatrix} \quad -\overline{A}^T = \begin{pmatrix} -a\text{i} & b-\text{i}c \\ -b+\text{i}c & -d\text{i} \end{pmatrix}$$

Heron Or Hero. Alexandrian mathematician and inventor (fl. 100 A.D.) who described a simple reaction turbine and republished the formula known by his name. He showed that a reflected light ray follows the shortest possible path.

Heronian mean *See* Heronic triples.

Heronic triples Sets of numbers $\{a, b, c\}$ such that b is given by $[a+\sqrt{(ac)}+c]/3$. The term b is also called the Heronian mean of a and c. If two parallel planes a distance d apart cut a cone at right angles to its axis, the volume intercepted between them is the product of d and the Heronian mean of the areas of circles intercepted.

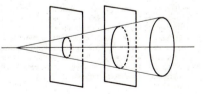

The second figure does not show a homeomorphism since the mapping is discontinuous and p of L maps on to both p' and p'' of M. A Mercator chart of the North Sea is a homeomorphism. A Mercator chart of the world is not.

homogeneous   Used of a function $f(x, y)$ of degree n for which

$$f(tx, ty) = t^n f(x, y)$$

That is, if the function has (or can be expanded into) separate terms, the sum of the powers of the variables in each term is equal to n. For this case the function may be written

$$a_0 x^n + a_1 x^{n-1} y + a_2 x^{n-2} y^2 + \ldots + a_n y^n$$

● $ax^2 + bxy + cy^2$

$$\frac{x^3 + y^3}{x - y}$$

Both of these are of degree 2.

The word is also used of separate expressions, for instance $3x^3$ and $2xyz$ are homogeneous terms of degree 3.
See also Markov chain.

homogeneous coordinates   1. Plane coordinates labelled by number triples (X, Y, Z), obtained by substituting

$$x = \frac{X}{Z} \quad y = \frac{Y}{Z}$$

into the equation relating (x, y) for points P on any given locus. Thus

$$x^2 + 2x + y^2 = 0 \tag{i}$$

gives $\qquad \left(\dfrac{X}{Z}\right)^2 + 2\dfrac{X}{Z} + \left(\dfrac{Y}{Z}\right)^2 = 0 \tag{ii}$

or $\qquad X^2 + 2XZ + Y^2 = 0 \tag{iii}$

which is homogeneous in X, Y, Z.
Any triple (X, Y, Z) where $Z \neq 0$ which satisfies (iii) corresponds to a unique finite point (x, y) on (i). Homogeneous equations of this form are used in projective geometry since, by taking $Z = 0$ for non-zero X, Y, points at infinity in the coordinate plane can be labelled.
2. A similar formulation transforms the labelling of points on a line by finite real numbers x to labelling by pairs of finite numbers (X_1, X_2), not both zero, such that $X_1 : X_2 = x$. The label $(a, 0)$ thus represents a point at infinity, but does so using real numbers.

homogeneous mesh gauge   *See* analytic projective geometry.

homography   Name sometimes given to an algebraic 1:1 correspondence between two sets X, Y. That is, if $x \in X$, $y \in Y$ then the function $f : x \mapsto y$ is algebraic. The general homography is given by

$$axy + bx + cy + d = 0 \ (bc \neq ad)$$

$$\text{or } f : x \mapsto \frac{bx + d}{ax + c}$$

homology   The relation between any pairs of elements in a homography.

homomorphism   A many-to-one mapping that preserves structure, particularly between groups. A map $\phi : G \mapsto H$ of a group G with operation ∗ into a group H with operation ∘, which for all $x, y \in G$, satisfies the condition $\phi(x \ast y) = \phi(x) \circ \phi(y)$.

● The set of logarithms, which for all $x \in \mathbf{R}$ maps $\mathbf{R} \mapsto \mathbf{R}^+$ by the relation $\phi(x) = e^x$. Since $e^{(x+y)} = e^x . e^y$ we get $\phi(x+y) = \phi(x) \times \phi(y)$.

A homomorphism which is one to one is called an isomorphism (as example above). Two isomorphic groups are equivalent to one other and have the same combination table or latin square. Thus we can perform multiplication in $\mathbf{R}$ by addition of logarithms.

homothetic transformation   A transformation with respect to a fixed point O, often called the centre of enlargement, such that configuration ABC ... becomes A′B′C′... and ratios are preserved.
The ratio $OA/OA' = OB/OB' = OC/OC' = \ldots$ is called the enlargement factor. The diagram shows homothetic triangles.

homotopic   Two paths between distinct points in any space, or two loops which start and finish at the same point, are homotopic if one can be deformed continuously into the other.

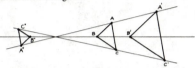

In (2) loop a can be deformed into loop b by shrinking it to a point and expanding again to coincide with b. The paths a and b in (3) and (4) are not homotopic.
See also connected.

horizon   The circle on the earth's surface formed by the points of contact of the tangents from any fixed point P above it. The line PH to the horizon is not horizontal, but has a dip angle θ dependent on the height h.

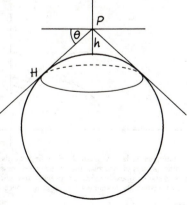

horizontal Any line or direction in or parallel to the tangent plane at any point P on the earth's surface.

horned sphere A topological construction in which two 'horns' arising from the surface of a sphere (which do not affect its topological properties) are split and fitted into one another as in the diagram.

The pairs of split horns are split again and arranged as before.

The process is continued indefinitely. The configuration remains a topological sphere on which any closed curve around any point may be collapsed to that point. The external space, however, is not simply connected. An elastic band B could not be removed from its horn unless the number of bifurcations were finite.

horn(like) angle Also cornicular angle. Translates the Gk. *keratoeides gonia*. Some Greek geometers (but not Euclid: see III, 16) held that an angle was intercepted between a circle and the tangent at any point, and hence that such angles could be ordered by magnitude. If so, they would be examples of actual infinitesimals. The confusion persisted till the 17th century, when Wallis described the configuration in terms of curvature.

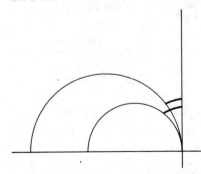

Huffmann code A method of coding words or other groups of symbols, so that the coded message is as short as possible and thus cheaper and quicker to transmit. By examining the language concerned probabilities are assigned to the occurrence of the letters, which are then arranged in order of likelihood. The code is then a systematic procedure for coding each letter with binary numerals so that the expected number of digits in each is a minimum. The code is not unique, and in any case could interchange 0 and 1 without effect.

Hull scale A method of transforming the z scores of the normal distribution curve to a measure given in points from 0 to 100. The formula is

$$\text{Hull points} = 14.28\, z + 50$$

It is often used for grading examination marks.

hunting A physical phenomenon associated with automatic control and regulation systems governed by servo mechanisms, in which the quantity controlled rises and falls periodically around the steady state value for which it is set. Such systems are described by linear differential equations and the hunting response, usually unwanted, should appear in their solution and thus be predicted. It was first observed by James Watt.

hydrodynamics *See* dynamics.

hydrostatics The study of fluids in static equilibrium, including the laws of fluid pressure, capillarity and surface tension, and the equilibrium of floating bodies.

hyperbola There are numerous equivalent formulations, of which three are commonly taken as definitions:

1. The section of a cone by a plane which is parallel to two of its generators, having two branches, one in each nappe of the cone.
2. The set of all coplanar points whose distance from a fixed point (the focus) of all coplanar points whose distance from a fixed point (the focus) is a constant multiple e of its distance from a fixed line (directrix) where $e > 1$. The quantity e is called the eccentricity. Both focus and directrix are in the plane of the points.
3. The curve given by the general equation

$$Ax^2 + Bxy + Cy^2 + Dx + Ey + F = 0 \text{ where}$$
$$B^2 - 4AC > 0.$$

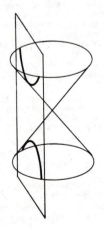

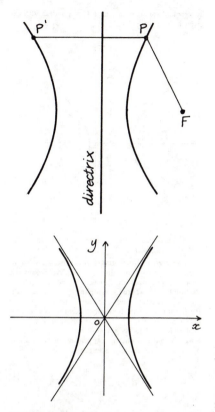

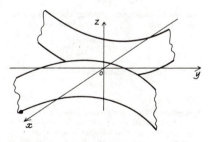

hyperbolic cylinder A cylinder whose cross-section is a hyperbola, having for suitable axes the equation

$$\frac{x^2}{a^2} - \frac{y^2}{b^2} = 1 \text{ for all } z.$$

hyperbolic functions These are defined as

$$\cosh\theta = \tfrac{1}{2}(e^\theta + e^{-\theta})$$
$$\sinh\theta = \tfrac{1}{2}(e^\theta - e^{-\theta})$$
$$\tanh\theta = \frac{\sinh\theta}{\cosh\theta}$$

From the definitions it follows that

$$\cosh^2\theta - \sinh^2\theta = 1$$
$$\frac{d\cosh\theta}{d\theta} = \sinh\theta$$
$$\frac{d\sinh\theta}{d\theta} = \cosh\theta$$

These and other expressions resemble those arising from the circular functions, except for differences of sign. If $x = \cosh\theta$ and $y = \sinh\theta$ we get $x^2 - y^2 = 1$, the equation to a rectangular hyperbola, corresponding to the circle $x^2 + y^2 = 1$, hence these functions are so named. The cofunctions $\operatorname{sech}\theta$, $\operatorname{csch}\theta$ and $\coth\theta$ are defined as for the circular functions, as are the inverses $\operatorname{arcosh}\theta$ etc. The set of functions can be used for integration by substitution.

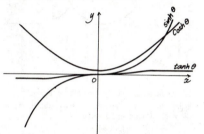

The curve $y = \cosh\theta$ is that taken by a flexible chain between two points, and is also called the catenary.

hyperbolic geometry The geometry of hyperbolic space, in which Euclid's Fifth Postulate is replaced by an axiom that infinitely many lines do not meet a given line when drawn through a point not on the line. The geometry was developed by Lobachevsky, but the name was given by Klein to contrast with Euclid's postulate that there is only one such line (Gk. *hyperbole*, an overshoot). The geometry corresponds to the first possibility of the Saccheri quadrilateral and can be realized as geodesics on a pseudosphere or by considering a closed plane region with a non-Pythagorean logarithmic distance function that sets any point on its perimeter at infinity.

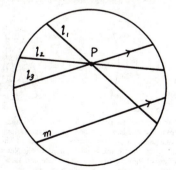

In the diagram line l_1 through P meets m, but lines $l_2, l_3, \ldots$ do not.

hyperbolic logarithms Name sometimes given to natural logarithms to the base e. If $x = \ln y$ then

$$y = e^x$$
$$= \cosh x + \sinh x$$

Here $\cosh x$ and $\sinh x$ are the hyperbolic functions.

hyperbolic paraboloid A non-central quadric and ruled surface given by

$$\frac{y^2}{b^2} - \frac{x^2}{a^2} - \frac{z^2}{c^2} = 0 \, (a, b, c \neq 0)$$

The cross-sections in planes parallel to $z = 0$ are hyperbolas degenerating into a pair of straight lines at $z = 0$, and parabolas in the x and y planes.

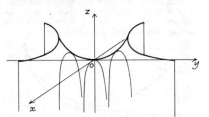

hyperbolic plane *See* hyperbolic geometry.

hyperbolic spiral The curve $r\theta = a$, the inverse of the Archimedean spiral $r = a\theta$.

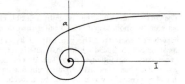

The curve spirals inwards to the origin as θ increases, and has an asymptote parallel to and a units from the base line.

hyperboloid of one sheet The quadric surface given by

$$\frac{x^2}{a^2} + \frac{y^2}{b^2} - \frac{z^2}{c^2} = 1$$

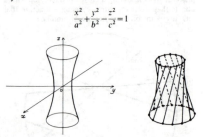

Planes parallel to the xy plane cut the surface in ellipses if $a \neq b$. If $a = b$ it becomes a hyperboloid of revolution. It is a ruled surface with a set of linear generators, and for this reason is used for the Venturi profiles of cooling towers, since these can then be constructed with straight reinforcing rods.

See minimal surface.

hyperboloid of two sheets The quadric surface given by

$$\frac{x^2}{a^2} - \frac{y^2}{b^2} - \frac{z^2}{c^2} = 1$$

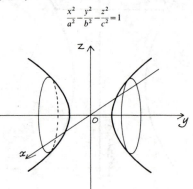

Its shape is best seen by allowing y and then z to take the value zero.

hypergeometric distribution A statistical distribution given by using a form of the hypergeometric series as a generating function. It corresponds to Bernoulli trials where the sampling is conducted without replacement, and therefore approximates to the binomial distribution only when the total sample taken is less than 5% of the population. If not, the probability of success p cannot be taken as constant for each trial and does not appear in the calculation. The probability of r successes is given by

$$P(r) = \frac{\binom{N-R}{n-r}\binom{R}{r}}{\binom{N}{n}}$$

Where N is the population, n the sample, and R the original number of 'successes' included in N.

hypergeometric series A geometric series of the form

$$1 + x + x^2 + x^3 + \ldots$$

modified by coefficients involving the positive non-zero constants a, b, c. Its general form is

$$1 + \frac{ab}{c}x + \frac{a(a+1)b(b+1)x^2}{c(c+1)2!} + $$

$$+ \frac{a(a+1)(a+2)b(b+1)(b+2)x^3}{c(c+1)(c+2)3!} + \ldots$$

The series converges for $x < 1$.

hyperplane The equation to a plane $ax + by + cz = d$ can be extended to any number of variables $ax + by + cz + dw + \ldots = r$ and is then said to represent a hyperplane, although it can no longer be physically realized.

hyperspace The abstract and mathematically valid extension of the concept of spaces of one, two and three dimensions, defined as the set of all ordered n-tuples $(x_1, x_2, x_3, x_4 \ldots)$ for $n > 3$. Such a space is made metric by defining a distance function, either by extending the Pythagoras relation to become

$$[D(x,y)]^2 = (x_1 - y_1)^2 + \ldots + (x_n - y_n)^2$$

where $x = (x_1, x_2 \ldots x_n)$, $y = (y_1, y_2, \ldots y_n)$, or otherwise. Theorems in n-spaces give many new insights into mathematics, and were studied by Cayley, Grassmann, Riemann and others.

hypersphere   Since the equation $x^2 + y^2 + z^2 = a^2$ is represented by a sphere in three-dimensional space, the hypersphere is represented by equations such as

$$x^2 + y^2 + z^2 + w^2 + \ldots = a^2$$

from which analagous mathematical properties can be deduced, although these cannot be physically realized.

hypocycloid   *See* epicycloid. Here the generating circle of radius a rolls inside the base circle. The equations are obtained from those of the epicycloid by taking a as negative

$$x = (b-a)\cos\theta + b\cos\frac{(b-a)}{a}\theta$$

$$y = (b-a)\sin\theta - b\sin\frac{(b-a)}{a}\theta$$

The four-cusp hypocycloid is the astroid.

hypothesis   From Gk., a foundation, and hence a supposition on which a logical structure is erected.

1. A tentative empirical proposal, often made the basis of a fully developed empirical theory, as Darwin's hypothesis of spontaneous small mutations.

2. In mathematics, usually a statement made merely as a starting point for logical argument, on the tacit assumption that it can be rejected or modified. It is often the protasis of a proposition, as in 'If ABC is an equilateral triangle, then ...'

3. In statistics, it is any provisional statement whose truth is unknown, concerning the probability distribution of given populations. Usually we have data drawn by sampling from the populations, and wish to test the evidence for one hypothesis rather than another.

See alternative hypothesis, null hypothesis.

hypothesis test   Sometimes taken as equivalent to a significance test, although it is more properly applied to statistical investigations where the null and alternative hypotheses are considered.

I

icosahedron *See* polyhedron.

ideal If S is any subgroup (submodule) of a ring R, such that the product of any element $x \in S$ and an element $r \in R$ is in S, then S is said to be an ideal of R. There are three cases which depend on the nature of the product operation $\otimes$

    (i) $r \otimes x \in S$
    (ii) $x \otimes r \in S$
    (iii) Both $r \otimes x$ and $x \otimes r$ are in S

These three give left, right and two-sided ideals.

ideal line Also ideal point. Any line or point, such as lines at infinity, which are not empirically realizable.

idempotent (Lat. *idem*, the same) A term describing any matrix A such that $A^2 = A$, and hence $A^k = A$ for all k.

● $A = \begin{pmatrix} \frac{1}{2} & \frac{1}{2} \\ \frac{1}{2} & \frac{1}{2} \end{pmatrix} \quad A^2 = \begin{pmatrix} \frac{1}{2} & \frac{1}{2} \\ \frac{1}{2} & \frac{1}{2} \end{pmatrix}$

identical Although Wittgenstein wrote 'to say of two things that they are identical is nonsense', the word can properly be used in context. For example, to say that $(x + y)^2$ and $x^2 + 2xy + y^2$ are identically equal means that they take the same value for all real x, y. The two solutions

$$\int \frac{dx}{\sqrt{(x^2 + 1)}} = \operatorname{arsinh} x + c$$

$$\int \frac{dx}{\sqrt{(x^2 + 1)}} = \ln \{ x + \sqrt{(x^2 + 1)} \} + c$$

are identical because one can be written as the other, and so on.

identity 1. An equation true for all values of its subjects, for example $(x + y)^2 = x^2 + 2xy + y^2$ ($x, y \in \mathbb{R}$). Some textbooks replace the equals sign by $\equiv$ and read 'is identically equal to'.
2. Describes an element I in a set with a binary operation $*$ such that for any element x, $I * x = x * I = x$.

● $3 + 0 = 3$ (addition of integers)
     $\binom{2143}{1234} = 2143$ (composition of permutations)

See also additive identity, multiplicative identity.

identity function If for any function f, $f(x) = x$ for all $x \in D$ where D is the domain of f, then f is called an identity function

● $f : x \mapsto \dfrac{x^2}{x} \quad x \neq 0$

identity transformation A geometrical transformation that leaves all points in space unchanged, or any abstract equivalent of this. It is represented, for n variables, by the $n \times n$ unit matrix. Thus

$$\begin{pmatrix} 1 & 0 \\ 0 & 1 \end{pmatrix} \begin{pmatrix} x \\ y \end{pmatrix} = \begin{pmatrix} x' \\ y' \end{pmatrix}$$

gives $x = x'$, $y = y'$, leaving the vector (x, y) unchanged.

ideogram A symbol which in writing replaces a complete concept, as in written Chinese. Our numeric symbols 0, 1, 2, 3 ... 9 are ideograms.

iff A convenient abbreviation for 'if and only if', corresponding to the symbol $\Leftrightarrow$ used when p implies q and q implies p. It must be distinguished from the one-way implication $p \Rightarrow q$ or the form of words 'if' or 'if – then'. Compare:

> If triangles ABC, DEF are congruent, then their angles are equal.
> Triangles ABC, DEF are equiangular, if their corresponding pairs of sides are in the same ratio.

See also implication, logical implication.

if – then A one-way relation symbolized by $\rightarrow$, $\supset$ or preferably $\Rightarrow$. Then $p \Rightarrow q$ can be read as 'if p then q'. Equivalent expressions are 'p implies q', 'q is necessary for p', 'p is sufficient for q' and 'p only if q' This may be seen by taking

> p = triangle T is equilateral
> q = triangle T is isosceles

If the order of p and q is changed the statement becomes false.
See also iff, implication.

i, j, k 1. Set of symbols used to denote unit vectors along the x, y, z axes in orthogonal cartesian coordinates, so that

$$\mathbf{i} . \mathbf{i} = \mathbf{j} . \mathbf{j} = \mathbf{k} . \mathbf{k} = 1$$
$$\mathbf{i} . \mathbf{j} = \mathbf{j} . \mathbf{k} = \mathbf{k} . \mathbf{i} = 0$$
$$\mathbf{i} \times \mathbf{i} = \mathbf{j} \times \mathbf{j} = \mathbf{k} \times \mathbf{k} = 0$$
$$\mathbf{i} \times \mathbf{j} = -\mathbf{j} \times \mathbf{i} = \mathbf{k}, \ \mathbf{j} \times \mathbf{k} = -\mathbf{k} \times \mathbf{j} = \mathbf{i}, \ \mathbf{k} \times \mathbf{i} = -\mathbf{i} \times \mathbf{k} = \mathbf{j}$$

2. In Hamilton's quaternions, which extended complex numbers of the form $a + ib$ to three-dimensional coordinates using expressions of the form $ai + bj + ck + d$, the coefficients are defined $i^2 = j^2 = k^2 = -1$.

ill-conditioned equations Any set of equations with constant coefficients whose solutions show big numerical differences corresponding to small changes in one or more of the coefficients (particularly arising from rounding of procedures). In physical applications they correspond to the equilibrium of unstable systems, such as frameworks which distort when subject to small changes of loading.
Graphically they are represented by nearly parallel lines or planes whose intersections are displaced considerably by very small changes of gradient.

image In any function or transformation that maps an entity x to a corresponding entity x', x' is said to be the image of x, and x the source of x'. Alternatively, in any binary relation $x \mathrel{R} y$, y is the image of x. If, for any relation, $x \in X$ and $y \in Y$, then Y is the image set of X. X and Y are also called the domain and range of the relation or function.

imaginary When Descartes solved quadratic equations by a geometrical construction of secant and circle, he found that for some equations the proposed secant failed to cut the circle. He then remarked that any roots were 'imaginary'. This name has unfortunately been retained in discussing complex numbers. *See* complex number, Argand diagram.

implication There is an ambiguity in use between logical implication and the relations $\Rightarrow$ and $\Leftrightarrow$ which are often read as 'implies' and 'implies and is implied by'. These are better termed 'conditional' and 'biconditional' relations, and read 'if ... then ...' and 'if and only if'.

94

Implication can then be taken as a relation between propositions in which the consequent follows logically from the antecedent, as a conclusion is logically deduced from a preliminary hypothesis. Thus the proposition $p \Leftrightarrow q$ implies the proposition $p \Rightarrow q$ but $p \Rightarrow q$ does not imply $p \Leftrightarrow q$. This is shown by the truth table

p	q	$p \Rightarrow q$	$p \Leftrightarrow q$
T	T	T	T
T	F	F	F
F	T	T	F
F	F	T	T

Here $p \Rightarrow q$ is true whenever $p \Leftrightarrow q$ is true, but the reverse is not so.

implicit definition One in which the term to be defined is given only in relation to other terms whose definition is given or known. Thus a circle may be defined explicitly as the set of all coplanar points equidistant from a point in the same plane, or implicitly as the intersection of a plane and a sphere.

implicit differentiation If two variables are related by an implicit function, the derivative of one with respect to the other can be carried out without expressing the dependent variable explicitly in terms of the other.

● $x^2 + y^2 = 4e^y$
Differentiating both sides with respect to x, using the chain rule,

$$2x + 2y\frac{dy}{dx} = 4e^y \cdot \frac{dy}{dx}$$

That is $\dfrac{dy}{dx} = \dfrac{2x}{4e^y - 2y}$

implicit function (*Compare* explicit function). An equation of the form $f(y, x, z, w, \ldots) = 0$ is said to define y implicitly in terms of $x, z, w, \ldots$, e.g. $2x^2 + 3xy + 5y^2 = 0$.
It may often be difficult or even impossible to express y explicitly in terms of the other variables.

implicit relation Any relation between entities that does not give the direct or explicit relation between them

● $x = y^2$ is explicit
$x^2 + y^2 = a^2$ is implicit

impossible The phrase 'which is impossible' is used by Euclid to signal a contradiction in proof by *reductio ad absurdum*, as Euclid III, 18.

improper integral If a function $f(x)$ has discontinuities in the interval $a \le x \le b$, then the corresponding integral $\int_a^b f(x)dx$ is improper. There are three possibilities:

1. Either a or b (or both) can increase without limit as in $\int_1^\infty e^x \, dx$
2. The function can increase without limit at one or both end points of the interval $[a,b]$, as in

$$\int_1^2 \frac{1}{x-2} dx$$

3. The function can increase without limit at one or more points within the interval $[a,b]$, as in $\int_1^3 \dfrac{1}{x-2} dx$. Such an integral can often be split and dealt with as 2 above.

impulse Defined as the product of a constant force F and the time for which it acts, and equal to the change in momentum δp produced

$$Ft = \delta p$$

Given generally by

$$\int F \, dt$$

the relation allows the computation of the very high forces produced in collisions, which destroy momentum over a very small time interval.

incidence See axioms of incidence.

incidence matrix An $n \times m$ matrix whose rows may correspond to the nodes or arcs of a graph or network, and whose columns may correspond to arcs or regions.

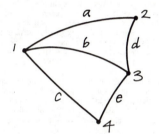

	arc				
	a	b	c	d	e
node 1	1	1	1	0	0
2	1	0	0	1	0
3	0	1	0	1	1
4	0	0	1	0	1

$$M = \begin{pmatrix} 1 & 1 & 1 & 0 & 0 \\ 1 & 0 & 0 & 1 & 0 \\ 0 & 1 & 0 & 1 & 1 \\ 0 & 0 & 1 & 0 & 1 \end{pmatrix}$$

table of connections   incidence matrix

Two incidence matrices are equivalent if the rows or columns of one is a permutation of the rows or columns of the other. Graphs or networks with equivalent matrices are isomorphic.

inclusion A set A, which may have only one member or none, is said to be included in B if every member of A is also a member of B. Inclusion is denoted by $\subset$, so that the relation is written $A \subset B$ or $A \subseteq B$ if $A = B$ is possible. A is also said to be a *subset* of B, and 0 is a subset of all sets.

inclusive See vel.

incommensurable Used of two quantities that have no common measure, so that no multiple of one can exactly equal a multiple of another. For example, one million diagonals of a square are more than 1 414 213 but less than 1 414 214 of its sides. It can be shown that this multiplication continues indefinitely,

and hence the diagonal and side of a square are incommensurable. If one of these quantities is taken as the unit and assigned the measure 1, the other is assigned a number said to be irrational; that is, not expressible as a ratio of integers. The statement that a number is irrational is equivalent to the statement that two quantities are incommensurable. Thus π is irrational, and the circumference and diameter of a circle are incommensurable.
See irrational number.

inconsistent equations A system of equations is inconsistent if there is no solution for the set as a whole.

The system $\left.\begin{array}{r}x+2y=3\\2x+4y=7\end{array}\right\}$

is inconsistent. Inconsistent linear equations in two or three variables are represented by parallel lines or planes with no finite intersections.

increasing sequence A sequence $\{a_n\}$ is said to be increasing if $a_n \leqslant a_{n+1}$ for all n.
If $a_n < a_{n+1}$ it is a strictly increasing sequence.

increment Any finite change in the value of a numerical quantity. Although general, it is usually used in the context of changes in variables, either positive or negative, which are small relative to their absolute values. In the delta notation, δx or Δx is used to express a change from the value x to $(x+\delta x)$, important in discussion of approximations and limiting values.
The differential notation $\mathrm{d}x$ is often used in applied mathematics for δx but in pure mathematics calls for a definition of differential. Often h is used instead of δx to avoid confusion, but has the disadvantage of not being visually related to the quantities concerned.

indefinite integral An integral on which no limits are given. The integral function $F(x)=\int f(x)\mathrm{d}x$ is called the indefinite integral of $f(x)$. Integration as the inverse of differentiation always yields indefinite integrals.

independent 1. Of events, A and B are said to be independent if the occurrence of one is in no way affected by or affects the occurrence of the other, or if the probability of A conditional on the occurrence of B is equal to the probability of A. That is $p(A|B)=p(A) \Rightarrow A$ and B are independent. Any event in a sequence of independent events is not affected by the outcome of any preceding event, and does not affect the outcome of any succeeding event.
2. Of variables. In any formula of the form $y=f(x)$ where a value of x may be selected or taken at random from the domain of the function, x is called the independent variable, y being the dependent variable. Where the inverse function exists the distinction is a convention of notation, but if the function models a physical situation the dependence is equivalent to causation. In plotting cartesian graphs, it is usual to allot the horizontal axis to the independent variable. See also response variable.
3. Of vectors. See linear dependence.

independent equations Any set of n equations in which one cannot be expressed in terms of the others.
● $3x+2y=4$ but not $x-y=3$
   $x-y=6$ $2x-2y=6$

indeterminate equation(s) Any equation(s) for which there is an infinite solution set. Thus $2x-y=0$ has the solution set $\{(x,y):x=\lambda, y=2\lambda\}$ for all real values of λ. In the special case where only integral values are permitted for the coefficients and the solution set of the equations, they are usually called Diophantine equations (Diophantos of Alexandria, c. 250 A.D., who proposed number problems equivalent to such equations).

indeterminate form Any expression which reduces to a quantity which is not defined in mathematics, such as $0/0$, $0°$ and so on. They may arise when functions are given values for which they are not defined, as

$$\frac{\sin(x+h)-\sin x}{h}h=0$$

and can often be expressed as limits, which in this example would be

$$\lim_{h\to 0}\frac{\sin(x+h)-\sin x}{h}$$

This has the value $\cos x$ and is no longer indeterminate.
Also called undetermined forms.

index 1. The index notation uses numbers written as subscripts or superscripts, as in x^2 or x_2. In the superior position an index n, where n is an integer, is defined as the product of n factors each x. See index laws. Superior indices are also used for contravariant coordinates.
2. A sequence of terms is said to be indexed, with respect to time for instance, if the successive values $x_1, x_2, x_3 \ldots$ correspond to times $t_1, t_2, t_3 \ldots$
3. Any conventional measure taken as a parameter, usually of an economic or social situation, as share price index, cost of living index.
4. An indexing symbol is any one used to identify terms in a set, as $\{x_1, x_2, x_3 \ldots\}$.

index laws The rules satisfied by the powers of given quantities under the binary operations multiplication and division, derived initially from the definition
$$a^n = a.a.a\ldots \text{ to } n \text{ factors } (n\in \mathbb{N})$$
It follows that
$$a^n \times a^m = a^{n+m}$$
$$a^n \div a^n = a^{n-m}$$
$$(a^n)^m = a^{nm}$$

Definitions for fractional, negative and zero powers can be formulated so that the laws hold good, and a^x ($x\in \mathbb{R}$) can be defined as a Cauchy sequence of rationals. If $y=a^x$ the inverse definition $x=\log_a y$ leads to the relation
$$\log pq = \log p + \log q$$
In general a^z ($z\in \mathbb{C}$) can be defined using Demoivre's theorem and hence the ordinary index laws appear as special cases.

indirect common tangent Also called transverse common tangent. The common tangent to a pair of non-intersecting circles which divides the line joining their centres internally.

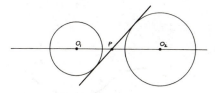

The ratio $O_1P:PO_2$ is the ratio of the radii of the circles, and P is one of the centres of similitude.

indirect isometry　*See* isometry.

indirect proof　A result or theorem which is not in the logical form of direct proof $p \Rightarrow q$ but in a form that is equivalent to it, for example, the contrapositive $\sim q \Rightarrow \sim p$.

● The theorem 'If n^2 is odd, n is odd' can be proved by showing that if n is not odd then n^2 is not odd. (Let $n = 2m$; then $n^2 = 4m^2$ which is not odd)

indirect reduction　A process in logic, equivalent to Aristotle's *reductio ad absurdum*, which is the usual term used in mathematics.

indivisibles　Any continuous quantity in mathematics can be subdivided indefinitely towards its limit zero. It does not of course follow that a physical entity of any kind can be subject to this process: the decision is empirical and not logical, so that physical indivisibles may possibly exist.

inductive definition　Any definition based on the properties of accumulated examples, as distinct from an analytic or axiomatic definition.

inductive inference　A conclusion which is inferred from a finite number of cases, but which does not follow *necessarily* from them. A stock example is the statement that the sun will rise tomorrow because it always has done in the past. The inference is useful in mathematics in suggesting conjectures for investigation. *See* four colour problem, proof by induction.

inequality　A binary relationship which has two forms:
1. indeterminate, denoted by $\neq$ and merely denying equality, as in $\sin(A + B) \neq \sin A + \sin B$ $(A, B \neq n\pi)$;
2. an irreflexive, antisymmetric, transitive relation, denoted by $<$ or $>$ stating that the first element is less than or greater than the second. If $<$ or $>$ replaces the equals sign in an equation, it becomes an inequality and may have a solution. The symbols $<$ and $>$ may be combined with $=$ to give $\leqslant$, $\geqslant$ read as 'less (greater) than or equal to'.
See also ordering relation.

inertia　More properly inertial mass. The property of matter that resists change of motion, measured by the force required to accelerate it if at rest or slow it down if in motion. It is numerically equal to the gravitational mass that determines the force between massive bodies postulated by Newton.

inertial framework　Any coordinate system S' is said to be an inertial framework with respect to another system S, if it is at rest or only in uniform rectilinear motion relative to S. The term 'framework' arises from Einstein, who defined such a system in terms of idealized rigid rods.

inference　The process of forming a conclusion by logically valid steps from given premises. The premises are then said to *imply* the conclusion. *See* implication.

inferior limit　Synonym for lower limit. *See* limit.

infimum　Synonym for greatest lower bound, written *inf*. Not standard.

infinite　Adjective. *See* infinity and infinitely many. If the elements of any set may be subjected to a counting process which proceeds without limit it is said to be denumerably infinite, as with the prime numbers

$$2 \quad 3 \quad 5 \quad 7 \; \ldots$$
$$\downarrow \quad \downarrow \quad \downarrow \quad \downarrow$$
$$1 \quad 2 \quad 3 \quad 4 \; \ldots$$

which may be counted or indexed without limit. If such a counting procedure cannot be established, as with the real numbers, the set is said to be non-denumerably infinite.

infinite group　1. Any group whose elements can be generated or numbered indefinitely, as the group $(\mathbb{Z}, +)$ of integers with respect to addition.
2. Any group whose elements are denumerably or non-denumerably infinite, as $(\mathbb{R}, +)$ the group of reals with respect to addition.

infinite integral　*See* improper integral.

infinitely many　A phrase used in mathematics of any objects which do not, either actually or in principle, result in a finite number when subject to a counting procedure or for which a counting procedure is not possible, as for numbers or points on a line interval. It should not, within mathematics, be used for very large numbers not definite or countable in practice, such as the grains of sand in a desert.

infinite product　The multiplicative equivalent of an infinite series. The product Πa_n is given by $\prod_{n=1}^{\infty} a_n = $
$a_1 . a_2 . a_3 \ldots$
An example is the Wallis product
$$\pi/2 = \tfrac{2}{1} . \tfrac{2}{3} . \tfrac{4}{3} . \tfrac{4}{5} . \tfrac{6}{5} . \tfrac{6}{7} . \tfrac{8}{7} . \tfrac{8}{9} \ldots$$

infinite roots　One root of a polynomial equation will increase without limit as the coefficient of the highest power tends to zero.

● $0.0001x^2 + 3x + 2 = 0$ has one very large root. and nearly coincides with $3x + 2$ in the region of the origin.

See also asymptote.

infinite series　A series consisting of a denumerably infinite sequence of terms.

● The sequence $a, a^2, a^3, \ldots$ gives the series $a + a^2 + a^3 + \ldots$

infinite set　Any set whose elements cannot be subjected to a terminating counting procedure that establishes its finite cardinal number.

infinitesimal calculus　A former name for analysis, usually held to comprise differential and integral calculus. The term arose after the early work of Newton and Leibnitz, before the modern concept of limit was established. The methods were explored in terms of 'infinitely small' changes in the values of variables, thought of as actual infinitesimals. These have returned to mathematics as entities in nonstandard analysis and sometimes occur in a discussion of the foundations of mathematics.

infinitesimals   The early analysts discussed differentiation and integration in terms of quantities taken to be less than any given quantity, eventually called infinitesimals. These were, tacitly rather than explicitly, held to be ordered in magnitude and hence to have ratios one to the other. Their use was supplanted by the later concept of limit. On the analogy of, say, $2 = \lim\limits_{x \to 1} \dfrac{x^2 - 1}{x - 1}$ a modern discussion (Tall 1980) *defines* an infinitesimal as $\lim\limits_{x \to 0} f(x)$ where $f(0) = 0$.
See also indivisibles, order of magnitude.

infinitude of primes   The theorem that the set of all primes has no largest member. Given in Euclid IX, 20, as 'prime numbers are more than any given multitude of prime numbers', and proved using line segments each measured by an arbitrary unit of length.

infinity   From Lat. *infinitus*, not finished.
1. Actual infinity. A concept tacitly assumed in many mathematical statements, as in $x^2 \geqslant 0$ for *all* real x. (*See* transfinite numbers.)
2. Potential infinity. A concept implied by any mathematical process, such as generating terms in a sequence or subdividing a line, that can proceed beyond any assigned finite limit, usually denoted by $\to \infty$, read 'approaches or tends to infinity'.
3. In the complex plane *the* point at infinity is defined as the point corresponding to the origin under the transformation $z \to \dfrac{1}{z}$.
4. Points in the cartesian plane labelled by the homogeneous coordinates (X, Y, Z) 'tend to infinity' as $Z \to 0$ so that the cartesian coordinates $(X, Y, 0)$ *define* a 'point at infinity' (which itself corresponds to a direction line along which a measure can increase without limit).
5. The line $Z = 0$ of the projective plane in homogeneous coordinates defines the 'line at infinity' in the Euclidean plane.

inflectional tangent   A tangent drawn at a point of inflection, at which it meets the curve in more than two coincident points, i.e. is the limit of a secant cutting the curve in three or a larger odd number of points.

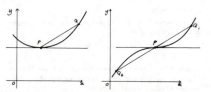

inflection (inflexion) point   A point (x_1, y_1) on any curve $y = f(x)$, such that there exists an open interval $a < x_1 < b$ containing x_1 where the derivative $f'(x)$ is increasing on one side of x_1 and decreasing on the other. If $y = f(x)$ and the second derivative is continuous at x_1, then x_1, if it exists, satisfies $f''(x_1) = 0$.

98

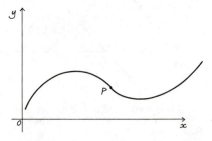

information theory   The mathematical analysis of the problem of transmitting signals or messages by any physical means. The word 'message' is taken in a very general sense, e.g. the pulse of current along a wire when a bell push is operated is a 'message', which may or may not satisfactorily activate the bell. Typical problems are analysing the result of extraneous signals or 'noise' on the required signals, or the construction of the most economical code for transmitting a message with the least number of distinct signal elements in the least possible time. Also called communication theory.
See Huffmann code.

initial conditions   When quantities are related by equations, the values of any constants that appear in the solutions will depend on the known values of the variables at a given point or points. Commonly used of differential equations at the instant $t = 0$.

initial term   In a sequence expressed as a general formula or a difference equation, the initial term (or terms) gives the starting values from which an actual sequence may be generated.

● The Fibonacci sequence
$a_n = a_{n-2} + a_{n+1}$
is generated as $1, 2, 3, 5, 8, \ldots$
for the two initial terms $a_1 = 1$, $a_2 = 2$.

initial value problem   Arises in solving differential equations. An equation $y' = f(x, y)$ can have a solution $f(x)$ such that it satisfies the initial value conditions $f(x_0) = y_0$.
See initial conditions.

injective   A function f is injective (or an injection) into Y if not more than one element of its domain X corresponds to any one image element contained in a subset of Y. The term 'one-one into' is also used.

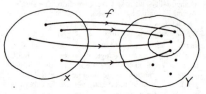

See also bijection.

inner product   Same as scalar product, but more frequently used when the vectors have more than three elements
$$\mathbf{a} = (a_1, a_2, a_3, a_4 \ldots) \quad \mathbf{b} = (b_1, b_2, b_3, b_4 \ldots)$$
$$\mathbf{a} \cdot \mathbf{b} = (a_1 b_1 + a_2 b_2 + \ldots)$$

Such a product cannot be put in the form $a.b = ab\cos\theta$ as for directed line segments in space.

input 1. Any signal fed into a gate whose operation is defined by a Boolean function.
2. Data, which reach a data processing system from a source outside itself, prior to transformation by the system.
3. Used generally of any form of energy, such as mechanical work, fed into a machine for obtaining an output in a different form, such as electrical energy.
4. By analogy with 3, the term input/output is sometimes used in discussing the values taken by functions or sets of equations.
5. The result of an input in any of the senses given is called *output*.
See function box or machine.

instant A difficult concept involving time, imperfectly abstracted from the intuitive concept of a time interval. Zeno's paradox of the arrow arises from the attempt to think of an instant as an interval of duration zero. For mathematical purposes the word is best defined in context, as in the value of x at an instant, or the 'instantaneous' position of a moving configuration A. ⋅
Then, using limits, if $x = x(t)$, the value of x at any instant t_0 is $\lim_{t \to t_0} x(t)$.
This definition need not correspond to any empirical fact in physics, in which any operational definition of duration might possibly require time intervals to be discrete.

instantaneous centre Used of rotation. If the point about which a body rotates is not fixed, and if $\dot{\mathbf{r}}$ or $\dfrac{d\mathbf{r}}{dt}$ is the velocity of any point P whose position vector is $\mathbf{r}$ then the instantaneous centre at any time t_0 is the point where $\dot{\mathbf{r}} = 0$.

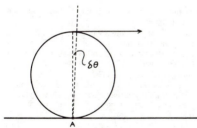

For a rolling disc the instantaneous centre is the point of contact A.
See tachnode.

integer A member of the set
$$\mathbb{Z} = \{\ldots -3, -2, -1, 0, 1, 2, 3 \ldots\}$$
$\mathbb{Z}$ is often divided into three subsets, positive integers, negative integers and zero. Integers can be defined formally as ordered pairs of natural numbers of the form (a, b). Given that the addition symbol in $(a + n)$ means 'form the nth successor to the natural number a', as in $5 + 3 = 8$, and $\times$ means 'continued addition', we can define new operations $+$, $-$, $\times$

between pairs as
$$(a, b) + (c, d) = (a + c), (b + d)$$
$$(a, b) - (c, d) = (a, b) + (d, c)$$
$$= (a + d), (b + c)$$
$$(a, b) \times (c, d) = (ac + bd), (ad + bc)$$

It can now be shown that $(a, 0)$ has the properties of the integer ^+a (positive a) and $(0, a)$ the properties of ^-a (negative a) as usually described.
See also algebraic integer, Gaussian integer.

integrable Used of any function $f(x)$ for which the symbol $\int f(x)dx$ can be given a meaning, either generally or over an interval containing x. The term is also applied to functions of more than one variable.

integral (n.) The result of finding the limiting value of the sum of an infinite series of quantities each of which differs from zero by less than any arbitrarily assigned small quantity. Denoted by the symbol $\int$, a modification of S used by the early analysts for summation, the concept is given precise formulation by Riemann or Lebesgue integration.
See also antidifferentiation.

integral (adj.) 1. Equivalent to 'whole' as in 'whole numbers', as in 'An expression in x can be true for integral values of x'.
2. As in 'integral calculus', the study of integration as the inverse of differentiation, or integral transform as transforms defined by integrals. Integral function is also used as a synonym for entire function.

integral calculus The branch of mathematics concerned with calculating areas, volumes, masses and other geometrical and physical quantities involving regions of vector space in one or more dimensions. The basic process divides the region into small parts and considers an overall quantity, the integral, as a sum or limit of a sum, as in Simpson's method or the Riemann sum. The Greek 'method of exhaustion' was in effect an integration process, but the methods did not develop as a calculus until integrals were related to derivatives in the 17th/18th century.

integral curves The set of curves given when the solutions of a differential equation $dy/dx = f(x, y)$ are plotted graphically.

integral domain A commutative ring with unity containing no divisors of zero. Such a ring has the same structure and many of the properties of the ring of integers $\mathbb{Z}$. It is a commutative group with respect to addition and also with the commutative operation of multiplication with identity 1, although in general it does not contain multiplicative inverses.

● The Gaussian integers $a + ib$; $a, b \in \mathbb{Z}$.
The ring of even integers $\{2n; n \in \mathbb{Z}\}$ is not an integral domain since it does not contain unity.
See also field, quotient field, ordered integral domain.

integral index An index or exponent n where $n \in \mathbb{Z}$, as in x^2, x^{-3}, x^0.

integral programming Linear programming in which the variables can only take integral values, as in many productive processes.

integral test A form of comparison test for the convergence of an infinite series. If a function f is positive and monotonically decreasing for all $x \geqslant 1$, the corresponding series

$$\sum_{n=1}^{\infty} a_n = f(1) + f(2) + f(3) + \dots$$

converges if $\int_1^{\infty} f(x)\,dx$ exists.

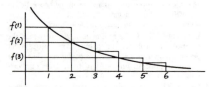

The diagram shows the intuitive basis for the theorem, and

$$\sum_{n=1}^{\infty} ne^{-n} \text{ converges because } \int_1^{\infty} xe^x\,dx = \frac{2}{e}$$

integrand   Any function which is being integrated.

integrating factor   Any function which, multiplying both sides of the differential equation $P\dfrac{dy}{dx} + Q = 0$, turns the left-hand side into an exact differential, that is, one which is the derivative of a function $f(x, y)$.

● $3y + x\dfrac{dy}{dx} = \cos x$

This has the I.F. x^2 since

$$3x^2 y + x^3 \frac{dy}{dx} = \frac{d}{dx}(x^3 y)$$

Then $\dfrac{d}{dx}(x^3 y) = x^2 \cos x$ which can easily be integrated by parts.

integration   The theory and processes of evaluating definite and indefinite integrals; for example, Riemann or Lebesque integration or algorithmic methods such as integration by parts or by substitution. Numerical integration discusses methods for obtaining values for definite integrals to any degree of approximation.
See also trapezoidal rule.

integration by parts   A method that arises from the product rule for differentiation.
Since $\dfrac{d(uv)}{dx} = u\dfrac{dv}{dx} + v\dfrac{du}{dx}$ we get

$$\int u\frac{dv}{dx}\,dx = uv - \int v\frac{du}{dx}\,dx + \text{constant}.$$

It is also written as

$$\int fg\,dx = f\int g\,dx - \int \left[\int g\,dx \right]\frac{df}{dx}\,dx + \text{constant}$$

● Taking $\sin x = f$ and $x = g$

$$\int x \sin x\,dx = x(-\cos x) - \int (-\cos x).1.dx$$
$$= \sin x - x\cos x + \text{constant}.$$

integration by substitution   Also known as integration by change of variable, arising from the chain

rule for derivatives. In Leibnitz notation, if $\dfrac{dy}{dx} = f(x)$

$$\frac{dy}{du} = \frac{dy}{dx}\cdot\frac{dx}{du} = f(x)\frac{dx}{du}$$

$$y = \int f(x)\frac{dx}{du}\,du$$

● $\displaystyle\int \sin^3\theta \cos\theta\,d\theta$

$$= \int u^3 \frac{du}{d\theta}\,d\theta \text{ if } \sin\theta = u$$

$$= \int u^3\,du$$

$$= \tfrac{1}{4}u^4 + c$$

$$= \tfrac{1}{4}\sin^4\theta + c$$

There are many standard substitutions covering a wide range of functions.

intension   Used in discussing definitions. The intension of a concept is the set of all qualities by which it is recognized, as 'triangle', which is plane, closed, has three straight sides, three angles. Compare extension of the concept, where is here the set of all entities recognized as triangles.

intercept   1. Part of a line or plane cut off by intersecting lines or planes.
2. Specifically, the intercepts on the x and y axes of $\dfrac{x}{a} + \dfrac{y}{b} = 1$ are a and b, the values corresponding to $y = 0$ and $x = 0$.

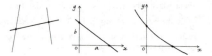

interior   Used of any point or line within any closed region.

interior point   1. Any point inside a closed curve or configuration of lines.
2. Any real point whose real polar line with respect to a conic has no real intersection with the conic.

intermediate value theorem   If the function f is continuous on the closed interval $a \leqslant x \leqslant b$ and if $f(a) \neq f(b)$, then for any number k between $f(a)$ and $f(b)$ there exists a number c between a and b such that $f(c) = k$.

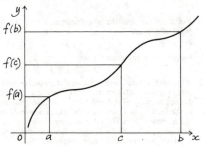

internal division *See* external division.

interpolation The insertion of intermediate values in a sequence of results, between those actually given or determined. It is frequently done by inserting points on a line drawn through plotted values on a graph, or, more rigorously, by using interpolation formulae to insert values between known values of a function (as with the table of differences for logarithmic or trigonometric functions).
See extrapolation.

interpolation formula Any formula which allows an estimate of the value of a function $f(x)$ for arguments lying between x_0 and x_1, when $f(x_0)$ and $f(x_1)$ are known.

● $f: x \mapsto \sqrt{x}$
$f(1) = 1.0000 \ldots$
$f(1.04) = 1.0198 \ldots$ to four decimal places.
By linear interpolation (which assumes f is linear over this small interval) $f(1.02)$
$= 1.0000 + \frac{1}{2}(0.0198)$
$= 1.0099.$

interquartile range *See* quartile.

intersection 1. The region in common between two or more overlapping regions. The intersection of two lines is a point, of two planes is a line.
2. The intersection of plane regions is the set of points common to the regions.

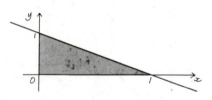

The shaded area is common to the half planes given by $x \geqslant 0$, $y \geqslant 0$, $x + y \leqslant 1$.
3. In general, for any sets $A, B, C \ldots$ the intersection, denoted by $A \cap B \cap C \cap \ldots$ is the set of elements X such that $x \in X \Rightarrow x \in A$ & $x \in B$ & $x \in C \ldots$ It is commonly represented by a Venn diagram.

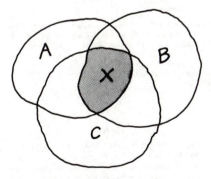

interval A region of linear space defined by two distinct points on a line, or a tract of time between two instants. It can be defined in three dimensions by

an equation such as

$$\delta s^2 = \delta x^2 + \delta y^2 + \delta z^2$$

See closed interval, open interval.

interval of convergence If a power series $\Sigma a_n x^n$ converges only for values of x lying between $\pm b$ where b is non-zero and real, then $-b < x < b$ is called the interval of convergence. The series will diverge for $x < -b$ or $x > b$.
See also circle of convergence.

interval scale In statistics, a scale of equal discrete intervals in a measure into which grouped frequencies are fitted, as income levels of a population:

Units of income	Number
0–1000	15
1001–2000	26
2001–3000	70
.	.
.	.
.	.

into mapping A mapping from S to S' whose range is not the whole of S'.

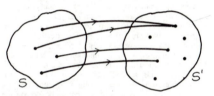

See also surjection.

intransitive relation Let R be a relation defined on a set of elements S. If a R b and b R c together do not imply a R c for some a, b, $c \in S$, then R is intransitive.

intrinsic curvature *See* intrinsic properties.

intrinsic equation Relates the distance s along the arc of any curve from the origin to a point P, with the angle ψ made by the tangent at P with Ox. The intrinsic equation of a cycloid is $s = 4a \sin \psi$ where a is the radius of the rolling circle; the intrinsic equation of a circle is $s = a\psi$

intrinsic geometry The geometry of a surface described in terms of configurations wholly within the surface, and without reference to external planes. On such a surface the straight line of Euclidean geometry is replaced by a geodesic, and distance as a measure taken along the geodesic between two points.
Thus, the angle sum of a spherical triangle bounded by three geodesics (great circles) is greater than two right angles.

intrinsic properties Are those properties of any configuration that are described with reference to itself and not to any external (or extrinsic) system of coordinates. The term intrinsic curvature is ambiguous, since it describes the intrinsic properties of configurations of 1, 2 ... n dimensions on the assumption that they are curves in 2, 3 ... $(n+1)$ dimensions, or at least by analogy with such curves.

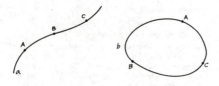

- On the line a considered as one-dimensional, B is between A and C, but A is not between B and C. This is not true for line b. That b is a closed curve in two dimensions is an extrinsic explanation of this intrinsic property.

intuition Usually as adverb 'intuitively'. Commonly used in mathematics of statements made in the course of proof or exposition whose truth does not appear to require (or is perhaps incapable of) formal proof. The usual phrase is: It is intuitively clear that ..., e.g., two straight lines cannot enclose a finite region.

intuitionism A theory of the nature of mathematics, largely due to the Dutch mathematicians Brouwer and Heyting. Mathematics is seen neither as arising from empirical experience (as in Euclid) or from formal logic (Russell, Hilbert), but from intuitive concepts shared by all — such as unity, duality, plurality. Since we have no direct intuitive concept of an actual infinity, only finitist constructions can be employed, but these can be extended by the acceptable intuition of potential infinity, that sequences of numbers or other mathematical entities may be extended without actual limit. Certain indirect logical proofs are excluded. In particular it is not possible to prove a proposition by showing that its negation leads to a logical contradiction, on the grounds that if indeed it does, it is a false proposition from which a true conclusion cannot be drawn. The standard proof that $\sqrt{2}$ is irrational is an example.

invariant Any specified quantity or property which does not change when subject to a specified transformation. Thus the area of a configuration is invariant in Euclidean space under translation or rotation but not under projection. The recognition of invariants as fundamental to the discussion of transformations was due to Cayley, and has also enabled physical theories to be restated. Newtonian mechanics states that all dynamic laws are invariant when transformed into coordinates systems in uniform relative translation, the general theory of relativity that all physical laws can be put into a form invariant when determined in any coordinate systems whatever. The property itself is called invariance.

inverse 1. In general, any process which works in an opposite direction from one already given. Thus the problem of finding cost, given selling price and percentage profit on cost, is inverse to the problem of finding selling price given the cost and profit.
2. Of operations. Used of the operation or process that reverses or 'undoes' the original operation. For real numbers multiplication and division are inverse to one another, and so are addition and subtraction. The inverse of an element will depend on the operation performed, and certain elements may be self inverse under particular operations. For example, if $\mathbf{m}$ is a reflection in a linear mirror,

$\mathbf{m} . \mathbf{m} = I$ where I is the identity, that is the element m is self inverse under the operation 'followed by'.
3. Of functions or mappings. For any function f consisting of the set of all ordered pairs (x, y) of which no two pairs have the same first element, the inverse, written f^{-1}, is the set of all pairs (p, q) for which (q, p) is in f. It follows that f must be one to one, otherwise pairs such as (p, q) (r, q) give the inverse pairs (q, p) (q, r). These have the same first element and cannot by definition be in the function f.

$$f: x \mapsto 2x + 1 \text{ gives } f^{-1}: x \mapsto (x - 1)/2$$
$$f: x \mapsto \ln x \text{ gives } f^{-1}: x \mapsto e^x$$

Functions such as $f: x \mapsto x^2$ or $f: x \mapsto \sin x$ have no general inverse according to this definition, but agreed or 'principal' values may be taken, such as $f: x \mapsto \arcsin x \, (-\pi/2 \leqslant f(x) \leqslant \pi/2)$. Since the inverse of (p, q) is (q, p) it follows that this is the mirror image of (p, q) in the line $y = x$.

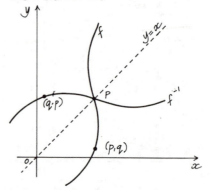

In the diagram P is self inverse.
4. Of binary operations. If a set S has a binary operation $*$ with an identity I, then any element $y \in S$ is the inverse of $x \in S$ if $x * y = I$. This inverse is often denoted x^{-1}

- $\begin{pmatrix} 1 & 2 & 3 & 4 & 5 \\ 3 & 5 & 4 & 2 & 1 \end{pmatrix}$ and $\begin{pmatrix} 1 & 2 & 3 & 4 & 5 \\ 5 & 4 & 1 & 2 & 3 \end{pmatrix}$ are inverse permutations.

inverse matrix A square matrix A^{-1}, such that $A^{-1} \times A = A \times A^{-1} = I$ where I is the identity matrix (unit matrix). A^{-1} always exists if A is non-singular. If any matrix transformation on a vector $\mathbf{x}$ is given by $A\mathbf{x} = \mathbf{x}'$, then $\mathbf{x} = A^{-1}\mathbf{x}'$.
For a 2×2 matrix

$$A = \begin{pmatrix} a & b \\ c & d \end{pmatrix} \quad ad \neq bc$$

$$A^{-1} = \frac{1}{ad - bc} \begin{pmatrix} d & -b \\ -c & a \end{pmatrix}$$

The inverse matrix is the adjoint matrix of A divided by $|A|$. It is also called the reciprocal matrix.

inverse permutation An example of an inverse relation. If three permutations are given by

$$P_0 = \begin{pmatrix} ABC \\ ABC \end{pmatrix} \quad P_1 = \begin{pmatrix} ABC \\ CAB \end{pmatrix} \quad P_2 = \begin{pmatrix} ABC \\ BCA \end{pmatrix}$$

then, by the usual rules for compounding permutations,

$$P_0 + P_1 = P_1$$
$$P_1 + P_2 = P_0$$

Hence P_2 is the inverse permutation to P_1, restoring P_0 to its original form. It follows that $P_1 + P_2 = P_0$, which is here the identity transformation.

inverse points If any transformation T transforms point P to point Q, and T^{-1} transforms Q to P, then P and Q are called inverse points.

inverse proportion If x, y are variables and $x = k/y$ where k is a constant, x is said to be inversely proportional to y, written $x \propto \dfrac{1}{y}$.

inverse relation If any entity A is related to B by any relation R, denoted $A \, \mathrm{R} \, B$, then the inverse relation R^{-1} specifies the relation of B to A.

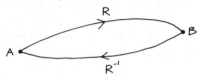

inverse square law Variables x, y are related by an inverse square law if $y = k/x^2$, where k is a constant. For example, the intensity of illumination is inversely proportional to the square of the distance from the source.

inverse transformation A common inverse relation. Any transformation $T^{-1}(B)$ that restores the transformation $T(A) = B$ to its original form A. The transformation $T = \begin{pmatrix} 2 & 1 \\ 0 & 1 \end{pmatrix}$ transforms the vector $\mathbf{a} = (x, y)$ into $\mathbf{a}' = (2x + y, y)$ and the inverse transformation $T^{-1} = \begin{pmatrix} \frac{1}{2} & -\frac{1}{2} \\ 0 & 1 \end{pmatrix}$ transforms $\mathbf{a}'$ to $\mathbf{a}$. Then the compound transformation $T \, T^{-1}$ leaves $\mathbf{a}$ unchanged, so that $T \, T^{-1}$ is the identity transformation given by $I = \begin{pmatrix} 1 & 0 \\ 0 & 1 \end{pmatrix}$.

inversion A conformal transformation of the plane into itself. Any point P transforms into P', where PP' passes through a fixed point O, called the centre of inversion, and $OP \cdot OP'$ is a constant K^2. Since K can be taken as the radius of a circle centre O, we can also speak of inversion with respect to a circle Γ.

- A straight line l not passing through O transforms into a circle C through O.

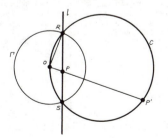

The points R, S are self inverse in this configuration.

involute The inverse of evolute; that is, if the evolute E of a curve is drawn, the original curve is the involute of E. It follows from the definition of evolute that any curve has an infinity of involutes, corresponding intervals of which have in the limit the same centre of curvature (i.e. are 'parallel' curves). Involutes may be mechanically constructed as the locus of a point on a stretched thread either unwound from or wound up on the profile of the curve. By taking various points along the thread the family of involutes may be obtained (Lat. *involutus*, wound up).

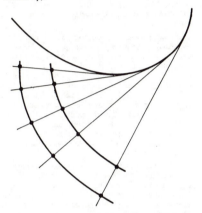

involution Any mapping which on repetition gives the identity, as reflection in a plane, multiplication by -1, pairs of corresponding points in an involutory hexad. Any two elements of such a mapping are said to be mates in the involution.

involutory hexad 1. The six points in which the opposite sides of a complete quadrilateral are cut by a transversal are said to form an involutory hexad, as PQRS forming the hexad (ABC, A'B'C') on the transversal m.

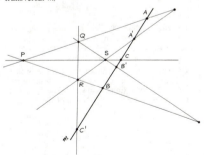

2. Six points A, A', B, B', C, C', form an involutory hexad, denoted (ABC, A'B'C'), if but only if the two cross-ratios (ABCA') and (A'B'C'A) are equal. The actual pairs of points AA', BB', CC' are then said to form an involution.

The two definitions are equivalent.

irrational exponent   An irrational number placed above a symbol in the position occupied by a rational index, as e^π, $5^{\sqrt 2}$, $i^{\sqrt 2}$. These cannot be defined in the same way as rational indices. For a real exponent b, a set of rational approximations defines a^b as the limit of the sequence $a^{b_1}, a^{b_2}, \ldots a^{b_n}, \ldots$ given that b can be expressed as the limit of a sequence of rational numbers $b_1, b_2, \ldots b_n \ldots$

● $5^{\sqrt 2}$ is the limit of the sequence
  $5^{1.4}$, $5^{1.41}$, $5^{1.414}$, $\ldots$

For a complex exponent of a complex number, as in

$$z^i \,(z, a \in \mathbb{C})$$

we can define $z^a = e^{a \ln z}$ but the ordinary index laws cannot be easily applied since this is a many-valued expression.

irrational number   A number which cannot be expressed in the form p/q where $p, q \in \mathbb{Z}$. The Greek concept of a number as a line interval which, in principle, could be 'measured by' a shorter line is said to have been disturbed by the Pythagorean discovery that the diagonal of a square is not commensurable with its side, which implies that $\sqrt 2$ is not expressible as a ratio between measures. The formal proof that $\sqrt 2$ is irrational in Euclid X, 117 is now regarded as an interpolation, but the relations between incommensurables as line intervals are discussed in Euclid X, 7–11. We now distinguish two classes of irrationals:

1. Algebraic, which can be expressed as roots of polynomial equations with integral coefficients.
2. Transcendental, which cannot be so expressed (*quod algebrae vires transcendit*). These include the values of exponential functions, logarithms and trigonometric functions.

A satisfactory definition of irrational numbers was not made till the 19th century, and the discussion is still open.
See also real number, Dedekind section.

irreducible polynomial   If $F[x]$ is a field of polynomials, any polynomial $f(x) \in F[x]$, except $f(x) = c$, is irreducible if it cannot be expressed as a product $g(x).h(x)$, where $g(x)$ and $h(x)$ are polynomials of lower degree.

● $x^2 + 5x + 6$ reduces to $(x+2)(x+3)$
  $x^3 - 3x + 1$ is irreducible

irreflexive relation   If there is a binary relation R on a set S between members $a, b \in S$, it is said to be irreflexive if it does not hold when $a = b$. For example $>$ and $<$ are irreflexive relations.

isochronic curve   A smooth curve down which a body will fall under gravity through equal vertical intervals in equal times. Shown by Huygens (1629–1693) to be a semi-cubic parabola of the form

$$x^2 + y^3 = 0$$

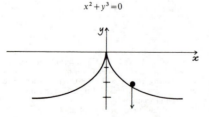

isocline   Given a differential equation of the form $y' = f(x, y)$ the isoclines are the curves for which y' is constant; that is, the family $f(x, y) = k$ for values of k.

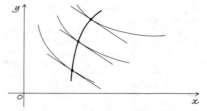

isogonal lines   Pairs of lines (also called isogonal conjugates) which make equal angles on opposite sides of a given line, which is thus the bisector of the angle between them.

isogonic point   The point P in any triangle ABC such that $AP + BP + PC$ is a minimum. Constructions have been given by the physicist Torricelli (1608–1647) and Steiner. The problem was first suggested by Fermat.

isolated point (or singularity)   *See* acnode.

isometric   A projection used in technical drawing in which linear dimensions are preserved by representing them in three orthogonal directions along axes inclined at $120°/60°$.

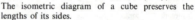

The isometric diagram of a cube preserves the lengths of its sides.

isometry   Any transformation that leaves angular and linear magnitudes unchanged relative to one another. It is more general than congruence in that it includes mirror images and is not overtly based on the intuitive concept of superimposition (as in Euclid). Plane isometries are classed as reflections, rotations or translations (or combinations of these); solid isometries can include central inversion. A direct isometry carries a configuration to a directly congruent figure, as indirect isometry corresponds to a reflection or mirror image.

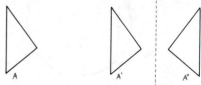

isomorphism *See* homomorphism.

isoperimetric point Also called Kimberling point. The point P relative to a triangle ABC for which triangles APB, APC, BPC have equal perimeters.

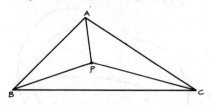

iterated integration The inverse process to the partial differentiation of several variables, including

as a special case successive integration with respect to the same variable

$$d^2 s/dt^2 = f(t) \text{ gives}$$

$$s = \iint f(t)\,dt\,dt$$

$$\iint f(x, y)\,dx\,dy = \int \left\{ \int f(x, y)\,dx \right\} dy$$

iteration Any method for arriving at a result by repeating (or iterating) a recursive procedure that gives successive approximations, as Newton's method for solving the equation $f(x) = 0$.

Jacobian determinant Also functional determinant. A determinant whose elements are partial derivatives of the form $\dfrac{\partial x_i}{\partial u_j}$. It vanishes if but only if there is a functional relation between the x_i for all i.

Jacobi, Carl Gustav Jacob German mathematician (1804–1851). He wrote a systematic treatise on determinants, investigated aspects of number theory and partial differential equations. He is best known for his work on elliptic functions.

join *See* lattice.

joint cost function Where quantities x and y of two different commodities are produced together, the term describes the total cost $C(x,y)$ expressed as a function of x and y.

joint frequency function For each pair of values (x,y) of the composite random variate (X,Y) let the probability of the event $(X=x \ and \ Y=y)$ be denoted $p(X=x, \ Y=y)$. The combined system of the values (x,y) and the corresponding probabilities p is called the joint probability distribution of (X,Y), having a joint frequency function $f(x,y)$ which gives the distribution of the x,y as a frequency surface.

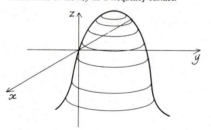

The concept can be extended to more than two variates.

joint probability The probability of two or more events occurring in the same trial, when throwing two or more dice.

joint probability distribution The distribution of two or more variates $X,Y \ \ldots$ If distribution is discrete, there is a joint probability function $f(x,y \ \ldots)$ which represents $P(X=x \ and \ Y=y \ and \ \ldots)$. For a continuous distribution there is a corresponding joint p.d.f.

joint variation Used when a quantity takes values related to other quantities which may vary *independently* of one another. It is analysed mathematically by keeping all but one of the quantities constant in turn.

● The pressure p of a mass of gas depends on the volume v and the temperature T, and is given by $pv=RT$ where R is a constant.

Jordan curve Any simple (i.e. non self-intersecting) closed curve that divides a plane into two regions, one wholly exterior and one wholly interior to the curve. Jordan's theorem states that any two interior points or any two exterior points can be joined by an arc which does not cut the curve.

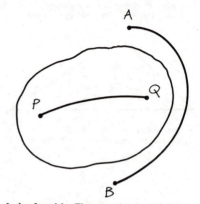

Jordan factorial The expression in x of degree n given by $(x)_n = x(x-1) \ldots (x-n+1)$. The factorial of an integer is a special case of this.

Joukowski aerofoil Under the Joukowski transformation a circle whose centre is not the origin and which passes through either $(-a,0)$ or $(+a,0)$ transforms to a closed curve with a cusp. Suitable choice of circle gives a shape resembling an aerofoil section. Streamlines past the circle, regarded as the cross-section of a body immersed in fluid, transform into those past the aerofoil section. The result is interesting for 'classical' hydrodynamics, but is not of practical value in actual aerodynamics.

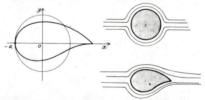

Joukowski's transformation This transformation is complex and given by $z=w+a^2/w$ where a is real positive. It is conformal except at $z=\pm a$. The transformation $z=a^2/w$ corresponds on the Argand diagram to the inversion of w in the circle of radius a, followed by reflection in the real axis, so that the transformation $z=w+a^2/w$ is easily constructed by the parallelogram law.

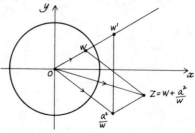

$$z = w + \frac{a^2}{w}$$

Concentric circles centred at the origin and not passing through $z = \pm a$ are transformed into confocal ellipses with foci at $\pm a$. Such a circle through $\pm a$ becomes a degenerate ellipse and appears as a straight line along the x axis.

Joule, J. P. English physicist (1818–1889) who showed the equivalence of electrical, mechanical and heat energy and demonstrated their conservation. The SI unit of energy is named in his honour.

j symbol Texts in science and engineering (particularly electrical engineering) use $j^2 = -1$ to avoid confusion with the symbol for electrical current. The form is now found in some school mathematical texts.

jump discontinuity *See* discontinuity.

juxtaposition Shorthand notation for multiplication or equivalent operations, whereby the two symbols are put side by side, omitting the operation sign.

- $a \times b$ written ab $(a, b \in \mathbb{R})$
  $x \& y$ written xy where x, y are statements in Boolean algebra.

K

Kármán vortices A set of small vortices forming alternately on each side of the wake when a fluid is in motion relative to an obstacle.

Their effect can be seen clearly when a flag flutters in the wind when extended from a pole.

Karnaugh maps Alternatives to the Venn diagram as adapted for sets. They are useful for describing Boolean or set functions involving larger numbers of terms that can conveniently be shown on intersecting rectangles. Introduced by M. Karnaugh in 1953 in an article 'The Map method for synthesis of combinatorial logic circuits'.

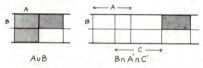

$A \cup B$ $B \cap \dot{A} \cap C'$

Kater's pendulum *See* compound pendulum. Kater (1817) determined g accurately, using the distance between reciprocal centres of oscillation as the length of an equivalent simple pendulum.

Kelvin scale A scale for temperature, based not on freezing or boiling points but on the laws of thermodynamics. It is derived by plotting the relation between the temperature and volume of gas at constant pressure. It is, however, calibrated against the triple point of water (the temperature at which ice, water and water vapour can exist in equilibrium). The unit is denoted by K ($K \approx C° + 273$).

Kendall, M.D. British statistician, whose work on advanced statistical theory has been of great influence.

Kendall's tau (τ) An index of rank order correlation in non-parametric statistics, which may also be applied to two sets of measures as well as their rankings. Given a set of n bivariate data $\{(x_1, y_1) (x_2, y_2)...\}$ consider all (unordered) pairs $\{(x_i, y_i)(x_j, y_j)\}$ where $i \neq j$. There will be $\frac{1}{2}n(n-1)$ of these binary pairs. Discarding equalities, each pair is concordant if $(x_i - x_j)(y_i - y_j)$ is positive, otherwise discordant. If N_c and N_d are the numbers of concordant and discordant pairs, Kendall (1938) gives, as an index of correlation

$$\tau = (N_c - N_d)/\frac{1}{2}n(n-1)$$

Critical values of τ for $n \leqslant 100$ are now available. *See* Friedmann's test.

Kenelly, A. E. British electrical engineer (1861–1939) who first extended alternating current theory by using complex numbers and hyperbolic functions.

Kepler, Johannes German mystic, astronomer and mathematician (1571–1630). The modern formal statement of his Laws of Planetary Motion neither follows their historical development nor the metaphysical arguments that accompanied his thinking. His later work shows many insights into Newton's physical science, anticipating but not formalizing universal gravitation and a mechanical explanation of the solar system. He worked for a year with the observational astronomer Tycho Brahe at Prague (1600), and from him obtained the accurate positional data for the planets that his laws eventually fitted.

Kepler-Poinsot solids The four stellated polyhedra, the three-dimensional analogues of the star polygons. Kepler discovered the stellated octagon and icosahedron. The two stellated dodecahedra, one of which is the mirror image of the other, were due to Poinsot (1777–1859).

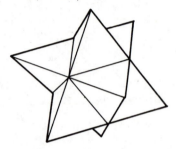

Kepler's Laws The three laws which were later shown by Newton to be deducible from his own Laws of Motion and an inverse square law of gravitational attraction.
I (1609) Planetary orbits are ellipses with the sun at one focus.
II (1609, but discovered earlier than I) The line joining the sun to a planet (the radius vector) describes equal areas in equal times.
III (1619) The squares of the periods of the planets are proportional to the cubes of their mean distance from the sun.
See also Brahe.

kernel *See* homomorphism. Under a homomorphic mapping, the subset which is mapped to the identity element of the image set.

● There is a homomorphism between the group of the symmetries of a square $G = \{1, r, r^2, r^3, a, b, c, d\}$ and the Klein four-group $\{1, r, a, b\}$
$\{1, r^2\} \mapsto 1$ $\{a, c\} \mapsto a$
$\{r, r^3\} \mapsto r$ $\{b, d\} \mapsto b$
Hence the kernel of G is $\{1, r^2\}$.

Khintchine's theorem The statistical case of the law of large numbers, stating that the sample mean $\bar{x}$ converges to the population mean μ as the size of the sample increases.

kinematics The branch of mathematics that deals with the motion of particles or bodies, without reference to the causes of motion or such concepts as force, mass, potential or kinetic energy. From Gk. *kinematos*, motion.
See also dynamics.

kinetic energy The energy possessed by a body by virtue of its motion. In Newtonian dynamics it is given by $\frac{1}{2}mv^2$.

kinetics The branch of mechanics dealing with bodies in motion, under the action of forces.
See dynamics, kinematics, statics.

Kiratowski's axioms A formal logical treatment for distinguishing a set $\{x, y\}$ from an ordered pair (x, y).

Klein, Felix German mathematician (1849–1923). His opinions on the teaching of geometry have had a deep and lasting influence on mathematical education throughout the world: he was, in teaching, the instigator of 'modern maths'. In his inaugural lecture at Erlangen University he presented geometries as the investigation of properties that remain invariant under different groups of coordinate transformations. His Erlanger Programme (1872) suggested the rewriting of Euclidean, non-Euclidean and projective geometries in terms of the relevant group properties, for example translation and rotation groups for Euclidean geometry.

Klein's bottle A closed non-orientable two-dimensional manifold or surface. It can be modelled in three dimensions by deforming a hollow cylinder in stages as shown, joining the ends to form a continuous sheet. The arrows shown on the cylinder are in opposite directions when the circles are brought together. The 'bottle' does not divide space into two regions: a line can be drawn on the surface from P to Q. It can, therefore, be described as a one-sided surface, the three-dimensional analogue of the Möbius band. Embedded in a manifold of four or more dimensions it becomes a closed non-intersecting surface, which does not separate the manifold into two regions. The name 'bottle' was originally a mistranslation of the German *Fläche*, surface.

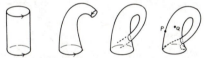

Klein's Four-group (*Viergruppe*) An abstract group $G = \{1, a, b, r\}$ of order 4, whose elements are self inverse, so that $a^2 = b^2 = r^2 = 1$. It thus contains 3 subgroups of order 2. These are $\{1, a\}$, $\{1, b\}$, $\{1, r\}$. It appears in a large number of realizations.

● The group of congruences of a rectangular lamina.
$G = \{1, 3, 5, 7\}$ under multiplication modulo 8.
The group of four permutations of a range of four points $A\,B\,C\,D$ that give the same cross-ratio.

knot 1. In mathematics, a closed curve in n-space which cannot be deformed into one of dimension $(n-1)$. In particular, a three-dimensional closed curve that cannot be deformed continuously into a circle.

2. A speed of one nautical mile per hour (originally determined by counting knots formed in a line with a float let out astern of a moving ship).

Kolmogorov, A. Russian mathematician, for many years director of a school for mathematically gifted children. He published (1933) an axiomatic treatment of probability that has greatly influenced all later work.

Kolmogorov-Smirnov test A one sample test for goodness of fit, developed in 1939. It is assumed that the random sample is from data whose measure may be considered a continuous distribution. It is, for example, required to correlate marks gained by students on an assignment with time spent in completing it, to establish whether they have the same distribution. The test statistic proposed is

$$D = \max |F_n(x) - F(x)| \text{ for each } x,$$

where $F_n(x)$ is the empirical distribution function (or cumulative observed proportion), $F(x)$ is the cumulative density function (or expected cumulative proportion).
D is thus the greatest difference between the pairs of cumulative proportions, $F_n(x)$ taken from the marks and $F(x)$ from the times in the example. A table of critical values is available (*see* Friedmann's test). A two sample variant of the test for the hypothetic identity of two distributions is similarly defined, based on the maximum difference between the empirical cumulative distribution function of the two samples.

Königsberg Former town in Prussia, now Kaliningrad in East Germany, source of the often quoted problem of the Seven Bridges which introduced the study of topology. Situated partly on islands at the confluence of the Old and New Pregel rivers, it once had seven river bridges: the problem was to devise a route crossing each bridge once and once only. Euler showed that the map of the bridges did not reduce to a unicursal network, and hence a route could not exist.

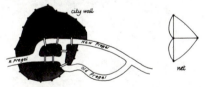

Königsberg in 1750

Kronecker delta The symbol δ_{ij} which has the values

$$\delta_{ij} = 0 \quad (i \neq j)$$
$$\delta_{ij} = 1 \quad (i = j)$$

Considered as a scalar, it can be used to define the unit matrix of order n whose elements are then δ_{ij}. If this square matrix is regarded as a tensor of order two the symbol is sometimes written δ_i^j and corresponds to $\dfrac{\partial x^j}{\partial x^i}$ where x^i, x^j are contravariant components. As before $\dfrac{\partial x^j}{\partial x^i} = 1$ if $i = j$, and since the components are independent $\delta_i^j = 0$ if $i \neq j$. These two values will hold for all coordinate systems in which the components are expressed.

Kronecker, L. German mathematician (1823–1891). An algebraist who refused to accept infinite processes and the contemporary work on the definition of real number. He made the celebrated remark: 'The good Lord made the whole numbers: all else is the work of man'.

Kruskal-Wallis test A non-parametric one-way analysis of variance analogous to the Friedmann two-way test. Used when samples $k \geqslant 3$ of sizes n_1, n_2, n_3 ... are to be compared to explore the null hypothesis H_0 that they are not significantly different with respect to some measure being investigated. For example, the final examination results of pupils originally put in four sets could be used to show whether setting is effective. The test statistic is

$$H = \frac{12S}{N(N+1)} - 3(N+1),$$

where $N = \sum n_i$, $S = \sum_{i=1}^{k} \left(\frac{R_i^2}{n_i} \right)$, $R_i = $ sum of the ranks

in the ith of the k samples. This statistic has chi-square distribution with $k-1$ degrees of freedom. Specially arranged tables are available for $3 \geqslant k \geqslant 6$. *See* Friedmann's test.

kurtosis An indication or measure of the shape of a distribution curve. It may be defined by μ_4/μ_2^2, where μ_2 and μ_4 are the second and fourth moments about the mean μ. Since the value of this measure is approximately 3 for a normal distribution, it is usual to define $k = \mu_4/\mu_2^2 - 3$. A distribution more peaked than normal has a positive value for k and is termed leptokurtic. If k is negative the distribution is platykurtic.

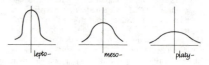

lepto-   meso-   platy-

L

lag When two periodic functions have the same period but different phases, the one which reaches its maximum or minimum values later in time is said to lag on the other. The first is then said to *lead* on the second.

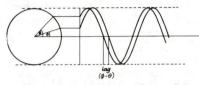

lag
$(\phi - \theta)$

The lag or lead is expressed as a difference of phase angle.

Lagrange, J. L. French mathematician (1736–1813), although born in Turin and at one time Euler's successor as professor in Berlin. One of the founders of the École Polytechnique. He worked in number theory and the systematic solution of differential equations. His major work *Mécanique Analytique* developed mechanics through the calculus. Lagrange boasted that it contained no diagrams.

Lagrange multiplier Arises in the problem of finding an extreme (maximum or minimum) value for a function in two or more variables $f(x, y \ldots) = k$ when there is an equation of constraint $\phi(x, y, \ldots) = 0$.

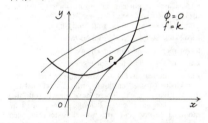

$\phi = 0$
$f = k$

The diagram in two dimensions shows the family of curves corresponding to various k values for $f(x, y)$ and the curve representing $\phi(x, y) = 0$. It can be shown that at the required point $P = (x_0, y_0)$,

$$\frac{\partial f}{\partial x} + \lambda \frac{\partial \phi}{\partial x} = 0$$

$$\frac{\partial f}{\partial y} + \lambda \frac{\partial \phi}{\partial y} = 0$$

$$\phi = 0$$

where λ is the constant called the Lagrange multiplier. The problem is the general case of the extreme values arising in linear programming.

Lagrange notation 1. The notation y' for the derivative of y with respect to another given variable

● $y = x^3$
  $y' = 3x^2$

2. A notation for a variation (which defines this word). A variation of a function $y(x)$ is any function $\delta y(x)$ which is added to $y(x)$ to give a new function $y(x) + \delta y(x)$. If $y(x)$ is an integral, giving say total time or total distance, the vanishing of the variation in the region of a point implies that the integral is stationary at that point and hence leads to the calculus of variations (Lagrange 1760).

● The principle of least action is expressed as

$\delta \displaystyle\int_{t_0}^{t_1} 2T \, dt = 0$ for a body moving with kinetic energy T.

Lagrange remainder *See* Taylor polynomial.

Lagrange's theorem If a finite group of order n has a subgroup of order m, then $n = rm$ where r is an integer.

lambda matrix A matrix whose elements are polynomials, conventionally taken to be of the variable λ. The general element is usually written $a_{ij}(\lambda)$. Lambda matrices arise in finding the eigenvalues and characteristic equation of a matrix transformation

$$A\mathbf{x} = \lambda \mathbf{x}$$

then $(A - \lambda I)\mathbf{x} = 0$ where I is the unit matrix. If

$$A = \begin{pmatrix} 4 & -2 \\ 1 & 1 \end{pmatrix} \quad A - \lambda I = \begin{pmatrix} 4 - \lambda & -2 \\ 1 & 1 - \lambda \end{pmatrix}$$

This is a λ matrix which gives the characteristic equation

$$\begin{vmatrix} 4 - \lambda & -2 \\ 1 & 1 - \lambda \end{vmatrix} = 0$$

or $\lambda^2 - 5\lambda + 6 = 0$

lamellar field Synonym for conservative field, so called because the region of the field can be divided into layers of equal potential — the three-dimensional equivalent being surface contours.

lamina A thin plate or sheet, usually of uniform thickness and density, but idealized in many problems as of negligible or zero thickness and of infinite rigidity. Not necessarily plane, it appears in hydrodynamics as an idealized surface embedded in a three-dimensional region, over which fluid flow is discussed.

laminar flow In hydrodynamics, flow which is entirely within a lamina of zero thickness and is therefore without turbulence or vorticity which would take the fluid into other layers.

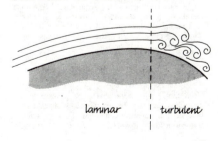

laminar   turbulent

Lamy's theorem A consequence of the sine rule applies to the triangle of forces, due to B. Lamy or Lami (1679). If three forces acting at a point are in equilibrium, each is proportional to the sine of the angle between the directions of the other two.

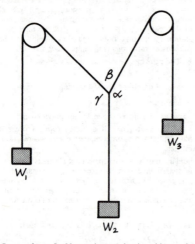

Lagrangian In Newtonian mechanics, this can be taken as the expression $L = T - V$, the difference between the kinetic and the potential energies of a system at any given time.

Laplace, Marquis de French mathematician and astronomer (1749–1827). He showed that the Newtonian planetary orbits are dynamically stable and developed a full theory of tidal action. He formulated the Nebula Hypothesis that the solar system had condensed from a cloud of gas, and published important work on probability.

Laplace's equation In 2, 3, ... n dimensions the partial differential equation

$$\frac{\partial^2 f}{\partial x_1^2} + \frac{\partial^2 f}{\partial x_2^2} + \ldots + \frac{\partial^2 f}{\partial x_n^2} = 0$$

where f is a continuous function. This is one of the important equations in mathematical physics, whose applications include fluid flow, heat flow and the study of electromagnetic fields related to x, y, z axes.

Laplace transform An integral transform named in honour of Laplace, from an analogy between its application in solving differential equations and Laplace's treatment of recurrence equations. Developed in this century by Bromwich, Jeffreys *et al.* from the original work of Oliver Heaviside. If $f(t)$ is an integrable function the Laplace transform of $f(t)$, denoted $L\{f(t)\}$ or $\bar{f}(p)$ is

$$\int_0^\infty e^{-pt} f(t) dt$$

given that $p > n$ where n is some positive integer depending on $f(t)$. In all the cases that arise in practice this integral converges. Lists of Laplace transforms for various $f(t)$ are available, as examples

$f(t)$	$\bar{f}(p)$
t^n	$n!/p^{n+1}$
e^{-at}	$1/(p+a)$
$\sin bt$	$b/(p^2 + a^2)$

There is a unique one-to-one correspondence between distinct functions and their transforms, so that each transform has a function as inverse. A differential equation involving $\dfrac{dx}{dt}$ written operationally as Dx can be solved by transforming both sides, rearranging terms, and finding the inverse transformations using tables. *See* Heaviside operator.

Laplacian operator If Laplace's equation is written with a differential operator acting on f this operator is called the Laplacian, and denoted ∇^2 so that

$$\nabla^2 f = \left(\frac{\partial^2}{\partial x_1^2} + \frac{\partial^2}{\partial x_2^2} + \ldots \right) f = 0$$

The symbol is read 'del-squared' or 'nabla-squared'. *See also* vector operator.

large A word used frequently in descriptive mathematics; e.g., 'terms in $1/x^2$ can be neglected if x is large'. Here *large* is very imprecise and merely means 'large enough for the statement to be true'. A similar objection applies to the word *small*. The objections can be met by assigning specific values to satisfy stated conditions. *See* limit.

large sample Any sample size for which the sample distribution of a statistic taken from a very large population is normal or approximately normal, usually taken as $n \geqslant 30$. Unless stated otherwise, a sample is assumed to be sufficiently large.

Laspeyres' index *See* weighted index.

latent root Synonym for eigenvalue.

latent vector Synonym for eigenvector.

Latin numerical prefixes The Latin numerals have four distinct forms: cardinal, ordinal, adverbial and distributive (n each). These have entered into the English language over a long period, often in modified forms, and are not consistent in their application as prefixes. The convention is to use the Latin prefixes with Latinic words, and Greek prefixes with Greek. The following forms are often found in mathematics

one	*un-, prim-, singul-*
two	*du-, duo-, secund-, bi-, bin-*
three	*tri-, tre-, terti-, tern-*
four	*quadri-, quart-, quartern-*
five	*quinqu-, quint-, quin-*
six	*sex-, sext-*
seven	*sept-*
eight	*octo-, octav-*
ten	*deci-, decim-, den-*
twelve	*duodeci-, duoden-*
sixty	*sexagesim-*
hundred	*centi-, centesime-, centen-*
thousand	*mill-*

latin square So called because it models an arrangement used by the Romans in tessellation designs. A latin square of order n arranges n distinct elements in n rows and n columns on a square grid, so that no element appears more than once in any one row or column. Thus, using the elements A B C D gives the squares

A	D	C	B
B	A	D	C
C	B	A	D
D	C	B	A

A	B	C	D
B	A	D	C
C	D	A	B
D	C	B	A

Latin squares are used in the design of certain experiments, such as seed trials with *n* varieties of seed. The pattern also occurs in the construction of group tables.

latitude Angle which fixes the position of any small circle on the earth's surface whose plane is parallel to the great circle of the equator. All points on this circle then have the same latitude.

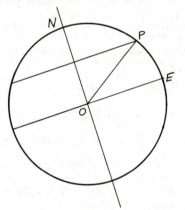

The latitude is the angle EOP where E, P are on the same meridian, and is measured from 0° to 90° North or South of the equator. Angle PON is the colatitude of P. The position of a point on the earth's surface is fixed uniquely by its latitude and longitude. Latitude is determined by measuring the altitudes of heavenly bodies whose declinations are known.

lattice A set of discrete points at a finite distance from each other, spaced according to some rule throughout a space of *n* dimension.

linear

rectangular

triangular

Three-dimensional lattices are used in the classi-fication of crystal structures.

lattice diagram 1. Any diagram formed by joining the points on a discrete lattice.
2. A device for quality control for discrete samples.

The horizontal and vertical lattice intervals represent acceptance or rejection of a sample. If the graph crosses into one of the regions marked 'acceptance' or 'rejection' sampling is discontinued and this action is now taken. The lines defining the regions can be calculated from the values P_0 and P_1 discussed under sequential analysis, of which this is a graphical form.

lattice multiplication *See* gelosia method.

latus rectum Lat. straight side. The chord PQ of a parabola perpendicular to its axis and passing through the focus.

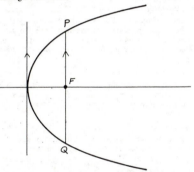

F is the mid point of this chord, and PF is called the semi-latus rectum.

law This word is used in logic and mathematics to describe the logically arbitrary rules which order the development of mathematical argument. The word 'rule' is often used in its place

- Law of excluded middle
  The commutative and associative laws of algebra
  The Four Rules of arithmetic

Such laws should be distinguished from physical laws such as Ohm's Law, in which, although given a functional mathematical form, $V = IR$ is abstracted from empirical observation and is at all times open to amendment.

law of composition Any rule by which two mathematical entities may be compounded to give a third. The set of entities is said to be closed to the process if the compound entity always belongs to the original set. The set N is closed with respect to addition but not to subtraction.

law of large numbers *See* probability. A formaliza-tion of the intuitive conviction that if an event occurs *r* times in *n* substantially identical trials then the ratio r/n if n is large is a measure of the probability p of the event. Where the ratio r/n is a determinate quantity μ, such as the mean of an existing population, the law expresses the probable convergence of the sample mean $\bar{x}$ to μ as the sample size increases. In the two cases

$$\text{Prob} \left(\left| \frac{r}{n} - p \right| > \epsilon \right) \to 0$$

$$\text{Prob} \ (|\bar{x} - \mu| > \epsilon) \to 0$$

where ϵ is any assigned value however small. For the trivial case of a finite population of size N, ϵ is actually zero if $n = N$. The above form is usually called the weak law of large numbers, developed for the statistical case by Khintchine (1929).
See also strong law of large numbers.

law of motion   Any laws that describe the motion of bodies under the action of forces, such as those of Newton.

lead   *See* lag.

leading coefficient   In any polynomial $P(x)$ of degree n, this is the coefficient of the term in x^n
● If $P(x) = 1 + 3x + 2x^2 + 5x^3$
the leading coefficient is 5.

leading diagonal   The set of elements a_{ii} in a determinant or square matrix that have the same row suffix as column suffix. That is, they run diagonally downward from left to right, forming a diagonal.

least action   *See* action.

least common multiple   The least number which is a multiple of every member of a set of positive integers; that is, all members are divisors of this number.
● 24 is LCM of $\{3, 4, 8\}$
Also called the least common denominator since it is used in the algorithm for adding fractions
● $\frac{1}{3} + \frac{1}{4} + \frac{1}{8} = \frac{8}{24} + \frac{6}{24} + \frac{3}{24} = \frac{17}{24}$
Here 24 is the l.c.d.

least upper bound   If B is an upper bound of a sequence $\{a_n\}$ and if, for every other upper bound C of the sequence, $B \leqslant C$, then B is the least upper bound. The greatest lower bound is defined similarly.

Lebesgue, Henri   French mathematician (1875–1941). He developed, in the form of a doctoral dissertation (1903), a theory of integration applicable to very general functions. This method is based on considering regions as measurable sets whose measures can be summed.
See also Riemann integration.

left derivative   *See* right derivative.

left-hand operator   In any non-commutative operation H where, $Hx \neq xH$, it is necessary to distinguish operations from the left Hx and from the right xH. The operation 'multiply by matrix A' should be designated by AB and not BA since, in general $AB \neq BA$. The distinction is not maintained in ordinary arithmetic, since the operation 'multiply' commutes.

Legendre, A. M.   French mathematician (1752–1833). He published a book on geometry which became a standard school textbook in the 19th

century, and did wide ranging work on analysis, number theory and elliptic functions. His integration of exp $(-x^2)$ was used by Gauss in developing the normal curve of errors.

Legendre polynomials   These arise as the solutions of the differential equation
$$(1 - x^2) y'' - 2xy' + n(n+1) y = 0$$
for $n = 0, 1, 2, 3, \ldots$
● for $n = 5$
$$P_5(x) = \tfrac{1}{8}(63x^5 - 70x^3 + 15x)$$
The general formula is
$$P_n(x) = \frac{1}{2^n . n!} \frac{d^n (x^2 - 1)^n}{dx^n}$$
This is known as Rodrigue's formula.

Leibnitz notation   In $y = f(x)$ Leibnitz considered infinitesimal changes in x and y and the ratio between them. He took the symbols dy, dx as actual infinitesimals, and symbolized their ratio as $\dfrac{dy}{dx}$. This ratio corresponds to the modern derivative.
See also derivative, differential coefficient, differentials, dot notations, Lagrange notation.

Leibnitz theorem   Name usually given to expression of the nth derivative of a product of two functions
$$(f.g)^{(n)} = f^{(n)} g + \binom{n}{1} f^{(n-1)} g^1 + \ldots$$
$$+ \binom{n}{r} f^{(n-r)} g^{(r)} + \ldots + f.g^{(n)}$$
It may also appear in the operational form:
$$D^n(uv) = uD^n v + \binom{n}{1} DuD^{n-1}v + \ldots$$
$$+ \binom{n}{r} D^r u D^{n-r} v + \ldots + vD^n u$$

Leibniz, Gottfried Wilhelm   (or Leibnitz) German mathematician, philosopher, lawyer, diplomat (1646–1716). Most of his mathematical work, published in the journal *Acta Eruditorum* that he himself edited, was done during ten years of his middle life. It included the introduction, independently of Newton, of the methods of the calculus. Leibniz held that the predicate of any proposition was contained in its subject, e.g. 'crows are black' is a tautology because being black is part of the *definition* of 'crow'. This view has been very influential for mathematical statements.

lemma   Originally, a proposition assumed to be true for the purpose of proving a proposition in part depending on it, from Gk. *lemma*, an assumption. Today it is always a proposition or theorem proved as a preliminary to a main theorem.

lemniscate   *See* Cassini ovals.

Lemoine circle   If three lines passing through the Lemoine point of a triangle are drawn parallel to the three sides, they intersect them in six concyclic points which lie on the Lemoine circle.

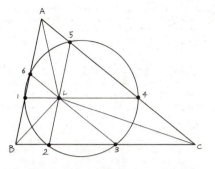

This is a special case of the Tucker circle.

Lemoine point   *See* symmedian.

length   This is an intuitive concept, defined in Euclidean geometry as the measure of a line or interval in terms of an arbitrary unit. Along any path S length may be defined as

$$\int dS$$

but the distance δS (or dS in differentials) between two points arbitrarily close can also be defined analytically.
See distance.

length of an interval   This is taken to be the difference between its end points even if they are not contained in the interval, and relates the interval to its geometric representation. Thus the intervals $2 < x < 3$, $2 < x \leqslant 3$, $2 \leqslant x \leqslant 3$ would each have unit length.

length of arc   A definition of length along a curve, arrived at by partitioning it into intervals and considering the straight line segments joining their ends. For a curve f over a closed interval $[a,b]$ with n line segments $d_r (r=1, 2, \ldots n)$ the arc length is defined as

$$L = \lim_{\substack{n \to \infty \\ d_r \to 0}} \sum_{r=1}^{n} |d_r|$$

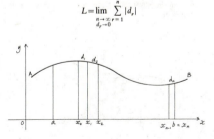

If both f and its derivative f' are continuous in the interval this will give

$$L = \int_a^b \sqrt{\{1 + [f'(x)]^2\}} \, dx$$

leptokurtic   *See* kurtosis.

less than   *See* inequality.

level   1. Used of a plane or a line drawn in a plane that is at right angles to the earth's gravitational force at any point.
2. Any instrument for determining levels in surveying.

level curve   *See* contour.

l'Hôpital, Marquis de   French mathematician (1661–1704) who wrote the first modern style textbook on the calculus. It was based entirely on the demonstrations of Johann Bernoulli.

l'Hôpital's rule   Discovered by Johann Bernoulli but not published by him, the method for finding the limiting value of a quotient of functions whose numerator and denominator both become zero or infinite at $x = a$. Both terms are replaced by their derivates.

$$\lim_{x \to a} \frac{g(x)}{f(x)} = \lim_{x \to a} \frac{g'(x)}{f'(x)}$$

The method is always valid if the limit of the second ratio exists.

Lie product   *See* cross product.

light path theorem   Given originally by Fermat, and equivalent to the theorem of least action. The path taken by a light ray between any two points is that in which the time of passage is a minimum. The familiar laws of reflection can be deduced from this principle.

likelihood   Sometimes used as a synonym for probability, although there is a useful distinction. Consider the Poisson distribution, which normally gives the probability of X successes in trials

$$P(X,\lambda) = \frac{\lambda^X}{X!} e^{-\lambda} \quad \begin{array}{l} (X = 0, 1, 2, \ldots) \\ (\lambda > 0) \end{array}$$

Here λ is a known parameter. If, however, λ is unknown but a sampled value for X has been obtained by trials, there is said to be a 'likelihood' that λ is given by the expression, although this is certainly not a probability distribution for λ. The larger the value of the 'likelihood', the more the supposed value of λ is supported by the observed X. The concept is fundamental to modern inference theory.

like terms   Terms in an expression which contain the same power of the same variable or the same function of the same variable. If two such expressions are identically equal, then the coefficients of like terms can be equated.

● $3x^2 + \sin x \equiv Ax^2 + B \sin x$
   implies that $A = 3$, $B = 1$

'Unlike terms' is used similarly, thus $3a + 2b$ and $x^2 + x$ contain unlike terms. Like terms can be combined by addition or subtraction, unlike terms cannot.

● $3a + 7a = 10a$
   $3a + 7b$ is irreducible.

limaçon   A trammel consisting of a rod of suitable length passes through a swivel at O. The centre P of the rod moves round a circle passing through O of radius a, starting and finishing at O. Points A, B on the rod are equidistant from P.

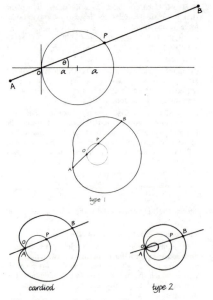

type 1

cardiod *type 2*

Then A, B trace the limaçon. There are three cases

1. $AP = PB = l > 2a$
The curve is a type one limaçon $r = l + 2a\cos\theta$
2. $l = 2a$ gives the cardioid $r = 2a(1 + \cos\theta)$
3. $l < 2a$ the curve is a type two limaçon with a loop and node at O.

The limaçon was first produced by Etienne Pascal in the 17th century.
See also trisectrix.

limit 1. The value of a function $f(x)$ at $x = a$ is given by $f(a)$ if this exists. The limit of $f(x)$ as x approaches the value a, written $L f(x)$ or $\lim f(a)$, is a
$$ {}_{x\to a} \qquad {}_{x\to a}$$
quantity defined in such a way that it may exist even if $f(a)$ does not, and may differ from $f(a)$ if it does. Thus $\dfrac{x^2 - 1}{(x-1)}$ is not defined for real x if $x = 1$, but $\lim_{x\to 1}$
$\dfrac{x^2 - 1}{(x-1)}$ can be shown to be 2. Consider any
arbitrarily small positive number ϵ and a positive number $\delta(\epsilon)$. If there exists both a number L and a value $\delta(\epsilon)$ so that
$$|f(x) - L| < \epsilon \text{ for } 0 < |x - a| < \delta(\epsilon)$$
then L is called the limit of f as x approaches the value a. Consider an example:
● Let $f(x) = (\sqrt{x} - 1)/(x-1)$
let $a = 1$ since $f(x)$ is not defined at $x = 1$.
Take $x = 0.99990$ hence $f(x) = 0.50001\ldots$, which suggests $L = 0.5$
Assign arbitrarily $\epsilon = 0.00002$
take $\delta(\epsilon) = 0.0001$
Then $|f(x) - L| < 0.0002$ as required, and L is a limit. It can be shown to be the limit by taking smaller and smaller values for ϵ so that it approaches zero.

It is possible that as x approaches a from a value b the limit when $b < a$ may be different from the value when $b > a$, as with the function
$$f = \begin{cases} x - 1 \text{ if } x < 3 \\ 2x + 1 \text{ if } x > 3 \end{cases}$$
Here limit is 2 if $x \to 3$ from the point $x = 2$ but 7 if the approach is from $x = 4$. The first is called the left limit or limit from below, usually denoted $\lim_{x\to a^-} f(x)$ the other the right limit (or from above) denoted $\lim_{x\to a^+} f(x)$.
2. For sequences of real numbers which are bounded above or below there may exist upper (or superior) or lower (inferior) limits, denoted lim sup or lim inf. These limits correspond to the greatest or least cluster points of the set of numbers, and will exist if the sequences are monotonically increasing or decreasing. The definitions resemble those for the limits of functions. Given a sequence $\{a_n\}$, an assigned positive ϵ however small, and an integer $n > N$ where N depends on ϵ then
$$a_n > \lim \inf \{a_n\} - \epsilon \text{ for all } n > N$$
There is nevertheless an infinite sequence of remaining values for which
$$a_n < \lim \inf \{a_n\} + \epsilon$$
Similarly $a_n < \lim \sup \{a_n\} + \epsilon$. Note that the limits are not necessarily equal to the greatest lower bound or least upper bound of the sequence, and that a real bounded sequence converges if but only if the inferior and superior limits are equal. The concept of limit is fundamental to mathematics.

limiting sum *See* sum to infinity, which is not the preferred term but suggests more vividly the nature of the process of formation.

limit point *See* cluster point.

limits of integration In a definite integral given by
$$\int_a^b f(x)\, dx$$
for a function f defined on a finite closed interval $a \leqslant x \leqslant b$ the numbers a, b are lower and upper limits of integration.

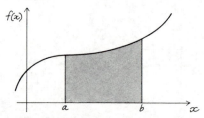

The geometrical representation is the area shaded.
Lindemann, C. L. F. German mathematician (1852–1939) who proved that π was transcendental, and hence the impossibility of 'squaring the circle' by Euclidean methods (which are equivalent to constructing polynomial roots).

line A concept abstracted intuitively from a thread (Lat. *linum*, flax) Proclus defined it as the 'flux of a

116

Trace each line of the diagram once and once only without lifting the pen from the paper. (This is impossible. The network is not unicursal since there are more than two odd nodes.)

Lobachevsky, N. I. Russian mathematician (1793–1856) Lobachevsky repeated the earlier work begun by Saccheri and showed that logically consistent geometries can be developed from alternative parallel postulates. In particular, he worked with the acute angle hypothesis, developing what later became hyperbolic geometry.

local Any property (e.g. of a function) which is only discussed over a region. Thus a local maximum of f at x is one that occurs in the interval $x \pm \delta$ where $\delta > 0$ is any assigned quantity.

localized vector *See* bound vector.

location measures *See* central tendency.

locus From Lat., a place. Originally defined as the path of a point having a law of motion (*see*, for example, conic sections) but in modern terms as the set of all points on a curve satisfying given conditions. This definition avoids the contradiction of a 'moving point', but makes it clumsy to define curves such as epicycloids which originated in descriptions of moving physical systems.

logarithm If $b^x = y$, x is called the logarithm of y to the base b, written $\log_b y$. It follows that the laws of indices apply

$$\log(xy) = \log x + \log y$$
$$\log(x/y) = \log x - \log y$$
$$\log(x^y) = y \log x$$

and hence tables of logarithms and antilogarithms may be used in computation.

The bases in practice are base 2, giving binary logarithms, used in communication theory, base 10, giving common logarithms, devised in 1624 by Briggs (1556–1630) and base e. It is usually assumed that log a means 'to the base 10'. Until recently these were used extensively for computation. Base e gives natural logarithms related to those devised in 1614 by Napier (1551–1617), usually written ln a, and important in analysis. The word logarithm means 'ratio number'.
See also Napier's analogies.

logarithmic function 1. The inverse of the exponential function, denoted $\log_e x$ or ln x. If $f(x) = e^x$ then $f^{-1}(x) = \ln x$. For $x > 0$ this defines a real valued function.
2. The function ln x given by

$$\ln x = \int_1^x \frac{dt}{t}$$

The two definitions are equivalent, and from both it can be shown that $f(xy) = f(x) + f(y)$ and hence the function behaves as a logarithm.

logarithmic growth Used of a physical increase modelled by the function $y = \ln x$. The rate of growth decreases as x increases since the derivative y' approaches zero as $x \to \infty$.
See also decrement, exponential growth.

logarithmic paper Graph paper printed with logarithmic scales. Single logarithmic paper has a natural scale on the horizontal axis, so that functions of the form $y = a^x$ or log $y = x \log a$ appear as straight lines and may conveniently be interpolated or extrapolated. Double logarithmic paper has logarithmic scales on both axes, and is used for plotting values which occur over wide numerical ranges.

logarithmic scale Any scale on which equal intervals represent the logarithms of the numbers labelling the intervals, so that the numbers themselves are not equally spaced. Two log scales sliding over one another, since the distance along each scale is proportional to the logarithm of the number represented, will give products and quotients: this is the principle of the slide rule, a device formerly used as an aid in computation.
Logarithmic scales are used where sets of values cover a wide numerical range, or are related by exponential laws not conveniently represented on linear scales.

$$y = ka^t$$

gives

$$\log y = \log k + t \log a$$

giving a linear relationship between log y and t.

logarithmic series The infinite series

$$x - \frac{x^2}{2} + \frac{x^3}{3} - \ldots + (-1)^{n-1} \frac{x^n}{n} + \ldots$$

where $-1 < x \leqslant 1$. For these values of x the series converges to $\ln(1+x)$. Any function of x (such as $-x$ or x^2) that remains between these limits for $-1 < x \leqslant 1$ can replace x, so that other forms of the series can be written down.

logarithmic spiral *See* equiangular spiral.

logic An investigation of the ways in which valid conclusions may be drawn from given premises. Systematized by Aristotle and later developed as a calculus using mathematical symbolism by Boole and others.

logical product If p and q are statements or propositions their logical product is the statement $p \,\&\, q$ or $p.q$.
The logical sum is similarly $p \vee q$ (p or q).
See connective.

longitude The angle which fixes a meridian (a great semicircle passing through the poles) with respect to the standard through Greenwich.

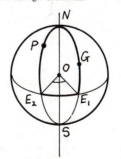

Longitude of P is the angle E_1OE_2, where E_1 is on the Greenwich meridian and E_2 on the meridian through P. Longitude is measured from 0 to 180°

East or West of Greenwich, and with latitude fixes a point uniquely on the earth's surface.

Longitude is determined by comparing the apparent position of heavenly bodies observed from a point on the earth's surface with their positions relative to the Greenwich meridian at Greenwich Mean Time, as given by astronomical tables. The process requires an accurate measure of time.

long term trend   Any trend of a time series, over a longer period of time, of values which may be masked by trends over a shorter period.

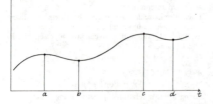

The diagram shows a general upwards trend although the trend is downwards between a, b and c, d.

loop   Part of a flowchart diagram or program in which a sequence of steps is repeated until the input meets some required condition expressible as a binary choice represented on the chart by a decision box.

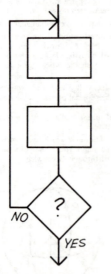

Lorentz covariant   Term used by Einstein to describe a physical law that takes the same mathematical form when transformed from a coordinate system $S(x, y, z, t)$ in which it is established, to another system $S'(x'y'z't')$. The system S' is moving with uniform velocity in a straight line relative to S, and the coordinates x, y, z, t are to be transformed by the Lorentz transformation.

Lorentz transformation   Name given by Poincaré to the transformations from a system of coordinates $S(x, y, z, t)$ to a system $S'(x', y', z', t')$ moving with uniform linear velocity relative to S.

They are $x' = \gamma(x - ut)$
$\qquad\quad y' = y$
$\qquad\quad z' = z$
$\qquad\quad t' = \gamma(t - ux/c^2)$

where $\gamma^2 = \dfrac{c^2}{c^2 - u^2}$ and c is the speed of light *in vacuo*.

The velocity u is along the x axis which coincides with the x' axis. The two origins O and O' coincide at $t = 0$.

Lorenz curve   Replaces cumulative frequency plot with a cumulative relative or percentage frequency (c.p.f). For example if c.p.f is plotted against a country's cumulative percentage total income, the plot would be a straight line if all incomes were equal, since any given proportion of the population would receive that proportion of the total income. Departure of the plot from a straight line between the end points indicates inequality of distribution.

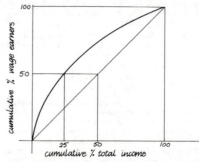

In the example 25% of a country's income is distributed among 50% of the population. The curves are useful for comparative studies in sociology.

loss function   If total profit P on sales is linearly dependent on quantity sold X, then $P = a + bX$ where a, b can be determined. If an alternative marketing system gives a different profit, Q say, where $Q = c + dX$ the two lines can be plotted and will intersect at X_0 if $b = d$.

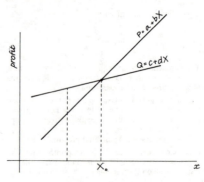

If sales are X_0 neither system is favourable. Above X_0 the P system is advantageous, but if adopted this leads to a greater loss of profit when sales fall below X_0. The expression of this loss of profit is the loss function.

lower bound   *See* upper bound.

lower limit   *See* limits of integration, limit.

lower Riemann sum   *See* Riemann sum.

loxodromic spiral   A line of constant bearing on the earth's surface, which will spiral in towards the pole. On the polar gnomonic projection it is the equiangular spiral.

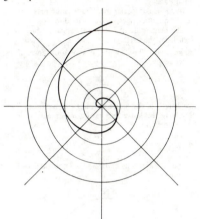

Lukasiewicz, J.   Polish logician (1878–1956) who introduced a modified notation for symbolic logic. For example, in place of $p \vee q$ (p or q) he wrote Apq, putting the logical connective as an operator before p, q. Written in reverse, this has since been adapted to some calculators as Reverse Polish notation.

machine In mechanics any device or apparatus which transforms work. Thus a lever is a machine, and so are two intermeshing gear wheels: in each case a given work input produces an equal output (less frictional or other losses) in a different direction or form. The word is also used very generally, as in Turing machine, which is a theoretical model only.

Machin's formula An adaptation of Gregory's series by John Machin (1680–1751) which produces a more rapidly convergent series from which π could be calculated. His formula was

$$\frac{\pi}{4} = 4 \arctan\left(\tfrac{1}{5}\right) - \arctan\left(\tfrac{1}{239}\right)$$

and each term was then expanded by Gregory's series for arctan x.

Mach number The ratio between the velocity of a body moving in air and the velocity of sound in air, under the same conditions of temperature and pressure.

Maclaurin's series A particular case of Taylor's series, giving the representation of a function in the neighbourhood of the origin as a power series. The coefficients of the series are given in terms of the values at 0 of the successive derivative of the function. Thus

$$f(x) = \sum_{n=0}^{\infty} \frac{f^{(n)}(0)x^n}{n!}$$

when $f^{(n)}(0)$ is the nth derivative of f evaluated at $x = 0$.

● If $f(x) = e^x$ then $f^{(n)}(x) = e^x$ and $f^{(n)}(0) = 1$ for all positive n, so that

$$e^x = \sum_{n=0}^{\infty} \frac{x^n}{n!}$$

Note that the series need not converge to the function it represents.

● $f(x) = e^{-1/x^2}$ for $x = 0$
Here $f^{(n)}(0) = 0$ and hence the first term is undefined and all other terms are zero.

Maclaurin's trisectrix See trisectrix.

magic square A square $n \times n$ array of numbers in which the sum of the n numbers in every row, column or diagonal is constant (usually called the magic number for the square).

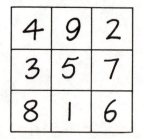

Legend ascribes the 3×3 square illustrated to a Chinese emperor, who found it inscribed on the back of a tortoise.

magnetic bearing The bearing of an object or track, measured in degrees clockwise from magnetic north at the point from which the bearing is taken.

magnification ratio The ratio between the linear measures of one figure or configuration and a similar configuration of a different size. It may be expressed as a fraction such as $1/n$ or a ratio as $p:q$.

magnitude 1. The numerical value or measure assigned to a mathematical or physical quantity, by which it may be compared numerically with other quantities.
2. In particular, scalar magnitude is the measure of a vector quantity irrespective of its direction.
3. The magnitude of a star is its apparent brightness seen from the earth.

major axis The longer axis of an ellipse. If the curve is given as

$$\frac{x^2}{a^2} + \frac{y^2}{b^2} = 1$$

the length of the major axis is twice max(a, b). Similarly the lesser axis is the minor axis which is twice min(a, b)

● $$\frac{x^2}{25} + \frac{y^2}{16} = 1$$

has a major axis of 10 and a minor axis of 8 units.

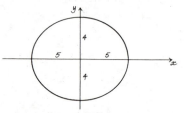

major premise See syllogism.

manifold In O.E. *manigfeald*, the suffix *-fold* as in threefold, added to *many*. Any entity constructed from a number of entities usually infinite, as a three-dimensional manifold constructed of all points with coordinates x, y, z or space time manifold involving x, y, z, t.

Mann-Whitney U test A non-parametric, distribution-free test. If X and Y are two variables whose cumulative distribution functions are $F(x)$, $F(y)$, then the null hypothesis under test is that their two means are the same. The test is applied as follows:

A and B are two samples of size n_A, n_B. Rank all the data of A, B together in one rank order list then determine the two sums R_A and R_B of the rank numbers for sample A and sample B. Compute the statistic

$$U = n_A n_B + \frac{n_A}{2}(n_A + 1) - R_A$$

or $$U' = n_A n_B + \frac{n_B}{2}(n_B + 1) - R_B$$

where $U + U' = n_A n_B$

For significance $U \geqslant \alpha_1$, or $U' \leqslant \alpha_2$, where α_1, α_2 are the critical values for n_A, n_B given by suitable tables at a specific significance level.

mantissa Lat. a makeweight. The fractional part of a logarithm, added to the characteristic or required integral power of the base.

$\log 49.1 = 1.6911 \ldots$: the mantissa is $0.6911 \ldots$

In logarithm tables only the mantissa is given.
See also characteristic.

many-one relation A correspondence that associates more than one member of a set S with each member of a set S'. Since one and one only member of S' corresponds with each member of S the relationship is functional (*see* function), but the inverse one:many relation is not a function.

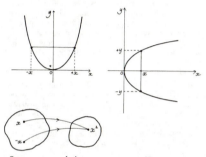

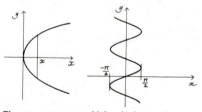

See one–one relation.

many valued function *See* function. In order that derivatives should be unique the modern definition of a function excludes correspondence of a point in the domain with more than one point in the range, hence this term is not strictly permissible. It does, however, describe the actual behaviour of real expressions such as $y = \sqrt{x}$ or $y = \arcsin x$ or complex expressions such as $\ln z$ defined as the inverse of e^z ($z \in \mathbb{C}$). It is usual to consider $y = \sqrt{x}$ as involving the positive root only, and to take $-\sqrt{x}$ as a separate branch of the function. Similarly $y = \arcsin x$ concerns only the *principal value* defined by $-\frac{1}{2}\pi < x < \frac{1}{2}\pi$. If such expressions are plotted in coordinates the multiple values are readily apparent.

The term many- or multiple-valued expression can be used.

many valued logic A generalization of three term logic as developed by Lukasiewicz in 1921. Post suggested m-valued logics ($m \in \mathbb{N}$) and Reichenbach (1932) developed an infinite value logic as a formulation of probability.

map, mapping A term broadly corresponding to 'function'. A transformation from one set S (the domain) to another S' (the range or image set) by means of some rule, formula or other procedure, whereby each element of S is assigned a unique image in S'. Mapping includes geometrical or non-numerical topological transformations, while the word function is usually used of those algebraically or analytically expressed.
See also surjective, injective, bijection.

map projection Any rule or process for putting the points of the whole or part of the spherical surface S of the earth into correspondence with those of a convenient plane P. The process is subject to the restriction that a one-to-one correspondence of the points of the spherical and plane surfaces, necessary if unique points on the earth are to be represented uniquely on the map, is not possible for the entire sphere. At least a hundred projections are described in textbooks, many of them devised to conserve individual terrestrial properties such as area, bearing, shape over large or small distances; usually each possible property at the expense of distorting the others. Examples of projections of distinct mathematical types are entered under Mercator, conical, stereographic, elliptical: many of the others can be described as variants of these.

marginal 1. A term used, especially in economics, of values, prices, quantities sold, etc., which are held to depend on such things as profit motives or propensities to buy or consume. It applies, for example, to the price above which sales will be lower than those required to break even on production costs.
2. Terms such as 'marginal frequency' or 'marginal probability' are sometimes used to denote total or other values inserted in columns alongside other tabulated values, i.e. in the marginal columns. This use is confusing and in best replaced by 'border values'.

marginal distribution In tables showing the distribution of more than one set of values, the distribution of the totals in the margins of the tables (marginal totals)

Score	Set A	Set B	Set C	Totals
1	3	2	0	5
2	10	11	5	26
3	15	20	9	44
4	7	12	10	29
5	1	4	3	8
Totals	36	49	27	112

Not to be confused with marginal values. The term border distribution, although less common, would be preferable.

Markov chain An ordered sequence of n discrete random variables $X_1, X_2 \ldots X_i, \ldots X_n$ (usually called *states* in the context of any physical system) such that the probability of X_i depends only on n and the state X_{i-1} which has preceded it. If it is independent of n the chain is said to be homogeneous, and the conditional probability given by $P(X_j|X_i)$ is called the transition probability from X_i to X_j. The values of P_{ij} can be given in a transition matrix for the chain:

$$
\begin{array}{c}
\\
X_1 \\
X_2 \\
X_3 \\
\cdot \\
\cdot \\
\cdot \\
X_n
\end{array}
\begin{array}{cccc}
X_1 & X_2 & X_3 & \ldots \quad X_n \\
\left(\begin{array}{cccc}
P_{11} & P_{12} & P_{13} & P_{1n} \\
P_{21} & P_{22} & P_{23} & P_{2n} \\
P_{31} & P_{32} & P_{33} & P_{3n} \\
\cdot & \cdot & \cdot & \\
\cdot & \cdot & \cdot & \\
\cdot & \cdot & \cdot & \\
P_{n1} & P_{n2} & P_{n3} & P_{nn}
\end{array}\right)
\end{array}
$$

An *ergodic* Markov chain is one in which it is always possible to pass from any one state to any other.
An *absorbing* Markov chain is one with a state it is impossible to leave which can always be reached from other states. That is, there are states X_i, X_j so that $P(X_j|X_i)=0$ for all $j=i$, so that the process described then terminates.
See also absorbing barrier, gambler's ruin, random walk.

mass　Formerly defined as amount of matter, it can now be considered as the intrinsic property of any object or entity that determines its change of velocity for a given effect, such as a Newtonian force. The mass of a body can be determined by comparing its behaviour with standard masses, for example in the pans of an equal arm balance in the earth's gravitational field or when accelerated by a known force. The international kilogram standard of mass is at present a metal cylinder kept at Sèvres in France, although it may eventually be defined in terms of a standard number of specified atoms.
Note that the mass of an object has a component due to the mass of any kinetic energy it may possess. This is usually negligibly small since the ratio energy/mass is 9×10^{16} (i.e. c^2), but for very energetic particles such as fast electrons it may be the major component.
See also weight.

mass-energy equation　The equations $E=mc^2$ or $m=E/c^2$, where c is the velocity of light, expresses the physical equivalence (but not identity) of mass and energy by giving them in units having the same dimensions. A system which acquires E units of energy thereby acquires E/c^2 units of inertial or gravitational mass, a system which loses m units of mass, as in radioactive decay, thereby dissipates mc^2 units of energy.

material implication　*See* implication.

mates　*See* involution.

mathematical induction　A formal method of proof which establishes the proposition $P(n)$ for all positive integers. The proposition $P(n+1)$ is proved to be true on the hypothesis that $P(n)$ is true. The proposition is then shown to be true for a given value a of n, and it follows that it is true for $a+1$, $a+2$... and hence for all positive integers greater than or equal to a. The value of a, which is usually 1, will depend on the proposition: for example, proof that the angle sum of a plane n-gon is $(n-2)$ needs a starting value $a=3$. The method can often, as with the binomial

theorem, be extended to $P(r)$ where r is rational. It is now usual to regard the validity of mathematical induction as an axiom.

mathematical programming　A general method of solving problems requiring the maximum or minimum values of functions subject to equations of constraint. Usually in the form of linear programming.

mathematics　This is what mathematicians study. There is no one definition of any value, although mathematical thinking tends to be structured, is usually symbolic and is frequently quantitative. The symbols used in mathematics tend to be operational, signalling a process to be completed, as $+$, $\int$, relational as in $x>y$, or to stand as ideograms for definable concepts, as the numerals $0, 1, 2,...$; but precise unambiguous description is not possible. Many see mathematics as a set of necessary logical deductions from arbitrary axioms, but others argue that it expresses intuitions founded in the empirical. To Plato, however, *mathēmata* — things learned or 'the studies' — was a general term for geometry, the study of number, astronomy and music. The word retains its platonic plural.
See also pure mathematics.

matrix　Originally formulated by Cayley. A rectangular $m \times n$ array of m rows and n columns of real or complex numbers (or other elements), usually denoted by a capital letter. The elements are denoted by a_{ij}, interpreted as the element occupying the ith row and the jth column. The matrix may then be denoted (a_{ij}). Thus for a $m \times n$ matrix A

$$
A=(a_{ij})=\begin{pmatrix}
a_{11} & a_{12} & \ldots a_{1n} \\
a_{21} & a_{22} & \ldots a_{2n} \\
\cdot & & \\
\cdot & & \\
\cdot & & \\
a_{m1} & a_{m2} & \ldots a_{mn}
\end{pmatrix}
$$

matroid　A concept in abstract algebra. A set of subsets from a finite universal set is called a matroid (by comparison with the rows in a non-singular sqaure matrix) if they are linearly independent.

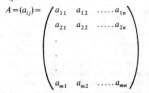

The joins of the vertices of graph (a) are independent, but those of (b) are not since $j_1 = j_2 + j_3$.

max (a, b)　$\max (a, b) = a$ if $a > b$
　　　　　　　　　　$= b$ if $a < b$

See min(a, b)

maximal ideal　*See* ideal. If R is any ring and M is a non-zero ideal of R, then M is maximal if $M \subset R$ and there is no other ideal N such that $M \subset N \subset R$.

maximal set　Contains the maximum number of elements permitted by its definition.
A set of consistent independent equations in four variables cannot contain more than four members, hence any set of 4 is maximal.

maximum　If f is any function and x is any point in an interval of the domain of f, then x is a maximum point if $f(x) \geqslant f(y)$ for all y in the interval. Similarly x is a minimum point if $f(x) \leqslant f(y)$. The diagram suggests there are two kinds of maximum and minimum.

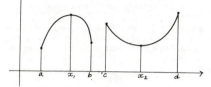

Here minima occur at a, b, x_2 and maxima at c, x_1, d, where a, b, c, d are the end points of closed intervals. At x_1, x_2, however, the maximum/minimum point is also that for an arbitrarily small interval $x \pm \delta$ where $\delta \to 0$. The point x is then said to be a *local* maximum or minimum. The function is not defined beyond its end points, and a, c, d give us *absolute* minima or maxima. At any local maximum or minimum $f'(x) = 0$ but the converse is not true.

maximum likelihood A criterion, in games or in any activity having elements of chance, by which decision is based on the event most likely to happen. In practice, of course, the possible consequences of the event or its non-occurrence would also be taken into account.

maximum value If a function f has a maximum at $x = a$ a maximum value is $f(a)$.

Maxwell, J. C. English mathematician and physicist (1831–1879). He made a major contribution to the kinetic theory of gases, and in 1873 published a mathematical theory which modelled all the then known properties of the electromagnetic field as investigated by Faraday, Ampère and others. His equations had a solution which required an electromagnetic disturbance to be propagated outwards with a speed of $3 \times 10^8 \ \mathrm{ms}^{-1}$. This suggested the identification of light with electromagnetic waves, and culminated in the discovery by Hertz (1888) of the lower frequency radio waves.

McNemar test A simple non-parametric statistical test to establish the significance of changes occurring after experimental treatment. For each subject (or test item) the direction of the change after treatment is noted, scoring $+$ for improvement, $-$ for deterioration and 0 for no change. It is not necessary to quantify the changes. If X, Y are the totals of positive and negative signs, the test statistic, ignoring zeros, is

$$\frac{(|X - Y| - 1)^2}{X + Y}$$

which has the chi-square distribution for one degree of freedom. The test statistic should be in excess of the critical value corresponding to a required significance level, if the null hypothesis H_0 is to be rejected.

mean 1. Any intermediate measure between two measures (or value between two values) formed according to some rule of procedure. See arithmetical mean, geometric mean, harmonic mean.
2. An average value or measure of central tendency for a set of data, often used as a population parameter.

For a sample of size n from any population it is given by

$$\bar{X} = \sum_{i=1}^{n} x_i \text{ for } i = 1, 2, 3, \ldots n$$

See also weighted mean.

mean curvature A measure taken along a finite interval $\triangle s$ of any curve.

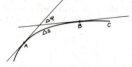

If $\triangle s$ is the interval along the curve C between points A and B, and $\triangle \psi$ is the acute angle between the tangents at A and B, the mean curvature from A to B is the ratio $\triangle \psi / \triangle s$.

mean deviation A measure of spread or dispersion, defined as the mean unsigned distance or deviation from the mean, either in a sample or a population. For a sample of n measures whose mean is $\bar{X}$ the mean deviation would be

$$\frac{1}{n} \sum_{i=1}^{n} |X_i - \bar{X}|$$

Note that, from the definition of mean, the mean algebraic deviation from the mean, $\frac{1}{n} \sum_{i=1}^{n} (X_i - \bar{X})$, would be zero.

mean point Any point constructed as the mean between two points at the ends of an interval. See arithmetical mean, geometric mean, harmonic mean.

mean proportional Formerly, as in Euclid VI, 13, the line of length m, gives lines of length a, b, constructed so that the ratio $a:m = m:b$. Now generally applied to any number m such that $a/m = m/b$ where a and b are numbers. Also called geometric mean.

mean square error This is the same as the variance for a distribution of sample means, for samples of size n with replacement. If $\bar{X}$ is the sample and μ the population mean for any set of observations, the mean square error is the expected value given by

$$E[(\bar{X} - \mu)^2] = \sigma^2 / n$$

where σ^2 is the population variance.

mean value theorem(s) 1. This expresses formally the intuitive statement that on at least one point on a continuous curve in an interval, the gradient is equal to the mean gradient over the interval.

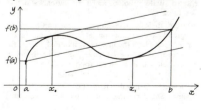

There is a value x_0, where $a < x_0 < b$, such that

$$f'(x_0) = \frac{f(b) - f(a)}{b - a}$$

The diagram suggests that $f'(x_1)$ also equals $f'(x_0)$, so that there can be more than one point. The theorem can be proved for functions continuous in the closed interval $[a, b]$, differentiable within the open interval (a, b).
2. The general or Cauchy mean value theorem. If functions f and g are continuous in $[a, b]$ and differentiable in (a, b), there is an x_0 in (a, b) such that

$$\frac{f(b) - f(a)}{g(b) - g(a)} = \frac{f'(x_0)}{g'(x_0)}$$

given that neither denominator vanishes.
3. There are also several mean value theorems for integrals. For example if a function f is continuous in $[a, b]$ and a function g is integrable and not negative, then for some x_0 in the interval

$$\int_a^b f(x) . g(x) \, dx = f(x_0) \int_a^b g(x) \, dx$$

Also if $f(x)$ is a positive monotonic decreasing function, if $f'(x)$ is integrable and $g(x)$ is continuous, then there is an x in $[a, b]$ such that

$$\int_a^b f(x) g(x) \, dx = f(a) \int_a^x g(x) \, dx$$

This is the Bonnet form.

measurable set If a number $r(x)$ or 'weighting' can be assigned to each member x of a set S so that $\Sigma r(x) = 1$, then the measure of any subset of S is the sum of the weights of its elements.

● The set of probabilities assigned to all the events of a sample space.

See also Lebesgue.

measure The number assigned to any physical quantity by comparing it with an arbitrary standard quantity of the same kind taken as the unit. In practice (*see* Appendix 1) units are constructed from a small number of units taken as fundamental, although many *ad hoc* units still exist.

measures of central tendency These are measures which describe the 'average' value of distributed data, and are used as parameters to describe statistical populations. The common measures (*see* separate entries) are arithmetic mean (or simply mean), mode and median.

measures of dispersion These measure the 'spread' of a distribution. Common measures of spread are entered under range, mean deviation, standard deviation.

measure theory Difficulties in integration if an integrand is discontinuous, at many points in the region over which the integral is required, even if the integral appears to exist, gave rise to the theory of measurable sets in point set topology. The theory of Lebesque integration is an application.

mechanics Originally from Gk. *mēchanē*, a contrivance, and hence the study of machines. Now used generally, as in Newtonian mechanics, for the study of the motion of bodies acted on by forces, and of the forces themselves when, but only when, these are transmitted by material contact.
See statics, dynamics, hydrostatics, hydrodynamics, kinematics.

median 1. The median of a triangle is the line joining the mid-point of one side to the opposite vertex. The medians meet in a point known as the centroid.

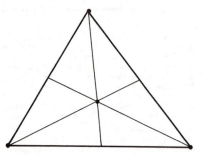

The centroid is also the centre of gravity if the triangle is cut from a uniform lamina.
2. The statistical measure determined by ordering the data and selecting the middle datum when there is an odd number of measures, or the arithmetic mean of the two central values if the number is even. The measure is often used in economics. Thus a person on median income has as many others earning less as there are earning more.

mediator *See* right bisector.

meet *See* lattice.

membership As in ordinary speech. Any given entity belongs to or is a member of a set if it meets the criteria for membership.

Menelaus' theorem If a transversal cuts the sides AB, BC, CA of any plane triangle at D, E, F, then the two products AD.BE.CF and BD.CE.AF are equal.

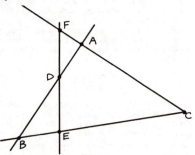

Result given by Menelaus (c. 100 A.D.). It can be extended to spherical triangles.
See also Ceva's theorem.

Mercator projection A projection of the earth's surface on a coordinate plane, such that point P of

latitude θ, longitude ϕ has the coordinates $x = a\phi$,
$y = a \int_0^{\theta} \sec\theta\, d\theta$, where a is a constant depending on
the equatorial scale of the map. It is a conformal
transformation of the earth's surface, so that lines of
constant bearing are straight lines (rhumb lines or
loxodromes) on the map.

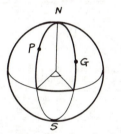

See alias transformation, meridional parts.

meridian   A great circle on the surface of the earth
passing through the N and S poles. By international
agreement the prime meridian is taken as the one
through Greenwich, and the longitude of any point
P is the angle between the plane of its meridian and
that of Greenwich, measured E or W from 0 to 180°.

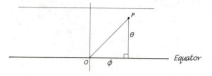

meridional parts   Determine the spacing of latitude
lines on a Mercator projection, and give for any
latitude the distance of the line from the equator
expressed in minutes of arc (i.e. nautical miles) on the
equatorial scale, i.e. the value of the integral
$\int_0^{\theta} \sec\theta\, d\theta$. The values are tabulated and may be
used to construct a Mercator graticule.

● $P = $ lat 20°, long 20° has the Mercator coordinates
$x = 1200$ $y = 1225$, to any convenient scale.

Mersenne, Marin   French monastic mathematician
(1588–1648), editor of Greek mathematical works
and discoverer of the Mersenne numbers, primes of
the general form

$$2^p - 1 \quad (p \text{ prime})$$

mesh gauge   *See* analytical projective geometry.

mesh system   A very general term for any coordinate system, however arbitrary, which serves to
specify points in physical space. A mesh system will
consist of intersecting sets of numbered lines whose
numbers will define regions of space, and by making
the mesh sufficiently fine the regions can be made
vanishingly small, approximating to mathematical
points. Cartesian axes with rational coordinates
(such as would arise in empirical measurement) are
an example of a mesh system. Any physical laws,
established for material systems in general, must be
independent of the mesh system adopted.

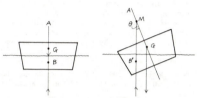

metacentre   If a body symmetrical about a vertical
axis AB is floating in a liquid the centre of buoyancy
B and the centre of mass G of the body will both lie
on this axis.

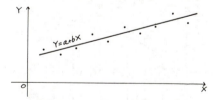

The upthrust through B will equal the weight acting
through G. If the body is given a small displacement
θ the centre of buoyancy will move to B'. The line of
upthrust is now the vertical through B', which cuts
AB at M. The limiting distance GM as θ becomes
vanishing small is called the metacentric height, and
M is then the metacentre. If GM is positive there is a
righting moment and the floating body is stable.

metamathematics   The attempt, largely by Hilbert,
to discuss the validity of mathematical systems from
a position completely outside them, so that circular
arguments do not arise. Thus the set of axioms,
postulates and theorems that constitutes Euclidean
geometry generates the non-geometrical metamathematical theorem that the set is internally consistent
and cannot produce two theorems which contradict
one another. A celebrated metamathematical
theorem due to Gödel proves that an internal proof
of the consistency of formal arithmetic (as developed
by Russell and Whitehead) is impossible.

method of least squares   Used by Gauss as a means
of fitting a curve (or line of best fit) to a set of
observations which appear scattered when plotted.

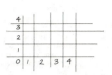

The points on the scattergram are defined by the
actual observations $(X_1, Y_1), (X_2, Y_2) \ldots (X_n, Y_n)$ and
it is assumed that each Y is given by $Y = a + bX + r$
where $f(x) = a + bX$ is the linear model and r is the
'residual', the difference between the model value and
the actual observed value. The least squares criterion
states that the line $a + bX$ is the best predictor of Y
given X if a and b are chosen so that the sum of the
squares of the differences between the observed and
predicted values is a minimum, that is, that

127

$\sum_{i=1}^{n} [Y_i - f(x_i)]^2$ is a minimum. The minimum value is found by differentiating partially with respect to a and b, equating the derivatives to zero, and solving the pair of simultaneous equations thus obtained. The method can be adapted to non-linear models. Gauss himself derived the theorem from his expression for normal distribution of errors.
See also regression line.

metrical geometry Any geometry based explicitly on the concept of measure; that is, that any line interval can be compared with another interval taken as the unit, which thus 'measures' the line. It is then possible to show that lines are equal or unequal, or can be bisected or divided in a given ratio, or that configurations are equal or unequal in area or volume. The discovery that some line intervals were incommensurable is met, in modern terms, by the definition of an irrational number.

metric space See distance. A metric space is any set of elements, such as points, for which such a function exists.

metric system A system of measures adopted by a French revolutionary convention in 1795, intended originally to be based on the metre as one ten-millionth part of the quadrant arc from the equator to the North pole. Difficulties of survey led to the eventual adoption of a standard rod legally defined as one metre. All submultiple and multiple units were in powers of ten, the submultiples denoted by Latin and the multiples by Greek prefixes. Volume, capacity and area were defined in terms of the linear metre or its multiples and submultiples, and mass in terms of one centimetre cubed of water. The system, in spite of the advocacy of engineers and scientists (among them James Watt and Lord Kelvin) failed to gain acceptance in Great Britain for political reasons. Later modifications were the centimetre-gram-second and the metre-kilogram-second systems which aimed at a wide range of derived units. It has now, with international definitions and agreed additional conventions, become the *Système International d'Unités* (SI).
See Appendix 1.

mid-ordinate rule Formerly used in numerical or graphical integration.

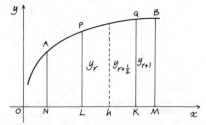

The area of strip $LPQK$ is estimated by calculating or measuring the ordinate midway between L and K, $y_{r+(1/2)}$ say. Then area $LPQK \approx h . y_{r+(1/2)}$ where h is the distance between the ordinates y_r and y_{r+1}. The total area NABM is then

$$\approx h(y_{1/2} + y_{1+(1/2)} + \ldots + y_{n-(1/2)})$$

That is, if the area is divided into equal strips, it is approximately the width of the strip multiplied by the sum of the mid-ordinates.
See Simpson's rule, trapezoidal rule.

mid-range The mid-way point between the minimum and maximum values of any measure in a given sample, often used as a rough indication of central tendency.

min (a, b) Defined as min $(a, b) = b$ if $a > b$
min $(a, b) = a$ if $a < b$
The definition may be extended to $f(x)$, $g(x)$
- min $(x, x^2) = x$ if $x \leqslant 0$ or $x \geqslant 1$
$= x^2$ if $0 < x < 1$

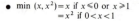

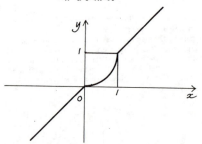

minimal surface The solution to Plateau's problem (J. B. Plateau, Belgian physicist 1801–1883) of finding the minimum area of any surface bounded by a closed curve or curves in three dimensions, simple or knotted. Many of the surfaces can be demonstrated physically by forming soap films on wires.

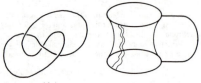

See catenoid.

minimax method Used in linear programming. A linear function in variables $x, y, z \ldots$ is to take a maximum or minimum optimum value, subject to the values of $x, y, z \ldots$ being held within a set of feasible values given by equations of constraint.

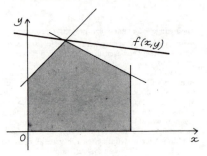

In the diagram $f(x, y)$ takes its maximum possible value.
See linear programming, feasible points, convex set.

minimum *See* maximum.

minimum axiom set A set of axioms which is both necessary and sufficient to generate the theorems of an axiomatic system. Thus Euclid has five axioms and five postulates from which the theorems purport to derive. Hilbert (1903) reformulated the axioms to avoid omissions and redundancies, and claimed that Euclidean geometry could derive from a minimum set of 21 axioms. Modern axiomatic formulations, for example of set theory, discuss the form and choice of their axioms in great detail.

minimum value If a function f has a minimum at $x = a$, a minimum value is $f(a)$.

Minkowski, H. German mathematician (1864–1909), born in Russia. He published work on number theory, but is chiefly remembered for his early exposition of Einstein's relativity theory in terms of 'space-time' in which the interdependence of the coordinates x, y, z, t were given geometric expression. His enthusiasm was largely responsible for establishing the concept of 'space-time' as a metaphysical entity rather than as a mathematical model.

Minkowski's inequality If $\{a_i\}$, $\{b_i\}, \ldots$ are sets of positive numbers, then for any positive non-zero number p, where $p > 1$

$$\left(\sum a_i p\right)^{1/p} + \left(\sum b_i p\right)^{1/p} + \ldots \geqslant [(a_i + b_i + \ldots)p]^{1/p}$$

If $p < 1$ the inequality becomes $\leqslant$.

Minkowski space A metric space with a distance function that depends on the orientation of the interval measured. According to relativity theory it describes the geometry of a real space S moving with uniform velocity relative to a Euclidean space S_0.

min-max approximation If an empirical function $f(x)$ is to be interpolated numerically using a polynomial approximation $p(x)$ fitted to a limited number of observations or data points, the method seeks to minimize the maximum value of the expression $|p(x_i) - f(x_i)|$ in a given interval.

minor 1. Generally, as in ordinary speech, in phrases such as 'minor arc', 'minor axis' as opposed to 'major arc' etc.
2. Specifically the $(n-1) \times (n-1)$ determinant produced by deleting the row and column of an $n \times n$ determinant containing a particular element. Thus in

$$\begin{vmatrix} a_{11} & a_{12} & a_{13} \\ a_{21} & a_{22} & a_{23} \\ a_{31} & a_{32} & a_{33} \end{vmatrix}$$

the minor of a_{21} is seen to be

$$\begin{vmatrix} a_{12} & a_{13} \\ a_{32} & a_{33} \end{vmatrix}$$

minor premise *See* syllogism.

minus Lat. *minus*, less.

1. In elementary arithmetic the word and its symbol $(-)$ denote substraction. Then $10 - 3 = 7$ can be read 'ten minus three equals seven'.

2. A synonym for negative, as -3 or $^-3$, read 'minus three' for 'negative three'. Many writers and teachers try to avoid this use, but it is still frequently met.

Miquel point If circumcircles are drawn to the four triangles formed by the complete quadrilateral, they intersect in the Miquel point.

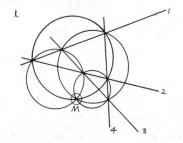

M.K.S.A. system *See* c.g.s. system.

Möbius, A. F. Swedish geometer (1790–1860). Pioneer in use of homogeneous coordinates (1827) which he introduced as barycentric coordinates. He considered polyhedral surfaces as sets of joined polygons and hence introduced the well known Möbius band.

Möbius strip (or band) A surface with one side and one edge obtained by putting the edge AB of a rectangle ABA′B′ as shown into coincidence with A′B′, so that A→A′, B→B′.

The strip can be modelled by a thin paper rectangle, but is to be considered as an intrinsically two-dimensional surface without thickness. The bounding curve of the band, as may be seen by following its edge, is a topological deformation of a single circle.

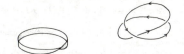

The circle can be obtained from the paper model by cutting the band along its dotted centre line, neglecting the width of the loop obtained.

modal class When a sample of data is large and its spread is fairly wide, then the data can be grouped to give a better indication of the underlying shape of the distribution.
The group or class having the greatest frequency is the modal ('o' long) class or group. The diagram shows the modal class in a distribution of heights.

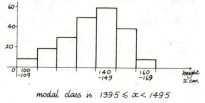

modal class is $139.5 \leqslant x < 149.5$

129

modal point That point on a frequency distribution at which the frequency is greatest.

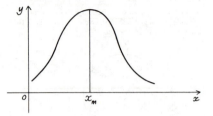

It corresponds to the mode of the data.

mode In any set of measures taken from a sample, the mode is the value that occurs most frequently, although this is often ill-defined or even misleading. In some circumstances it is the best measure of central tendency — for example, in footware manufacture the modal shoe size for any section of the population clearly dictates production. In a probability distribution it is the x value for which the density function reaches its maximum.

model Also mathematical model. This has two distinct meanings:
1. A physical three-dimensional construction which reproduces the forms of abstract mathematical configurations such as solids, surfaces, intersections of lines and planes in space and so on, often used in demonstration and teaching.
2. Generally (and since c. 1960 more commonly) a mathematical expression or formulation whose abstract behaviour is 'models', either in fact or as a proposed hypothesis, that of a physical system being described or investigated. A model may be developed in stages to account for properties that emerge as the result of increasing experimental knowledge, as for example the three expressions

$$PV = C, \ PV = RT, \ \left(P + \frac{a}{V^2}\right)(V - b) = RT$$

which were proposed in turn to describe the empirical properties of gases.
3. It is now accepted that one mathematical formulation can model another, generally produced at a higher order of abstraction. Thus the set of axioms that defines 'group' is modelled (or realized) by any one group that obeys the axioms.
4. The name is also applied to idealized real objects, for example, the behaviour of a rigid body models for some purposes the behaviour of real solids. Note that the model may exhibit properties which do *not* correspond to the physical situation modelled: thus model discontinuities may be physically continuous although they suggest the existence of regions in which the rate of physical change is very high.

modular arithmetic Also finite arithmetic. Integers of the form $r + km$ ($k = 0, 1, 2 \ldots$) where $r < m$ will give a remainder or residue r when divided by m. Integers having the same remainder r when divided by m are said to be congruent modulo m (Lat. abl. of *modulus*) and are written $a \equiv b$ mod m.

● $2 \equiv 13 \equiv 24$ mod 11

Since the possible values of r are $\{0, 1, 2 \ldots (m-1)\}$

and congruence is an equivalence relation, the process partitions the set of integers into m equivalence or residue classes congruent with $\{0, 1, 2 \ldots (m-1)\}$. This set will be closed with respect to addition modulo m, and hence generates a finite arithmetic.

●

+	0	1	2	3
0	0	1	2	3
1	1	2	3	0
2	2	3	0	1
3	3	0	1	2

Addition table modulo 4.

The algebra of congruences is used extensively in number theory.

module An additive abelian group, whose subgroups are then termed submodules.

modulo See modular arithmetic.

Modulor A set of scales or tabulated values devised by the architect Le Corbusier. He took a standard measure, the height of a man with his arm raised, and multiplied and divided this repeatedly by the golden ratio $\frac{1}{2}(\sqrt{5}+1)$, rounding off each result to a whole number. This gives an approximation to a Fibonacci sequence. Le Corbusier claimed that this scale or multiples of it should give the measures of furniture, rooms, buildings and their fittings, which would then be automatically adapted for human use.

modulus (Lat. a measure) 1. Synonym for absolute value.
2. For a complex number $z = x + iy$ the modulus of z denoted by $|z|$ is $\sqrt{(x^2 + y^2)}$, or the length of the representative vector in the Argand diagram. Then $|z_1 - z_2|$ gives the distance between the points representing z_1 and z_2. As a special case when z_1, z_2 are real $|z_1 - z_2|$ is simply their positive difference.
3. A divisor (from Euclid's concept of one number as the 'measure' of another). See modular arithmetic.
4. Of logarithms. The number by which logarithms in one base are transformed into those in another.

modulus of elasticity See Young's modulus.

Mollweide's projection See elliptical projection.

moment 1. Originally, the tendency of a force to produce movement about an axis, later quantified as the product of the force and its perpendicular distance from the axis. More generally, if the line of action of any force $\mathbf{F}$ passes through a point P whose position vector is $\mathbf{r}$, the moment of $\mathbf{F}$ about any point Q whose position vector is $\mathbf{r}_0$ is given by the vector product $(\mathbf{r} - \mathbf{r}_0) \times \mathbf{F}$. That is, it is normal to the plane of PQ and $\mathbf{F}$, in a direction given by the advance of a right-hand screw rotating in the sense of $\mathbf{F}$.

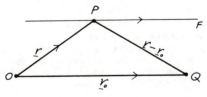

This quantity is also called the first moment of F. The product of the force and the square of its perpendicular distance is called the second moment of the force. Third and higher moments can be defined similarly. Since moments are additive the total moment of parallel forces of magnitudes F_1, $F_2 \ldots F_n$ acting at perpendicular distances d_1, $d_2 \ldots d_n$ from an origin 0 is $\sum_{i=1}^{n} F_i d_i$.

2. By analogy, statistical quantities similarly expressed are called moments. The rth moment about the origin is defined as

$$\mu_r' = E[X^r] = \int_{-\infty}^{\infty} x^r f(x)\,dx,$$

where $f(x)$ is a probability density function, for continuous data and, for discrete data

$$\mu_r' = \sum_{\text{all }i} X_i^r p(X_i)$$

$\mu_1' = E[X]$ defines the mean of the population.
The rth moment about the mean μ is defined as

$$\mu_r = E[(x-\mu)^r] = \int_{-\infty}^{\infty} (x-\mu)^r f(x)\,dx$$

for continuous data and, for discrete data

$$u_r = \sum_{\text{all }i} (X_i - \mu)^r p(X_i).$$

$$\mu_1 = \int_{-\infty}^{\infty} (x-\mu) f(x)\,dx = 0$$

$\mu_2 = E[(X-\mu)^2] = $ population variance σ^2.
This is usually more easily determined using moments about the origin. It can be shown that

$$\sigma^2 = \mu_2 = E[(X-\mu)^2] = \int_{-\infty}^{\infty} (x-\mu)^2 f(x)\,dx$$
$$= E[X^2] - (E[X])^2$$
$$= \mu_2' - (\mu_1')^2$$

moment generating function This can be denoted $M(t)$, and for any probability density function $f(x)$ of a continuous variable gives the expected value of e^{tx} or $E(e^{tx})$

$$M(t) = E(e^{tx})$$
$$= \int_{-\infty}^{\infty} e^{tx} f(x)\,dx$$

It is used to determine statistical moments about the origin, the rth moment being

$$\left. \frac{\partial^r M(t)}{\partial r_t} \right|_{t=0} = \mu_r'$$

See moment.

moment of inertia 1. Of a particle about an axis. The product of the mass of the particle and the square of its perpendicular distance from the axis. The moment of inertia of a system of particles is the sum of their individual moments, defined as

$$I = \sum_{i=1}^{n} m_i r_i^2$$

2. Of a continuous body. The limit of the sum of the moments of inertia about any axis of small regions into which the body is divided, as these regions become vanishingly small. It is thus given by an integral. In the dynamics of rotation, I plays the same part as mass in linear motion.
See also radius of gyration.

momentum *See* linear momentum, angular momentum.

monoid Synonym for hemigroup.

monomial An expression consisting of a single term.

monotonic function If the function f is either increasing or decreasing over an interval (but not both) then f is said to be monotonic over the interval.

monotonic sequence A sequence of terms $\{a_n\}$ which either increases or decreases for all n, so that $a_n \leqslant a_{n+1}$ or $a_n \geqslant a_{n+1}$. Sometimes the term strictly increasing or decreasing is used for $a_n < a_{n+1}$, $a_n > a_{n+1}$. From the axiom of completeness for real numbers it follows that a monotonic sequence bounded above or below must converge.

Monte Carlo methods Approximate solutions to problems in mathematics, statistics, .physics, operational research and so on by means of 'artificial sampling' or simulation, using random number tables or random numbers generated *ad hoc*. For example, the optimum stock level at which an essential item in fluctuating demand should be reordered to minimize the chance of running out of stock and maximize economy of storage can be estimated by using random numbers to simulate calls on the item (within the range shown to apply by past records) and taking into account the known range of delivery times. Named from a conference on random simulation held at Monte Carlo. There is no connection with any other activity associated with this locality!

morphism Same as homomorphism.

motion If the vector fixing the position of a body relative to an origin changes with time, the body is said to be in motion relative to the origin. There are three kinds of motion:

1. If the magnitude but not the direction of the vector changes, the motion is translatory or linear. Linear motion can be uniform or accelerated.
2. If the direction changes, the body is said to rotate about the origin. Rotatory motion can have a uniform or non-uniform angular velocity, and can be combined with translation.
3. A special case of rotation occurs when a body rotates about an axis within the body (as the earth about its N–S axis). This is often called spin. The body as a whole can then be stationary relative to an external origin.

moving average If the observations in a time series are given by $y_1, y_2, y_3 \ldots$ the moving average of length k is formed by taking the mean of the first k terms

$$\bar{y}_1 = \frac{y_1 + y_2 + \ldots + y_k}{k}$$

The next value $\bar{y}_2$ is obtained by subtracting y_1 from the total of the first k terms and adding y_{k+1}, so that

$$\bar{y}_2 = \frac{y_2 + y_3 + \ldots + y_{k+1}}{k}$$

This process is repeated to obtain a sequence $\bar{y}_1$, $\bar{y}_2$, $\bar{y}_3$,... of moving averages, and is used to smooth fluctuating data to show trends.

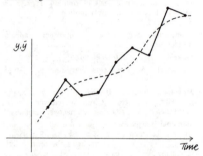

moving total   The sum of values over a given period, updated and taken forward at regular intervals, used in time series analysis for calculating moving averages.

multinomial distribution   *See* binomial distribution. If more than two events can occur with probabilities $p_1, p_2, p_3, \ldots p_n$ then the probability that the events will occur respectively $x_1, x_2, x_3, \ldots x_n$ times in N trials is given by

$$\frac{N!}{x_1! \, x_2! \, x_3! \ldots x_n!} \, p_1^{x_1} \cdot p_2^{x_2} \cdot p_3^{x_3} \ldots p_n^{x_n}$$

where

$$\sum_{i=1}^{n} x_i = N$$

This expression is, as with the binomial expansion, the general term in $(p_1 + p_2 + p_3 \ldots + p_n)^N$.

multinomial theorem   An extension of the binomial expansion of $(a + b)^n$ to more than two variables, as $(a + b + c + \ldots)^n$.

multiple   The result of multiplying a number by an integer. If a is a multiple of b then b divides into a without remainder. Successive multiples of a would be given by na ($n = 1, 2, 3, \ldots$).

multiple angle formulae   In elementary trigonometry, formulae such as $\sin 3A = 3 \sin A - 4 \sin^3 A$.

multiple correlation coefficient   1. A measure of the correlation, (usually taken as linear) between a response variable Y and two or more independent variables $X_1, X_2 \ldots$ It corresponds to the Pearson correlation coefficient, but is not easily computed and is difficult to interpret, since the partial correlation coefficients (determined by holding X_1 or X_2 constant) may be of opposite sign or dependent on the X chosen as constant.

2. A special case arises where the observed values of a response variable Y are correlated with the predicted values Y' given by a regression equation expressing the correlation of Y' with another variate X. The square of the multiple correlation coefficient between Y, Y' and X is the multiple determination coefficient.

multiple integral   The integral of a function of more than one variable over a given region of space.

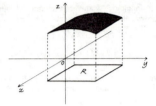

The volume enclosed by the surface $z = f(x, y)$ can be represented, with suitable limits, by the double integral

$$\iint f(x, y) \, dx \, dy$$

The limits correspond to the planes in the diagram which also define the volume.

multiple point   *See* double point.

multiple regression   *See* linear regression. This occurs where there is more than one independent variable, so that the response variable is modelled by $Y = a + bX_1 + cX_2 + \ldots$ Here b and c taken singly are the *partial regression coefficients* of Y on X_1 and X_2, since each vanishes in turn if X_1, or X_2 is held constant during a set of trials. Any actual values of Y are given by $a + bX_1 + cX_2 + \ldots + r$ where r is the residual, usually assumed to be normally distributed.

multiple roots   If m of the possible n roots of a polynomial equation of degree n are identical, it is said to have m multiple roots $x_1, x_2, \ldots x_m$.

● $x^2 - 2x + 1 = 0$ has two roots, $x_1 = x_2 = 1$.

The x axis is tangential to the curve representing the equation at the point where multiple roots occur.

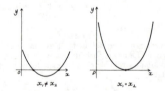

multiple valued function   Originally used for expressions such as $\sqrt{x}$ or arcsin x that have more than one value corresponding to each value of the argument or variable. The modern definition of real functions now excludes such expressions, but it remains in considering the functions of complex variables.

multiplication   A binary operation on a set or between members of two sets, denoted by $\times$, $.$, or by juxtaposition as $ab = a \times b$. Originally defined as an

132

operation between integers equivalent to repeated addition. (2×3) may be read as 2 lots of 3 or $(3+3)$ or 2 multiplied by 3, implying $(2+2+2)$.

The process can then be defined recursively for natural numbers given that addition is defined, using the concept $(n+1)$ or 'successor to n'.

$$\left. \begin{array}{l} a \times (b+1) = (a \times b) + a \\ a \times 1 = a \end{array} \right\} \text{Definition}$$

By putting $b=1$ this generates the product $1 \times 2 = 2$ if $a=1$, $2 \times 2 = 4$ if $a=2$ and so on. In this way multiplication is made a logical outcome of Peano's axioms, even if its origins are in fact empirical.

The process is then extended by definition and analogy to many other classes of mathematical entities:

Between rationals as $a/b \times c/d = ac/bd$ $(a, b, c, d \in \mathbb{Z}; b, d \neq 0$.

Between reals, after defining them as Dedekind sections of rationals.

Between complex numbers (r_1, θ_1) (r_2, θ_2) as $[r_1 r_2, (\theta_1 + \theta_2)]$.

Multiplication of two numbers or other entities is said to give their product. If the operation is not commutative (as with matrices) we distinguish right multipliers from left multipliers.

See also cross product, logical product, scalar product, vector product, multiplicative identity.

multiplication law of probability *See* probability. If A and B are independent events which occur with probabilities $p(a)$ and $p(b)$ then the probability of the joint event (A and B) is given by

$$p(A \text{ and } B) = p(A) \cdot p(B)$$

This law may be deduced from the Kolmogorov axioms and may be extended to any number of independent events.

A more general law for non-independent events gives

$$p(A \text{ and } B) = p(A) \cdot p(B|A)$$
$$= p(B) \cdot p(A|B)$$

where $p(A|B)$ is the probability of A given that B has occurred.

This reduces to the first expression if A, B are independent and $p(A|B) = p(A)$.

multiplicative group Any group for which the binary operation may conventionally be represented by juxtaposition or the multiplication sign.

● The operation of compounding the six elements of the permutation group P_3.

multiplicative identity For the multiplicative operator $\times$ on a set S the multiplicative identity I is a unique element of S such that

$$a \times I = I \times a = a \text{ for all } a \text{ in } S.$$

For the multiplication of real numbers the identity is 1, for 2×2 matrices the identity is the unit matrix $I = \begin{pmatrix} 1 & 0 \\ 0 & 1 \end{pmatrix}$

See also additive identity.

multiplicative inverse When a binary operation between elements of a set containing an identity element I is multiplication, the multiplicative inverse of any element a is written a^{-1}. It has the property that $a \times a^{-1} = I$

● 1/3 is the multiplicative inverse of 3 in $\mathbb{Q}$.
Since

$$\begin{pmatrix} 5 & 3 \\ 3 & 2 \end{pmatrix} \times \begin{pmatrix} 2 & -3 \\ -3 & 5 \end{pmatrix} = \begin{pmatrix} 1 & 0 \\ 0 & 1 \end{pmatrix}$$

each of these matrices is the inverse of the other.

multiplicative notation Any binary operation between elements that has a similar formal structure to multiplication between numbers can be denoted by a multiplication symbol. Sometimes $\otimes$ or $\odot$ is used to distinguish this from numerical multiplication. The process may be non-commutative so that

$$a \otimes b \neq b \otimes a$$

The notation is commonly used to represent operations in a group or between matrices. With vectors, more than one multiplicative process can be defined.

multiply connected 1. A network is so described if one or more points can be deleted from its arcs (or if its arcs may be cut) without separating it into two portions. Otherwise it is simply connected. The connectivity N is given by $1+n$, when n is the maximum number of points that can be deleted.

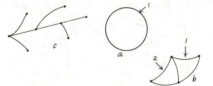

Loop a can be cut at 1, so $N=2$. Net b can be cut at 1 or 2, so $N=3$. Net c cannot be cut anywhere and is simply connected with $N=1$.

2. Similarly, a surface is multiply connected if one or more closed cuts can be made without separating it into two regions; otherwise it is singly connected.

A torus d is multiply connected, $N=2$.

multivariate distribution *See* bivariate distribution.

multivariate normal distribution A vector variate $X = (X_1, X_2, X_3 \ldots)$ where the R.H. brackets enclose an ordered set of random variables, is said to have a multivariate normal distribution if, but only if, all linear combinations of the form $a_1 X_1 + a_2 X_2 + a_3 X_3 + \ldots$ have normal distributions.

mutually exclusive Used of two conditions when each excludes the other. Thus, odd numbers and even numbers form mutually exclusive classes, but odd numbers and primes do not.

nabla The symbol ∇. *See* differential operator, divergence, gradient.

naive set theory The mathematical structure based on the definition of set which allows membership to any distinguishable entities, subject to a test for membership. It is open to Russell's paradox, and invites replacement by an axiomatic set theory.

NAND Name now given to the complement (or negation) of AND in Boolean algebra, equivalent in logic to $\sim (p.q)$, not both p and q. It is defined by the truth table

a	b	a NAND b
0	0	1
0	1	1
1	0	1
1	1	0

It has the important property of logical completeness, i.e. any function in Boolean algebra or its equivalents can be written using this connective only.

napierian logarithms *See* logarithm.

Napier, John Scottish mathematician and polymath (1550–1617). Inventor of 'Napier's bones' (1617) and the first user of the decimal point in its modern form. He described in 1614–1619 a system of logarithms often, although wrongly, identified with natural logarithms. Napier did not arrive at the modern concept of a logarithm as the index of a base number, but began with the correspondence of the terms of an arithmetic series and a geometric series having a fractional multiplier. His first tables were logarithms of trigonometric ratios, and were, in modern terms, to base 1/e.
See also Briggs, logarithm.

Napier's analogies Name originally given to Napier's tables of logarithms, from the root meaning of the Greek *analogia* as describing ratios.
See Euclid Book V Def 8.

nappe A name given to the parts of a double cone as generated so that one complete cone consists of two nappes A and B.

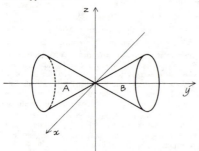

natural logarithms *See* logarithm.

natural numbers The set of symbols $\mathbb{N} = \{1, 2, 3, 4 \ldots\}$ whose structure is given by Peano's axioms. The set is a mathematical formalization of the undefined empirical sequence of number words used in most developed languages for tallying or ordering sets of objects.
See also integers.

nautical mile A distance equal to the length of arc along a meridian that subtends one angular minute at the centre of the earth. It is so chosen that the angular latitude scale on charts will correspond to distance. It varies from approximately 2004 m at the poles to 1984 m at the equator.

n-dimensional A mathematical entity is n-dimensional if it requires a set of n numbers to specify it completely. Thus position in physical space has dimension 3, and on a surface 2; the phase space giving the temperature and pressure at any point in a volume of gas has dimension 5.
See space.

N (μ, σ^2) distribution *See* normal distribution curve.

necessary and sufficient If the truth of proposition p depends on the truth of proposition q, then q is said to be a necessary condition for p.

$$p = \text{triangle ABC is equilateral}$$
$$q = \text{triangle ABC is isoscles}$$

Proposition q may not, however, be a sufficient condition for p, and further information may be needed

$$r = \text{triangle ABC is equiangular}$$

r is now a necessary and sufficient condition for p. Also expressed as 'if and only if'.

negation If p is any proposition then the proposition not p, denoted $\sim p$ (or p', $\rightarrow p$ or $\bar{p}$) is called the negation of p. Negation can be defined by the truth table

p	$\sim p$
1	0
0	1

Negation is symbolized in traditional logic by e

$$A \, e \, B \text{ reads no A is B}$$

negative After a long history of imprecise use, negative is now defined in terms of ordered pairs or couples of natural numbers (*see* integers). Thus ^-a appears as the pair $(0, a)$ with the combination rules of difference couples. Any other negative, such as ^-x ($x \in \mathbb{R}$) is then given as $(^-1)x$. The common use of this word as equivalent to 'null', (e.g. 'a negative response') should be avoided in mathematical contexts. The word should also be clearly distinguished from 'negation' in mathematical logic.

negative binomial distribution In a set of Bernoulli trials, the probability that x failures occur before the rth success is recorded is

$$\binom{r+x-1}{x} p^{r-1} q^x$$

where p, q are the probabilities of success and failure. The name follows from the expansion of $(p+q)^{-r}$.

negative correlation If one variate tends to increase

while another decreases (or vice versa) the variates are said to be negatively correlated. This corresponds to a negative value for the linear correlation coefficient.

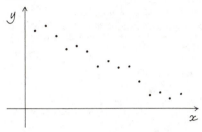

neighbourhood   1. A generalization to space of n dimensions of the Cauchy ϵ criterion for the convergence of sequences. Suppose X is any space, x any point in it, and the distance between x and any other point denoted by $d(x, y)$. Let ϵ be any arbitrarily small value of d. Then the set P of all points y such that $d(x, y) \leqslant \epsilon$ is called a neighbourhood (or ϵ − neighbourhood) of X. The neighbourhood in two and three dimensions is a circle or sphere of radius ϵ surrounding the point; in one dimension it is the interval $x \pm \epsilon$.
2. The concept is further generalized in topology. A neighbourhood of x in a topological space is any subset of the space that contains an open set that contains x.

nephroid   An epicycloid of two cusps, the set of positions of a point on a circle of radius a which rolls around another of radius $2a$. It is also the envelope of any diameter of a circle that rolls around another of the same diameter. The parametric equations are

$$x = a\,(3\cos t - \cos 3t)$$
$$y = a\,(3\sin t - \sin 3t)$$

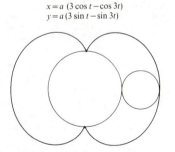

nested intervals   A sequence of intervals or sets of points I_n such that $I_{n+1} \subset I_n$ for all $n \in \mathbb{N}$. If all the

intervals are bounded and closed, then $\bigcap_{n=1}^{\infty} I_n = \phi$; that is, there is at least one point that lies in each of the intervals.

Certain properties of continuous functions can be proved by repeated bisection of an interval to produce a sequence of nested intervals.

net   A plane configuration of precisely measured lines and angles which when drawn on paper and cut out will fold up into a given solid.
See also Schlegel diagram.

network   1. A set of points, called nodes, which are joined by lines drawn between them (sometimes called arcs). The network is defined solely by the connections existing between its nodes, not by their spatial distribution or the form of the lines, which may or may not cross at points other than the given nodes.

2. Any set of entities and relations between them that can be represented diagrammatically by the above, as in a telephone or railway network.

neutral element   Synonym for identity element.

newton   *See* Appendix 1.

Newtonian mechanics   The study of mass systems involving motion, force, energy, momentum, impact (but not electromagnetic effects) using the Laws of Motion and the inverse square gravitational law. There is also the assumption that inertial frameworks transform by the Galilean transformation. The name is used to distinguish the results from those of relativistic mechanics.

Newton, Isaac   English mathematician (1642–1727). His contributions to both mathematics and physics changed the direction of these studies decisively. The success of his gravitational hypothesis, that masses m_1, m_2 whose distance apart is d experience a force of attraction given by

$$F = \frac{G m_1 m_2}{d^2}$$

where G is a universal constant, established a consistent account of the solar system. He made major advances in most mathematical topics of his day, and discovered the analytical methods that formed the basis of the calculus. His gravitational theory is still valid after 300 years, although it is now held to be a limiting case when d is large and at least one of the masses comparatively small, as in actual solar orbits.

Newton-Leibnitz controversy   The long dispute whether Newton or Leibnitz first discovered the calculus and its uses. The dispute began in publications by other writers but both Newton and Leibnitz were eventually involved. The modern view is that the two discoveries were completely independent, using fundamentally different notational approaches. That of Leibnitz has proved most useful in general, but Newton's dot notation survives in mechanics to indicate derivates with respect to time.

Newton-Raphson method   As for Newton's method (q.v.). By taking extra terms in the Taylor series, it can be established that the successive solutions have quadratic convergence.

135

Newton's laws of motion   The three laws or postulates which begin Newton's *Principia*. They can be paraphrased informally as:

1. Bodies persevere (Newton's word) in a state of rest or uniform rectilinear motion unless under the action of forces.
2. The rate of change of their 'quantity of motion' or momentum is proportional to any force which may be acting, and takes place in the force's line of action.
3. Reaction to the body exerting force is equal and opposite to its action.

Law 1, due originally to Galileo, describes inertia and, in effect, defines force. Law 2 establishes the fundamental equation of dynamics, Force = mass × acceleration. Law 3 corresponds to the conservation of linear momentum.
The exact status of these 'laws' and the assumptions on which they are based has been and is a matter of continuing controversy; but by using them and adding subsidiary hypotheses about conservation, elastic collision and gravitational attraction, Newton and his followers were able to give a substantially complete account of terrestrial and planetary mechanics. The later discovery of electromagnetic phenomena lead to a reassessment of Newton's principles, but they are still valid for all practical applications of mechanics where velocities are small compared with that of electromagnetic radiation.
See momentum, action, force.

Newton's method   An iterative method for solving an equation $f(x)=0$

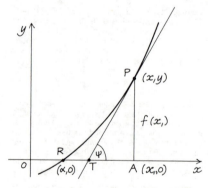

$OR = \alpha$ is an exact root, $OA = x_1$ an approximate root obtained, say, by inspection. The tangent at $P = (x_1, y_1)$ cuts the x axis at T. Then

$$OT = OA - AT$$
$$= x_1 - f(x_1) \cot \psi$$
$$= x_1 - \frac{f(x_1)}{f'(x_1)}$$

Hence if x_1 is a first approximation, by repeating the iteration (with OT a better approximation to OR than OA)

$$x_2 = x_1 - \frac{f(x_1)}{f'(x_1)}$$

and so on for successive approximations $x_1, x_2, \dots$ $x_r, \dots$ A more rigorous analytical derivation of the formula may be seen from the first two terms only of Taylor's series in the form

$$f(a+h) \approx f(a) + hf'(a)$$

where a is the first approximation and $f(a+h)$ is the exact root. Thus the Newton method ignores all terms in h of power two or more.
See iteration for example of use.

n-gon   A polygon with n sides

Nicomedes   Greek geometer (c. 230 B.C.), who described a mechanical linkage (equivalent to a conchoidal trammel) which allowed, theoretically, the exact trisection of an angle.

nilpotent   A term describing any matrix A such that $A^k = 0$ for some positive k.

$$A = \begin{pmatrix} 0 & 1 & 0 \\ 0 & 0 & 1 \\ 0 & 0 & 0 \end{pmatrix} \quad A^2 = \begin{pmatrix} 0 & 0 & 1 \\ 0 & 0 & 0 \\ 0 & 0 & 0 \end{pmatrix} \quad A^3 = \begin{pmatrix} 0 & 0 & 0 \\ 0 & 0 & 0 \\ 0 & 0 & 0 \end{pmatrix}$$

Nim   A simple two-person game played with three or any greater number of rows of sticks or matches. Each player can take in turn all or some of the matches in any one row: the loser is the one removing the last match. It is interesting mathematically because a strategy for winning can be devised by recording the number of matches in each row in binary notation; this strategy can readily be programmed for a digital computer. If both players know the strategy the first is bound either to win or lose according to the number of matches set out in the rows.

nine point circle   The circle which, for any triangle, passes through the midpoints of the three sides, the feet of the perpendiculars from the vertices to the opposite sides, and the midpoints of the lines joining the vertices to the orthocentre.

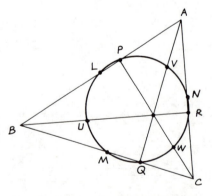

nine point geometry   A finite geometry consisting of nine elements called points and a number of associated elements called lines. Terms such as *parallel* and *intersection* are defined, and axioms are set up, such as:

There are three points not on the same line.
Every line is on exactly three points.

A sequence of theorems is generated. The crucial theorem is that all the derivable theorems require not more than 12 lines associated with the points.

node 1. In any network, a point where paths or loops begin or end.

2. In an oscillating system, a point distinct from fixed boundary points, where the amplitude is zero.

3. A cusp or isolated singular point on a curve.

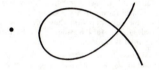

Noether, Emmy German (later American) mathematician (1882–1935). She did much of the early work on abstract axiomatic algebra, particularly on non-commutative algebras and algebraic number theory.

nomogram Also called alignment chart. A diagram constructed from linear or logarithmic scales which allows numerical values to be read off for conversion and other formulae. A simple example for converting miles to kilometres is shown.

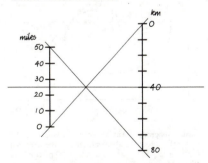

A ruler is passed through the mile value and the pole P: it then cuts the kilometre scale at the required point. Some engineering texts use nomograms to give the numerical values of the subjects of formulae corresponding to the various values of the variables. Like other such devices they are being displaced by simple computer programs or pocket calculators.

non-denumerable *See* denumerable infinity.

non-empty sets Since the null set is regarded as a subset of all sets, it may sometimes be necessary to specify that a set should be non-empty. A non-empty set contains at least one member.

non-Euclidean geometry Any consistent system of geometrical theorems based on axioms other than Euclid's, often differing by an alternative Fifth Postulate, which then implies a non-Pythagorean distance function or metric.
See hyperbolic geometry, elliptic geometry.

non-intersecting lines The term includes both parallel and skew lines.

non-negative Term used to distinguish the two sets of numbers $\{x : x$ is positive$\}$ and $\{x : x$ is positive or zero$\}$. These are denoted as $x > 0$ or $x \geqslant 0$ for all $x \in \mathbb{Z}$.

non-orientable *See* orientable surface. A surface such as that of the Möbius band or Klein bottle cannot be given an orientation in three-dimensional space that can distinguish right and left, or inside and outside.

non-parametric methods More properly 'distribution free' methods. These are inference methods valid irrespective of the underlying distributions, and are usually handled by ranking the variates in order of magnitude. The 'traditional' methods use parameters such as mean and variance which assume a distribution.

non-singular matrix Any $n \times n$ matrix A whose determinant $|A|$ is not zero. The set of simultaneous equation $A\mathbf{x} = c$ has no unique solution if the matrix A is singular. A matrix is non-singular if it has an inverse A^{-1} such that $AA^{-1} = A^{-1}A = I$, where I is the identity matrix of order n: the converse is also true.
See Cramer's rule.

non-terminating decimal A decimal representation of a number having infinitely many non-zero digits. They are either periodic or non-periodic. Periodic decimals represent rational numbers, non-periodic represent irrational numbers. (*See also* recurring decimal.)

- $\frac{1}{3} = 0.3333\ldots$ or $0.\overline{3}$
  $\pi = 3.1415926535\ldots$

non-uniform convergence *See* uniform convergence.

NOR The negation of OR in Boolean algebra or its equivalents, denoted NOR or $\sim(p \vee q)$. It is defined by the truth table

a	b	a NOR b
0	0	1
0	1	0
1	0	0
1	1	0

It has the important property of logical completeness.
See NAND.

NOR gate A mechanical or (usually) electronic device which gives an output for the inputs a NOR b, but not otherwise.

normal 1. To a curve or surface. A line drawn at any point perpendicular to the tangent of a curve or the tangent plane of the surface at that point.
2. Of a subgroup. A subgroup H of a group G is called a normal (or invariant) subgroup of G if $gHg^{-1} = H$ for all $g \in G$.

normal approximation A discrete probability or frequency distribution, such as the binomial or Poisson for n trials, may be shown to approach a continuous normal distribution as n increases without limit. It is often convenient to calculate values from this rather than from the original discrete distribution, especially if n is large.

normal component The unit vector $\hat{t}$ is resolved into a unit vector $\hat{n}$ normal to a curve at P, so that the component is in the direction of the normal at P, together with a tangential component.

normal curve of error See normal distribution curve.

normal deviation The expression $z = \dfrac{x - \mu}{\sigma}$ is known as the normal deviation, deviate or z-score. It is a measure of the deviation of a score x from the mean of the population μ, expressed in terms of the standard deviation of the population.
Also known as standard normal score, z score, normalized score.

normal distribution curve Also Gaussian distribution curve, normal curve of error. A frequency distribution of a continuous variate of the general form $y = Ae^{-\frac{1}{2}x^2}$. Derived by Gauss in calculating the probable orbits of asteroids from a limited number of intermittent observations subject to error, although an earlier formulation was due to Laplace (1778). Since e^{-x^2} is a maximum when x^2 is a minimum, Gauss was able to deduce the method of least squares for constructing the line of best fit to the observational data. The function is of importance because it is applicable to many real processes and because of its connection with the Central Limit Theorem. The function is continuous, symmetric, unimodal, with a domain extending over all real values. The general form given is written specifically as $y = e^{-(x - \mu)^2/2\sigma^2}$ or $y = \exp[-(x - \mu)^2/2\sigma^2]$ where μ and σ^2 are the mean and variance of the set of values. The x values can be transformed to the standardized or z values given by $z = \dfrac{x - \mu}{\sigma}$ and the distribution could be written $y = e^{-\frac{1}{2}z^2}$

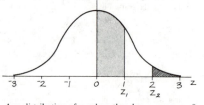

Any distribution of z values then has a mean $\mu = 0$ and standard deviation $\sigma = 1$. For normally dis-

tributed data 68.7% of the values lie between $-1 \leqslant z \leqslant +1$, 95.4% between $-2 \leqslant z \leqslant +2$ and 99.7% between $-3 \leqslant z \leqslant +3$. The notation $N(0, 1)$ is used for this form, called the standard normal distribution. For a probability density function the total area under the curve must be unity. Since the area under the curve is

$$\int_{-\infty}^{\infty} \exp\left[\frac{-z^2}{2}\right] dz = \sqrt{(2\pi)}$$

the function becomes a probability distribution function $f(x)$ of area unity if $f(z) = \dfrac{1}{\sqrt{(2\pi)}} \exp\left[\dfrac{-z^2}{2}\right]$ and this is its final form. Normal probability tables are used in practice. The area under the curve $f(z)$ is tabulated for small increments of z, and gives the cumulative probability, and hence the expected proportional frequency, as z increases. Since the curve is symmetrical about the vertical axis only positive values need to be tabulated. The diagram shows the areas for 0 to z_1 and z_2 to ∞.

normalized score See normal deviation.

normalizer See stabilizer. When the binary operation that defines a stabilizer is replaced by the operation of raising to a power, i.e. $x \circ a$ is replaced by a^x, the subgroup $G(a)$ thus formed is called a normalizer. Thus for the group $\{\mathbb{Z}, x\}$ the normalizer of any $a \in A$ is the identity.

normal matrix A matrix A which multiplies commutatively with its transpose, so that $AA^T = A^T A$.

normal region A closed region in the x, y plane which is convex in both the x and y directions, although it may show concavities obliquely.

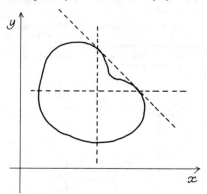

normal subgroup Any subgroup in which the left and right cosets are identical, such as the subgroup $\{1, r^2\}$ in $D_4 = \{1, r, r^2, r^3, a, b, c, d\}$. The combination tables are

$\otimes$	a	c
1	a	c
r^2	c	a

$\otimes$	1	r^2
a	a	c
c	c	a

northing The distance between two points on the earth's surface can be resolved into two components, the *northing*, the angular or actual great circle distance along a meridian in a direction towards the north pole, and the *easting*, a similar measure easterly along a latitude. The terms are also used for distances or coordinates so measured on the grid or graticule of a map from a suitable origin.

not 1. As a prefix in symbolic logic it indicates the negation of a proposition p. Not p is written $\sim p$, $\bar{p}$, p' or $\rightarrow p$. In logic $\sim (\sim p) \Rightarrow p$. Not can be defined by a truth table

p	$\sim p$
0	1
1	0

2. In a switching circuit a NOT-gate is any circuit with an output if there is no input, but no output if there is input. It is sometimes called an inverting circuit.

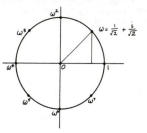

notation Any set of symbols used systematically and according to agreed conventions, to represent numbers, operations and mathematical entities generally, as in denary notation, matrix notation, Leibnitz notation.

nought Colloquial equivalent to zero, the cardinal number of the empty set, also the symbol 0 representing it. Often used in reading decimals.

● 0.0006 point three noughts six.

nowhere dense Used of a set of numbers, e.g. $\mathbb{N}$, which contains no cluster points.
See dense.

n-space The set of ordered n-tuples $\{x_1, x_2 \dots x_n\}$ where $x_i \in \mathbb{R}$ and $n \in \mathbb{N}$. If $n=3$ this describes ordinary physical space on the assumption that the x_i are independent of time. Euclidean or other geometries and the laws of vector algebra can be generalized for values of $n > 3$.
See sample space, phase space, vector space.

nth roots of unity The roots of the equation $x^n = 1$ ($z \in \mathbb{C}$). Plotted on an Argand diagram, these lie on the vertices of a regular n-gon with one vertex at $(1, 0)$ inscribed in a unit circle centre $(0, 0)$.

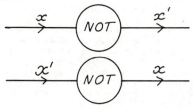

Hence the roots, from the diagram, can be given as

$$\cos \frac{2\pi k}{n} + i \sin \frac{2\pi k}{n} \quad (k = 0, 1, 2 \dots (n-1))$$

From this it follows that if the roots are 1, ω for $k = 0$, 1 the set of roots is 1, ω, ω^2, $\omega^3 \dots \omega^{n-1}$ and that $1 + \omega + \omega^2 + \omega^3 + \dots + \omega^{n-1} = 0$. The set of roots forms a multiplicative group of order n. Geometrically they divide the circumference of the unit circle into n parts (Gauss 1831) and $z^n - 1 = 0$ is sometimes called the cyclotomic equation.

null distribution The probability distribution of any test statistic under the assumption that the null hypothesis is true.

null hypothesis Usually denoted H_0, it is the central hypothesis in a significance test, acting as a criterion against which the evidence for the alternative hypothesis H_1 can be assessed. It often, but not necessarily always, relates to the maintenance of the status quo, and is the hypothesis that there is no difference between the measures being compared, or that a strategy being evaluated has had no result.

null matrix Also called zero matrix. Any matrix all of whose elements are zero. The set of $n \times m$ matrices includes a distinct zero matrix for every value of n and m.

null method Used of a physical experiment or measurement which is arranged to give a zero reading at a required outcome and non-zero otherwise. It is easier to detect no outcome than to measure a given outcome. The non-zero conditions must be observed concurrently since they are the only check that the experiment is working.

null sequence A sequence whose limit is zero, e.g. the set $\left\{\frac{1}{2}, \frac{1}{4} \dots \frac{1}{2^n} \dots \right\}$ where $n \rightarrow \infty$. Also written as $\left\{\frac{1}{2^n}\right\}$ $n = 1, 2, 3 \dots$

null set *See* empty set.

null space The null set when considered as a member of any given space, as sample space, phase space, vector space, etc.

null vector The vector of a given order or dimension, all of whose components or elements are zero, and denoted **0**.

number The word itself is older than mathematics and refers to more than one concept. Greek philosophers saw that the idea of a 'unit' was arbitrary, and early Greek geometry attempted to express number as the ratio between measures of length, taking any convenient length as the unit. This work led to the apparent contradiction of incommensurable numbers which do not agree with intuition. Mathematics has now largely solved the philosophical and intuitive problems by defining numbers of different logical types, always, at least in principle, referred to in context with a suitable adjective. *See* integer and 'number' prefixed by algebraic, cardinal, complex, irrational, natural, ordinal, rational, real, transcendental, transfinite.

Numbers, however, have properties in common, and may, for mathematical purposes, be defined axiomatically as a set of entities having these properties. A suitable axiom set which defines a set of entities that represent a number system S is

1. If $a, b \in S$ there is a relation $+$ such that $a+b = b+a = c \in S$
2. There is an identity I_+ such that for all x, $x + I_+ = I_+ + x = x$
3. For all $a, b, c \in S$ $(a+b)+c = a+(b+c)$
4. For all $x \in S$ there is an inverse $x^{-1} \in S$ such that $x + x^{-1} = I_+$

These four axioms are repeated for $a, b, c, \ldots \in S$ for a second relation $\times$ with an identity $I_\times$.
Any one kind of number may be deficient in meeting all the axioms, e.g. the set N has no element x^{-1} for the relation $+$ and the identity I_+.

number bonds An important concept in teaching and learning **a**rithmetical processes. All standard algorithms 'for addition, subtraction, multiplication and division of larger numbers depend on knowing by heart the sums and products of single-digit integers. These necessary results are called 'number facts' or 'number bonds' in discussing elementary mathematical education.

number field A field whose elements consist of numbers, and is therefore closed to the four operations of ordinary arithmetic, as in the sets Q and R. Number fields permit a set to be extended by adjoining elements not in the set.

- $S = \{a + b\sqrt{3}; a, b, \in Q\}$ is a field extension of Q although $\sqrt{3}$ is irrational, because an operation between any two elements of S gives an element of S, as in $(1 + 2\sqrt{3})(2 + 3\sqrt{3}) = (20 + 7\sqrt{3})$.

number-line A straight line on which real or other numbers are represented by intervals marked to scale. By convention positive numbers are set out to the right and negative to the left of the point chosen as origin and labelled zero.

number pair An ordered pair of numbers from a specified set, as (a, b) $a, b \in N$ or (x, y) $x, y \in R$.
They may be used to define points in a plane, vectors, physical states or members of a more general kind than those specified, e.g. complex numbers if the elements of the pair are real.

number system 1. Sometimes used for a system of numbers, as Babylonian or Indo–Arabic systems.
2. The natural numbers N form a number system, in which not all the processes of arithmetic can be applied to all members; that is the set, which is closed to addition and multiplication is not closed to subtraction, division and the extraction of roots. Number systems in general are logical constructions which become closed to one or more of these operations. The principal systems are

Naturals	N	closed to $\{+, \times\}$
Integers	Z	closed to $\{+, \times, -\}$
Rationals	Q	closed to $\{+, \times -, \div\}$
Reals	R	closed to $\{+, \times, -, \div\}$ and taking of roots iff positive
Complex	C	closed to all five operations

Transfinite and infinitesimal number systems are also proposed.
See number.

number theory The branch of mathematics that deals with the properties of numbers and the structure of number systems. Elementary theory would include topics such as Highest Common Factor, Least Common Multiple, decomposition into primes and modular arithmetic. More developed theory studies algebraic structures to determine the properties of all possible number systems. A famous conjecture in number theory due to Gauss was that the number of primes up to and not exceeding x approached $x/\ln x$ as x becomes large. This was proved in 1896 (Hadamard and de la Vallée Poussin).
See also prime pairs and Goldbach's conjecture.

numeral A sign or symbol denoting a number, as Indo–Arabic or Roman numerals. A finite set of numerals may represent any number in a system by means of a notation, as decimal or binary notation. Tally marks are not regarded as numerals.

numerator Lat. *numerare*, to number. The first number in a fraction expressed as a/b, which gives the number of parts taken after the unit has been divided, as two in two-thirds, $2/3$.
See denominator.

numerical coefficients The numbers which appear in an algebraic expression, associated as multipliers with the variables. In algebra such coefficients may be represented by letters, usually from the beginning of the alphabet.

- The coefficients of the polynomial in x, $5x^2 + 3x + 2$ are 5, 3, 2.
  The coefficients of $\dfrac{ax+b}{cx+d}$ are a, b, c, d.

Since a coefficient is always a numerical value or a literal symbol that can take a set of values the term is pleonastic but is useful for emphasis, as in 'identical but for a numerical coefficient'.

numerical integration *See* integration.

numerical methods Any methods for arriving at a direct numerical answer to a problem without first producing a general solution in which numerical values can afterwards be substituted. They are often applicable to problems to which general solutions cannot be found, and are then calculated to required degrees of approximation. Available for integrals, differential equations, polynomials and equations generally, and now of great importance since they can be programmed into digital computers.

O

oblate spheroid The surface produced by rotating an ellipse about its minor axis. A special case of the ellipsoid, having the equation

$$\frac{x^2}{a^2}+\frac{y^2}{a^2}+\frac{z^2}{c^2}=1 \quad \begin{array}{l}(a,c>0)\\(c<a)\end{array}$$

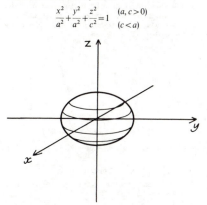

oblique coordinates Cartesian coordinates not at right angles to one another.
See also covariant, contravariant.

oblique projection 1. A parallel projection onto a plane not at right angles to the axis of projection.

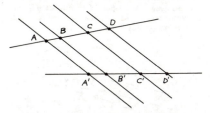

2. Used of any map projections in which the graticule is not in one of the standard positions relative to the earth's surface. Thus the standard Mercator projection coincides with the globe at the equator, so that distortion approaches zero near Latitude 0°. An oblique Mercator graticule is assumed to touch the globe along a great circle other than the equator or a meridian, and neither meridians nor latitude circles project as straight lines.
See also transverse Mercator.

obtuse angle An angle greater than one but less than two right angles, from L. *obtusus*, blunted. If the measure of an angle A is θ degrees, then A is obtuse iff $90° < \theta < 180°$.
See also acute angle.

obtuse angle hypothesis *See* Saccheri quadrilateral.

occupancy problem Any problem which can be modelled by a set of r balls, which may or may not be distinguishable by size, colour etc., which are to be put into a labelled set of n boxes or cells, according to any specified rules of distribution. Examples cover a wide range. In each the thing or event

modelled by 'ball' precedes that represented by 'box'.
● Machine breakdowns occurring each day of a year
  Disintegration among radioactive atoms
  Deaths associated with age groups
  Misprinted words in any text
  Identification of queen bee in a swarm ($r = 1$)

occurrence ratio *See* probability.

octahedral group The group S_4 of permutations on four symbols, also called the symmetry group of degree 4. The group has $4! = 24$ elements and is realized by the set of symmetries and rotations that map an octahedron on to itself.
See also permutation group.

octave Any group of eight. Since western music divides the interval between a fundamental note and its first harmonic (*see* harmonic) into eight (counting both first and last notes) this harminic is said to be an octave above the fundamental.

odd function A function not taken at its zeros, whose sign changes when the sign of the variable changes. If the sign does not change the function is even. Thus $y = x^3$ is odd, $y = x^2$ is even.

odd number A non-zero integer not divisible by two. If it is divisible it is called *even*.

odd permutation *See* permutation.

offset In surveying small areas such as archaeological sites, distances measured at right angles from measured intervals along a straight base line, and serving to fix points relative to this line.

ogive From the name used in architecture for a curve having this shape. The curve of the cumulative normal frequency distribution.

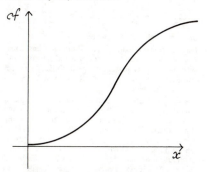

one The number one, denoted 1 in our numerals, was given metaphysical status by the Greeks. It is now taken as a proper noun, the name of the natural number corresponding to the concept 'cardinal of the unit set', where a unit set is defined by some logical process that expresses the concept of singularity, such as:

A unit set I is such that there exists an $x \in I$, and if $x, y \in I$ then $x = y$.

Alternative, one is the cardinal of the set of all empty or null sets. Since the empty set is a realization of the concept 'unique', the set of all empty sets is a con-

141

venient conceptual realization of a unit set or single-ton.

one-many relation   A correspondence that relates more than one element of a set B with some members of A. Since each $x \in A$ does not have a unique image in B, the relationship is not now regarded as a function in analysis.

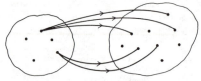

See also many-one relation, function.

one-one correspondence   A fundamental but very general concept, a relation that associates each single member of any set S with a unique member of S' and vice versa. There is one-one correspondence between registered cars and their allotted registration numbers, or between x and $\sin x$ if $0 \leqslant x \leqslant \pi/2$.
See also many-one relation, one-many relation.

one:one function   A function whose inverse is also a function. Also called one : one mapping.

one-one mapping   Also called a bijection. A one-one correspondence between mathematical entities, often called a one-one function if the entities are algebraic or analytical.

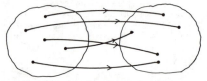

See also single valued functions.

one:one transformation   Any kind of transformation that maps each element of a set onto one and one only element of another, as in the isometries of translation, rotation or reflection which transform given configurations.

one sample location problem   If only one sample of size n can be taken from a population a rough measure of the median may be made. By subtracting a hypothesized value of the population median from each observation X the sign test may be applied, since on the hypothesis that the sample is fair the distribution of differences will have a zero median. If this is not so a new median value may be chosen to estimate the population median.

one sample test   Any statistical test or investigation of a population which uses one sample of any appropriate size. It does not mean that the sample consists of only one representative of the population.

one sided operator   An operation symbol which is only defined when written either to the right or the left of the operand, but not for both positions.

● For scalar multiplication by a, $ax = xa$ are both defined.
For the differential operator D, Dy is defined but yD is meaningless.

one-sided test   Also, sometimes misleadingly, called a one-tailed test. A test in which the alternative hypothesis H_1 indicates a particular direction or sense of difference from the null hypothesis H_0. For example if H_0 is $\theta_1 = \theta_2$, the alternative hypothesis $\theta_1 > \theta_2$ (as distinct from $\theta_1 \neq \theta_2$) gives a one-sided test. The term two-sided or two-tailed test is used for contrast, where critical values on both sides of the mean need to be considered.

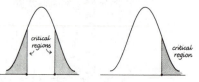

two sided and one sided tests

only if   A condition necessary if a proposition is to be true.

$$x = +2 \text{ only if } x^2 = 4$$

Note that the converse of this is not true, since $x^2 = 4 \Rightarrow x = {}^{+}2$ or $x = {}^{-}2$.
See iff.

on-off servo   Any mechanical or electrical control device that has two states corresponding to on/off, active/inactive, open/shut etc., capable of being symbolized by 1 and 0, as with a thermostat which switches on a heater at a preset temperature and switches it off when the temperature is regained.

onto mapping   A mapping of set A to set B is onto (or surjective) if $f(A) = B$, that is, for each $b \in B$, $b = f(a)$ for some $a \in A$.

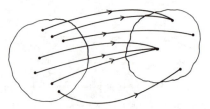

Note that more than one element of A can map onto each element of B.

open ball   *See* ball.

open disc   *See* disc.

open interval   An open subset of the set $\mathbb{R}$ of real numbers considered as part of a number line. If a, $b \in \mathbb{R}$ then the set of all real numbers x such that $a < x < b$ is called an open interval and denoted (a, b). Such an interval may be represented by a finite section of the real number line, but without the end points a and b, which are nevertheless limit points of the interval. Open intervals are important in analysis, where a function f may be undefined at $f(a)$ but defined for $x < a$. They are often represented by line intervals between open dots.

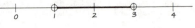

open neighbourhood *See* neighbourhood, which as defined is open if $d(x, y) < \epsilon$, that is $d(x, y) = \epsilon$ does not apply. *Compare* open interval.

open set 1. Of real numbers. Any subset $A \subset \mathbb{R}$ such that for each point $a \in A$ there is a positive number h for which every point in the interval $(a - h)$ to $(a + h)$ belongs to A.

● $A = \{x : 1 < x < 2\}$

If equality is allowed the set is not open since the criterion fails for $a = 1$ or $a = 2$.
2. Any subset of a metric space that does not contain its limit points, or, equivalently, any subset that is a neighbourhood for each of its points.

● The open disc $x^2 + y^2 < 1$

3. In a topology without a metric, a space and its subsets can be arbitrary collections. Such subsets are usually called 'open sets' since their properties are related to those of subsets of metric spaces.
See closed interval.

operation The carrying out of any procedure on a set or subsets of its members, using assigned rules such as addition of integers, differentiation of functions, evaluation of definite integrals, extraction of square roots.

operation table A two-way tabulation of the result of applying a binary operation, usually taken as closed to all members of a given set, as in

$\otimes$	1	r	r^2	r^3
1	1	r	r^2	r^3
r	r	r^2	r^3	1
r^2	r^2	r^3	1	r
r^3	r^3	1	r	r^2

where $\otimes$ denotes 'followed by' and 1, r, r^2, r^3 are rotations through $0°$, $90°$, $180°$ and $270°$. An operation table is a generalization of the usual multiplication table for numbers

$\times$	1	2	3	4
1	1	2	3	4
2	2	4	6	8
3	3	6	9	12
4	4	8	12	16

operator A symbol for an operation on a set, whereby each element is transformed according to some rule or procedure. Also an entity such as a matrix or a multiplier, that acts on the elements of a set. The index notation is often used for repeated application of the operator.

● The differentiation operator Df, D^2f giving f', f''.
The difference operator Δ^n for members of a sequence.
Transformation of a vector $\mathbf{x}$ by a matrix operator A^n.

See also binary operation.

optimization Any procedure used to find the best solution to a problem with more than one solution.

Mathematical techniques of optimization include linear programming and the calculus of variations.

or *See* vel and aut.

orbit (Lat. *orbita*, track) The path of any particle or body which travels around another, as planetary orbits. Physics is mainly concerned with central orbits, in which a body tends towards a pole.

orbital The supposed orbit of an electron around the atomic nucleus, as modified by quantum mechanics. An orbital is the region around a nucleus in which the probability of locating an electron is not negligible.

order In mathematics, a number given to each member of a set of similar entities, serving to classify it in relation to the other members, and often allowing the members to be put into an order in the usual sense of the word.

● The order of a group is the number of elements it contains.
The order of a derivative is the number of times the operation of differentiating has been repeated.
The order of a differential equation is that of the highest derivative contained in it.

See also ordering relation.

order axioms Statements that formalize the intuitive basis of a total ordering relation R on a set S.

1. If $a, b \in S$ and $(a R b \, \& \, b R a)$ is true, then $a = b$.
2. Only one or else all of the relations $a = b$, $a R b$ or $b R a$ is true for all $a, b \in S$.

ordered field A field F is said to be ordered if there is an ordering relation on F, such as $\leqslant$, so that for all a, b, $c \in F$ either $a \leqslant b$ or $b \leqslant a$, and also $a \leqslant b \Rightarrow a + c \leqslant b + c$ for all c, and $a \leqslant b \Rightarrow ac \leqslant bc$ for all $c > 0$.

ordered integral domain An integral domain is said to be ordered if its elements are or may be termed positive so that the following criteria hold:

1. If the defined additive or multiplicative process is carried out between two positive elements the result is positive.
2. If, for any element e of the domain one and only one of these statements is true

    (i) $e = 0$
    (ii) e is positive
    (iii) $-e$ is positive [i.e. $e + (-e) = 0$]

In such an integral domain the terms *less than* or *greater than* have a meaning and the elements can thus be ordered.

● The integral domain whose elements have the form $(a + b\sqrt{2})$ a, $b \in \mathbb{Z}$ is ordered, the domain of Gaussian integers is not.

ordered pair A set of two elements $\{a, b\}$ whose serial order is specified. It is then written (a, b) and is, in general, different from (b, a). Examples are coordinates (x, y) or (r, θ).

ordered set Any set of entities with an ordering relation that establishes them in a specified order. Different orderings may be imposed on the same set, as with people arranged by height or alphabetically by name. An ordered pair is an ordered set having only two members.

See also partially ordered set, totally ordered set, well ordered.

ordered triples   A set of three numbers (a, b, c) in which the order is specified, so that $(a, b, c) \neq (b, a, c)$. When a, b, $c \in \mathbb{R}$ the triple may be taken as the coordinates of a point in space of three dimensions.

ordering relation   Any binary relation between members of a set that is transitive but not symmetric or reflexive. It will therefore serve to put them in unique order.

● The set $\mathbb{N}$ can be ordered 1, 2, 3 ... by the relation 'is less than'.

order of magnitude   1. Informally, a rough approximation, to one significant figure or often as a power of ten, which gives an indication of the size of a quantity. Thus the mass of an electron, given as 9.108×10^{-31} kg to 4 significant figures, would be given as 9×10^{-31} kg or 10^{-30} kg. The mass of a hydrogen atom, given as 2×10^{-27} kg or 10^{-27} kg, would then be of a different order of magnitude. This is usually taken to mean that they differ by at least a factor of 10^n $(n = 1, 2, 3 \ldots)$
2. If functions f and g take numerical values which increase without limit or tend to a limit as $x \to \infty$ or $x \to 0$ there are two possibilities:

(i) The ratio $\dfrac{f(x)}{g(x)} \to 0$

(ii) The ratio $\dfrac{f(x)}{g(x)}$ remains finite.

For (i) f is said to be of a smaller order of magnitude than g written $f = o(g)$.
For (ii) f has the same order of magnitude as g, written $f = O(g)$.

●
$$x^2 = o(x^3) \qquad x \to \infty$$
$$\sin x = o(1) \qquad x \to \infty$$
$$x + x^2 = o(x) \qquad x \to 0$$

ordinal numbers   The set of words expressing order of precedence, {first, second, third ...} corresponding to the names of the cardinal numbers $\{1, 2, 3 \ldots\}$ in their usual order. The ordinal words are not 'numbers' in the arithmetical sense, since they cannot be combined by addition or multiplication.

ordinate   *See* abscissa.

OR gate   *See* gate. The term is always used for the inclusive or – *see* vel.

orientable surface   Any surface of which two sides can be distinguished, corresponding to upper/lower, left/right or, with closed surfaces, inside/outside. Examples are planes, cones, spheres, toroids.
See also, non-orientable.

oriented area   Any plane area whose normals are in a specified direction, in particular in an area given as the vector product $\mathbf{a} \wedge \mathbf{b}$ or $\mathbf{a} \times \mathbf{b}$. The parallelogram $P(\mathbf{a}, \mathbf{b})$ has a scalar area given by $|a_1 b_2 - a_2 b_1|$ in terms of the components of $\mathbf{a}$, $\mathbf{b}$, and the vector product orientates it relative to the coordinate system.

origin   In any coordinate or mesh system, the arbitrary point from which the coordinate values are plotted, and thus having the coordinates (0), $(0, 0)$, $(0, 0, 0) \ldots$ in 1, 2, 3 ... dimensions.

orthocentre   The unique point in a triangle where the perpendiculars from the vertices to opposite sides intersect.

orthogonal   At right angles to one another, or in some way relating to right angles (as in definitions which follow).

orthogonal circles   Circles which intersect at points where tangents (and hence radii) are perpendicular.

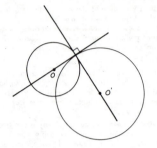

Circles $\quad x^2 + y^2 + 2g_1 x + 2f_1 y + c_1 = 0 \quad$ and $x^2 + y^2 + 2g_2 x + 2f_2 y + c_2 = 0$ are orthogonal if $g_1 g_2 + f_1 f_2 = \frac{1}{2}(c_1 + c_2)$.

orthogonal complement   If $\mathbf{V}$ is a real vector space, $\mathbf{a} . \mathbf{b}$ the inner product of vectors $\mathbf{a}$ and $\mathbf{S}$ a subspace of $\mathbf{V}$ then the orthogonal complement of $\mathbf{S}$, denoted $\mathbf{S}^{\perp}$ is $\mathbf{S}^{\perp} = \{\mathbf{x} \in \mathbf{V} : \forall \mathbf{y} \in \mathbf{S}, \ \mathbf{x} . \mathbf{y} = 0\}$. That is, every vector in $\mathbf{S}^{\perp}$ is orthogonal to every vector in $\mathbf{S}$.

If in $\mathbb{R}^3$, $\mathbf{S} = \{$points in the x, y plane$\}$ and $\mathbf{x} . \mathbf{y}$ is the usual scalar product, then $\mathbf{S}^{\perp} = \{$position vectors of points on z axis$\}$.

orthogonal group   The group O_n formed by the set of $n \times n$ orthogonal matrices under the operation of matrix multiplication. The special orthogonal group SO_n is the subgroup formed by the set of matrices whose determinant is $+1$.
See also unitary group. ·

orthogonal matrix   Any matrix A that describes an orthogonal transformation, having the property that its inverse A^{-1} is identical with its transpose A', so that $A A' = I$.
The determinant of an orthogonal matrix has the value ± 1.

orthogonal projection   For any configuration in three dimensions, the two-dimensional figure formed on a plane by the feet of perpendiculars from points of the configuration. Also a similar projection from a plane figure to a line in the plane, as in the diagram.

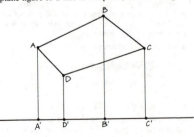

orthogonal transformation Any transformation T which preserves angles and lengths unchanged. The domain and range of T will be subsets of Euclidean space.

orthogonal vector(s) Used of two vectors **a**, **b** whose representations in the cartesian plane are at right angles to one another; that is, the inner, dot or scalar product $\mathbf{a}.\mathbf{b}=0$.
In three dimensions a vector can be orthogonal to two vectors skew to one another. The vector given by

$$\begin{vmatrix} \mathbf{i} & \mathbf{j} & \mathbf{k} \\ a_1 & b_1 & c_1 \\ a_2 & b_2 & c_2 \end{vmatrix}$$

is at right angles to both $\mathbf{l}=(a_1, b_1, c_1)$ and $\mathbf{m}=(a_2, b_2, c_2)$. The term is extended to two vectors of any dimensions whose inner product is zero.

orthographic projection Projection of the surface of a hemisphere on to a plane by parallel projection.

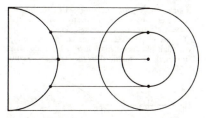

It is commonly used in the construction of star maps.

orthopole The vertices of a triangle ABC have orthogonal projections A' B' C' on to any given line. Perpendiculars are drawn from A', B', C' to the sides opposite A, B and C. These are concurrent at P, the orthopole. If the line of projection is a diameter of the circumcircle, the orthopole lies on the nine-point circle.

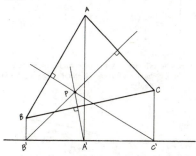

Osborn's Rule Allows an identity in circular functions to be replaced by the corresponding expression in hyperbolic functions (or vice versa) by changing the sign of the square of a sine if explicitly present (or implied as by $\tan x = \sin x/\cos x$)

$$\cos^2 x + \sin^2 x = 1 \rightarrow \cosh^2 x - \sinh^2 x = 1$$
$$\sec^2 x - \tan^2 x = 1 \rightarrow \mathrm{sech}^2 x + \tanh^2 x = 1$$

oscillating See sequence.

oscillating function Any function defined for a sufficiently large continuous variable x or integral variable n which neither has a limit as $x \rightarrow \pm\infty$ nor tends to $+\infty$ or $-\infty$ as $x \rightarrow \infty$ or $n \rightarrow \infty$, is said to oscillate. Oscillation may be finite if all values of $|f|$ are less than an assigned value k, or infinite if such a k does not exist.

- $f(x)=\sin x$ oscillates finitely
  $f(n)=n(-1)^n$ oscillates infinitely

A periodic function is a special case.

oscillating sequence See oscillating function. A sequence which behaves in the same way is said to oscillate.

- $u_n = \sin n$ $(n=1, 2, 3 \ldots)$

oscillation 1. Movement of a body or system about a central point or state, which may or may not have a regular period or amplitude (see simple harmonic motion, compound pendulum, wave motion).
2. See also oscillating sequence.

osculating circle A name given to the circle which defines the radius of curvature of any curve at a point, from Lat. osculatio, a kissing. The verb osculate is also used of any two curves that touch (or cut) at three coincident points. It is sometimes applied to higher order contacts such as a conic cutting a curve at four coincident points.

parabola through four points   osculating parabola

osculating polynomial The derivatives of an osculating polynomial equal that of the given curve at common points, so that, in contrast to the collocation polynomial, it shares tangents as well as points. The order of osculation is the order of the highest derivative shared with the curve.

ostensive definition Definition by showing or demonstrating. Many formal statements in mathematics purporting to define a particular in terms of a more general concept, as 'a rectangle is a parallelogram with one angle a right angle' are in fact abstracted from concepts that children have acquired ostensively, from statements such as 'this is a square' or 'we call this shape a rectangle'.

Oughtred, William English parson and teacher (1574–1650), who published works on proportion and trigonometry. He devised the logarithmic slide rule and introduced the sign $\times$ for multiplication.

outcome space The set of all possible results of trials or experiments. See sample space, event space.

output See input.

oval Not a defined curve in mathematics unless specific, as in Cassini's ovals. An oval is any closed curve or surface roughly elliptical and symmetrical about two axes at right angles.

overlapping sets Term sometimes used to describe sets which are not disjoint, that is, their intersection is not the empty set.

P

Paasche's index *See* weighted index.

pair *See* ordered pair.

pairwise disjoint A term that describes a set of subsets U such that no two of them have any element in common.
If $A_1, A_2, A_3 \ldots \in U$ then for all $i \neq j$ $A_i \cap A_j = \emptyset$

pantograph An instrument of six rods linked by pin joints, used for copying a diagram to any desired scale.

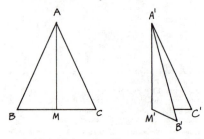

P is a fixed pivot, A traces the diagram, B is a pen tracing the copy. The scale depends on the relative lengths of the rods.

paper folding A useful physical realization of geometrical or general symmetry properties got by folding sheets of paper having the shape of plane configurations.

The properties of an isosceles triangle ABC are realized by folding A'B'C' about the median A'M' where M' is the mid-point of the side B'C'.

A right angle is produced by two folds of a single sheet.

Pappus' theorem *See* Guldinius' theorem.
Pappus only discussed a special case, but the theorem is commonly named after him.

Papy, Georges Belgian mathematician and teacher who introduced the study of abstract and linear algebra and axiomatics into Belgian schools early in 1960, using many striking visual representations. He wrote a set of books *Mathématiques Moderne* which have been very influential in shaping the so-called 'modern mathematics syllabuses'.

Papygram A name used for the representation of a binary relation by a directed graph, used extensively in the textbooks of Papy (often with coloured lines to distinguish various relations).

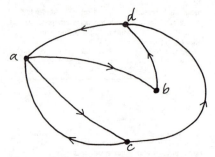

The example shows the set of binary relations $\{(a,b),\ (a,c),\ (c,a),\ (b,d),\ (c,d),\ (d,a)\}$ on the set $\{a,b,c,d\}$.

parabola 1. A plane curve formed by the intersection of a cone by a plane parallel to a generator. (Gk. *parabole*, a throwing or placing alongside).
2. The set of points in a plane equidistant from a fixed point (the focus) and a fixed line (the directrix).
3. It can also be described by the cartesian equation $y^2 = 4ax$.

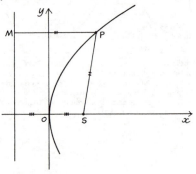

See also conic sections.

parabolic cylinder A cylinder whose directrix is a parabola, having, for suitable axes, the equation $y^2 = 4ax$ for all z.

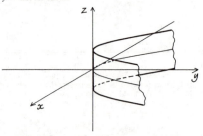

parabolic rule Synonym for Simpson's rule.

parabolic space (or geometry) The name given by

Klein (1871) to Euclidean space or geometry, since the Fifth Postulate specifies a line between the 'excessive' and 'defective' cases he termed 'hyperbolic' and 'elliptic'. *See* these entries and 'conic sections' for a full account of the nomenclature. Parabolic geometry corresponds to the third case of the Saccheri quadrilateral which gives all the possible results.

parabolic spiral The family of curves whose equation in polar coordinates is $r - a = b\theta^n$.
Special forms of these are

Archimedian spiral $a = 0$, $n = 1$
Hyperbolic or reciprocal spiral $a = 0$, $n = -1$
Lituus $a = 0$, $n = \frac{1}{2}$

paraboloid 1. The surface formed by rotating a parabola one complete turn about its axis.
2. A quadric surface given, in cartesian coordinates, by the equation

$$Az = Bx^2 + Cy^2$$

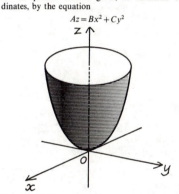

See also elliptic paraboloid.

paradox Any argument, apparently valid, that leads to a contradiction. *See*, for example, Zeno and *heterologisch*. A paradox usually arises from tacit assumptions made before the argument is developed.

parallel Two straight lines in the Euclidean plane are said to be parallel if they either coincide or have no point in common. The first condition has only been recognized since the development of analytical geometry. The word parallel is frequently left undefined or defined implicitly in context, and is often taken as meaning 'in the same direction'.

parallel axis theorem If the moment of inertia of a body of mass m about an axis through its centre of mass is I, then the moment of inertia about a parallel axis at a distance h is $I + mh^2$.

parallelepiped (note spelling) A six-sided prism, all of whose faces are parallelograms.
See also cuboid.

parallel motion *See* four-bar linkage.

parallelogram law The law by which vectors, considered as directed line segments, are to be combined. If $\overrightarrow{OP}$, $\overrightarrow{OQ}$ are vectors their sum is given by $\overrightarrow{OR}$, the diagonal of the parallelogram, having OP, OQ as adjoining sides.

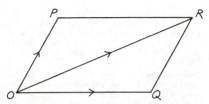

The law arises by definition, but does of course model the empirical relationships of vector quantities as in displacement or the parallelogram of forces. *See also* vector polygon.

parallelogram of forces An alternative form of the triangle of forces drawn with localized vectors.

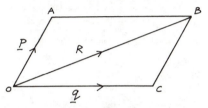

Since CB is parallel and equal to OA it can also represent **p**. The diagram then becomes the triangle of forces.

parallel postulate The fifth postulate given in Euclid's elements, which states in verbal form that if and only if the sum of the angles α and β in the diagram is less than 180°, the two lines meet at a point when produced.

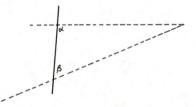

From early times (e.g. Proclus 410–485) this has been taken to have the form of a theorem, and the continuing attempts to prove it using Euclid's other definitions and axioms lead eventually to the formulation of non-Euclidean geometries in which other postulates are stated. In 1868 Beltrami proved that the truth of the postulate could not be demonstrated. Many alternatives, more acceptable in wording, were suggested over the centuries, of which one due to Proclus was restated by Playfair (1748–1819) as *through a given point only one straight line can be drawn parallel to a given straight line*. The modern form of this, due to Hilbert, replaces the term 'parallel to' with 'which does not intersect'.
See also parabolic space, hyperbolic geometry, elliptic geometry, Saccheri quadrilateral.

parameter A variable to which other variables are related. This can be used either to obtain the other variables if required, as in parametric equations, or, in statistical parameters such as mean or standard deviation, to describe a set of variables collectively. In physics a parameter is a variable which remains constant for a system whose behaviour depends on the value of the constant, as pressure/volume relationships in a gas kept at a constant temperature which is then the parameter.

parameter space Corresponds to a phase space in physics. The set of all parameters whose values define a state. The dimensions of the space are the number of parameters, and each set of values gives a point in the space.

parametric coordinates If f and g are functions whose domain is a subset of R, then for each t in the domain the pair $[f(t), g(t)]$ are said to be parametric coordinates

● If $f(t)=t/(1+t)$, $g(t)=t^2 (t \neq -1)$
Then $t=2$ gives the parametric coordinates $(\frac{2}{3}, 4)$.

parametric equations Express a relation between two or more variables in terms of two or more equations involving a single variable which is the parameter.

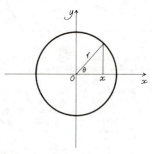

● Using θ as a parameter the two equations
$x=r\cos\theta$
$y=r\sin\theta$ $\quad 0 \leqslant \theta \leqslant 2\pi$
are equivalent to the equation $x^2 + y^2 = r^2$.

Many equations can be written more simply and conveniently in parametric form.
See, for example, folium of Descartes.

parity Functions which are symmetric about the y axis, that is, for which $f(x)=f(-x)$, are said to have even parity or to be even functions, those symmetric about the origin for which $f(x)=-f(-x)$, have odd parity, or are said to be odd functions.

● $y=x^2$, $y=\cos x$, $y=\cosh x$ are even
$y=x$, $y=\sin x$, $y=\sinh x$ are odd

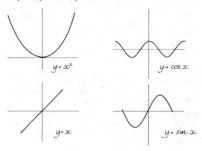

partial correlation In a situation involving multiple variation, this is the correlation between any two variates when the others are either held constant or their effect eliminated by experimental design.

partial derivative The result of applying the process of differentiation to a function of two or more variables $f(x_1, x_2 \ldots)$ with all variables but one held constant, to which the limiting process is applied, using the symbol $\dfrac{\partial f}{\partial x}$

Thus $\dfrac{\partial f}{\partial x_1} = \lim_{h \to 0} \dfrac{f[(x_1+h), x_2, \ldots] - f(x_1, x_2, x_3 \ldots)}{h}$

● $z = y\sin x + y^3$

$\dfrac{\partial z}{\partial x} = y\cos x, \quad \dfrac{\partial z}{\partial y} = \sin x + 3y^2$

For $z=f(x, y)$ the partial derivatives may be shown diagrammatically as slope functions. Thus $\tan\theta$ below is $\dfrac{\partial z}{\partial x}$ and $\tan\phi$ is $\dfrac{\partial z}{\partial y}$

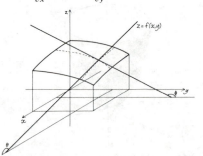

The process is of importance in physical applications where dependence on several variables occurs. For this reason the modified Leibnitz notation is usually used since it is easier to read. Otherwise, for variables $x_1, x_2 \ldots$ notations such as $D_1 f$, $D_2 f \ldots$ or f'_1, $f'_2 \ldots$ are used. Second partial derivatives are represented in Leibnitz notation by $\dfrac{\partial^2 f}{\partial x^2}$ or $\dfrac{\partial^2 f}{\partial x \partial y}$

The second form denotes the process $\dfrac{\partial}{\partial y}\left(\dfrac{\partial f}{\partial x}\right)$ which can also be written $D^2_{x,y} f$.
The individual symbols ∂f, ∂x, ∂y have no useful interpretation as differentials, since in general their value depends on the values at which the other variables are held constant.

partial differential equation An equation that expresses a relationship between a function of more than one variable $f(x_1, x_2 \ldots)$ where the x_i are independent, the partial derivatives

$\dfrac{\partial f}{\partial x_1}, \dfrac{\partial f}{\partial x_2}, \ldots, \dfrac{\partial^2 f}{\partial x_1^2}, \ldots \dfrac{\partial^2 f}{\partial x_1 \partial x_2} \ldots$, and the variables x_1, $x_2 \ldots$ An important example is Laplace's equation

$$\dfrac{\partial^2 S}{\partial x^2} + \dfrac{\partial^2 S}{\partial y^2} + \dfrac{\partial^2 S}{\partial z^2} = 0$$

which arises in such studies as the flow of heat.

partial fractions   A rational function of the form

$$Q(x) = \frac{\phi(x)}{f(x)}$$

where $\phi(x)$ is a polynomial of degree m and $f(x)$ is of degree n, where $m < n$ and $f(x)$ can be split into linear or quadratic factors, can be expressed as the sum of terms having the form

$$\frac{A}{(x-\alpha)}, \frac{B}{(x-\alpha)^2}, \frac{Cx+D}{x^2+\beta x+\gamma}, \cdots$$

It is then said to be resolved into partial fractions. The resolution often enables the integral of $Q(x)$ to be conveniently found, given that x does not take a value that makes any denominator zero.

The values of A, B, C, ... can be found by multiplying out the partial fractions and equating coefficients in both numerators. Any function $f(x)$ is factorizable in principle, but the method is only practicable for small m, n. If $m > n$ the denominator must first be divided into the numerator to obtain a polynomial quotient and a remainder whose degree is less than n.

partially ordered set   If a binary ordering relation R between elements of a set S does not apply to all pairs $a, b \in S$ it is not a total ordering relation on S. It is then a total ordering on a subset of S. Unlike a total ordering, a partial ordering is not represented by points arranged on a line.

● The relation R 'divides into' totally orders the set $\{2, 4, 8, 16\}$ but not the set $\{2, 4, 5, 8, 16\}$

partial regression coefficients   If the variation in X depends on its relation to two or more variables $\{Y, Z \ldots\}$ the partial regression (or correlation) coefficients are obtained by measuring X as Y varies with Z held at a constant value, then X as Z varies with Y held constant, and so on. *Compare* partial derivative.

partial sum   A series, either infinite or terminating, is given by

$$S_n = \sum_{i=1}^{n} u_i \text{ or } S_\infty = \sum_{i=1}^{\infty} u_i.$$

Then the partial sums $S_1, S_2, S_3 \ldots$ are given by

$$S_1 = u_1$$
$$S_2 = u_1 + u_2$$
$$S_3 = u_1 + u_2 + u_3$$

and, in general $S_j = u_1 + u_2 + \ldots u_j$.

particle   An ideal construction normally having mass but no dimensions. If required it can also possess angular momentum and electric charge, and can have zero mass if it carries the corresponding energy equivalent. A particle is realized in practice by any entity whose dimensions can be neglected for the purpose in hand, and which can be considered to occupy a point or small region in space.

particular affirmative   *See* universal affirmative.

particular integral   Any solution v, often found by trial, that satisfies a linear differential equation

$$ay'' + by' + cy = P(x)$$
$$\text{so that } av'' + bv' + cv = P(x)$$

Together with the complementary function w this gives the general solution $y = u + v$.

particular negative   *See* universal negative.

particular solution   *See* complete primitive.

partition   The expression of a set S as the union of a set of disjoint subsets, such that every element of S is in precisely one subset. The sets may be finite or infinite.

● The set of all triangles may be partitioned into the three disjoint sets of right, obtuse and acute angled triangles.
Division mod n partitions the set $\mathbb{N}$ into n equivalence classes.

See also division.

Pascal, Blaise   French religious mystic and mathematician (1623–1662). From the age of 12 onwards he produced many results in mathematics, discovering known theorems independently. He invented an adding machine, did original work on the cycloid and on what is now projective geometry and probability theory, and is remembered for his *Treatise on the Arithmetical Triangle*.

Pascal, Etienne   French mathematical amateur (1588–1640) father of Blaise, and discoverer of the limaçon.

Pascal's theorem   The points of intersection of the three pairs of opposite sides of a hexagon inscribed in any conic are collinear. Conversely, if the intersections are collinear, a conic will pass through the vertices of the hexagon.

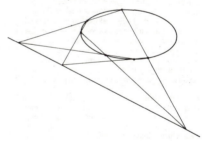

Pascal's triangle   The infinite triangular array of integers,

in which each entry is the sum of the two numbers diagonally above it. Many number patterns can be identified in its rows, columns and diagonals. In particular, the entries in the $(n+1)$th line are the binomial coefficients from the expansion of $(a+b)^n$.

Described by Pascal and named after him, but known as a pattern to both Chinese and Arabic mathematicians by about 1300.
See also binomial theorem.

path The track of a moving body or particle between any two points, or any set of points that can be occupied by a body so moving. At one time mathematicians spoke of the 'path' of a moving point, but since any one point is only specified by its position it is now usual to restrict 'path' to physical motion.

Peano, Guiseppe Italian mathematician and logician (1858–1932), associated with Frege, Hilbert and Russell in pioneering mathematical philosophy. He suggested an international academic language, Interlingua, consisting of Latin forms shorn of terminations and used synthetically.

Peano's axioms A set of five axioms for the natural numbers considered as an arbitrary set N of symbols, developed by Peano to allow the processes of arithmetic to be built up logically without unstated assumptions:

1. 1 is a number.
2. The successor to any number is a number.
3. There are no distinct numbers with the same successor.
4. 1 is not a successor.
5. Every property of 1, which also belongs to the successor of any number having this property, belongs to all numbers.

Of these, axiom 1 can be realized using the symbol 0, but some mathematicians do not regard 0 as a member of N. Axiom 5 allows number theorems to be proved by mathematical induction. The symbol 1 is arbitrary as far as the axioms are concerned, and it is necessary to define it extrinsically if arithmetic is to be applied without logical discontinuity to the real world. (The symbols 1 ... 5 on the left of the above list are arbitrary labels to distinguish the axioms.)
See also Frege, natural numbers, number, unity.

Pearson, Karl English applied mathematician (1857–1936). Pioneer in applying statistical methods to biological problems, particularly those of heredity.

Peaucellier's linkage Devised by a French engineer in 1873 as part of a pump mechanism, this is a four-bar linkage constrained in such a way that it constructs straight lines or circles. It is in fact an inversion mechanism.

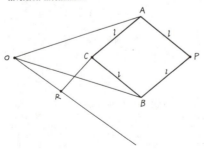

It consists of four equal links of length l forming a rhombus $APBC$. A and B are linked by equal rigid rods OA, OB to a pivot O, and C by a rod CR to a point R about which it can rotate. The distance OP can be adjusted. If $OR \lessgtr OC$ the path of P is a circle, if $OR = OC$ it is a straight line. In each case P is the inverse point of C with respect to O. Although P describes a straight line the links themselves need not be straight.
See also ruler postulate.

pedal curve If perpendiculars are drawn from any fixed point P to a set of tangents $t_1, t_2, t_3 \ldots$ of a given curve Γ the feet of the perpendiculars R, S, $T, \ldots$ lie on the pedal curve Γ_1 (usually called the first positive pedal) with respect to that point.

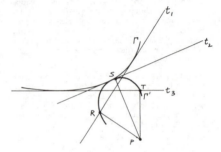

If Γ is a circle and P is on its circumference Γ_1 is the cardioid. If Γ is a parabola and P its focus, Γ_1 is the tangent at the vertex.

pedal equation If the perpendicular of length p from the origin to the tangent of any curve at the point whose polar coordinates are (r, θ) is drawn, the relation between p and r is the pedal or p, r equation of the curve.

For the circle $r = 2a \sin\theta$, $p/r = r/2a$ and hence pedal equation is $2pa = r^2$

Pedal equations are used in calculating central orbits.

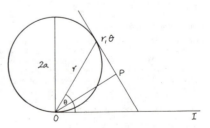

pedal line Also called Simson's line. The perpendiculars to the sides of a triangle from any point on its circumcircle are collinear. The line on which they fall is the pedal line.

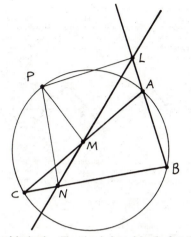

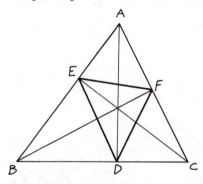

pedal triangle The triangle formed by the feet of the perpendiculars from the vertices to the opposite sides of any triangle. It is the triangle of least perimeter with its vertices touching the three sides of the original triangle.

pencil A configuration of lines on a point, frequently generalized to all the lines on a point.

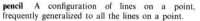

pendulum A body that oscillates about a fixed point under the influence of a gravitational field. The simple pendulum is an idealized arrangement in which a point mass swings at the end of a weightless thread under the influence of gravity only, and is realized approximately by a small heavy sphere attached to a light thread. For large swings the period varies with the amplitude θ, but as θ→0 the

period becomes

$$t = 2\pi \sqrt{\frac{l}{g}}$$

where l is the length of the pendulum and g the acceleration due to gravity. For a small sphere l can be measured from its centre.
See also compound pendulum, conical pendulum.

pentagonal number Any number in the sequence 1, 5, 12, 22, ... given by

$$\{a_n\} = \frac{n}{2}(3n - 1)$$

$n = 1, 2, 3, \ldots$ This is represented geometrically by pentagons nested within successive gnomons.

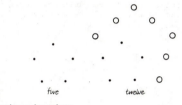

See polygonal numbers.

pentagram Also pentacle. A plane figure formed by joining alternately the five points arranged at the vertices of a pentagon.

pentomino *See* polyomino.

percentage Parts per hundred. A ratio expressed so that its second term is 100, as 1:4 = 25:100. This is denoted 25%, the symbol % being a modification of p/c written quickly by hand.

percentage error Expresses the error in any one calculation or measurement as a proportion, given as a percentage of, usually, the calculated or measured value finally accepted.

percentiles These are defined as for quartiles, but the total range is divided into one hundred parts. Percentiles should only be given for a discrete distribution if the total number of measures is large. Common phrases such as 'the top ten per cent' should refer to a percentile division of statistical data, but frequently deciles are meant.

151

perfect number A number n which is the sum of all its divisors except n itself, as $6 = 1 + 2 + 3$, $28 = 1 + 2 + 4 + 7 + 14$. (Euclid Book, VII Def. 22). The next two, given by Nicomachus, are 496 and 8128. He also defines 'over perfect' and 'defective' numbers, where the sum exceeds or is less than n. All known perfect numbers are even, but this has not been generally proved.

perfect square Any number or expression which is the square of another. Thus $9 = 3^2$ and $a^2 + 2ab + b^2 = (a + b)^2$ are perfect squares. Perfect cube is similarly defined.
See also completing the square.

Perigal's dissection The dissection of a square into four congruent quadrilaterals. Taken with a smaller square the five shapes assemble to form a larger square, and hence provide a constructional demonstration of the Pythagoras theorem.

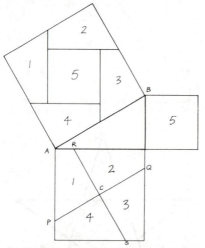

The line PCQ, passes through the centre C of the given square and is parallel to the hypotenuse AB of a right angle triangle. SCR is perpendicular to this. The smaller square is the one on the remaining side, the large square the one on the hypotenuse.

perimeter Gk. *peri* around, *metron*, a measure. The distance around a closed plane curve or the sum of the sides of a plane polygon. The perimeter of a circle is called the *circumference*. The symbol π is the Greek initial letter of *peri*.

period *See* harmonic motion.

periodic decimal *See* recurring decimal.

periodic function A real or complex valued function is said to be periodic of period A if for all z $f(z + A) = f(z)$ and A is the minimum value for which this is true.

● The sine function $\sin x$ has period 2π since $\sin(x + 2\pi) = \sin x \,(x \in \mathbb{R})$.
  The 'saw-tooth' function $y = [\![x]\!]$.
  The exponential function e^z has a period $2\pi i$ since $e^{z + 2\pi i} = e^z \,(z \in \mathbb{C})$.

For e^z the period is a multiple of i and is said to be

'imaginary'. Some functions, such as elliptic functions, have two periods, one real and one imaginary. Any periodic function $\mathbb{R} \to \mathbb{R}$ will have a coordinate representation and properties that will repeat themselves after the interval A, so it is only necessary to study the function in the interval.

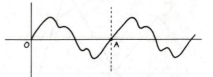

permutation 1. The arrangements of n distinct objects (usually symbols) taken r at a time in all possible orders, and whose number is given by

$$_nP_r \text{ or } ^nP_r = \frac{n!}{(n - r)!}$$

Other formulae may be derived when some of the n are not distinct.
2. The number of ways in which r objects from a set of n can be labelled by r distinct labels.
The two definitions are equivalent.

permutation group Term usually used for a subgroup of the symmetric group S_n, including S_n itself.

● The four permutations (1234), (4123), (3412), (2341) form a group of order 4 which is a subgroup of S_4.

Cayley's theorem states that any finite group of order n is isomorphic to a permutation group on n symbols, and hence such groups have a central role in group theory.

perpendicular In mathematics, used of a line drawn at right angles to another line or to a plane, as the perpendicular from a vertex to the opposite side of a triangle. In technical usage, a perpendicular or perpend is always at right angles to the gravitational horizontal as shown by a spirit level or plumb line.

perspective 1. A convention by which points on distant objects or configurations are transformed into or projected onto points on a plane, considered to be interposed between the objects and the eye, as in painting or drawing.

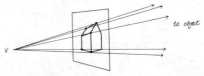

See works by Dürer (c.1500) and Magritte for early and modern examples which make the convention explicit. Ruskin, in *Elements of Perspective* (1859), showed that conventional perspective as constructed did not correspond to true optical images, particularly for large architectural features.
2. Two configurations $ABC \ldots$ and $A' B' C' \ldots$ are said to be in perspective if the lines $AA', BB', CC' \ldots$ meet at a point called the centre of perspective or projection.

See also centre of perspective, projectivity, perspectivity.

perspectivity   The relation between sets of collinear points when the lines joining them meet in a centre or vertex.
See centre of perspective.

Pfaffian   Since a skew symmetric determinant of even order $2n \times 2n$ expands to a polynomial which is a perfect square, such a determinant has a square root. This root is called a Pfaffian.

$$\begin{vmatrix} 0 & a \\ -a & 0 \end{vmatrix} \text{ gives, trivially, } \pm a$$

$$\begin{vmatrix} 0 & a & b & c \\ -a & 0 & d & e \\ -b & -d & 0 & f \\ -c & -e & -f & 0 \end{vmatrix} \text{ gives } \pm(af-be+cd)$$

phase   See harmonic motion.

phase angle   See harmonic motion. If quantities are given in the form $a \cos(\omega t + \epsilon)$ then ϵ is the phase angle, giving the initial value at $t=0$.

phase space   The set of all vectors which specifies the complete state of any physical system. Each vector represents a 'point' in the multidimensional phase space, referred to an origin at which all measures are taken as zero; e.g. an element at position (x, y, z) in the atmosphere could also have measures of pressure (p) temperature (T) and humidity (h) at time (t), and hence be given by the vector

$$\mathbf{a} = (x, y, z, p, T, h, t)$$

pi (π) From initial letter of Gk. *perimetros*, first used consistently by Euler. The ratio between the circumference and diameter of a circle, believed but not known to be irrational until so proved by Lambert (1761) and then shown to be transcendental in 1882 by Lindemann. Well-known rational approximations to π are $22/7$, $355/113$ and 3.1416. A verse originally published as a letter to the editor of 'Nature' gives π to 30 places:

> Sir, I send a rhyme excelling
> In sacred truth and rigid spelling.
> Numerical sprites elucidate
> For me the lesson's dull weight.
> If Nature gain, I'll not complain,
> Tho' Dr. Johnson fulminate.

An IBM computer produced over 100000 decimal places in 1961. Because of the analytic importance of the circular functions and circular measure, π appears in many contexts not obviously related to circles.

pivotal condensation   See Gaussian condensation.

placeholder   1. In a system of numeration in which the position of the numerals in a sequence determines their value, any symbol that has no value attached to itself but is used to indicate the assigned columns, and hence positional values, of the other symbols. Normally used of the symbol 0 (or zero) in the Hindu-Arabic system.

- In 302.007 the zeros show the positional values of the digits 3, 2, 7

Note that zero may be used to show a zero value or the cardinal of the empty set: it is not then a placeholder

- $x^2 + x = 0$
  2.0
  absences 0

2. For any expression $P(x)$ the variable x is a symbol which acts as a place holder for any of the elements in the domain of P. $P(x)$ then takes values $P(a)$, $P(b)$ ...
See dummy variable.

place value   The numerical value assigned to a digit by virtue of its position in any multidigit number written in a positional notation. Thus the four digits in 476.3 have the values

4 four hundreds
7 seven tens
6 six units
3 three tenths

when the denary/decimal fraction notation is used.
See also zero, decimal point.

planar network   A network which can be drawn so that its connecting lines do not cross.

A is planar, since it can be redrawn as B, C is not planar.

plane   A surface passing through three non-collinear points such that straight lines can be drawn on it in any direction. The lines will either be parallel or intersect at finite points, and are wholly enclosed within the plane.
In Cartesian coordinates any plane is given by

$$ax + by + cz = k \ (a, b, c, k \in \mathbb{R})$$

plane geometry   Usually taken as Euclidean geometry in two dimensions: the study of configurations drawn on a flat surface or plane with a Pythagorean metric.

plane numbers   See polygonal numbers.

plane vector   See vector. A plane vector $\mathbf{r}$ is one having two elements only: $\mathbf{r} = (x_1, x_2)$, often written as a column $\mathbf{r} = \begin{pmatrix} x_1 \\ x_2 \end{pmatrix}$. It can be interpreted geometrically as a position or displacement relative to an origin given by $(0, 0)$.

planimeter   A mechanical integrator designed by Amsler, used to measure the area of any closed region, such as a country represented on a map.

Plateau's Problem   See minimal surface.

Plato   Greek philosopher and teacher (427–347 B.C.). Founded the Academy in Athens during the later stages of Athenian political influence, and for 50 years directed *mathēmata*, the studies: arithmetic, geometry, astronomy and music. The geometry in Euclid's Elements (c.300 B.C.) is a formal logical exposition of the work of this period, which included the study of irrationals and the theory of proportion. The traditional problems of trisecting an angle, duplicating a cube (the Delian problem) and quadrature of a circle were also discussed. The extensive works of Plato do discuss the nature of mathematics but do not include mathematical texts, and like Pythagoras before him Plato's name has been attached, as in the Platonic solids and the Platonic restriction, by later writers to ideas that probably originated much earlier than the Academy.

Platonic ideas   (or ideals, or forms). Important for interpreting the Greek attitude to mathematics. According to Plato 'real' (that is 'thinglike') entities were, at least metaphorically, imperfect 'models' of the ideal forms or entities which existed outside or transcending the visible world. The concept of, say, *triangle*, which a geometer could separate from an actual drawn example, took temporal 'reality' closer to the ideal triangle than any non-mathematical construction such as a bed (Plato's example) could approach its ideal. Hence mathematics came closer to true knowledge than any other study. *The Republic*, Book VII, should be consulted for Plato's own exposition.

Platonic restriction   The entirely arbitrary rule of Plato that the only permissible instruments (trammels) for a geometrical construction are a straight edge and compasses. The straight edge was not to be graduated or marked in any way, and it was not permissible to use the compasses to transfer a length, as with dividers as now used. It is still a matter of contention whether this rule was fruitful or stultifying in the development of geometry. In algebraic terms the restrictions on construction become rectrictions of calculation to the four rules of arithmetic and the extraction of square roots.
See also ruler postulate.

Platonic solids   The five regular polyhedra considered by Euclid in Book XIII, but first studied systematically by Theaetetus (c. 380 B.C.), the cube, tetrahedron, octahedron, dodecahedron and icosahedron. This is the last book of the Elements and probably Euclid saw his earlier books as culminating in the theorems about these solids. They are described by the Schäfli numbers 3^3, 3^4, 3^5, 4^3, 5^3, and can all be constructed from plane nets. They have played a role in early pre-scientific thinking, as for example, in Kepler's use of nested Platonic solids to define the radii of planetary orbits, or the opinion that primitive atoms had these shapes. A known virus particle is indeed icosahedral. The solids are discussed in Plato's dialogue *Timaeus*, but were known much earlier.

platykurtic   *See* kurtosis.

Playfair's Axiom   One of the many proposed versions of Euclid's Fifth Postulate. Through a given point only one straight line can be drawn parallel to a given straight line. Despite its attribution, it is not a modern formulation, and was recorded by Proclus (410–485 A.D.).

Plücker coordinates   Due to Plücker (1801–1868), who took as the fundamental entity of coordinate geometry not the point (x, y) but the line whose intercepts on the axes are given. Since the cartesian line in terms of its intercepts is $\frac{x}{a} + \frac{y}{b} = 1$ Plücker took

as his coordinates $\left(\frac{1}{-a}, \frac{1}{-b}\right)$ giving the line $ax + by + 1 = 0$. A Plücker point now becomes a linear equation relating all lines with given co-ordinates passing through it. The theorems of geometry in analytical form can now be recast in a dual form in which lines and points interchange. This proved of importance in projective geometry. Plücker himself was also an experimental physicist of distinction.

plus   Word used in reading the positive sign (as $+2$ or $+2$, plus two) or in verbalizing a binary addition (as $a + b$, a plus b). Also used informally to indicate an indefinite number greater than a given number, as 10^+, equivalent to 'at least 10'. From Lat. *plus*, more. *Compare* minus.

Poincaré, Henri   French mathematician and philosopher of science (1854–1912). He made important advances in many branches of mathematics, particularly in functional periodicity, in the integration of linear differential equations, the theory of orbits and the dynamics of the electron. In a paper delivered in 1904 he made an explicit reference to the principle of relativity as applicable to all physical phenomena. He did not, however, accept the logical consequences of this, and rejected Einstein's theoretical development.

point   1. The primitive intuitive concept was originally abstracted from the act of marking a surface by a prick from a needle, via L. *punge*, *punctum*, prick or stab, translating the Gk. *stigma*, a puncture. Euclid uses *semeion*, a mark. Attempts to define the intuitive concept in simpler terms were not successful, e.g. 'that which has no part' (Euclid) or 'position without magnitude' (adapted from Aristotle). These definitions arose because the Greeks tried to separate the concept from its representative marks.
2. An undefined concept in mathematics, taken to be any entity for which propositions involving the word 'point' have a meaning.

● The ordered number pair (x, y)
A position on a plane referred to coordinate axes
The intersection of two lines
A phase state in a physical system

Points are represented in diagrams by dots, small crosses or circles, or by labelling lines at intersections or elsewhere to mark the points referred to. Labelling includes the use of sets of coordinates. *See also* dot notations.

point at infinity   *See* infinity.

point of accumulation   *See* cluster point.

point of symmetry   A configuration is symmetric about a point P if any line through P which cuts it at Q, also cuts it at R where $PQ = PR$. The point of

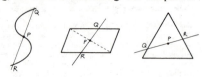

PQ = PR   PQ = PR   PQ ≠ PR

154

symmetry coincides with the centre of rotation for rotational symmetry if the configuration is of even order, but otherwise does not exist.

point projection *See* centre of perspective.

point-slope equation Describes a line of slope m passing through the point (x_1, y_1), and is given by $y - y_1 = m(x - x_1)$.

Poisson distribution The discrete probability distribution given by the probability function

$$p(X) = \frac{e^{-\lambda}\lambda^x}{x!} \quad x \in \{0, 1, 2, \ldots\}$$

It arises as the distribution of the number of events in a Poisson process and is used in place of the binomial distribution when $n \to \infty$ and $p \to 0$. The mean and variance of the distribution are both given by λ.

Poisson, S-D French geometer and physicist (1781–1840). He wrote on a wide range of topics in magnetism, astronomy, the theories of viscous flow, elasticity and gravitational potential. He also contributed to probability theory.

polar If straight lines through a point P_0 cut a conic at points Q, R, the set of all points P such that P is the harmonic conjugate of P_0 with respect to QR is the polar of P_0 with respect to the conic. It is a straight line.

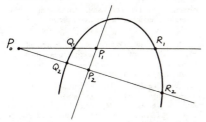

Alternatively, if a line through any point P cuts a conic at X and Y, then the intersection Z of the tangents at X, Y lies on a line m called the polar of P. P is then the pole of the line m.

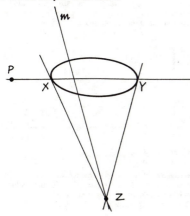

polar axis The axis through the true N and S poles of the earth, about which it rotates.

polar coordinates 1. An ordered pair (r, θ) of real numbers which labels points in a plane relative to a pole (or origin) O on a fixed base (or initial) line. The line OP is sometimes called the radius vector of P.

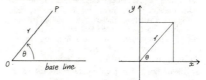

Positive is taken in an anticlockwise direction and r is unsigned. Polar coordinates are transformed to cartesian by the equations

$$x = r\cos\theta$$
$$y = r\sin\theta$$

2. In three dimensions, the triplet (r, θ, ϕ) is referred to a pole 0 on a fixed base line in a fixed base plane,

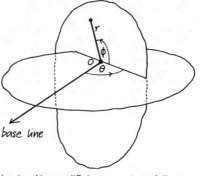

base line

but is subject to differing conventions of direction, base line and plane. θ and ϕ correspond to latitude, longitude, Greenwich hour angle, declination or other angular measures used in geography and astronomy.

See also cylindrical coordinates.

polar curve Any curve given by an equation in polar coordinates (r, θ)

polar equation Any relation between the polar coordinates (r, θ) of a set of points.

● $r = 2\cos\theta$ is the polar equation of a circle referred to a pole on its circumference and its diameter as an initial line.

polar spherical triangle In navigation, the PZX triangle, one of whose vertices is the true N or S pole.

pole 1. Any point selected as a fixed position from which to take measurements, set up coordinates, or establish relationships with other points. Examples are the pole of polar coordinates, the pole of a polar line in the relation pole–polar. The word 'origin' normally applies to a selected point on linear axes, but is otherwise synonymous with pole in coordinate systems.

2. One of the two points on a sphere through which

all the meridian or longitude circles pass, which on the earth are taken as the points through which the axis of rotation passes.
3. *See* polar.

polygon   A plane or skew configuration of straight lines meeting at angles, said to be *regular* if plane and with equal sides and angles. From Gk. *polys+gonia*, having many angles. Some specified polygons, apart from the triangle and quadrilateral, are given the Greek numerical prefixes, the others are not usually named. A general notation is *n*-gon, where *n* takes integral values, as 9-gon, 23-gon. Polygons may be convex or re-entrant.

polygonal law   The parallelogram law for vectors represented as line segments, extended to any number of vectors.

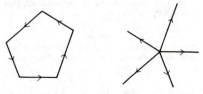

If a set of forces acting at a point is represented in magnitude and direction by the sides of a closed polygon taken in order, the forces are in equilibrium.

polygon numbers   Discussed by Plato and later by Nichomachus. The representation of numbers by patterns of dots (pebbles, according to Aristotle) arranged in geometrical configurations, and generated as sequences by constructing their gnomons. Thus for squares we get

1   4   9

See pentagonal number, triangular numbers. In the earlier Greek treatment only the dots in the gnomons were counted, so that the square numbers were given as 1, 3, 5, ..., and so on for other shapes.

polygonal region   Any region, usually taken to be convex, enclosed by a set of straight lines. If the lines represent equations of restraint in cartesian coordinates the polygon contains all permissible values of the variables.
See linear programming.

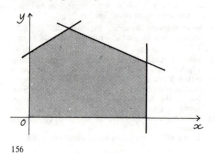

polyhedral angle   The solid angle enclosed between three or more planes that intersect at a point, measured in steradians.

polyhedron   A closed configuration or solid having plane faces, from Gk. *polys*, many, *hedra*, seat or side. Specific polyhedra are named using the Greek numerical prefixes, e.g. tetrahedron. The regular polyhedra have faces which are regular polygons. The word dihedron is used for a plane polygon oriented on an axis not in its own plane, and thus having two 'faces'.
See also Platonic solids.

polynomial   Any expression containing only powers of a variable, and hence of the form

$$P(x)=a_0+a_1 x+a_2 x^2+a_3 x^3+\ldots+a_n x^n$$

The highest power present is the degree of the polynomial. Many other expressions such as exponentials or circular functions can be represented as infinite polynomial series.

polynomial equation   Any equation in the form $P(x)=0$ where $P(x)$ is a polynomial of degree n. Gauss showed that a polynomial $P(x)$ where $x \in \mathbb{C}$ has n roots. Abel showed that a quintic cannot in general be solved using radicals, and Galois demonstrated the conditions under which any polynomial had exact and complete solutions.

polynomial regression   Used for data to which linear regression techniques do not apply. Polynomials are chosen which provide a curve of best fit when data are plotted.

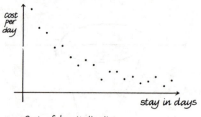

Cost of hospitalisation

polyomino   *See* Greek numerical prefixes. A polyomino of order *n* is the set of all distinct configurations formed by putting *n* squares edge to edge. Thus the five possible tetrominos are

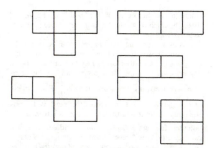

Any isometries of these are not considered to be distinct. There are 12 possible pentominos and 35 hexominos. Polyominos can be used in studying tessellation.

(*Note*: plural is -os or -oes).

polytope   The abstract generalization of the concept of a polyhedron in real space to a postulated space of dimension four. As polygons are the faces of polyhedra, so polyhedra are regarded as the 'cells' of polytopes. Certain three-dimensional structures made with rods can be regarded as the non-linear 'projections of' polytopes into real space.

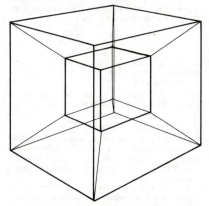

Poncelet, J. V.   French military engineer (1788–1867). He produced the first recognizably modern account of projective geometry (1822) which formulated the principle of duality. Most of his work was done while a prisoner of war in Russia.

Popper, Karl   Austrian, now English philosopher of science and mathematics (1902–   ). He argued that the acceptance of a scientific theory stood not on the accumulation of facts which it could explain, but on the possibility of constructing experiments that could prove it false but in fact fail to do so. He has written extensively on the nature of probability and the development of an axiomatic approach to this study.

Popper's axioms   A set of axioms for probability proposed in 1938. They are substantially equivalent to those of Kolmogorov, but are more general in that they do not specify sets of events as the arguments of probability functions.

population   In statistics this is a conventional term for any set of entities or source from which samples are taken. This may be an actual population of objects, beings or measures, or may simply refer to a probability distribution.

population mean   The mean (usually arithmetic mean) of a given population, found not by sampling but by measuring *all* members of the given population. Usually denoted by μ (compare sample arithmetic mean denoted by $\bar{X}$).

population parameters   These are functions of a set of data for an entire population, used in place of the individual values in discussing and formulating statistical results. Examples are the population mean μ, the variance σ^2 and the standard deviation σ. Such functions as the normal probability density are formulated in terms of μ and σ^2.

porism   Term used by Euclid for a theorem whose truth appears at once from another theorem which has been proved.

- *Theorem:* If two straight lines intersect, the vertically opposite angles are equal (Euclid I, 15).
  Porism: If two straight lines intersect, the sum of the angles formed is four right angles.

position   Used of a point or particle, and can only be given unambiguously relative to an arbitrary coordinate system. Usually stated in the form of an ordered set whose elements, distances or angles, are given in a conventional order, as with Cartesian coordinates, latitude and longitude, bearing and distance, position vectors.

position line   *See also PZX* triangle. If a single navigational observation of altitude of the sun or a star is possible, the point *Z* can lie anywhere on the circle on the earth's surface, from which the altitude is constant at any given time. The arc of this circle intercepted on the area covered by an ordinary chart where the ship is known to be can be plotted as a straight line within the limits of observational error. The position of the vessel will be somewhere along this line. An observation of a second body, or of the same one at a later time, gives a second position line, whose intersection with the first (transferred if necessary using the known course and speed of the ship since the last observation) then gives the required latitude and longitude. Method developed by Capt. H. Sumner 1843.

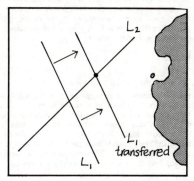

position vector A vector from an origin O to a point P may be used to fix the position of P with respect to a coordinate system. $\overrightarrow{OP} = \mathbf{r}$ is then called the position vector of P.

positive 1. *See* integer.
2. A real number x is positive if $x > 0$, and is represented on the real number line by an interval drawn to the right of the origin.

positive definite form A quadratic form given generally by

$$\sum_{i, j = 1}^{n} a_{ij} x_i x_j$$

is positive definite if it is always positive for all real values (not all zero) of the set of variables $\{x_i\}$.

● $ax^2 + 2bx + c$ is positive for all x if $a, c > 0$, $ac > b^2$

positive integer *See* integer. A member of the set $\mathbb{Z}^+ = \{+1, +2, +3 \ldots\}$ which excludes zero. *See* non-negative.

posterior probability *See* prior probability, Bayes' theorem.

postmultiplication *See* premultiplication.

postulate This word is not now distinguished precisely from axiom. The verb 'to postulate' is equivalent to 'propound as an axiom'. In Euclid, however, a postulate is a preliminary statement of what can be done within the context of geometry; e.g., a straight line can be indefinitely produced; a circle can be drawn with any centre and radius. This contrasts with the axiom as a 'common notion'; e.g., the whole is greater than the part, or the axiom as a necessarily unproved preliminary assumption. *See also* parallel postulate, axiom.

potential If a system of particles have gravitational masses or electrical charges given by $m_1, m_2 \ldots$ and are at distances $r_1, r_2 \ldots$ from any point P, then the potential at P due to the masses or charges (which give rise to a field) is defined as

$$\sum_{i=1}^{i=n} k \frac{m_i}{r_i}$$

where k is a constant depending on the units. For a continuous distribution of mass over a region relative to axes x, y, z a triple integral is required, but for a uniform spherical shell of radius r and mass M the potential at a distance $s > r$ is $\phi = M/s$, that is, as if the mass were concentrated at its centre. The gravitational attraction F on a mass m at a distance s from such a shell is given by

$$F = Gm \frac{d\phi}{ds}$$

where G is the gravitational constant.

potential energy 1. A measure of the work that can be done by a body by virtue of its position in a gravitational (or electromagnetic) field, were it to move from that position to a point at a different height above datum. It is equal to the work done in taking the body initially from the lower to the higher level, so that for small distances above the earth's surface gravitational potential energy is given by

$$E = mgh$$

where m is the mass of the body, h the height through which it is raised and g the acceleration due to gravity.
2. A similar formulation applies to a body moved from one position taken as origin to any other against a conservative force or system of forces (as in compressing a spring, or a gas within a cylinder by means of a piston). The work done is $\int_0^a \mathbf{F} . d\mathbf{s}$, and in any conservative system of force this work is done by the body on returning to its zero position from a.

potential function *See* potential gradient. If a field of force $F(x, y)$ is formed from the gradient $\nabla \phi(x, y)$ of a scalar function $\phi(x, y)$, then $\phi(x, y)$ itself is the potential function, so called because it gives the potential of F at (x, y). The concept may be extended in general to analytic functions.

potential gradient Given a scalar potential function S, as of a gravitational or electrical field, which has a constant value over a surface in the field, then the rate of change of the potential is greatest in the direction of the unit normal $\hat{\mathbf{n}}$ to the surface. Then the quantity

$$\frac{\partial S}{\partial n} \hat{\mathbf{n}}$$

is called the potential gradient grad S at this point. In cartesian coordinates it is given by

$$\text{grad } S = \frac{\partial S}{\partial x} \mathbf{i} + \frac{\partial S}{\partial y} \mathbf{j} + \frac{\partial S}{\partial z} \mathbf{k}$$

where $\mathbf{i}, \mathbf{j}, \mathbf{k}$ are unit vectors. The given partial differential operators form the vector operator del or ∇, so grad $S = \nabla S$.

power 1. A term used for the exponent or (frequently) the sum of the exponents of a product.

● x^2 is 'x to the power 2'
$x^2 y^2 z$ is a term of power 5

2. In dynamics, the rate at which work is done. The unit of power is the watt (W) defined as one joule (J) per second. If the point of application of a force $\mathbf{F}$ moves with velocity $\mathbf{v}$, the power developed is the scalar product $\mathbf{F} . \mathbf{v}$.
3. Used in statistics of the probability that a test rejects the null hypothesis at a specified significance level.
In this sense it is usual to speak of one test having greater power than another. The word is also used generally in mathematics of any process of wide applicability or scope.

power efficiency Also power. A term used in statistics, usually to assess distribution free (non-parametric) tests. It is the probability that a test will reject the null hypothesis H_0 at a specified level of significance, relative to a parametric test using a relevant distribution. It is often expressed as a percentage of the latter.

power function The power function of a statistical test involving any parameter θ is the probability $p(\theta)$ that the sample point will fall in the critical region of the test, when θ is the true value. That is

$$p(\theta) = 1 - \beta(\theta)$$

where $\beta(\theta)$ is the size of the type II error produced by the test.

power of the continuum Any set S whose members can be placed indefinitely into one-to-one correspondence with the set $\mathbb{R}$ of real numbers, is said to have the power of the continuum (or the same cardinal number as the set $\mathbb{R}$, usually denoted by c). *See also* Cantor, transfinite numbers.

power series If $\{a_n\}$ is a real or complex sequence $a_0, a_1, a_2, a_3 \ldots$ then a power series is one of the form

$$a_0 + \sum_{n=1}^{\infty} a_n z^n \quad (z \in \mathbb{C})$$

such that $1 + x + x^2 + x^3 + \ldots$

or $\quad 1 + z + \dfrac{z^2}{2!} + \dfrac{z^3}{3!} + \ldots$

Within but only within its circle of convergence a power series is absolutely and uniformly convergent, and hence may be differentiated or integrated term by term to give a series with the same radius of convergence, having as its limiting sum the derivative or integral of the original limiting sum. This can be shown by the behaviour of

$$S = \sum_{n=0}^{\infty} \frac{x^n}{n!} = 1 + x + \frac{x^2}{2!} + \frac{x^3}{3!} + \ldots$$

$$= e^x$$

Differentiating term by term gives

$$\frac{dS}{dx} = 0 + 1 + x + \frac{x^2}{2!} + \ldots$$

$$= e^x$$

precession *See* gyroscope. Used generally of any periodic motion in space where corresponding phase points are in advance of one another. Thus, in precession of the equinoxes, the equinoctial points are reached $1/26\,000$ of a year earlier each year. For a gyroscope, the point A on the wheel rotating with period t' is next reached at A' as it precesses through the angle ωt.

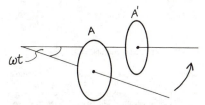

predicate In logic, a proposition has the structure of a sentence, with subject and predicate. Thus, in 'all circles are similar', the predicate is 'are similar'.

predictor-corrector methods 1. Used for the numerical solution of differential equations. One of the standard methods, say the Euler formula, is used to obtain the first value, and a modified formula is applied to find a more accurate or corrected value. The process can be repeated to obtain numerical results to any degree of accuracy, which depend finally on the accuracy of the corrector formula.

• To solve $\dfrac{dy}{dx} = f(x, y)$.

Use $y_{k+1} \approx y_k + hf(x_k, y_k)$

to obtain an approximation (see Euler's formula). Then use

$y_{k+1} \approx y_k + \frac{1}{2}h\left[f(x_k, y_k) + f(x_{k+1}, y_{k+1})\right]$ as a corrector where $f(x_{k+1}, y_{k+1})$ is obtained from the first approximation.

2. Used in statistics when an estimator or predictor is found to be biased. Thus the expected variance s^2 of a sample gives a biased prediction of the population variance σ^2, so that the best estimate $\hat{\sigma}^2$ of the population variance is

$$\hat{\sigma}^2 = \frac{n}{n-1} s^2$$

then s^2 is the predictor and $\dfrac{n}{n-1}$ the corrector.

premise A basic assumption in a logical argument, or a proposition taken as true from which a conclusion is drawn by valid logical inference. An argument may have two or more premises: if two they are called major and minor. If one of the premises is false a valid argument may produce a false conclusion

• Major premise: Prime numbers are odd
Minor premise: Two is not odd
Conclusion: Two is not prime

premultiplication When multiplication or any multiplicative operation (such as compounding) is not commutative (as with matrices where $AB \neq BA$) it is necessary to distinguish a multiplier A on the left from that on the right of the multiplicand B. The terms left multiplication and premultiplication are synonymous: so are right multiplication and postmultiplication.
See also multiplication.

p, r equation *See* pedal equation.

pressure 1. The force acting per unit area on any surface in a direction normal to the surface. The force may be transmitted by a fluid as in a boiler or through another surface. For a given total force it is then inversely proportional to the areas in contact (compare stiletto heels and snowshoes).
2. The total resultant force acting on an area, e.g. on a dam.

price function A mathematical model which purports to give the price of a commodity as a function of other factors, such as unit distribution costs, taken to be quantifiable.

prime A positive integer is prime if it has two but only two distinct factors, itself and 1. Euclid (Books VII, VIII) regards a number as a line interval compounded of units, and defines a prime as a number which can only be measured by the unit (not itself a number). It follows from both definitions that 1 is not a prime: the smallest prime is 2. The study of primes and their distribution has been an important topic in number theory.
See also coprime.

prime factors If the factors of a composite number are themselves factorized into primes the number then becomes the continued product of a sequence of prime factors.

• $60 = 5 \times 12$
$= 5 \times 6 \times 2$
$= 5 \times 3 \times 2 \times 2$

This factorization is unique (Euclid IX, 14).

prime field (subfield). A field which has no subfield other than itself and the trivial $\{1\}$ is called a prime field. It follows that the least subfield of any field is a prime field.

The field of rationals $\mathbb{Q}$ is a prime subfield of the field of reals $\mathbb{R}$ since it has no subfields other than $\{1\}$

prime number theorem If $\pi(x)$ is the number of primes less than or equal to x (where x is not necessarily an integer) then

$$\lim_{x \to \infty} \frac{\pi(x).\ln x}{x} = 1$$

The theorem has a long history beginning with Legendre, and was finally proved by Hadamard in 1896.

prime pairs If the primes are set out in order of magnitude it is found that many pairs occur of the form p, $(p+2)$ where p is prime.

● $(11, 13)$, $(27, 29)$, $(71, 73)$, $\ldots$

It is an unproved conjecture that there is an infinity of prime pairs.

prime rich quadratic An expression of the second degree in n whose values are prime for a substantial range of n values. An example is

$$Q(n) = n^2 + n + 41$$

which generates primes for 80 consecutive values from $n = -40$ to $n = +39$. Polynomials of higher degree can be constructed, but there is no general expression. It is conjectured that no quadratic can generate more than 80 primes for *consecutive n* values.

primitive modular roots *See also* primitive roots. The positive integers a $(1 < a < m)$ which are relatively prime to m, together with unity, form a multiplication group G_m modulo m, whose order is $\phi(m)$, the Euler function. Thus $\phi(8) = 4$ and $G_8 = \{1, 3, 5, 7\}$. If but only if this group has generators, then these generating integers are called primitive roots modulo m. Thus 3 is a primitive root mod 7 since it generates $G_7 = \{1, 2, 3, 4, 5, 6\}$ but 2 is not. The only values of m that produce primitive roots are 2, 4, p^n and $2p^n$, where p is an odd prime and $n = 1, 2, 3 \ldots$

primitive proposition One of a set of preliminary assertions prefixed to a systems of propositions (especially in *Principia Mathematica*) for which formal proof is inappropriate or impossible. They are usually more detailed and specific than axioms, and denoted P_p

$$\vdash p \vee q \to q \vee p \; P_p$$

This reads: Assert that $(p$ or $q)$ implies $(q$ or $p)$: this is a primitive proposition.

primitive roots Of the n roots of unity, $1, \omega, \omega^2 \ldots \omega^{n-1}$ any one root z is primitive if $z^m \neq 1$ where $0 < m < n$. Thus ω and ω^3 are primitive eighth roots of unity, but 1, ω^6 are not (since $(\omega^6)^4 = \omega^{24} = 1$). Any root ω^p is a primitive root if but only if its exponent p is either unity or is relatively prime to n. The number of these exponents for any n is the Euler function $\phi(n)$, once called the totient function. Thus $\phi(9) = 6$ from the set of exponents $\{1, 2, 4, 5, 7, 8\}$.

principal argument *See* argument.

principal axis A line through the focus of any conic perpendicular to a directrix. The major axis of an ellipse lies on the principal axis

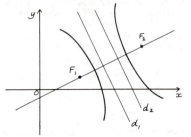

If a conic has two foci the principal axis passes through both.

principal branch The curve formed by principal values of a function. The modern definition of a function requires that each of such branches should be regarded as a separate function.

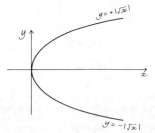

principal minor *See* minor. Any minor whose elements are symmetric with respect to the principal diagonal of the determinant or matrix from which they are formed.

● The unit matrix of order 3 $\begin{pmatrix} 1 & 0 & 0 \\ 0 & 1 & 0 \\ 0 & 0 & 1 \end{pmatrix}$

has two principal minors, each $\begin{pmatrix} 1 & 0 \\ 0 & 1 \end{pmatrix}$

principal root If the roots z_1, $z_2 \ldots$ of a complex equation are written in the form $z_1 = r_1$, θ_1, $z_2 = r_2$, $\theta_2 \ldots$ the principal root is the one for which θ_i is least and non-negative. The Argand diagram shows a typical case. If $z^n = 1$ the principal root is 1 with $\theta = 0$.

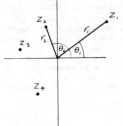

principal value   When an equation such as $f(x)=c$ is not satisfied by a unique $x\in\mathbb{R}$ it is often convenient to take one member of the set of x values, usually the smallest or the one in a given interval about the origin, and to take this as the principal value

Thus for $\sin x = 0.5$ x has the values $\dfrac{\pi}{6}, \dfrac{5\pi}{6}, \ldots$

The principal value is $\pi/6$ and this is normally taken as the solution of $\sin x = 0.5$, written $\sin^{-1} 0.5$ or arcsin 0.5.

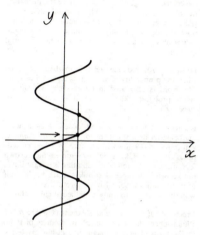

Principia Mathematica   *See* Russell, Bertrand.

prior probability   A probability assigned to events, prior to sampling or holding trials, on the basis of previous records, subjective assessment or arbitrary decision. These are combined with probabilities arrived at by the result of trials or sampling to give an amended posterior probability using Bayes' theorem. If, for example, the prior probability of an event is very low, its occurrence in a small sample gives, by Bayes' theorem, a much lower posterior probability than a simple occurrence ratio derived from the sample would suggest.

probabilistic models   These are known theoretical probability distributions against which a random variable, such as the throw of dice or the incidence of traffic accidents, can be compared using some form of 'best fit' analysis, such as

1. The binomial distribution $P[X=x,n]=\dbinom{n}{x}p^{x}q^{n-x}$ where $n=0$, 1, 2, ..., $p=$ probability of occurrence of event, $q=(1-p)=$ probability of non-occurrence.

2. The Poisson distribution $P[X=x,\lambda]=\dfrac{e^{-\lambda}\lambda^{x}}{x!}$ where λ is the mean and $x=0$, 1, 2, 3, ...

3. The Normal distribution $N(\mu,\sigma^{2})$.
See separate entries.

probability   Formalizes the intuitive notion of chance events; that is, whether or not a given outcome will in the future result from a given action. If a sample space S is the set of all possible outcomes of the action considered, and A is any possible event or set of events such that $A\subseteq S$, a theory of probability will discuss a probability function that assigns a unique number to each A. The function is defined so that

$$0\leqslant p(A)\leqslant 1$$
$$p(S)=1$$
$$p(\emptyset)=0$$

where $p(A)$ denotes the probability of A and $p(S)=1$ corresponds to certainty (from the definition of S). There are three current formulations.

1. Classical definition
If a trial can lead to N mutually exclusive and 'equally likely' outcomes, and if a number $n(A)$ of these have the attribute A, then the probability of A is $p(A)=\dfrac{n(A)}{N}$.

The term 'equally likely' is not formally defined but remains an intuitive concept.

● A pack of cards is cut. What is the probability of showing a spade (event A)?
$n(A)=13$
$N=52$
$p(A)=\frac{13}{52}=\frac{1}{4}$

This formulation requires the total outcome space to be known to give the value of N. It was first discussed by de Moivre and Laplace.

2. Frequency definition
If event A occurs $n(A)$ times in N trials of a random experiment, a frequency (or occurrence) function $R(A)$ is defined as

$$R(A)=\dfrac{n(A)}{N}$$

This is an empirical result. The probability of A is then defined as

$$p(A)= \lim_{N\to\infty} R(A)$$
$$= \lim_{N\to\infty} \dfrac{n(A)}{N}$$

This behaviour of $R(A)$ is one form of the Law of Large Numbers, and its successive values need not form a Cauchy sequence.

3. Axiomatic formulation
A modern approach (by Kolmogorov, 1933, and others) allows an axiom set to be operationally justified by formulations 1 and 2 but from then on develops probability as a topic in pure mathematics. It assigns to any event $A\subseteq S$ a real number $p(A)$ in the closed interval $(0,1)$ such that

$$p(A)\geqslant 0$$
$$p(S)=1$$

together with an operational axiom:

If A_1, A_2, A_3, ... A_n are mutually exclusive events, then $p(A_1\cup A_2\cup\ldots A_n)=\sum_{j=1}^{n} p(A_j)$.

This axiom corresponds to the addition of discrete probabilities, but, since n can increase without limit, applies to a denumerable infinity of events. Other sets of axioms have been proposed, e.g. by Popper. Formulations 1 and 2 make it clear that a probability cannot properly be assigned to any events that have actually occurred. It leads to the expected value of a 'future occurrence function' which only has meaning for a large number of instances and which will necessarily (unless $p = 1$ or 0) have a dispersion about this value. Some discussions of probability regard it as expressing the operation of 'hidden variables', which if known would replace probabilistic statements by exact predictions.

probability density function   Often written p.d.f. The most usual specification of a continuous probability distribution, having an analogy with the probability function of a discrete variable. It is the derivative of the cumulative distribution function (c.d.f.) and gives the probability that the variate X lies between given limits. That is

$$\text{prob } (a \leqslant X \leqslant b) = \int_a^b f(x)\,dx$$

$$= F(b) - F(a)$$

where f is the density function and F the c.d.f. The density function is represented by the ordinate of the probability distribution curve at any point.

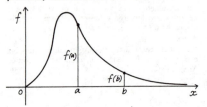

The function f is non-negative and the total area under the curve is unity for any p.d.f., that is

$$\int_{-\infty}^{+\infty} f(x)\,dx = 1$$

probability function   The function $p(X)$ giving the probabilities in a discrete distribution. That is, $p(x)$ is the probability that $X = x$ if X is the relevant variate. It can be represented as a histogram whose total area is unity.

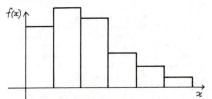

As an example, consider the counts x of plant species obtained by throwing quadrats, which then provide a working mean λ. The Poisson distribution will then give, using

$$p(x) = \frac{\lambda^x e^{-\lambda}}{x!} \quad (x = 0, 1, 2, 3 \ldots)$$

If the species is randomly scattered over the area, the histogram of the counts would then approximate to that of $p(x)$.

probability generating function   Often written p.g.f. A function which expands into a *power series* in t which converges over $|t| < t_0$ so that

$$\phi(t) = a_0 + a_1 t + a_2 t^2 + \ldots a_r t^r + \ldots$$

It is then a p.g.f. if, for any set of variates X (for example a set of trials with successes $0, 1, 2 \ldots r \ldots$), the coefficients $a_0, a_1, a_2 \ldots a_r \ldots$ give the probabilities of $x_0, x_1, x_2 \ldots x_r, \ldots$. The probabilities are thus the coefficients of t^x in the expansion. The function is normally discussed only for non-negative integral values of x. It can also be used to obtain factorial moments.

probable   An undefined term in mathematics, used when the probability of an event is regarded as high. The word is also used in terms such as probable error, probable value, where it is equivalent to 'expected'.

problem   A word often used loosely in elementary mathematics as a synonym for exercise or example, whose result is known in advance by whoever proposes it. The Gk. *problema*, something thrown forward, is a question whose solution is sought but is not known in advance. A problem in the application of mathematics is solved when formulated in such a way that it yields to known mathematical methods.

Proclus   Of Alexandria and Athens (410–485 A.D.). Philosopher who reformulated the theories of Plato in the form of highly imaginative occult mysteries. He is of major importance in the history of mathematics as the writer of a *Commentary on Euclid* (450 A.D.) which quotes from a lost treatise by Eudemus, said to be a pupil of Aristotle. Much of the mathematics commonly associated with Pythagoras and other early mathematicians is drawn from Proclus, writing nearly 1000 years after their deaths.

product   The result of a multiplicative operation, as in 'the product of two numbers' or by analogy as 'the product of two permutations'.

product-moment correlation coefficient   Also named Pearson coefficient (Karl Pearson 1857–1936). *See* linear correlation coefficient.

product rule for differentiation   If $f(x)$, $g(x)$ are differentiable then $\phi(x) = f(x) \cdot g(x)$ is differentiable and $\phi'(x) = f(x) \cdot g'(x) + g(x) \cdot f'(x)$. The result is also written, for $y = uv$ where u, v are functions of x

$$y' = uv' + vu'$$

or

$$\frac{d(uv)}{dx} = \frac{u\,dv}{dx} + \frac{v\,du}{dx}$$

The expressions can be extended to n factors, e.g.

$$y' = uvw' + uwv' + vwu'$$

See Leibnitz theorem.

product set   *See* cartesian product.

programmable calculator   *See* calculator.

programming The reduction of any quantitative process to a sequence of operational instructions each of which involves a binary choice. Such instructions, in the form of punched tape, a keyboard sequence struck by an operator, or magnetic signals stored on discs or held within computer circuits, enable data to be processed electrically or mechanically without further human computation. Examples of programmed operations are the solution of equations, the keeping of bank accounts, the analysis of statistics, the production of graphs and other diagrams on video display units. Criteria which decide whether or not a given process can be programmed for a computer were discussed by Turing.

projectile Any body having mass launched or projected in some way and then allowed to move freely in a gravitational field, usually of the earth. If the projectile is fired into the atmosphere, the mathematical analysis of the ensuing motion may take into account the resistance of the air or may ignore it to a first approximation.

projection 1. The transformation of any configuration of points C into a configuration C' by straight lines which join each $P \in C$ into $P' \in C'$. The direction of PP' and the position of P' on it are determined in some well-defined manner. The correspondence may be one-one or many-one. Under central projections the lines originate from a vertex or pole, orthogonal or parallel projections are transformations by parallel lines. The shadows of solid objects, plans, elevations, isometric views and so on are all examples of projections. For a formal discussion of projection *see* perspectivity.
2. Specifically as map projection. Any transformation whatever that represents the surface or part of the surface of a sphere on a plane. Some of these, such as the gnomonic, are projections as defined above, but many are topological mappings or use non-linear coordinate transformations.

projective geometry 1. Originally the synthetic geometry which studied the properties of projected configurations, in which Euclidean distances were replaced by ratios between distances and a number of non-metrical theorems were developed, such as Desargues' or Pascal's theorems. In this geometry pairs of intersecting lines became parallel when their point of intersection was projected towards infinity.
2. Analytic or algebraic projective geometry, in which points and lines are defined as sets of numbers and very general theorems are formulated using homogeneous coordinates or complex numbers. Projection then becomes a set of abstract transformations, of which Euclidean and synthetic projective geometries are special cases.
See also Klein.

projectivity The relation between two sets of collinear points

$$\{A, B, C, D \ldots\} \ \{A', B', C', D' \ldots\}$$

when one transforms into the other by a sequence of perspectivities.

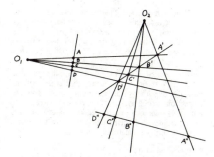

prolate cycloid *See* cycloid. The radius a of a circle centre C is produced to P so that $CP = b$ $(b > a)$. If the circle rolls along a straight line the point P describes the prolate cycloid, given by the equations

$$x = a\theta - b \sin \theta$$
$$y = a - b \cos \theta$$

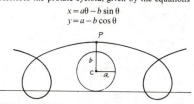

The motion of P is retrograde when below the line, as with the wheel flanges of a railway train.

prolate spheroid The surface produced by rotating an ellipse about its major axis. A special case of the ellipsoid, having the equation

$$\frac{x^2}{a^2} + \frac{y^2}{a^2} + \frac{z^2}{c^2} = 1 \qquad \begin{matrix} (a, b, c, > 0) \\ (c > a) \end{matrix}$$

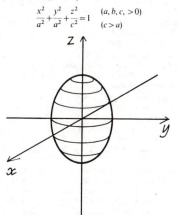

proof The proof of a proposition or theorem is a sequence of statements each of which is agreed to follow logically from its predecessor. If the initial statement is agreed to be true, the final statement in the sequence establishes the truth of the theorem.

proof by contradiction Also called *reductio ad absurdum.* A method of proving a proposition by showing that the hypothesis of its negation leads to a contradiction. The validity of such arguments has been queried.

163

proof by exhaustion This is not the same as the method of exhaustion used by the early geometers, but is simply a result established by testing all possible cases. Its validity depends on the possibility of showing that every case has been, or in principle can be, tested.

proof by induction A method of formal proof for a theorem $P(n)$ where $n \in \mathbb{N}$. Although it begins with an inductive hypothesis (that is, one obtained by trial or inspection) proof by induction is not equivalent to inductive inference, where general conclusions are drawn from specific instances. There are two forms of proof, each of which has three stages

1. Weak induction
(a) Prove that if the hypothesis $P(n)$ is postulated as true for any given n, then $P(n+1)$ is true.
(b) Verify or demonstrate that $P(n_0)$ is true for the smallest integer n_0 for which $P(n)$ is postulated true.
(c) Conclude that $P(n)$ is true for n_0, $n_0 + 1$, $n_0 + 2 \ldots$ and hence all $n \geqslant n_0$.

● $P(n)$ is $1^3 + 2^3 + 3^3 + \ldots n^3 = \frac{1}{4}n^2(n+1)^2$
If this is true $P(n+1) = \frac{1}{4}n^2(n+1)^2 + (n+1)^3$
$$= \frac{1}{4}(n+1)^2(n+2)^2$$
But $P(1)$ is certainly true, hence $P(n)$ is true for $n = 1, 2, 3, 4 \ldots$ and hence all $n \geqslant 1$.

2. Strong induction
This differs only in assuming as a hypothesis $P(n)$ for a *range* of values n_0, $n_0 + 1$, $n_0 + 2$, $\ldots n_0 + m$ and then in showing that $P(n_0 + m + 1)$ is true if $P(n_0)$, $P(n_0 + 1) \ldots P(n_0 + m)$ are true. Hence, as before, $P(n)$ is shown after the initial verification to be true for all $n \leqslant n_0$. This form can be used when $P(n_0)$ is trivially true, and thus gives no information.

proper divisor All positive integral divisors of a number N except N itself.
See also aliquot parts.

proper fraction A positive fraction less than unity, a fraction in the form a/b where a, b are non-zero natural numbers and $a < b$. It is also a positive rational less than unity.

proper length A term used in relativity theory, the length of an object measured in the coordinate system in which it is at rest.

proper subset A subset of any set that excludes at least one member of the set. If P is a proper subset of S, $P \subseteq S$ but not $P \subseteq S$. The term applies in the same way to proper subgroups, subrings, etc.

proper time A term used in relativity theory. The time interval between two events measured by a clock at rest relative to a coordinate system in which the events successively occur at the same point.

proportion Two quantities are said to be proportional, in proportion or in direct proportion, if the ratio between them is constant. The word is also used loosely for fraction, ratio, or sometimes part.

● At an hourly wage a person will receive an amount proportional to the hours worked.
See inverse proportion.

proportional division The process of dividing a number (or a line) into two or more parts which are proportional to a given set of numbers.

proportional parts If a line segment AB is divided internally and externally at L and P so that $AL:LB = AP:PB$, L and P are said to divide AB into proportional parts. The concept is generalized to any linear expression. Thus distances d_1, d_2 ... along a route traversed at constant speed in times t_1, t_2 ... are given by

$$\frac{d_1}{t_1} = \frac{d_2}{t_2} = \ldots$$

and the route is thus divided into parts proportional to the times taken. More generally, if the value of $f(x)$ is known in the interval $[a, b]$ only at a, b, and it is assumed that $f(x)$ is linear over this interval (that is, there is a linear function $g(x)$ such that $g(a) = f(a)$ and $g(b) = f(b)$ and $f(x)$ behaves like this function) then approximate intermediate values of $f(x)$ in the interval can be calculated, using the linear equation

$$g(x) = \frac{f(b) - f(a)}{b - a}(x - a) + f(a)$$

This expression is commonly used to calculate intermediate values in mathematical tables such as logarithms between $f(a)$ and $f(b)$, given as tables of differences.

proposition Has a wide range of uses, of which four are important for mathematics.

1. A statement about entities whose relationships form a branch of mathematics.

● If the product of two real numbers is zero, then at least one of them must be zero.

A proposition can be considered as undecided when formulated, and it is then the task of mathematics to show whether it is true or false. Some propositions, e.g. Goldbach's conjecture, are still undecided. A proposition must always be meaningful. 'All square circles are congruent' is not subject to proof or disproof and is without meaning, an 'empty concept' in our terminology.

2. An existential proposition states that an entity which is the subject of a proposition does or does not exist.

● 'There is no greatest prime' (Euclid). The truth of this proposition implies that any proposition about the greatest prime (such as 'the greatest prime is the sum of two cubes') is not properly formulated.

3. A proposition in classical geometry, whose traditional Euclidean form has greatly influenced the development of mathematics. This recognizes six stages:

(i) *protasis* or the general enunciation,

● In any triangle ...

(ii) *ekthesis* or the specific data,

● Given triangle ABC ...

(iii) *diorismos* or what is to be done,

● Prove AB = ...

(iv) *kataskenē* or construction if needed,

● Draw AM ...

(v) *apodeixis* or proof, using (ii), (iii) and (iv)

(vi) *symperasma* or conclusion,

● Hence AB = ... and the protasis is true.

Not all the stages need be present in any one proposition.

4. Modern logic sometimes restricts the use of the word to compound statements whose truth follows from the truth values of the components.

- $(2+1=3)$ *or* $(2+1=5)$ is a true proposition if at least one of the two constituent statements is true.

See propositional calculus.

propositional calculus That branch of mathematics that deals with propositions or statements, the formal relations between them and compound statements made up from them. Statements, which may be arbitrarily true or false, are denoted by $p, q, r \ldots$ and are linked by the propositional connectives. The calculus then aims to give a formal demonstration of the truth or falsehood of the compounded or derived propositions.

propositional connectives *See* connective.

propositional function The equivalent in logic of a function in mathematics. In the expression $f(x)$ the f denotes some sort of mathematical process, such as taking the sine or squaring, and the x states that this process operates on the variable x, which can take values $a, b, c, \ldots$ if but only if these are in the domain of the function. In the propositional function $F(x)$, F is any possible predicate and x a member of the set of entities of which it may meaningfully be asserted. Thus if F is 'is a mammal' $F(x)$ is the statement 'x is a mammal', which is meaningful if x denotes an animal. Its truth or falsehood can in principle be determined.

pseudometric *See* distance, metric space. A space or set of elements $S = \{x, y, z \ldots\}$ is pseudometric if, of the four conditions that define the distance function, the condition $d(x, y) > 0$ for $x \neq y$ does not necessarily hold.

- The space of many-valued expressions is pseudometric, since $y(x_1) = y(x_2)$ for some x_1, x_2 where $x_1 \neq x_2$.

pseudo-random numbers Numbers generated in a computer by printing out digits 0–9 from a formula involving congruences modulo m, where m is a very large number, usually at least 2^{24}. The digits generated are statistically random, but the sequence would repeat after m steps (or earlier).

See also quasi-random numbers.

pseudoscalar A term sometimes used to differentiate a true scalar such as mass from a magnitude such as volume whose sign will change if the coordinate system in which it is represented is changed from a right-handed to a left-handed set, or alternatively if it is transformed to occupy a quadrant of the coordinates having an odd number of negative axes (one or three). An example is given under scalar triple product, which expresses the volume of the parallelepiped whose edges are the vectors **a**, **b**, **c**. Here four of the eight quadrants formed by the x, y, z axes have an odd number of negative axes, and in these $[\mathbf{a}, \mathbf{b}, \mathbf{c}]$ is negative. These axes change places if the set of coordinates is made left-handed. The change of sign is only a mathematical convention, and it is usual to treat volumes etc. as unsigned quantities. Sometimes the convention is useful: it distinguishes, for example, between the upper and lower faces of a lamina whose area is given.

pseudosphere A surface of constant negative curvature on which triangles described by geodesics have an angle sum less than 180°. The properties of configurations on its surface correspond to 'hyperbolic geometry'.

See tractrix.

Ptolemy, Claudius Alexandrian mathematician, astronomer and geographer (known to have been alive in 161 A.D.). He developed the geocentric theory of planetary motion in terms of cycles and epicycles. Ptolemy did not make maps, but data collected by him enabled a map of the Mediterranean region and beyond to be constructed which, although subject to systematic errors of position, was superior to anything produced during the next 1000 years.

Ptolemy's theorem If ABCD is a cyclic quadrilateral then the sum of the products of opposite sides AB.CD and BC.AD is equal to the product of the diagonals AC.BD. The converse is true.

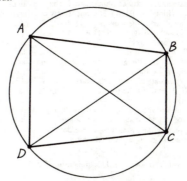

If one side of ABCD is a diameter the theorem becomes the addition rule for $\sin(\theta + \phi)$. The products are then expressed in terms of the angles subtended by the sides at the centre of the circle.

punctured neighbourhood *See* deleted neighbourhood.

pure mathematics The distinction between pure and applied mathematics, between manipulating a consistent symbolic calculus according to arbitrary rules, and obtaining results valid in the physical world as modelled by some of the symbolic structures, was developed in the 19th century. In so far as pure mathematics uses concepts which may not model physical reality — real numbers as distinct from rationals, for example — this distinction may be maintained, but it is no longer of great value. Some of the concepts of pure mathematics, such as real numbers or infinite series, may represent the failure of the human mind to adjust its intuitions to the structure of the physical world. A proposition in mathematics requires the assignment of one of the concepts true, false, undecided or undecidable: these are intuitive concepts outside mathematics and not therefore 'pure'.

See also mathematics.

pyramid A generic name for solids or three-dimensional configurations having a plane polygonal base, the vertices of which are joined to a point (the vertex) not in its plane. They are named individually from the shape of the base, e.g. square pyramid. If the vertex is vertically over a point equidistant from the vertices of the base, the pyramid is a right pyramid: otherwise it is skew. From Gk. *puramis*, hellenizing the Egyptian name of the tomb structures built in Egypt on a square base.

Pythagoras Early Greek philosopher (c. 582–500 B.C.) whose school of followers was moral and religious rather than academic. It was credited with producing results in number theory and observational astronomy which formed the basis of the flowering of Greek mathematics some two centuries later. Much learning that is associated with the Pythagoreans, including the famous Pythagoras theorem, is mere attribution by later writers, particularly Plutarch (c. 100 A.D.) and Neoplatonists such as Proclus of the 4th century.

Pythagoras' theorem This theorem, which first appears as Euclid 1, 47, is part of the mythology of mathematics. Its attribution to Pythagoras is quite late (Plutarch c. 100 A.D.), but it was certainly well known as a theorem before 300 B.C. There is no evidence whatever that it was known to the Egyptians, although they may have had the 'Pythagorean triple' $3^2 + 4^2 = 5^2$ as a number fact not associated with geometry. The theorem was also known in India and China, but its first recorded versions are also late (Bhaskara c. 1150 A.D.). Euclid VI, 31 extends the theorem to any similar and similarly placed figures drawn on the sides of the right angled triangle. E. S. Loomis (1940) has recorded 370 proofs and visual demonstrations. In coordinate geometry the distance, d, of the point (x, y) from the origin is given, using Pythagoras, by

$$d^2 = x^2 + y^2$$

This is extended, for three dimensions, to

$$d^2 = x^2 + y^2 + z^2$$

and generally to

$$d^2 = \sum_{i=1}^{n} x_i^2$$

A space for which this relation is postulated is said to have a Pythagorean or Euclidean metric.

Pythagorean triples Sets of whole numbers $\{a, b, c\}$ such that $a^2 = b^2 + c^2$. Each triple specifies a right angled triangle with integral sides.

PZX triangle The spherical triangle fundamental to astro-navigation. Lines from the centre of the earth towards the celestial pole, the zenith and an observed astronomical object cut the earth's surface at P, Z and X. The position of X, the sub-stellar point at the time of observation, is given by astronomical tables, and hence the latitude and longitude of Z can be found from suitable observations. *See* position line.

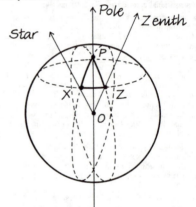

Q

Q.E.D. and Q.E.F. Traditionally added to the end of proofs or constructions in Euclidean geometry, abbreviated from the Latin *quod erat demonstrandum* (which was to be demonstrated) and *quod erat faciendum* (which was to be done). Euclid uses without contraction the phrases '*Oper edei deixai* and *oper edei poiēsai* which also have these meanings.

quadrangle *See* complete quadrangle.

quadratic equation Is of the type $ax^2 + bx + c = 0$ $(a \neq 0)$. It always has two roots if the domain of x is complex, but one or both of these may be suppressed if x is real, rational or an integer. The general solution is

$$\frac{-b \pm \sqrt{(b^2 - 4ac)}}{2a}$$

For real x, the discriminant $b^2 - 4ac$ indicates the nature of the roots. If $b^2 - 4ac > 0$ there are two real distinct roots, if $b^2 - 4ac = 0$ the two roots coincide. If $b^2 - 4ac < 0$ the equation has no solutions for real x and the curve $y = ax^2 + bx + c$ does not cut the x axis. If $x \in \mathbb{C}$ it then has two complex roots of the form

$$\frac{-b \pm i\sqrt{(4ac - b^2)}}{2a}$$

quadratic form The general expression $ax^2 + 2bx + c$ where $a, b, c \in \mathbb{R}$ and $(a \neq 0)$. The forms whose values are always positive when x is real are called positive definite quadratic forms.
See also general quadratic form.

quadratic residue If p is an odd prime the set of $(p-1)$ non-zero squares $\{1^2, 2^2, 3^2 \ldots (p-1)^2\}$ will give $\frac{1}{2}(p-1)$ distinct remainders when divided by p. These are the quadratic residues modulo p.
● If $p = 11$ the quadratic residues form the set $\{1, 4, 9, 5, 3\}$, congruent with $\{1^2 \ldots 5^2\}$ modulo 11. The remaining five non-zero integers, the set $\{2, 6, 7, 8, 10\}$ are not generated from the set $\{1^2, 2^2 \ldots 10^2\}$

quadratrix Curve, generated by Hippias (c. 425 B.C.), as the locus of the intersections of two lines.

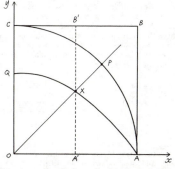

OP moves uniformly in a circular arc from OA to OC, A′B′ moves uniformly parallel to AB from AB to OC. Both motions start together and take the same time. The set of all points X where A′B′ cuts OP is the quadratrix. Its cartesian equation is the positive principal branch of

$$y = x \cot \frac{\pi x}{2a}$$

where OA is the x axis and OP $= a$.
Since the limiting value of y as $x \to 0$ is OQ or $2a/\pi$ we get $\pi OQ^2 = 2OP$. OQ, a rectangle equal in area to a circle (Dinostratus 350 B.C.). (Note that the side OQ is not commensurable with OP). Moreover, by trisecting any interval moved through by A′ or B′, the corresponding positions of X trisect the angle through which OP has rotated in the same time. The curve is accordingly a trisectrix. A similar curve given by

$$y = \cos \frac{\pi x}{2}$$

is the quadratrix of Tchirnhausen.

quadrature A term formerly used for finding an area bounded by curves using a limiting process and thus corresponding to integration. Quadrature of a circle is not the same as 'squaring the circle', which requires a geometrical construction with straight edge and compasses.

quadric surface The general surface corresponding in three dimensions to a conic in two. The cartesian representation of the general quadric equation of the second degree in three variables is $ax^2 + by^2 + cz^2 + dxy + exz + fyz + gx + hy + iz + j = 0$. By a suitable choice of origin and axes this equation takes the form

$$Ax^2 + By^2 + Cz^2 + D = 0$$

where A, B, C, D are positive, negative or zero coefficients. There are nine general types of quadric surface: the parabolic, elliptic and hyperbolic cylinders, the ellipsoid, the elliptic hyperboloid of one and of two sheets, the elliptic and hyperbolic paraboloids and the elliptic cone. Special cases of these appear as cones, spheres and other solids of revolution. A central quadric is symmetric with respect to a central point, which with a suitable choice of axes becomes the origin. It then has the general form

$$\pm\frac{x^2}{a^2} \pm \frac{y^2}{b^2} \pm \frac{z^2}{c^2} = 1 \ (a, \ b, \ c > 0)$$

quality control chart *See* control chart.

quantifier 1. In logic, one of the terms *all, some, none* and *not-all* which are said to quantify a proposition, and denoted traditionally by *a, i, e, o* the vowels in *AffIrmo*, I affirm and *nEgO*, I deny. An unquantified proposition is rarely in a form in which it can be discussed. Examples of the four forms are

    all whole numbers are prime
    some whole numbers are prime
    no whole numbers are prime
    not all whole numbers are prime

If S is {whole numbers} and P is the predicate 'is prime' the four forms can be written

    S a P, S i P, S e P, S o P

a and e are universal, i and o particular quantifiers.

2. In mathematics, symbols which quantify the number of elements to which a statement refers. Common quantifiers, taken from earlier logicians and popularized by Bourbaki, are ∀ 'for all' and ∃ 'there exists'.

Thus

$$\forall x \in \mathbb{R}^+ \; \exists \; y \in \mathbb{R}^- : y^2 = x$$

is read: 'For all x belonging to the set of positive real numbers, there is a y belonging to the set of negative reals, such that $y^2 = x$.'

quantity A general term, more commonly used of a physical measurement, equivalent to amount, size or numerical magnitude. It is sometimes used mathematically in phrases such as negative or complex quantities, where numbers are meant. Also in scalar quantity, vector quantity, tensor quantity.

quarter Lat. *quatarius*, a fourth part. Although this is now denoted by $\frac{1}{4}$ or 0.25 the word itself antedates mathematical notation or the study of arithmetic.

quarter turn Rotation through one right angle, $90°$ or $\pi/2$ radian.

quartile 1. For a continuous statistical distribution. If the range of the observations or scores is divided into four parts with the probability $\frac{1}{4}$ that a given variate will lie in any one part, then the three points of division are the three quartiles Q_1, Q_2, Q_3 ... Q_1 is called the lower and Q_3 the upper quartile, Q_2 coinciding with the median. The quantity $Q_3 - Q_1$ is the interquartile range, $(Q_3 - Q_1)/2$ is the semi-interquartile range or quartile deviation.
2. For a discrete distribution the definition is nominally the same and the quartiles can be found by listing in order and counting. If the total number of values is not divisible by four there is some indeterminancy about the exact values to be taken. This is not important unless the number of observations is small.

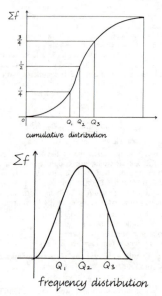

cumulative distribution

frequency distribution

quartile deviation The same as semi-interquartile range. For any distribution this is half the difference between the first and third quartiles $Q = \dfrac{Q_3 - Q_1}{2}$. It is a measure of variability around the median of a distribution, and one quartile deviation on each side of the median contains half of the population considered.

quasi-random numbers Apparently random sequences of numbers which have a particular statistical distribution of some or all of the digits, relevant to some Monte Carlo problem for which they are to be used.
See also pseudo-random numbers.

quasi-stable Used of a subsystem which develops within a larger physical system in such a way that it tends to maintain itself over a finite period once it has developed. An example is a cold or warm spell in a variable climate, or a vortex within a turbulent air stream.
See also chaotic.

quaternion group The finite multiplicative group formed by the eight elements ± 1, $\pm \mathbf{i}$, $\pm \mathbf{j}$, $\pm \mathbf{k}$ given that

$$\mathbf{i}^2 = \mathbf{j}^2 = \mathbf{k}^2 = -1$$
$$\mathbf{ij} = -\mathbf{ji} = \mathbf{k}$$
$$\mathbf{jk} = -\mathbf{kj} = \mathbf{i}$$
$$\mathbf{ki} = -\mathbf{ik} = \mathbf{j}$$

The quantities 1, $\mathbf{i}$, $\mathbf{j}$, $\mathbf{k}$ and their products define Hamilton's algebra of quaternions, appearing as coefficients to the ordered quadruples. They can also be represented by 2×2 matrices whose elements are in terms of 0, 1, i where $i^2 = -1$ as

$$1 = \begin{pmatrix} 1 & 0 \\ 0 & 1 \end{pmatrix} \; \mathbf{i} = \begin{pmatrix} -i & 0 \\ 0 & i \end{pmatrix} \; \mathbf{j} = \begin{pmatrix} 0 & 1 \\ -1 & 0 \end{pmatrix} \; \mathbf{k} = \begin{pmatrix} 0 & i \\ i & 0 \end{pmatrix}$$

quaternions A system of ordered quadruples (a, b, c, d) and the associated algebra for combining them. As developed by Hamilton and Tait one element was intended to represent the scalar magnitude, and three the directional coordinates of physical systems. This application has now been replaced entirely by modern vector methods, since quaternions proved to be algebraically clumsy in use.

queue Any sequence of elements or events a_1, a_2, a_3, ... a_n ... associated with arrival times t_1, t_2, t_3 ... t_n ... such that the first to arrive is the first to be dealt with (or be deleted from the sequence). This contrasts with a *stack*, in which the last to arrive is the first to be dealt with. Both sequences are discussed in queuing theory.

queue   stack

queuing theory The branch of statistics or operational research that studies the behaviour of queues and stacks, arrival and departure times, service functions and the supply of components. In a few straightforward cases, such as arrival times modelled by a Poisson process and service times exponentially distributed — a situation found approximately at bank counters and Post Office queues — a full mathematical treatment is possible. Often Monte Carlo methods are the only practicable strategy. *See* stochastic.

quinary Pertaining to five (*see* Latin numerical prefixes). Usually as a base in numeration. The Romans used a denary base in counting, but a mixed denary/quinary base in their notation for numerals. The Chinese *suan pan*, the Japanese *soroban*, and the 'counting board' of the Middle Ages, all use beads or counters whose value is five units.

quintic A polynomial equation of degree five, whose general solution is famous for having defied the efforts of mathematicians such as Euler and Lagrange. A proof that a general solution in radicals did not exist is due to Abel; a comprehensive theory of solvability in which the quintic appears as a numerical case was presented by Galois.

quotient *See* division.

quotient field If R is an integral domain such as the ring of integers it may be used to construct the field F consisting of the rationals $\mathbb{Q}$. Since every field behaves as an integral domain R is said to be embedded in F, which is then called the quotient field of R.
Thus the integers $\{\pm 1, \pm 2, \pm 3 \dots\}$ are embedded in their quotient field $\{\frac{0}{1} \pm \frac{1}{1}, \pm \frac{2}{1}, \pm \frac{1}{2}, \pm \frac{3}{1}, \pm \frac{2}{2}, \pm \frac{1}{3} \dots\}$

quotient group *See* factor group.

quotient ring *See* difference ring.

quotient rule Given any function $f(x)$ in the form u/v where u and v are functions of x, then the quotient rule, in the Leibnitz notation, gives

$$\frac{df(x)}{dx} = \frac{v\dfrac{du}{dx} - u\dfrac{dv}{dx}}{v^2}$$

More formally, if functions f, g have derivatives at $x = a$ and $g(a) \neq 0$, then f/g has a derivative given by

$$(f/g)'(a) = \frac{g(a)f'(a) - f(a)g'(a)}{g(a)^2}$$

quotient set For any multiplicative group G having a subgroup H, the (right) quotient set $G|H$ of G is the set of all right cosets of the form Hx where $x \in G$. The left quotient set $H|G$ is defined using left cosets of the form xH where $x \in G$. The right and left quotient sets are identical if the group is commutative.

● If G is the set of all permutations of 3 numbers $P_0 = (123)$, $P_1 = (231)$, $P_2 = (312)$, $P_3 = (132)$, $P_4 = (321)$, $P_5 = (213)$ and $H = \{P_0, P_3\}$ then the right quotient set is
$G|H = \{(P_2, P_3), (P_1, P_5), (P_2, P_4)\}$.
This contains only three elements since the cosets occur in pairs $H.P_1 = H.P_5 = (P_1, P_5)$.

quotient test *See* remainder theorem. The polynomial $f(x)$ has $(x - a)$ as a factor if $f(a) = 0$.

quotition *See* division.

radian   *See* circular measure.

radical   A root of an imperfect power, such as the square root of a number which is not a perfect square. Denoted by $\sqrt[n]{x}$ where n is the index of the radical and x the number (the sign $\sqrt{\ }$ was originally R_x from Lat. *radix*, a root). Any combination of numbers, powers and roots such as $-b \pm \sqrt{(b^2 - 4ac)}$ is also called a radical. A problem solvable in radicals is equivalent to a Euclidean construction.

radical axis   The line from every point of which the tangents to two circles are equal. If the circles intersect their radical axis is the line through their points of intersection. If the equations of the two circles (coefficients only) are (g_1, f_1, c_1) and (g_2, f_2, c_2) the radical axis is the line

$$(g_1 - g_2)x + (f_1 - f_2)y + (c_1 - c_2) = 0$$

See coaxial circles.

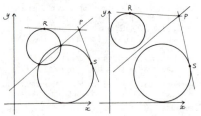

radical centre   The point of intersection of all three radical axes of any three circles taken in pairs.

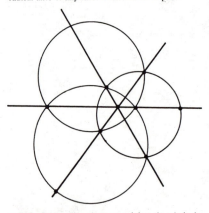

radical plane   The plane containing the circle in which two spheres intersect. Any other plane cutting both spheres intersects the radical plane in the radical axis of the two circles of intersection. *See* coaxial circles.

radius of convergence   *See* circle of convergence.

radius of curvature   At any point P of a curve this is the radius r of the osculating circle at P, i.e. of the circle having a triple intersection with the curve at P, defined as the limiting circle passing through three points A, P, B in that order on the curve as A, B approach P.

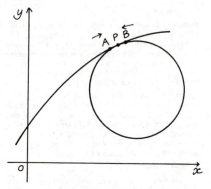

The osculating circle is also called the circle of curvature and has a common tangent with the curve at P. Its centre is the centre of curvature. *See also* curvature.

radius of gyration   Also swing radius. If the moment of inertia of a solid body of mass m about an axis is Mk^2, the distance k is called the radius of gyration.

radius vector   Synonym for position vector, but usually in referring to a point on a curve or surface with respect to an origin. If the radius vector is given its variation can be used to specify the curve. Thus the equation of a straight line through AP is

$$\mathbf{r} = \mathbf{a} + t\mathbf{b}$$

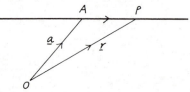

where b is any vector in the direction AP.

radix   Synonym for number base. Decimal notation uses radix 10. Also an obsolete term for square root.

random   Used generally of any process involving a finite or infinite sample space in which all elementary events have the same probability. Thus in sets of single digits chosen at random from N, 1 is as likely to occur as 9, but the sequence $1, 1, 1, 1, 1, 1, \ldots$ is not likely to occur. In a sequence of sets of six digits $\{1, 1, 1, 1, 1, 1\}$ is as likely as $\{2, 7, 3, 4, 4, 1\}$ or any other set specified in advance, and so on.

random digits   (or random numbers) A sequence of digits given in a table or produced by a randomized generating process, where at each term each of the ten digits 0–9 has the same probability of occurrence. Tables of random digits are useful for simulations of random processes or the selection of random samples.

random number A number having random digits, which may be generated by mechanical means, as a rotating number wheel or icosahedral dice, or by a suitable computer program which produces pseudo-random numbers (q.v.).
See also quasi-random numbers.

random sample When taken from a finite population a random sampling process is one that ensures that all possible samples of a given size are equally likely to be selected. From an infinite or continuous population, a random sample is a sequence of observations not dependent on one another, taken from the probability distribution of the population.
See also stochastic.

random trials A succession or sequence of trials or experimental determinations, the individual results of which are independent.

random variable Often called *variate* to distinguish it from a functional variable. A variable quantity whose behaviour is governed by a probability distribution.

random walk A stochastic process in which a notional 'particle' moves in a succession of steps, the direction of each at any one point being given by a probability distribution independent of previous steps. The size of each step can also be a variate. In most applications the particle moves over a lattice of points in one or more dimensions. By reducing the probability of further steps to zero at any point, line or plane in the lattice the system can model 'sinks' or 'absorbing barriers'. A particle entering such a state takes no further part in the process. Similarly, by introducing a reflecting barrier particles are returned to the lattice interior. Such a system can model the movement of molecules of gas in a closed vessel fitted with a porous plug through which the gas can diffuse.

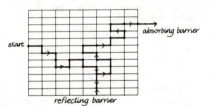

range 1. Of a function. The set of all image or output values corresponding to the values of the permitted input or domain.
For $f:x \mapsto x^2$, $x \in \mathbb{Z}$ the range is the set $\{0, 1, 4, 9, 16 \ldots\}$
2. The difference between the greatest and the least in any set of measures, often made more precise by using interquartile or interpercentile ranges.
See also dispersion.

rank 1. One of the ordinals 1st, 2nd, 3rd ... nth allotted to the positions of individual values of a set of measures, when these are arranged in order of magnitude.
2. A matrix A is of rank r if it contains at least one minor having a non-zero determinant of order r while all minors of order $r+1$ have zero determi-

nants. Consider

$$A = \begin{pmatrix} 1 & 1 & 0 & 0 \\ 0 & 0 & 1 & 1 \\ 1 & 1 & 1 & 1 \end{pmatrix}$$

Then $\begin{vmatrix} 1 & 1 & 0 \\ 0 & 0 & 1 \\ 1 & 1 & 1 \end{vmatrix} = 0$, $\begin{vmatrix} 1 & 0 & 0 \\ 0 & 1 & 1 \\ 1 & 1 & 1 \end{vmatrix} = 0$ but $\begin{vmatrix} 1 & 0 \\ 0 & 1 \end{vmatrix} \neq 0$

hence A is of rank 2.
3. Any matrix transformation maps a set of vectors into another. The rank of such a transformation, and hence the rank of the matrix, is the number of linearly independent vectors in the image set, that is, the dimensions of the image space. Thus

$$\begin{pmatrix} 4 & 7 \\ 3 & 1 \end{pmatrix} \begin{pmatrix} x \\ y \end{pmatrix} = \begin{pmatrix} x' \\ y' \end{pmatrix}$$

generates the two-dimensional vector space whose elements are x', y'. The rank of a matrix can also be found by casting it into echelon form by row transformation and counting the non-zero rows.

rank order correlation A measure of the correlation between two variates, calculated by comparing their ranking.
See also Kendall's tau, Spearman's rho.

rank-sum test *See* Wilcoxon rank sum test.

rank tests Any test arranged by ranking observations in a numerical order and not by analysis of the actual measures. The ranks can be compared by non-parametric tests.

rate of change This commonly expresses the way in which one quantity varies as a second quantity varies. The term is only defined if both quantities are stated, but the second of these is usually understood from context. The use of the word 'rate' often suggests an intuitive reference to time, which could be avoided by the word 'ratio'. Thus if y is a linear function of x the 'rate of change of y with respect to x' is the ratio of the y increment to the x increment that produces it. This, if y is any function $f(x)$, becomes the derivative or 'slope function' when the x increment $\to 0$. Behind this expression is the 'picture' of the abscissa changing with respect to time, with the slope function giving the corresponding rate of change of the ordinate.

ratio The result of dividing one quantity by another, usually expressed either in the lowest convenient terms or with one term unity. Ratios are denoted by: or the fraction solidus /

- The ratio between 14.62 and 21.93 is written
  $14.62:21.93 = 2:3$
  The ratio $2.3:9.798 = 1:4.26$

The ratios between fractional quantities can also be expressed as the ratios between whole numbers.

- $4.761:2.3 = 4761:2300$

Euclid used the word *logos* to express the comparison between two measures expressed as line intervals or areas. By choosing a suitable common measure as unit, he gave constructions equivalent to

171

expressing many ratios as whole numbers, the commensurable or 'rational' ratio (*rhētos logos*). Other measures could not be compared in this way, giving rise to the incommensurable or irrational ratio (*arrētos logos*) such as the side and diagonal of a square.
See irrational number.

rational function A function which is the ratio of two polynomials, that is

$$R(x) = \frac{P(x)}{Q(x)}$$

where $Q(x) \neq 0$, as $R(x) = \frac{4x-1}{3x^2 - 5x + 2}$ $x \notin \{2/3, 1\}$

rationalized A radical numerator (or denominator) of a fraction is rationalized by multiplying both numerator and denominator by a conjugate radical

$$\frac{a + \sqrt{b}}{c + \sqrt{d}} = \frac{(a + \sqrt{b})(c - \sqrt{d})}{(c + \sqrt{d})(c - \sqrt{d})}$$
$$= \frac{(a + \sqrt{b})(c - \sqrt{d})}{c^2 - d}$$

which rationalizes the denominator. One of the two parts remains irrational.

rationalized units Since the early work of Faraday and Ampère there has been a long history of controversy over electrical and magnetic units and many attempts to standardize them. Because of the geometry of electromagnetic fields many important equations contained π as a factor. Heaviside and later Giorgi proposed a system of units that began by redefining certain quantities so that they contained this irrational, which consequently disappeared from other and more commonly used equations. The system of units is then said to be rationalized. The SI system is a rationalized system that has now replaced all other systems by international agreement.
See Appendix 1.

rational number Three definitions are equivalent.
1. Any number which may be constructed as an integral multiple of another number taken as unit. In Greek geometry the unit was the measure of a line interval.
2. Any number of the form p/q where $p, q \in \mathbb{Z}$ and $q \neq 0$.
3. An ordered pair (a,b) of signed integers, $a, b \in \mathbb{Z}$, $b \neq 0$ with defined criteria for equality and operational rules.

(i) $(a,b) \lesseqgtr (c,d)$ if $ad - bc \lesseqgtr 0$
(ii) $(a,b) + (c,d) = \{(ad + bc), bd\}$
(iii) $(a,b).(c,d) = (ac, bd)$

It can be shown that those definitions correspond to the Four Rules applied to fractions. Analytic mathematics begins with the Greek discovery that the diagonal of a unit square cannot be expressed as a multiple of some submultiple of its side, and is not therefore a rational quantity.

ratio test A criterion for the convergence of a series. There are several forms
1. If the terms u_n and v_n of two series are strictly

positive, that is, $u_n > 0$, $v_n > 0$ and the ratio $\frac{v_{n+1}}{v_n} \leqslant \frac{u_{n+1}}{u_n}$ is true for sufficiently large n, then Σv_n is convergent if Σu_n is convergent. Conversely, if $\frac{v_{n+1}}{v_n} \geqslant \frac{u_{n+1}}{u_n}$ is true for sufficiently large n, then Σv_n diverges if Σu_n diverges.

2. The series Σv_n converges if $\frac{v_{n+1}}{v_n} \leqslant r$ where $r < 1$ for all sufficiently large n (d'Alembert's test).

3. If $\lim_{n \to \infty} \frac{v_{n+1}}{v_n} = k$ where $k < 1$ then Σv_n converges.

ratio to moving average A method used to determine seasonal variations in long-term time series. The value for each interval, say one month, is expressed as a ratio of the moving average centred on that month. Examination of the mean ratios for any month over a longer period, say several years, will show whether the variations are random or likely to be the result of seasonal factors.

• If the ratio to moving average of sales for December is consistently greater than unity over a long period, this suggests a seasonal increase at this time.

It is usual in commercial practice to express the ratios in terms of an index of 100 (corresponding to unity).

ratio to trend As for ratio to moving average, except that the ratios of observations or data are calculated with respect to values on the trend line, usually as percentages or in terms of an index of 100. Since the trend line smooths out seasonal variations the method is of less value for separating seasonal from other possible cyclic variations. The diagram shows a plot of data, moving average and trend line. The required values are the ratios of the ordinates, expressed as percentages.

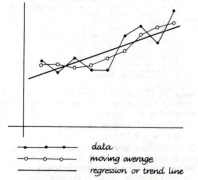

•——•——•	*data*
○——○——○	*moving average*
	regression or trend line

ray A half line or line drawn in one direction only from a point taken as origin, as distinct from a 'line' which extends indefinitely in both directions.
See also line segment.

reaction The property postulated by Newton's third law of motion. If, for example, a body A presses against a body B with a force F, then at the same time B presses against A with an equal force in the opposite direction. The law does not apply in all cases to the forces between electrical charges moving within conductors.

real axis Do not confuse with real number line. In the Argand representation of a complex number, the (horizontal) axis along which the real part $x = \mathrm{R}(z)$ of a complex number is represented. The corresponding vertical axis $y = \mathrm{Im}(z)$ is the so-called 'imaginary' i or j axis. Then the complex number is $z = x + iy$ or $z = x + jy$.

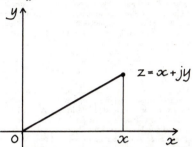

real Euclidean plane The representation of all members of the set $\mathbb{R} \times \mathbb{R}$ or $\mathbb{R}^2$, by assigning each ordered pair of numbers to a point in a Euclidean plane given by its cartesian coordinates, orthogonal or oblique. The two axes of the coordinate system then represent the duplicated set $\mathbb{R}$. Conversely, each point in the plane represents a unique pair of $\mathbb{R} \times \mathbb{R}$.

realization A term used to describe an actual example or physical structure which corresponds to an abstract mathematical entity. Thus Klein's four-group is 'realized' by the symmetries of a rectangular lamina. The use is often extended to any abstract or conceptual structures which illustrate other concepts.

real number The Greek discovery that the diagonal of a square was incommensurable with its side, equivalent to the statement that the equation $2q^2 = p^2$ has no solution in integers, implied that entities such as $\sqrt{2}$ could not be realized as the ratio of line intervals and hence were not numbers. It was not till the 19th century that logical definitions were constructed, and real numbers proved to obey all the arithmetical operations. The set $\mathbb{R}^+$ of positive real numbers is then closed to the operation of extracting roots. There are two main approaches to definition, the Cauchy sequence and the Dedekind section, both of which have given rise to more modern formulations at high levels of abstraction.

real number line A continuous line, on which every real number can be represented by a point. The line is usually taken as straight and as representing numbers on a linear scale. A useful informal definition of a real number is any number that can be so represented: this is equivalent to the converse statement that every point on the line represents a real number.

real parameters Parameters which are always real numbers, as in the ellipse given by

$$x = a \cos t \qquad y = b \sin t$$

where t is the parameter.

real part That part of a complex number in the form $(a + ib)$ which is not multiplied by i, i.e. the real number a. The term 'real' arises in distinction to the term 'imaginary' unfortunately bequeathed by Descartes. In the Argand diagram of $z = (a + ib)$, a gives the horizontal and b the vertical displacement of the point representing z.

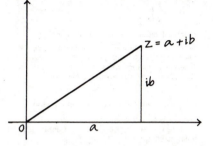

real valued function Any function whose codomain (or range or image space) is $\mathbb{R}$ or a subset of $\mathbb{R}$

$$f(x) = x^2$$

$$g(x) = \begin{cases} 0 \text{ if } x \text{ is rational} \\ 1 \text{ if } x \text{ is irrational} \end{cases}$$

rearrangement Used of a permutation, particularly if it arises incidentally, as in the statement: *these sets are the same since one is merely a rearrangement of the elements of the other.*

reciprocal The reciprocal of $x \neq 0$ is the number $p = 1/x$. Then $xp = 1$ and $x = 1/p$. The term reciprocal is widely used for any relations having a similar pattern, where the reciprocal of the reciprocal is the original element.

reciprocal diagram In two reciprocal diagrams the lines of one are parallel to the lines of the other, and the lines that form closed regions in one form vertices in the other. The diagrams have application in statics.

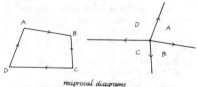

reciprocal diagrams

See also Bow's notation, duality.

reciprocal elements The subjects of reciprocal theorems that can be mutually interchanged. Points and lines are reciprocal (also called *dual*) elements in many theorems.
See duality.

reciprocal equation A polynomial equation of the form

$$a_0 x^n + a_1 x^{n-1} + a_2 x^{n-2} + \ldots a_n = 0$$

where $a_0 = a_n$, $a_1 = a_{n-1}$, $a_2 = a_{n-2}, \ldots$ If n is odd, say $2m + 1$, the equation has a root $x = -1$. Dividing both sides by the factor $(x + 1)$ then leaves a reciprocal equation of degree $2m$. If we now substitute $y = x + 1/x$ it then reduces to an equation of the lower degree m and the equation $x^2 + xy + 1 = 0$. The process may be repeated.

reciprocal matrix   *See* inverse matrix.

reciprocal relation   Any relation between quantities x, y is reciprocal if it is not altered by changing x into $1/x$ or y into $1/y$

- $y\left(x + \dfrac{1}{x}\right) = y^2 + 1$

reciprocal spiral   *See* hyperbolic spiral.

reciprocal theorem   Two theorems are reciprocal if the mutual interchange of two words naming two elements of the theorems converts one into the other. Reciprocal theorems involving lines and points are often called dual theorems.

reciprocal transformation   A transformation $z \to \dfrac{1}{z}$, where z is real or complex. If $z \in \mathbb{R}$, zero is excluded from the domain; if $z \in \mathbb{C}$ the origin transforms to the point at infinity.

Record, Robert   English doctor and teacher (1510–1558), who published a work on arithmetic, *The Ground of Artes*, in 1542. A later book contained the first introduction of the symbol $=$ for 'is equal to'.

rectangular coordinates   A cartesian coordinate system in which the axes are perpendicular to one another

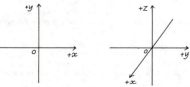

For three dimensions the convention is now established that a turn from positive x to positive y gives positive z as the direction of travel of a right-handed screw thread.
See also oblique coordinates.

rectangular distribution   *See* uniform distribution.

rectangular hyperbola   A hyperbola with perpendicular asymptotes. Its equation, referred to the asymptotes as cartesian axes, is $xy = c^2$.
See also conic sections.

rectilinear   A general adjective bringing the term 'straight line' into a description

rectilinear motion, rectilinear coordinates, rectilinear regression, rectilinear graph.

recurrence relation   An equation relating two or more consecutive terms in the sequence $u_1, u_2, u_3 \ldots u_n \ldots$, as

$$u_{n+1} - 3u_n = 0$$

This can be expressed using the difference between any two successive terms given by

$$\Delta u_r = u_{r+1} - u_r$$

The example then becomes

$$(u_{n+1} - u_n) - 2u_n = 0$$

or

$$\Delta u_n - 2u_n = 0$$

Hence recurrence relations are often called difference

equations. A relation involving more than two terms will require higher order differences.
Given a recurrence relation and the initial term or terms the sequence can be generated. Using the example:

$$u_{n+1} - 3u_n = 0$$

for $\qquad u_1 = 1 \quad u_2 = 3$

$$u_2 = 3 \quad u_3 = 9$$

and the sequence is 1, 3, 9, 27 ...

recurring decimal   Also circulating or periodic decimals. A decimal representation of a number in which a digit or sequence of digits is endlessly repeated, as $\frac{1}{3} = 0.333 \ldots \frac{4}{7} = 0.571428571428 \ldots$ Notations such as $0.\dot{3}$, $0.\dot{5}7142\dot{8}$, $0.(571428)$ are used, and the repeated digits are called the period. A mixed recurring decimal is one whose period develops only after initial non-periodic digits, as $1/24 = 0.041666 \ldots$
A terminating decimal can be defined as a mixed recurring decimal whose period is zero: this avoids confusion with rounded decimals. A recurring decimal (or any n-based fraction) always represents a rational number, and conversely a rational number is always a recurring decimal (or n-based fraction). The fraction can always be made terminating by a suitable choice of base.

$$2/3 = 0.666 \ldots \text{(base 10)}$$
$$= 0.2000 \ldots \text{(base 3)}$$

See also non-terminating decimal.

recurring sequence   Any power sequence of the form

$$a_1, a_2 x, a_3 x^2, \ldots a_n x^{n-1}$$

whose coefficients satisfy a linear equation, as $3a_n - 5a_{n-1} + 2a_{n-2} = 0$.
The sequence generates a series $a_1 + a_2 x + a_3 x^2 + \ldots + a_n x^{n-1}$ by the addition of terms.
See also generating function.

recursive definition   A method of defining a function logically so that, with non-negative integers as arguments, all its values may in principle be calculated. The definition gives a rule for calculating the value corresponding to an argument $(n + 1)$ given the value corresponding to n. By defining a starting value for $n = 0$ or $n = 1$, the sequence of values for all n may be generated, without the need for an explicit functional relation. For example, to define a^n where $n \in \mathbb{Z}^+$, $a \in \mathbb{R}$, $a \neq 0$ we can take the pair of definitions (or rules).

$$\left. \begin{array}{l} a^0 = 1 \\ a \cdot a^n = a^{n+1} \end{array} \right\} \text{Definition}$$

By using the second rule we get $a^{0+1} = a \cdot a^0$
and from the first this is $a^1 = a \cdot 1$
$$= a$$
and hence generate $a^2 = a \cdot a$, $a^3 = a \cdot a \cdot a, \ldots$
The method is used to give logical definitions of the processes of arithmetic such as addition and multiplication, consistent with Peano's axioms. It requires the processes to be defined as a sequence: the example given assumes both addition and multiplication.

recursive function Any function involving natural numbers (or non-negative integers) as arguments or values, defined so that it generates those values for successive values $0, 1, 2, 3, \ldots$ of the argument, which is called the recursive variable. It is the general expression for the example discussed under recursive definition.

reducible conic *See* degenerate conic.

reducible loop A loop or closed circuit in any region is reducible if it can be progressively contracted to a point within the region, in effect if it does not enclose an internal 'obstacle' not part of the region.

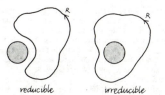

reducible   irreducible

reducible polynomial *See* irreducible polynomial.

reductio ad absurdum Also called *reductio ad impossibile* or indirect reduction. A form of argument used by Euclid which offers the proof of a proposition by assuming its negation and showing that this entails an unacceptable or impossible conclusion, contradicting the assumption and thus an absurdity (*adunaton*). An example discussed by Aristotle is, in modern algebraic notation

Let $\sqrt{2} = p/q$ where at least one of p, q is odd,
Then $q^2 = p^2$ so that p is even, $2r$, say,
Then $q^2 = 4p^2$ so that q is even,
Hence at least one odd number is even.
The logical absurdity of this conclusion forces the rejection of the proposition that $\sqrt{2}$ can be expressed as a ratio of integers, so that $\sqrt{2}$ is irrational.
The logical status of this method of proof has been challenged by those who hold that one cannot argue validly from a false proposition.
See conditional.

reduction A process or formula whereby in logic an argument set out in one form is transformed into another which arrives at the required conclusion. The first form, direct reduction, can be shown by an example.

All equiangular triangles are isosceles.
No scalene triangles are isosceles.
Therefore scalene triangles are not equiangular.

This can be transformed into

No isosceles triangles are scalene.
All equiangular triangles are isosceles.
Therefore no equiangular triangles are scalene.

For indirect reduction, *see reductio ad absurdum*.

redundant 1. Used of a definition that contains more information than is needed to specify.

A square is a parallelogram with four equal sides and four right angles.

2. Also describes a set of equations which, although consistent, is numerically larger than solution requires.

- $\left.\begin{array}{l} 3x + 2y = 6 \\ x - 3y = 4 \\ 5x + 7y = 8 \end{array}\right\}$

referent *See* relation.

reflecting barrier *See* random walk.

reflection *See* bilateral symmetry.

reflexive relation A binary relation between members of a set such that it holds between any member and itself, such as 'is a factor of' between integers. It is shown by a loop on a Papygram. *See also* identity.

region If S is a plane, any subset R of S is called a region if each pair of points in R can be joined by an arc all of whose points lie in R. A similar definition applies to a configuration in three dimensions.

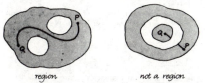

region   not a region

regression curve As for regression line, but representing an assumed non-linear relationship, involving higher powers than unity, exponents, logarithms etc.

regression line 1. Synonym for line of best fit for the pairs (X, Y) of a bivariate distribution (*see* scattergram).
2. In the plural, a pair of lines fitted to a distribution of X and Y. If X and Y are discrete, or are made so by considering class intervals, then one can plot independently on X, Y axes:

(i) The mean X_m of the X values corresponding to any one value of Y to which is fitted the line of regression of X on Y.
(ii) The mean Y_m of the Y values corresponding to any one value of X, to which is fitted the line of regression of Y on X.

This will give two distinct sets of scattered points, to each of which corresponds a line of best fit. These lines will predict a value X' for any given Y and a value Y' for any given X. The lines are given by

$$X' = aY + b$$
$$Y' = cX + d$$

The coefficients a, b are obtained from the equivalent form

$$X' - \bar{X} = \frac{\text{covariance}\,(X, Y)}{\text{variance}\,Y}\,(Y - \bar{Y})$$

where $\bar{X}$, $\bar{Y}$ are the means of the observations, and similarly for c, d.

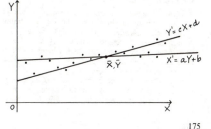

The lines intersect at $\bar{X}$, $\bar{Y}$, and may be plotted with this point as origin. The regression lines coincide with the axes if there is zero correlation between the two attributes X, Y.

The term 'regression' is due to Galton (1822–1911) who used it to express the tendency of measurable biological characteristics genetically transmitted to 'regress' (Lat. *regrussus*, a return) towards the mean of the population. For example, the children of very tall parents tend to be tall, but less tall than their parents.

regular A very general word in mathematics, meaning 'well-behaved' or 'conforming to a pattern'.

● Regular polygons have all their sides and angles equal. A function of a complex variable which is single-valued and differentiable in some domain D is regular in D.

The transition matrix T of some Markov chain is regular if some power T^n has positive non--zero elements

$$T = \begin{pmatrix} 0 & 1 \\ \frac{1}{2} & \frac{1}{2} \end{pmatrix} \quad T^2 = \begin{pmatrix} \frac{1}{2} & \frac{1}{2} \\ \frac{1}{4} & \frac{3}{4} \end{pmatrix}$$

regular point Any point on a curve which has no intrinsic properties other than that of being on the curve. Thus all points on $y = \sqrt{x^3}$, $x > 0$ are regular points, but at $x = 0$ there is a cusp, hence $(0, 0)$ is not a regular point.

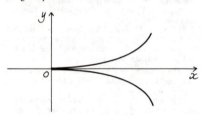

regular solids The five three-dimensional closed configurations having congruent regular polygons as faces, often called the platonic solids.

Name	Shape of face	Number of faces
tetrahedron	triangle	4
cube or hexahedron	square	6
octahedron	triangle	8
dodecahedron	pentagon	12
icosahedron	triangle	20

If the faces are allowed to interpenetrate the number of possible solids is much larger.
See Kepler–Poinsot solids.

relation A binary relation on a set S is any subset of the cartesian product $S \times S$, having a defining property that associates the members of S in pairs. Non-mathematical relations such as 'A is the father of B' have the same structure as mathematical relations like 'X is the square of Y'. In a relation aRb a is the *referent*, b the *relatum*.

Relations involving more than two elements, as in 'the man put the book on the table' occur in mathematics in statements such as 'b is the mean of a and c'.

Similarly functions of several variables and general linear relationships are also multiple relations.
See also symmetric, reflexive and transitive relations.

relative error The ratio of the probable absolute error $\pm e$ to the expected value E of the quantity measured.

$$\text{relative error} = \frac{\pm e}{E}$$

It is a number and not a unit.

relatively prime Two integers such as 5 and 8 are relatively prime if they have no factors in common other than ± 1.

relative motion The motion of a body M measured in any coordinate system S is its motion relative to that system. If another coordinate system S' is moving relative to S then the motion of the body relative to S' will be different. For the simple case of uniform rectilinear motion, let M have velocity v relative to S', and S' have velocity u relative to S in the same sense and direction.

Newtonian mechanics assumes that the measured velocity of M relative to S will be $u + v$, that is, that physical velocities are directly additive. This is an empirical assumption which need not be true.

relativity 1. Special relativity. Maxwell (1831–1879) subsumed all known electromagnetic phenomena into a set of equations whose solution required a *constant* quantity c. This had the dimension of a velocity which would (*see* relative motion), vary according to the motion of the coordinate system in which it was measured. Lorentz (1904), in a paper on moving electrons, transformed the coordinates (x, y, z, t) of a system S to (x', y', z', t') of a system S' moving relative to S, in such a way that the constant c survived. Einstein (1905) saw that if this Lorentz transformation was to be valid it must apply to *all* physical laws. He therefore *postulated* c as a constant and derived the transformation without direct reference to Maxwell's equations. He was then able to reformulate the laws of mechanics and electromagnetics so that they held good in any coordinate systems in uniform relative movement. This reformulation is now called special (or restricted) relativity. The name was given by Planck in 1908.

2. General relativity. Einstein (1916) was later able to extend this formulation of physical laws to a form which held good for all coordinate systems, even if accelerated relative to one another. Special relativity then appeared as a limiting case when the acceleration was zero, and gravitational phenomena involving acceleration were explained without postulating, as Newton had done, an inverse square law of attraction over a distance.

relatum See relation.

relaxation method Introduced by R. Southwell (1935) as a means of solving sets of equations numerically to a sufficient degree of approximation. A trial solution for the set

$$a_1 x + b_1 y + \ldots + d_1 = 0$$
$$a_2 x + b_2 y + \ldots d_2 = 0$$
$$\ldots\ldots\ldots\ldots\ldots = 0$$

gives the 'residuals' r_1, r_2, ... in place of the zeros. The trial values are then 'relaxed' in turn by suitable changes Δx, Δy,... to examine the effect on the residuals. An operation table is set up to record the effect of the deltas, which are manipulated to reduce the residuals to zeros within the required approximation. The method proved useful for differential equations in engineering calculations, but has now been completely superseded by computer algorithms and iterations. It is still of mathematical interest.

remainder 1. The residue or part remaining, $38 \div 3$ gives the quotient 12 and remainder 2. Formally, if a is an integer and b is a positive integer less than a, then there is a unique pair of integers q, $r(0 \leqslant r < q)$ such that $a = bq + r$. The integer q is the quotient and r is the remainder.
2. The concept is extended to a ring of polynomials R. If $a(x)$, $b(x)$, $q(x)$, $r(x) \in R$, $a(x) \neq 0$ and $b(x)$ is of a lower degree m than $a(x)$ where $m \geqslant 1$, then $a(x) = b(x) + q(x) + r(x)$.
• $x^3 + 4x^2 + 2x + 1 = (x+3)(x^2 + x - 1) + 2$

remainder term *See* truncation error.

remainder theorem If a finite polynomial $f(x)$ is divided by $(x - \alpha)$ to give $Q(x)$ and a remainder, the remainder is equal to $f(\alpha)$ because $f(x) = Q(x)(x - \alpha) + R$. Hence $f(\alpha) = R$ if $x = \alpha$.
• $(x^2 + 3x + 2)/(x - 2) = (x + 5)$ rem 12
  and $f(2) = 12$
If $f(\alpha) = 0$ it follows that $(x - \alpha)$ is a factor of the polynomial, so that the theorem provides a test for the divisibility of algebraic expressions.

repeated addition A definition of multiplication for whole numbers, in which the adding together of n equal quantities is equivalent to multiplication by n.
• $2 + 2 + 2 + 2 = 4 \times 2$
  $\qquad = 8$
The operation $4 \times$ can be read as 'four lots of'. The definition follows from Peano's axioms and the rule of associativity.
• $\quad 1 + 1 + 1 + 1 + 1 + 1 = 6$
  $(1 + 1 + 1) + (1 + 1 + 1) = 3 + 3$
  $\qquad\qquad\qquad\qquad = 2 \times 3$
  $\quad$ Hence $2 \times 3 = 6$

repeated integral If $\displaystyle\int_a^b f(x, y)\, dx$ is a function of y defined in the interval $c \leqslant y \leqslant d$ and is integrable in $[c, d]$ this integral can be denoted by
$$\int_c^d \left[\int_a^b f(x, y)\, dx \right] dy$$
or
$$\int_c^d dy \int_a^b f(x, y)\, dx$$
This is a repeated integral.

repeated roots A polynomial equation in x of degree n has exactly n roots ($x \in \mathbb{C}$), as shown by Gauss (1797). These correspond to n factors.
$$(x - \alpha_1)(x - \alpha_2)\ldots(x - \alpha_n) = 0$$
where α_1, $\alpha_2 \ldots \alpha_n$ are the roots. If fewer than n distinct solutions exist, m say, where $m < n$, then $n - m$ factors appear more than once, and the equation is said to have repeated roots. The order of a repeated root is the number of times each corresponding factor appears.

Thus the quintic $(x - 3)^2(x - 4)^3 = 0$ has one root of order 3 and one of order 2.
A repeated root of odd order corresponds to a point of inflexion on the x axis.

repeated subtraction *See* division.

repeated trials The repetition of a random experiment in statistics. If the probability of the event being investigated is constant from trial to trial, and if the experiment can have two but only two outcomes, such an experiment would be called repeated Bernoulli trials.

repeating decimals *See* recurring decimal.

representative Given any set $S\{x_1, x_2 \ldots\}$ on whose elements there is an equivalence relation R, then any x_i may be chosen as an example of an entity that will have the property given by R.
In the set of primes $S = \{2, 3, 5, 7, 11 \ldots\}$ each element is prime to every element, and any one may be selected to demonstrate the general properties of a prime number.
That 2 is even is not a *general* property, although 2 is representative of the set of *even* primes.

representative fraction Used in describing the scale of a map, it expresses as a fraction the ratio of a distance measured on the map and the corresponding distance on the earth's surface (taken as the geosphere). Thus an R.F. of $\frac{1}{50\,000}$ means that one unit on the map is 50 000 units on the ground. It is a measure independent of the units used.

reproductive Used of families of distributions having the property that sums of two or more random variables within the distributions are also distributed in the same form. Thus two sets of normally distributed variables have a normally distributed sum, and thus are reproductive.

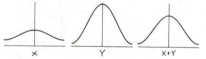

residual 1. Usually the difference between a predicted and observed value in a regression problem (*see* linear regression). Also, in the analysis of variance, the residual variation is what remains when the components of the various factors have been subtracted from the total variation.
2. A term introduced by Southwell in discussing relaxation methods.

residual variance The variance σ^2 of the residuals or 'error terms' in a linear or other regression. Not to be confused with residual variation.

residue class ring Let R be a ring and I an ideal in R, and R/I the set of cosets of I in R. Let r, $s \in R$ and $I + r$, $I + s$ be two of the cosets of I and define addition and multiplication of the cosets by
$$(I + r) + (I + s) = I + (r + s)$$
$$(I + r)(I + s) = I + rs$$
Then the set R/I is called a residue class ring.
• R is the set of all polynomials with real coefficients, I the set of multiples of $(x^2 + 1)$. Then

R/I is effectively the remainders when polynomials in R are divided by (x^2+1).

residues *See* modular arithmetic, quadratic residues.

resisting moment The moment of a force acting as a retarding or braking agent to a rotational motion.

resolutes *See* component. Two or more vector quantities may be compounded by vector addition into a single vector of which they are then the components, and conversely a single vector may be split into resolutes. These are usually in directions at right angles to one another.

resolution of forces A particular case of the use of resolutes. If two directions are given in a plane containing a force $\mathbf{F}$, its resolutes or components in these directions are the forces $\mathbf{F}_1$ and $\mathbf{F}_2$ given by the parallelogram rule for vectors. $\mathbf{F}$ is then $\mathbf{F}_1 + \mathbf{F}_2$ and is the resultant of its resolutes.

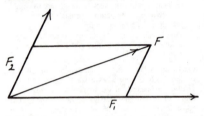

It is often convenient to resolve a force into two directions at right angles. If $\mathbf{F}$ makes an angle θ with the first direction

$$|\mathbf{F}_1| = |\mathbf{F}|\cos\theta$$
$$|\mathbf{F}_2| = |\mathbf{F}|\sin\theta$$

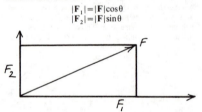

response variable A dependent variable when considered statistically as a random variable or variate; that is, a variate whose probability distribution depends on the values of one or more others. The ordinary dependent variable y in any physical formula of the form $y = f(x)$ is considered as a response variable if a large number of observations are taken and subjected to statistical analysis based on probability distributions.

rest Newton held that a state of rest was relative to the system in which motion was measured, and took as an example movement on the deck of a ship. He did, however, consider rotation to be absolute, always detectable by centrifugal effects caused by departure from his first law of motion. Most modern discussions of motion, as in relativity theory, postulate a system S taken arbitrarily as the resting system. Nothing can be stated about the 'absolute' movement or state of rest of S.

restitution A measure of loss of kinetic energy by moving bodies after elastic impact. Consider bodies of mass m_1, m_2 moving with velocities u_1, u_2 before impact and v_1, v_2 after impact, taking velocities to the right as positive. Then, according to Newton, the ratio of the relative velocity of separation after impact and approach before impact is constant, that is

$$\frac{v_2 - v_1}{u_1 - u_2} = e$$

This constant is the coefficient of restitution. It is an empirical result, but holds good for many practical situations.

restraint Also constraint. Any external limitation placed on the possible values of a function or quantity by the circumstances in which it is used, usually in the form of equations of restraint (or constraint)

$$3x + 2y = 4 \text{ subject to the restraints } x \geqslant 0, y \geqslant 1$$

resultant The sum of two or more vectors. If the vectors represent forces, velocities or accelerations the resultant is the single quantity which has the same effect. The resultant can be obtained by applying the parallelogram law to the graphical representation of the vectors taken in pairs.

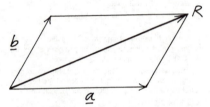

return to origin *See* random walk. The particle may return to the origin after n steps, and may repeat this indefinitely since all paths are equally likely. In a set of Bernoulli trials, such as in repeatedly spinning a coin heads or tails, the return to origin corresponds to the first and subsequent times that the total number of heads equals the total number of tails.

Reuleaux polygons Described by the engineer Franz Reuleaux in *The Kinematics of Machinery* (1875/6). They are formed from regular polygons having an odd number of sides by arcs described on each side and centred on the vertex immediately opposite, as AB centred at O.

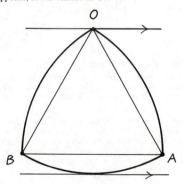

Since the configuration has a constant width between parallels it can be used as the cross-section of a roller, or, more usefully, as a coin to operate slot machines. The English 50p and 20p coins are Reuleaux heptagons.

reverse Polish notation A parenthesis-free logical notation adapted for use in some computer languages and electronic calculators. *See* Lukasiewicz. In reverse Polish a calculation is broken down into a series of two-number operations. The numbers are entered and followed by the operator. Thus $2+3$ and 2×3 are performed by the key sequences

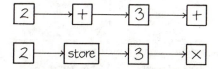

revolution Consider a fixed direction OA relative to an origin O, and any vector $\overrightarrow{OP}$ lying initially along OA. If $\overrightarrow{OP}$ now changes its direction so that the angle AOP is no longer zero, $\overrightarrow{OP}$ is said to rotate about O, in a sense clockwise or anticlockwise, through the angle AOP. When $\overrightarrow{OP}$ first returns to the direction OA in the same sense it is said to have made one revolution about O, and the angle AOP is one complete turn. The magnitude of $\overrightarrow{OP}$ need not remain constant throughout the rotation.

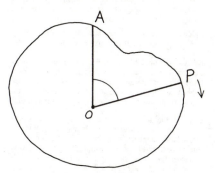

Rhind papyrus A papyrus (c. 1650 B.C.) obtained from Egypt by A. H. Rhind and published in 1927. It contains mathematical problems copied from an earlier lost work, and is one of our chief sources of knowledge, apart from speculation, about Egyptian mathematics.

rhombohedron A hexahedron whose six faces are congruent rhombuses, a rhombic parallelepiped.

rhumbline *See* Mercator projection.

rider A subsidiary proposition (often set as an exercise in textbooks of geometry) which follows from theorems already established.

Riemann integration A method of integrating without using antiderivatives. If a bounded function f is defined over a closed interval $[a,b]$ and S_n is the nth Riemann sum of f over this interval, then the Riemann integral is $\lim_{n \to \infty} S_n$. All continuous functions

are Riemann integrable, but the method applies to other classes of bounded functions which need not be continuous.

Riemann sum The theoretical basis of Riemann integration. If a bounded function f is defined over a closed interval $[a,b]$ and this interval is divided into n non-overlapping, but not necessarily equal intervals, then

$$b-a = \delta x_1 + \delta x_2 + \delta x_3 + \delta x_4 + \ldots + \delta x_n$$
$$= \sum_{r=1}^{n} \delta x_r$$

An arbitrary point ζ_r is chosen in each interval δx_r and the sum S_n is formed by taking

$$S_n = \sum_{r=1}^{n} f(\zeta_r) \delta x_r.$$

This is called the *general* Riemann sum, otherwise it is taken that the intervals are equal.

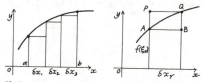

If the point ζ_r is taken at the beginning of the interval δx_r for a monontonically increasing function the area $ABCD$ which represents the term $f(\zeta_r)\delta x_r$ will be a minimum. If it is taken at the end of the interval it will be a maximum given by $PQCD$. The values of S_n thus obtained are called the *lower* and *upper* Riemann sums. Riemann sums can exist for non-continuous functions or functions with singularities.

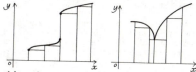

right angle 1. One quarter of a complete turn.
2. If a straight line meets another to form two adjacent angles which are equal, then each is called a right angle (Euclid Def. 10).

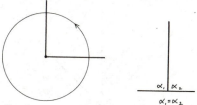

If angles are measured in degrees, one right angle is $360°/4 = 90°$.

If in radians a right angle is $\dfrac{2\pi}{4} = \dfrac{\pi}{2}$ radians.

right angle hypothesis *See* Saccheri quadrilateral.

right ascension The celestial equivalent of longitude, the angle between any celestial meridian and

179

the standard meridian that passes through the first point of Aries (◔) which is an arbitrarily agreed point on the celestial equator corresponding to the vernal equinox.

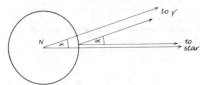

See also Greenwich hour angle.

right bisector   Also called the mediator or perpendicular bisector. A straight line which bisects a given line segment AB at right angles. The usual construction is not open to demonstrative proof within the Euclidean axiom system; it is only an intuitive assumption that arcs of circles centred on A, B actually intersect.

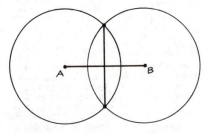

right derivative   *See* derivative. The R.H. derivative of $f(x)$ at x is defined as $\lim_{h \to 0^+} \dfrac{f(x+h)-f(x)}{h}$ where the symbol 0^+ denotes that h is always positive, and thus approaches 0 from the positive or right-hand half of the real number line. Similarly the left-hand derivative is given by replacing 0^+ by 0^- when h is always negative.

● $f(x)=|x|$
Then R.H. derivative $=1$
L.H. derivative $=-1$
These two limits exist but there is no derivative at 0.

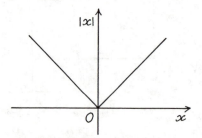

right-handed system   Three-dimensional cartesian axes Ox, Oy, Oz, drawn so that a right-handed screw turned in the direction from Ox to Oy would move in the direction Oz.

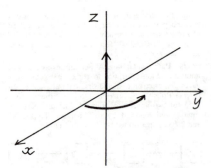

Usually Oy is horizontal and Oz vertical, but some texts may use other conventions.

right-hand operator   *See* left-hand operator.

rigid body   A rigid body is defined as one that it is not deformed by any applied force however great. Its actual existence implies logical paradoxes. In practice it means any body whose dimensional or other internal changes may be neglected relative to its movement as a whole, so that its behaviour as a model is often (but not always) an approximation to the behaviour of real bodies, in some contexts. Rigid bodies may be specified as rods, laminas or solids. The word rigid is often applied informally to mathematical abstractions such as triangles, whose shape is invariant if their three sides are held constant.

rigidity   The ratio of the shearing stress on a solid body to the shearing strain it produces.

rigorous   Applied in mathematics to any formulation or demonstration in which all relevant conditions and assumptions are sought out and made explicit, as compared with a non-rigorous exposition which merely arrives cheerfully at the required result.

ring   An additive abelian group or module $\{G, \oplus\}$ with a second multiplicative binary operation $\odot$ between its elements, such that multiplication distributes over addition and the multiplicative operation is associative. That is, together with the usual additive group properties, if a, b, $c \in R$
$$a \odot (b \oplus c) = (a \odot b) \oplus (a \odot c)$$
$$a \odot (b \odot c) = (a \odot b) \odot c$$
The ring R is commutative if the operation $\odot$ is commutative, and is called a division ring if its non-zero elements form separately a multiplicative group. A commutative division ring is called a field.

> The set $\mathbb{Z}$ of integers forms a commutative ring; the set $\mathbb{Q}$ of all rationals forms a division ring. Since multiplication in $\mathbb{Q}$ is commutative, the set is also a field.

Rodrigue's formula   *See* Legendre polynomials.

Rolle's theorem   For a function $f(x)$ which is continuous for $a \leqslant x \leqslant b$, everywhere differentiable for $a < x < b$ and for which $f(a)=f(b)$, there exists a number c with $a < c < b$ for which $f'(c)=0$. It is a special case of the mean value theorem.

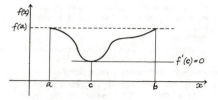

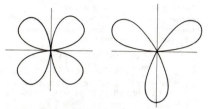

Roman numerals   Current from c. 500 B.C. to c. 1600 A.D. and from then on used for clockfaces, inscriptions, dating, tabulating etc., as a convenient or decorative system.

Initially, one symbol represented each power of ten and was repeated as often as necessary, but later symbols for 5, 50, 500 were introduced, with a subtractive rule to reduce the number of symbols required.

M	1000	L	50	I	1
D	500	X	10		
C	100	V	5		

The symbols are written from left to right in order of magnitude, but any symbol out of this order is subtracted from what follows

$$DCLXV = 665$$
$$MCMXLIX = 1949$$

Sometimes the symbols ⊂ı⊃ and ı⊃ are used for 1000 and 500. The system does not easily allow algorithmic computation.

root   1. Used for 'square root of'. Root two ($\sqrt{2}$) is the real number which when squared equals two. Similarly for cube, fourth ... n^{th} roots.
2. A root of an equation is any member of its solution set, a value of its variable that satisfies the equation, or a set of values if it has more than one variable.

root mean square   Also RMS. For a set of discrete values $x_1, x_2 \ldots x_n$ the RMS value is $\sqrt{\dfrac{\sum\limits_{i=1}^{n} x_i^2}{n}}$.

The RMS value is in practice of importance for continuously variable quantities. For example, a current I flowing through a resistance dissipates power as heat at a rate proportional to I^2, so that if I is variable, as with alternating current, the mean power dissipated is proportional to the mean of I^2. It follows that the RMS value of the variable current is the same as that of a steady direct current dissipating the same power. If $I = f(t)$ this gives $\lim\limits_{dt \to 0} \Sigma I^2 \, \delta t$ or $\int [f(t)]^2 \, dt$.

root mean square deviation   The same as standard deviation.

rose-petal curves   Named by Grandi (1723). Curves of the form $r = a \sin n\theta$ which form n loops if n is odd and $2n$ loops if n is even.

rotary reflection   The result of combining a rotation about a point C with a reflection in a line m. It is equivalent to a glide-reflection.

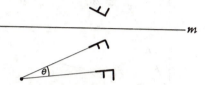

rotation   1. *See* revolution
2. A rotation is a direct isometry relative to a fixed point called the centre of rotation. If P is any point on a plane configuration and O a fixed point in the plane, then if $OP = OP'$ and $POP' = \theta$ measured anticlockwise, the mapping $P \to P'$ is a rotation centre O of magnitude $^+\theta$.

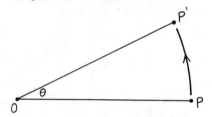

rotational symmetry   A plane configuration has rotational symmetry if there is a point O, not necessarily within it, such that if the configuration is rotated through any positive angle $\theta \leqslant 360°$ about O, it will then be congruent with itself. The point O is called the centre of symmetry, and the configuration has rotational symmetry of order $n = 360°/\theta°$ where θ, which must divide into 360 without remainder, is the smallest positive angle with the required property. If there is no smallest value for θ the configuration has circular symmetry (and is a circle). A three-dimensional configuration may have symmetries in more than one plane; a sphere has circular symmetry in any plane that intersects it.

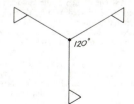

rotation group   *See* cyclic group.

rotation matrix   A 2×2 matrix which, when it premultiplies a column vector, rotates it through a given angle about the origin

$$\begin{pmatrix} \cos \alpha & -\sin \alpha \\ \sin \alpha & \cos \alpha \end{pmatrix} \begin{pmatrix} x \\ y \end{pmatrix} = \begin{pmatrix} x' \\ y' \end{pmatrix}$$

rotates the point (x, y), and the line segment joining (x, y) to $(0, 0)$, through a positive angle α about the origin.

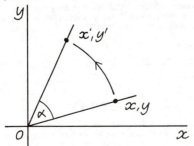

rotation of axes   A set of coordinate axes Ox, Oy is considered to rotate through a positive angle α about the origin O to become the set OX, OY. The result is then equivalent to two sets of axes $Ox, Oy; OX, OY$ such that angles xOX, yOY are both α.

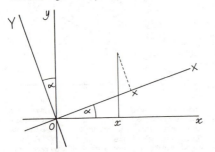

If $P = (a, b)$ relative to Ox, Oy and $P = (A, B)$ relative to OX, OY, then

$$a = A \cos \alpha - B \sin \alpha$$
$$b = A \sin \alpha + B \cos \alpha$$

If these equations transform (a, b) to (A, B) the axes of the coordinates of P are said to have been rotated. The transformation is also given by a rotation matrix.

roulette   Any curve, such as the cycloid, produced when a curve, considered as a rigid configuration, rolls on another without slipping. The point tracing the roulette may be on the curve or any other point on its plane, as in the curtate cycloid.
See tachnode.

rounded   A numerical value is said to be rounded when it is given to an agreed number of significant figures or decimal places. The difference between the rounded and the actual value is the rounding error.
See truncated.

route independent   A quantity which changes during motion from point A to point B is said to be route independent if its value at B is the same for all possible paths from A to B.

● The total work done in taking a mass from A to B in a gravitational field.

Otherwise, the quantity is route dependent.

● The total work done against friction in sliding a mass from A to B over a rough plane.

row canonical matrix   *See* echelon matrix.

row transformation   1. The transformation of the rows of a matrix by one of the three operations:

(i) Interchange of rows
(ii) Multiplication of the elements of any row by a scalar $k = 0$
(iii) Addition of a scalar multiple of the elements of any row to the corresponding elements of another.

Matrices A, B related by such a transformation are said to be row equivalent. A similar transformation can also be on the columns of a matrix. A and B are then column equivalent.
2. The row and column transformations (i)–(iii) can also be applied to determinants. Under (i) the determinant changes sign, under (ii) it is multiplied by k, under (iii) it is unchanged.

row vector   An ordered set of n elements obeying the rules of vector algebra, but considered as a matrix of one row and n columns, and hence operated on by the rules of matrix algebra. It follows that the inner (dot or scalar) product of two vectors requires one of them to be written as a column vector, or matrix of n rows and one column: this product then proceeds like ordinary matrix multiplication.

$$(a_1 \; b_1 \; c_1) \times \begin{pmatrix} a_2 \\ b_2 \\ c_2 \end{pmatrix} = a_1 a_2 + b_1 b_2 + c_1 c_2$$

Row or column vectors are sometimes called row or column matrices.

rule   Used generally and informally of an established procedure in mathematics which has been shown to lead to the required result, as the rule of three, Osborn's rule.

ruled surface   A curved surface through each point on which there is at least one straight line lying wholly within the surface, such as the cone, the elliptic hyperboloid of one sheet and the hyperbolic paraboloid. The sets of straight lines are also called the generators of the surface. Such surfaces are used in constructions: they can, for instance, be thin curved shells reinforced with straight rods, or supported by straight beams as seen in some modern roofs. They can also be modelled with straight stretched threads.

rule of five   In traditional arithmetic, a problem requiring a sixth term to be calculated when five are given, also called the Double Rule of Three since it is equivalent to two applications of this rule. An example from 1865:

If 800 soldiers require 5 sacks of flour in 6 days, how many will consume 15 sacks in 2 days?

rule of signs Due to Descartes, it gives information about the number and position of the roots of the polynomial equation

$$f(x) = x^n + a_1 x^{n-1} + \ldots + a_n = 0$$

Suppose $a_n \neq 0$. Putting the non-zero signed coefficients 1, a_1, a_2, ... a_n in order and counting the sequential changes of sign gives the number V. The rule states that the number of positive roots of $f(x) = 0$ is not greater than V and differs from V only by zero or a multiple of 2.

● $x^4 - 4x^3 + 3x^2 + 2x - 1 = 0$
  The coefficients are 1, -4, $+3$, $+2$, -1, showing three changes of sign.
  Hence the number of positive roots of this equation is either 3 or $(3-2) = 1$. The process does not tell us which is true.

rule of three In 19th century elementary arithmetic, the method for determining the fourth term in a proportion when three are known, corresponding to the solution of

$$\frac{a}{b} = \frac{c}{x}$$

where a, b, c are given.
This is written, using the numerical quantities given, as $a:b::c:x$ and the 'rule', usually stated without explanation, was 'multiply the second and third quantities together and divide by the first'.
It was also taught as the 'unit' method:

  if a articles cost b pence
  1 article costs b/a pence
  c articles cost bc/a pence

See also rule of five.

ruler postulate There was no geometrical construction for a straight line, equivalent to using compasses for a circle, until Peaucellier's linkage in 1873. The straight edge is not an instrument to construct lines: it is a guide for the pen and is itself constructed empirically. The ruler postulate is that an ideal ruler can exist, so that the straight lines required by Euclidean geometry can be drawn. It corresponds to Euclid Book I Post. 1.

run A term used in probability studies to describe the repeated occurrence of one possible result, as a run of heads in spinning a coin, or a run of zeros in generating random numbers.

Runge-Kutta methods Used for the numerical solution of differential equations, obviating the preliminary computation of higher order derivatives as required by Taylor series approximations. The method is illustrated for an equation of the form $y' = f(x, y)$ such as $y' = 2y$.

  Put $y_{n+1} \approx y_n + \frac{1}{2}k_0 + \frac{1}{2}k_1$
  where $k_0 = hf(x_n, y_n)$
    $k_1 = hf(x_n + h, y_n + k_0)$

and h is the difference between successive x values. Given an initial value $y(x_0) = y_0$ this generates values y_1, y_2, y_3 ... directly. The methods are adapted for other equations by defining terms k_2, k_3 and k_4 in terms of their predecessors to give a modified equation for y_{n+1}.

Russell, Bertrand Philosopher and mathematician, third Earl Russell (1872–1970). With A. N. Whitehead he initiated the study of the foundations of mathematics in England, publishing jointly *Principia Mathematica* (1910–1913) which identified mathematics and symbolic logic. The authors tried to avoid logical paradoxes that arose, particularly in set theory, by a theory of types and an axiom of reducibility. The work was very influential in opening discussion of the nature of mathematics, but did not succeed in generating mathematics as a complete system.

See Gödel's theorem, paradox.

Russell's paradox One of the constructed paradoxes of set theory that lead to the replacement of set definitions by undefined quantities satisfying axioms. A set is either of the 'first kind' if it contains itself or of the 'second kind' if it does not (e.g. a set of sets contains sets, but a set of triangles does not contain sets, only triangles). Let M be the set of all sets of the second kind; then M cannot include M because it is itself a set. Hence it must be of the first kind. But if it is of the first kind it must contain itself, which by the initial assumption it does not. The paradox arises because the accepted definition of a set requires a rule for including or excluding *any* given entity so that one *must* assign a place for M. Russell tried to remove the contradiction by the theory of types, which specified certain entities, such as sets of sets, excluded as the subjects of certain propositions. It is now accepted that the initial problem in set theory is to decide what kind of rules define sets.

See fuzzy set, axiomatic set theory, naive set theory.

S

Saccheri, Gerolamo Italian mathématician, member of the Society of Jesus (1667–1733), who wrote a book on Euclid's theory of parallel lines which inadvertently anticipated modern geometry. He developed what were in effect non-Euclidean theorems in an unsuccessful attempt to find contradictions in them that would prove the Parallel Postulate.
See also Lobachevsky, Riemann, Legendre, Bolyai.

Saccheri quadrilateral A quadrilateral ABCD with $AD = BC$ and right angles at A, B.

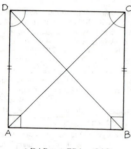

Then $\triangle DAB \equiv \triangle CBA$ (SAS)
so $\triangle DAC \equiv \triangle CBD$ (SSS)
and $\angle D = \angle C$

There are then three hypotheses:

1. The angles at D, C are acute
2. The angles at D, C are obtuse
3. The angles at D, C are right angles

The third hypothesis is equivalent to Euclid's parallel axiom. Saccheri attempted to show that the other two yielded logical contradictions but was unable to do so. Later his postulates became the basis for non-Euclidean geometries.
See hyperbolic geometry, elliptic geometry, parabolic space.

saddle point A point on a surface given by a function $f(x, y)$ so named because the shape of a saddle provides an example.
If there is a point $P = (a, b)$ on $z = f(x, y)$ such that

$$\frac{\partial f}{\partial x} = 0 \text{ and } \frac{\partial f}{\partial y} = 0$$

at (a, b), and if for every circle centre (a, b) there are some points (x, y) such that $f(x, y) > f(a, b)$, and some points (x, y) such that $f(x, y) < f(a, b)$, then P is a saddle point.

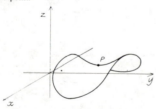

In effect, these conditions means that the stationary value at P is neither a maximum or minimum, since it increases or decreases according to the direction taken away from P.

sample A subset of a population, whose size is dictated either by practical convenience or the requirements of statistical significance. Samples are investigated statistically on the assumption that measures based on them can yield valid inferences about the characteristics of the population.

sample distribution function Another name for empirical distribution function.

sample mean (or sample arithmetic mean). The mean of a sample n of a population of size N, where $n < N$. Usually the arithmetic mean is intended, and for a sample $x_1, x_2 \ldots x_n$ the sample mean

$$\bar{x} = \frac{1}{n} \sum_{i=1}^{n} x_i.$$

The quantity $\bar{x}$ is a good (or unbiased) estimator of the population mean μ.
See also population mean.

sample mean distribution A random sample $\{x_1, x_2, x_3 \ldots\}$ of size n taken from a population having a mean μ and variance σ^2 will have a mean $\bar{x}$ and variance s^2. If a succession of samples are drawn the values of $\bar{x}$ will have a distribution. If all possible samples of size n are taken, this distribution is normal with mean μ and variance σ^2/n.
See also Cauchy mean value theorem.

sample space The set of all possible samples which can be taken from a population P, and includes by definition the empty set and P itself.
For explanation of this term *see* space.

sample standard deviation The standard deviation S for a sample of size n from any population, given by $S^2 = \frac{1}{n} \sum_{i=1}^{n} (x_i - \bar{x})^2$. It can be used as an estimator for σ, the population standard deviation. The best estimator $\hat{\sigma}$ or S replaces n by $n - 1$ in the above expression, since $\hat{\sigma}^2 = \frac{ns^2}{n-1}$. The sample standard deviation is the square root of the sample variance.

sample variance For a sample $X_1, X_2 \ldots X_n$ of size n the variance s^2 can be defined as the mean square deviation from the sample mean $\bar{x}$

$$s^2 = \frac{1}{n} \sum_{i=1}^{n} (X_i - \bar{X})^2$$

For purposes of calculation this formula is usually rewritten as

$$s^2 = \frac{1}{n} \sum_{i=1}^{n} X_i^2 - (\bar{X})^2$$

See variance.

sampling error The difference between the sample mean $\bar{X}$ and the population mean μ for any one sample. The expected value of $\bar{X}$ is given by

$$E(\bar{X}) = \mu$$

Hence $E(\bar{X} - \mu) = 0$ so that the errors in successive samples distribute about a value zero. Then $E[(\bar{X}-\mu)^2]$ is the variance of this distribution, and is given by σ^2/n where σ^2 is the population variance and n the sample size.

saw tooth function A function described by its name, whose graph is composed of straight line segments whose gradients are alternately of opposite signs.

The function $F(t)$ is periodic, continuous but not differentiable at its peak values (which are thus not stationary values). The period is usually expressed as $2\pi/\omega$ where ω is the angular frequency of a simple harmonic motion having the same period. Fourier analysis expresses this function as an infinite trigonometric series. It describes the voltage variation on the X (or horizontal sweep) plates of an oscilloscope's cathode ray tube, although this does not show the singularities at the peaks since it is continuous.

scalar Originally a physical quantity such as temperature or density that could be completely represented on a scale without reference to direction. Now generalized as a member of the field over which a vector space is defined, and hence a real or complex number.

scalar field A term used in applications of mathematics to describe a physical field defined by a numerical valued function given, at each point of some region in space, independently of direction, as atmosphere pressure or temperature.
See also conservative field, vector field.

scalar matrix A diagonal matrix whose elements are equal. Multiplication by such a matrix is equivalent to multiplication by a scalar. The unit matrix is a special case.

scalar multiplication A binary operation, seen as analogous to the multiplication of a measure by a scale factor, whereby a scalar is combined with a vector to give another vector. The operation must satisfy axioms in the structure of a vector space, such as that of associativity or distribution over addition. Do not confuse with the scalar product.

scalar product One of the two binary multiplicative operations defined for vectors, sometimes called the inner or dot product to avoid confusion with scalar multiplication. The form of the definition allows vector methods to handle physical concepts such as work.

(i) If **a**, **b** are vectors in Euclidean space, **a.b** or $\langle \mathbf{a}, \mathbf{b} \rangle$ can be defined as $|\mathbf{a}|.|\mathbf{b}|\cos\theta$, where θ is the angle between the vectors and $|\mathbf{a}|$, $|\mathbf{b}|$ are their scalar magnitudes, often written simply as a, b.

(ii) If $\mathbf{a}=(a_1, a_2, a_3 \ldots)$
$\mathbf{b}=(b_1, b_2, b_3 \ldots)$
then $\mathbf{a.b}=(a_1 b_1 + a_2 b_2 + a_3 b_3 + \ldots)$
The two definitions are equivalent for vectors in Euclidean space of two or three dimensions.
It follows that the formation of these products is commutative but not associative with a third vector,

although the process distributes over vector addition. The results for the base vectors **i**, **j**, **k** are important

$$\mathbf{i.i=j.j=k.k}=1$$
$$\mathbf{i.j=j.k=k.i}=0$$

The product **a.a** is sometimes written $\mathbf{a}^2$.
See also vector product, cross product.

scalar triple product A vector function usually written $[\mathbf{a,b,c}]$ and defined for a specific application of vector methods, by the non-associative expression

$$[\mathbf{a,b,c}]=(\mathbf{a}\times\mathbf{b}).\mathbf{c}$$

From the definitions for scalar and vector products this becomes

$$ab\sin\theta\hat{\mathbf{n}}.\mathbf{c}=abc\sin\theta\cos\phi$$

The R.H. expression is the product of the base area and perpendicular height of a parallelepiped whose base is defined by a and b and whose third edge is c and hence is the volume of this solid. In terms of the components or coordinates of a, b, c this is also given by

$$\begin{vmatrix} a_1 & a_2 & a_3 \\ b_1 & b_2 & b_3 \\ c_1 & c_2 & c_3 \end{vmatrix}$$

If $[\mathbf{a,b,c}]=0$ the volume vanishes and hence a, b, c are coplanar (or two of the vectors coincide).

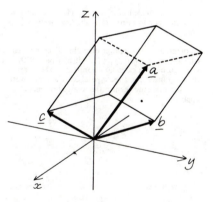

Since vector products are not commutative (or since one interchange of the rows or column of a determinant produces a change of sign) it follows that the six expressions formed by permuting the elements of **a**, **b**, **c** are numerically equal but three of them are negative.
See pseudoscalar for further information.

scale The numerical ratio, however expressed, between a measure and the quantity used to represent it. Examples can be taken showing many useful conventions.

● A plan on a scale of 1:10

A scale on an axis of 10 mm per 1000 units
A half scale model
A diagram enlarged × 25
The angular movement of the pointer expresses current as one ampere per 10°

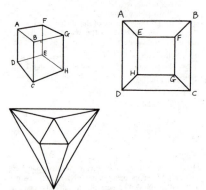

scale factor   The term refers to an enlargement, and is expressed as a multiplying fraction λ. If O is a fixed point, an enlargement is a mapping that transforms P to P' so that

(i) for $\lambda > 1$, OPP' are in that order on a straight line, and $OP' = \lambda OP$
(ii) for $\lambda > 0$, P' is at O for all P
(iii) for $\lambda < 0$, OPP' are in a straight line with O between P and P' and $OP' = \lambda OP$, the image being inverted
(iv) for $-1 < \lambda < 1$, $\lambda \neq 0$, $OP' = \lambda OP$, hence a reduction occurs.

The number λ is called the scale factor of the enlargement, which reproduces any configuration of points P to one of points P' on a larger or smaller scale. The word 'enlargement' is taken to cover all cases, including reduction.

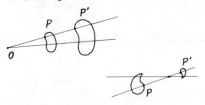

The concept 'scale factor' is sometimes used in teaching arithmetic to introduce multiplication by a fraction.

scattergram   Also scatter diagram. Given bivariate data $(x_1, x_2, \ldots)$ and $(y_1, y_2 \ldots)$ it is a plot of these values, usually in cartesian coordinates. The forms of the diagrams suggest the type of correlation between the variates, and hence the regression model to apply.

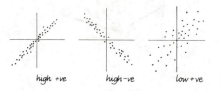

high +ve   high −ve   low +ve

Schäfli number   A method of classifying polyhedra due to Schäfli. Each is denoted by an ordered pair (p, q) having p-gonal faces of which q meet at each vertex. Thus a tetrahedron is $(3, 3)$, a cube $(4, 3)$, a dodecahedron $(5, 3)$. These are sometimes written 3^3, 4^3, 5^3.

Schlegel diagram   Plane networks which represent the faces, vertices and edges of polyhedra, and having the same connectivities. If a wire model of a polyhedron is viewed from a point just outside the centre of one face the perspective view approximates to the diagram (as shown for the cube).

Schwarz' inequality   For two vectors $\mathbf{a}$, $\mathbf{b}$ the inequality given by $|\mathbf{a} . \mathbf{b}| \leqslant |\mathbf{a}| \times |\mathbf{b}|$. Note that . on the left denotes the scalar or inner product, the × on the right ordinary multiplication. The inequality can also be written

$$|\mathbf{a} . \mathbf{b}| \leqslant ab$$

where a, b are the scalar magnitudes.

scientific notation   Any expression of a decimal fraction in the form $d_1 \ldots d_n . d_{n+1} \ldots d_m \times 10^N$ where d_r is a decimal digit and N any integer including zero. The decimal separator point can appear between any digits, and is sometimes called floating point notation.

● 23.4×10^{-3}
  0.0234
  0.234×10^{-1}

In *standard form* the decimal part is always expressed as a number between 1 and 10.

secant   *See* circular functions.

sech   *See* hyperbolic functions.

second derivative   The function obtained by differentiating a given function twice, that is, by finding the derivative of its derivative. If f' (or Df) is the derivative the second derivative is denoted by f'' (or $D^2 f$). It can thus be defined, given that the limit exists, as

$$\lim_{h \to 0} \frac{f'(x+h) - f'(x)}{h}$$

The process can be extended to third or higher order derivatives, but the notation is then adjusted to f, $f^{(1)}, f^{(2)}, f^{(3)}, \ldots$ The Leibniz notation for these is

$$\frac{dy}{dx}, \frac{d^2 y}{dx^2}, \frac{d^3 y}{dx^3}, \ldots$$

second moment   Also second moment about origin or second central moment.

second order linear differential equation   An equation of the form $ay'' + by' + cy = P(x)$ containing second derivates, which arises in many physical applications. It can be solved by splitting y into two parts such that $y = u + v$, and hence replacing the equation by the equations

$$av'' + bv' + cv = P(x)$$
$$au'' + bu' + cu = 0$$

The first of these is the particular integral, the second the complementary function, which are solved separately.

section　1. The configuration produced by cutting a solid by a plane, as in conic section, cross-section.
2. See Dedekind section.

sector　1. That part of any polar curve enclosed by two radii and an arc of the curve, specifically any part of a circle enclosed by two radii.
2. Plural, or as sector compasses. A once common instrument used in draughtsmanship and surveying, consisting of two linear scales pivoted together at their zero point, often with other non-linear scales such as areas or chords marked on the arms.

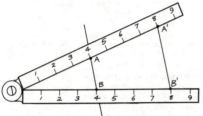

In the example a distance AB intercepted between the marks 4 is transferred on a 2:1 scale to $A'B'$ by joining marks 8. Originally devised by Galileo.

selection　The act of choosing. In mathematics it is usually taken that, within the limits set by requirements, selection is random, as in 'select any point P on AB', 'select any value of x greater than b'.

self adjoint　Any matrix which is the adjoint (or adjugate) of itself, as the unit or the null matrix.

self contradiction　Arises in two term logic if a proposition asserts and denies the same predicate. 'A is B and A is not B' or 'P is both rational and irrational'. Note that an inverse relation in mathematics is not necessarily the denial of a relation. In set algebra $A \subset B$ and $B \supset A$, for example, is possible and defines $A = B$.

self correspondence　Used of elements in a set, or any subsets of its elements, which under any given relationship correspond to themselves. Thus, in any transformation of the point (p, q) of a cartesian coordinate system by a 2×2 matrix A, the point $(0, 0)$ corresponds to itself.

self dual　See duality. A statement whose dual is represented by the same configuration or diagram

There are three points on three lines.
There are three lines on three points.

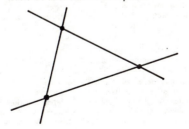

Compare 'there are six points on four lines', whose dual requires a different diagram.

self evident　Used of any result that appears intuitively obvious, as any curved path between A, B is longer than the straight line path AB.

It is more commonly used of moral and political issues than in mathematics where ingenious counter examples can often be devised. A reasonable criterion of 'self evident' in a mathematical context is that no-one is likely to argue otherwise.

self inverse　See inverse. If G is a group with the operation $*$ and e is its identity, then any element x of G is self inverse if $x * x = e$, that is $x = x^{-1}$.

semicubic parabola　A curve in the form of $y^2 = x^3$, having a cusp at the origin. The evolute of the parabola $y^2 = 4ax$ is the semicubic $27ay^2 = 4(x - 2a)^3$. The curve can be used as the approach curve to bends in rail or highways, since, for uniform velocity along the track, the rate of increase of the inward acceleration (and thus the force experienced by passengers) is constant.

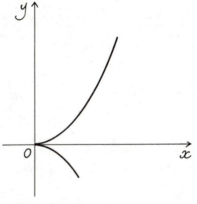

semi-interquartile range　See quartile.

semi *latus rectum*　The *latus rectum* (Lat. a straight side) is the chord through the focus of a conic perpendicular to the axis of symmetry through the focus. It is usually given as the semi *latus rectum*. For the parabola $y^2 = 4ax$ its equation is $x = a$.

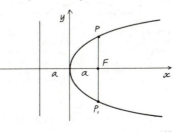

sense Used of direction or rotation, most commonly in the term 'of opposite sense', defining a reciprocal direction or reverse rotation.

separation of variables A method of solving differential equations. If the R.H.S. of $y' = f(x, y)$ can be written as $g(x) h(y)$, so that factors involving y only can be collected on one side and x only on the other, integration may be possible.

● $$xy \frac{dy}{dx} = 1 + y^2$$

$$\frac{y}{1 + y^2} \frac{dy}{dx} = \frac{1}{x}$$

$$\int \frac{y}{1 + y^2} \frac{dy}{dx} dx = \int \frac{1}{x} dx$$

$$\tfrac{1}{2} \log (1 + y^2) = \log |x| + \text{constant}$$
$$1 + y^2 = Ax^2$$

sequence A fundamental concept in mathematics. Many expressions can be expressed as a set of terms by taking particular points or values, for example

The series $\frac{1}{2} + \frac{1}{4} + \ldots + \frac{1}{2}n + \ldots$ gives the set of partial sums $\frac{1}{2}, \frac{3}{4}, \frac{7}{8} \ldots$
The expression $x^2 (x = 1, 2, 3 \ldots)$ gives the set of terms 1, 4, 9 …

Such sets of terms, which have in common the existence of a rule or procedure for generating successive members, are called sequences, usually denoted by $\{a_n\}$ where a_n is the nth term.
The value of the terms in a sequence may increase numerically without limit, approach a finite limit, remain constant, oscillate between two values, or take values at random. They are accordingly known as divergent, convergent, oscillating or random sequences.

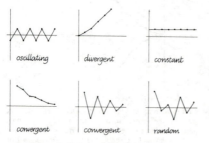

oscillating | divergent | constant

convergent | convergent | random

sequential analysis (or sampling) A decision procedure based on taking successive samples. Also called probability ratio analysis, because it compares the occurrence ratio of the event sampled with the associated probabilities. Take H_0 as the null hypothesis, H_1 the alternative hypothesis (e.g. that production tolerances are being exceeded) and let P_0, P_1 be the maximum acceptable probabilities of erroneously rejecting or accepting H_1 respectively. For each additional sample beyond the first compute the ratio

$$R = \frac{\text{events supporting } H_0}{\text{events supporting } H_1}$$

The decisions are then

1. If $R > \dfrac{1 - P_1}{P_0}$ accept H_0

2. If $R < \dfrac{P_1}{1 - P_0}$ accept H_1

3. If neither holds continue sampling.

See also lattice diagram.

sequential probability ratio test Due to A. Wald (1945). A method for comparing two sequential tests to select the one most likely to give a reliable result. By arranging for observations from each sequence to count as successes, the method compares the ratios of successes from the two sets of trials.

sequential test (or trial) Any sampling scheme in which observations are taken one at a time. The evidence is examined cumulatively to decide whether to accept or reject the hypothesis being tested or to take one more observation.

serial relation Any relation that puts entities into a serial order. A synonym for ordering relation. 'Greater than' is a serial relation on $\mathbb{N}$.

series Any expression formed by summing the terms of a sequence in succession. The value of this sum after n terms have been added is the sum to n terms S_n

$$S_n = \sum_{i=1}^{n} a_i$$

An infinite sequence generates the corresponding infinite series whose partial sums S_n as $n \to \infty$ may converge, diverge or oscillate. The rational approximation values of many important functions and constants such as $\sin x$ or π may be calculated by expressing them as a series to a sufficient number of terms.

set This word has many synonyms (collection, assembly, class …) but cannot be defined in simpler terms. In mathematics, however, a collection of entities, considered as a whole, is taken as a set if but only if

1. The entities are distinct.
2. There is a rule for deciding unambiguously whether an entity x is or is not a member of the set.

The word 'set' translates the original '*Menge*' of Dedekind (1858), but was defined by Cantor in 1895. The definition has yielded logical paradoxes (*see* '*heterologisch*') which axiomatic set theory seeks to avoid.
See fuzzy set.

set operation If $\mathcal{E}$ is a given universal set and A, B are subsets of $\mathcal{E}$ they may be combined in various ways to give new sets, for example

$$C = \{x : x \in A \text{ or } x \in B \text{ or both}\}$$

This operation is the *union* of A and B, written $A \cup B$. Other operations are set intersection, complementation, set difference, symmetric difference.

sets of coordinates A single coordinate will fix a point on a given base line, but in general, using cartesian, polar, cylindrical or other coordinate systems, an element or state is represented by an ordered set of coordinates. Both the number and the order of the coordinates is important: the order is governed by arbitrary conventions, e.g. a point in a plane is the ordered pair (x, y) where x is the primary axis and the y axis is at a given angle (usually $90°$) to the x axis. In physical applications, a set of coordinates fixes an element relative to a given frame of reference.

set theoretical   Pertaining to the theory of sets, and used of any development of a topic in mathematics, such as the approach to analysis in Bourbaki, which is based on the concept of set.

sexagesimal   (Lat. *sexagesimus*, sixtieth) The notation for degrees, minutes and seconds in angular measure, and also any number system using sixty, either wholly or in part, as its base.
See Babylonian numerals.

Shanks, William   Mathematical amateur, who in 1873 calculated π to 707 decimal places. The task, using a form of Gregory's series, took 15 years, and the result was cut into Shanks's tombstone. It was later shown that only the first 528 places were correct.

sheaf of planes   A set of parallel planes, as given by the cartesian equation

$$ax + by + cz = r$$

where r can take any real value but a, b and c are constants.

Sheffer stroke function   The function of two propositions p, q denoted by $p|q$ which reads p is incompatible with q. The truth table is thus

p	q	$p|q$	or	$p \wedge q$	$p|q$
T	T	F		T	F
T	F	T		F	T
F	T	T			
F	F	T			

By selecting this as a primitive function negation is made a derived function since $p|p = \sim p$.

Sheppard's correction   If a variance $\bar{\sigma}^2$ is calculated from grouped data, a correction for variance within the groups was given by Sheppard as

$$\sigma^2 = \bar{\sigma}^2 - n^2/12$$

where σ^2 is the true variance and n the class interval. It is rarely used and in any case computer methods obviate the need to group data for smaller samples.

shift   The operation, or result, of moving any digit or set of digits one or more places to the left or right in a positional notation, relative to its radical point (usually decimal or binary). A left shift of n places multiplies, and a right shift divides, the digit represented by r^n where r is the base of the number system.

shortest distance   *See* distance. Any path between points A and B for which the distance function $D(A, B)$ is a minimum. For Euclidean space this path has the intuitive properties of the otherwise undefined 'straight line', for a spherical surface the path is an arc of a great circle.

SI   (*Système International d'Unités*) *See* Appendix 1. SI is sometimes found as an adjective in the expression 'SI units', but this is not international usage.

sidereal day   The elapsed time between two transits of the same sidereal body over the same meridian, the period of revolution of the earth relative to the fixed stars.
See solar day.

sigma notation   The uses of the Gk. Σ, *sigma* to denote a sum, normally of related terms or quantities.

$$\sum_{\text{all } i} X_i = X_1 + X_2 + X_3 + \ldots$$

If the indexes of the first and last terms to be added are required, they are placed below and above the Σ and are called the limits of summation. Here ∞ is taken to have the meaning 'continue indefinitely'

$$\sum_{r=1}^{n} r^2 = 1^2 + 2^2 + 3^2 + \ldots + n^2$$

$$\sum_{r=0}^{\infty} x^r = 1 + x + x^2 + \ldots + x^n + \ldots$$

In some cases it is necessary to state the domain of the summation in words

$$\sum_{\text{all primes}} x^2 = 2^2 + 3^2 + 5^2 + 7^2 + 11^2 + \ldots.$$

See summation.

sigma scale   *See* normal distribution curve. A method for dividing the $N(\mu, \sigma^2)$ curve. This redistributes the usual scores on a linear scale from 0 to 100, and thus covers the range -3 to $+3$ standard deviations approximately. The sigma score is given by

$$\Sigma = \frac{50z}{3} + 50$$

where z is the z score.
The scale is regarded as more straightforward if the results of tests and examinations need to be discussed with laymen or examiners in arts.

sign   One of the two symbols $+$ or $-$, read plus, minus or positive, negative. They correspond to the signs $+$, $-$, denoting the binary process of addition and subtraction, but are associated with single numbers which are then termed *signed* quantities. For example a signed integer is defined as an ordered pair of natural numbers with rules of addition and subtraction. If two pairs are (a, b), (c, d), then, by definition

$$(a, b) + (c, d) = (a + c), (b + d)$$
$$(a, b) - (c, d) = (a + d), (b + c)$$

where the symbol $+$ on the right-hand side is the ordinary binary operation between natural numbers. Then the pair $(a, 0)$ is written $+a$ or ^+a, the pair $(0, b)$ is written $-b$ or ^-b. The rules for adding, subtracting, multiplying and dividing signed numbers can be developed from these definitions. In particular $^+a - {^-b} = {^+(a+b)}$.
Although most texts do not distinguish (except by brackets) between the uses of $+$, $-$ as binary operations or as labels, a recommended notation for signed quantities, at least for elementary texts, is to use them as raised prefixes, $^+1$ not $+1$, $^-2$ not -2.

189

The definitions for signed integers are carried over into the definitions for rational and real numbers. Sign is an ordering property and $^-a <{}^+b$ for all a, $b \neq 0$. Complex numbers and vectors are not ordered quantities and are not signed, although by convention a vector $-\mathbf{x}$ is taken to be the vector $\mathbf{x}$ multiplied by the scalar $^-1$.

sign convention The arbitrary agreement whereby positive and negative values are assigned to any representation of signed quantities, or to any sense in which physical measures may be so taken. Thus on Cartesian axes positive is to the right and above the origin, negative to the left and below. A positive angle is taken as anticlockwise, and rotation is signed accordingly. Any temperature above a given arbitrary zero (as on the Celsius scale) is positive. Such conventions must be consistent.

significance level The probability of rejecting a null hypothesis H_0 in a significance test, when in fact H_0 is true.

significance testing The analysis of data to determine whether or not they support a given hypothesis. There is usually a control or null hypothesis H_0 which denies that the data are significant: the actual hypothesis under test is the alternate hypothesis H_1. The data are summarized by a test statistic which characterises the test and whose probability distribution is known if H_0 is true.
A range of values for the test statistic which would support H_1 over H_0 is called the critical region, whose boundaries are the critical values. More informatively, given a value for the test statistic, one can identify the size of the critical region into which it would fall for a given significance level. Tests are often referred to by the type of distribution of the probability of H_0, or by the names of the devisers of the test (F, t, chi-squared, Friedmann, etc.).

significant figures A formal definition covering all cases is obscure and prolix. The term is best defined by examples, where it will be seen that they are in general the number of digits required to express a number to any required degree of accuracy.

3.14159 to 3 sig. figs. is 3.14
287643 to 4 sig. figs. is 287600
0.1032 to 3 sig. figs. is 0.103
0.002479 to 3 sig. figs. is 0.00248

Zeros do not count as significant except where they occur between other digits. The last significant digit is rounded up if necessary.

sign test A non-parametric test of the difference of population medians from which the two sets of random variables are drawn.

similar Two or more configurations are said to be similar when a dilatation of one makes it congruent with the other. This requires angles to be preserved and corresponding linear dimensions to be increased or decreased in the same ratio. All circles are similar. Figures are said to be *similar and similarly placed* if their orientation is preserved, that is, their corresponding sides are parallel.

similitude Synonym for enlargement or dilatation. A centre of similitude is the same as centre of enlargement.

simple field extension *See* field extensions.

simple harmonic motion *See* harmonic motion.

simplex The generalization (due to Schäfli) of the simplest closed configuration of straight lines in plane and three-dimensional regions to k dimensions. The simplest configuration of straight lines in a plane is a triangle, and is called a 2-simplex; the simplest region in space, a tetrahedron, is called a 3-simplex. A line segment is then a 1-simplex and a point a 0-simplex. The four-dimensional analogue to a 3-simplex (that is, the corresponding polytope) is a 4-simplex and has for '3-faces' five tetrahedra. In general, the boundary of a k-simplex is composed of simplexes of dimensions $0, 1, \ldots k-1$ and has

$k+1$ 'vertices' (0-simplexes)
$\frac{1}{2}k(k+1)$ 'edges' (1-simplexes)

$$\frac{(k+1)!}{(i+1)!} \quad (k-i) \text{ '}i\text{-faces' } (i\text{-simplexes})$$

If $k > 3$ the simplexes cannot be realized by constructions.

simplex method Used in linear programming to determine the optimum (min-max) solution of a linear function of a set of variables subject to a set of linear inequalities, when the number of variables is large. The inequalities are replaced by equations having slack variables and set out in a tableau or matrix of coefficients. A trial solution is taken and improved by continued iteration. It is a method suitable for a computer program.

simply connected *See* connected.

simply periodic Also singly periodic. *See* periodic function, which is simple if it has only one fundamental period.

● e^z has one fundamental period $2\pi i$
  $\cos \theta$ has one period 2π

Simpson's rule If a curve (empirically derived or otherwise) is plotted on cartesian coordinates, or if the cartesian equation of a curve is known, this is a method for estimating the area bounded by the curve, the x axis, and any two ordinates at a, b. It is thus an approximation to a definite integral.

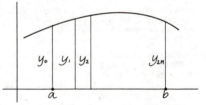

The interval $[a, b]$ is divided into $2n$ equal subintervals each of length $h = \dfrac{b-a}{2n}$, inserting the ordinates to divide the area into strips. Let the first subinterval begin at $x_0 = a$ and the last end at $x_{2n} = b$, with the corresponding ordinates $y_0, y_1, y_2 \ldots y_{2n}$. These can be calculated or measured from the graph. Then

$$\text{Area} \approx \tfrac{1}{3}h(y_0 + 4y_1 + y_2) + (y_2 + 4y_3 + y_4) + \ldots + (y_{2n-2} + 4y_{2n-1} + y_{2n})$$

Expressed verbally the rule becomes: Form the sum of the first and last ordinates (y_0 and y_{2n}), four times the odd ordinates and twice the remaining even ordinates, then multiply this sum by one-third of the width of the interval.

The rule was used for empirically plotted curves for which no integrable function is available, but is now absorbed into numerical methods generally.

Simpson, T. English mathematician (1710–1761). He began life as a weaver, but later became a professor of mathematics at the Woolwich Military Academy. He published works on Newton's method of fluxions.

Simson, R. Scottish mathematician (1687–1768) whose editions of the works of Greek geometers were standard for many years.

Simson's line Synonym for pedal line of a triangle.

simulation Used of a system which is made to behave in some particular in a similar way to another system either continuously or in discrete steps. This may be done with a physical model, but is often a mathematical model, analytic or probabilistic or some combination of the two. The simulation, which may be programmed for a computer, allows the behaviour of the second system to be studied on a different scale (as with a model of an economy) or, as with an aircraft simulator, without involving the risks of operating with actual physical systems.

simultaneity Formerly taken as an intuitive concept. Einstein (1905) pointed out that simultaneity or synchronicity of events at distinct points could only be defined operationally by an arbitrary procedure for the measurement of time, involving the transmission of time signals between the points. This met the earlier doubts of Poincaré (1900) who had denied objective meaning to exact simultaneity.

sine *See* circular functions.

sine curve (*also* **sine wave**) A curve having the shape of any stretch or translation of the graph of $y = \sin x$. Such a graph can be generated by projection of a point P moving with constant angular velocity ω round a reference circle of radius A with centre C on the base line COX, such that $\angle XCP = \alpha$ at $t = 0$. It then has the form $y = A \sin \omega t + \alpha$ where $x = \omega t$.

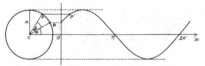

The constant A is called the *amplitude*, the angle α the *phase*, the time t the *epoch* of the sine function. *See also* harmonic motion.

sine formula The expression in spherical trigonometry given by

$$\frac{\sin a}{\sin A} = \frac{\sin b}{\sin B} = \frac{\sin c}{\sin C}$$

where a, b, c, are arcs of the spherical triangle measured as angles subtended to the centre of the sphere, and A, B, C are its angles.

sine rule Connects the sides and angles of a triangle by the expression

$$\frac{a}{\sin A} = \frac{b}{\sin B} = \frac{c}{\sin C} = 2R$$

where R is the circumradius of the triangle.

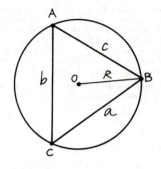

See also Lamy's theorem.

singleton A set $\{a\}$ having only one member, and hence having cardinality one, such as the set of even prime numbers.

single valued functions (or mappings) *See* function.

singly connected *See* multiply connected.

singularity 1. Used of the functions of a complex variable. A singularity of an analytic function is a point at which it is not analytic, but in every neighbourhood of the point there are points at which it is analytic.

● 0 is a singularity of $\dfrac{1}{z}$ $z \in \mathbb{C}$

0 is a singularity of $\tan \dfrac{1}{z}$

2. A singularity of a second order linear differential equation is any point at which its leading coefficient is zero

● $x(x-1)\dfrac{d^2 y}{dx^2} + x\dfrac{dy}{dx} + y = 0$ has singularities at

$x = 0$ and $x = 1$.

singular matrix Any $n \times n$ matrix whose determinant is zero.

singular point A general term for any point on a curve which is not a regular point. Nodes, multiple points, isolated points and cusps are examples of singular points.

● $(0, 0)$ is a singular point on the semi-cubic parabola curve $y = \sqrt{x^3}$.

singular solution Refers to a non-linear first order differential equation. It is any solution that is not a special case of the general solution and is, at each of its points, tangent to some element of the family that comprises the general solution.

● $y^2(y')^2 - a^2 + y^2 = 0$
has $y = a$ and $y = -a$ as singular solutions, and has the general solution $(x-c)^2 + y^2 + a^2$ where c takes any value.

sinh *See* hyperbolic functions.

sink 1. A 'negative source', a point in a hydrodynamic system from which fluid is being removed or 'annihilated'.
2. A comparable point in a hot body, at which it is

supposed to be in contact with a large cold reservoir that absorbs the heat without rise of temperature.

sinusoidal Used of any variation or shape corresponding to a sine wave of the form $y = a \sin(bx + \epsilon)$ and hence applies to any harmonic oscillation or its graphical representation.

skew field A field such as that of quaternions, in which multiplication is not commutative.

skew Hermitian matrix *See* Hermitian matrix.

skew lines Straight lines in different planes which are not parallel and do not intersect.

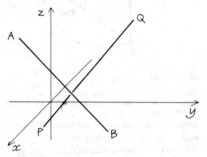

skewness Extent of asymmetry of a probability or frequency distribution about a modal value. If, on cartesian axes, the distribution has a 'tail' to the right, it is positively skewed; if to the left, negatively. There are various formal measures of skewness, one of which is $\mu_3/\mu_2^{3/2}$ where μ_2 and μ_3 are the second and third moments.

positively skewed   negatively skewed   symmetrical

skew polygon Any polygon (with more than three sides) whose sides are not in the same plane.

skew quadrilateral A configuration formed by four straight lines which do not lie in the same plane. Adjacent pairs of sides define planes which intersect along the diagonals.

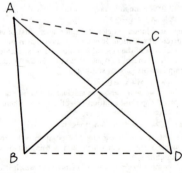

skew symmetric Used of a matrix (or its determinant) for which $a_{ij} = -a_{ji}$, so that its transpose $A' = -A$. It must have all elements zero in the principal diagonal

$$A = \begin{pmatrix} 0 & a & b \\ -a & 0 & c \\ -b & -c & 0 \end{pmatrix}$$

Sometimes called antisymmetric.

slack variable Or auxiliary variable. Used in linear programming to convert a restraint given as an inequality into an equation. Thus

$$2x - y \leqslant 8 \quad (x, y \geqslant 0) \text{ is written as}$$
$$2x - y + z = 8 \quad (x, y, z \geqslant 0).$$

It is usually more convenient to solve a set of such equations than the corresponding inequalities. If $z = 0$ the equation corresponds to $2x - y = 8$, and if $z > 0$ it corresponds to $2x - y < 8$.

slide rule A calculating device using the juxtaposition of two scales, one of which is slid along the other. Devised by Oughtred (1622) with two logarithmic scales to permit multiplication and division, but later extended with scales for reading powers, reciprocals, trigonometric ratios and other functions. They are now superseded by electronic pocket calculators.
See also Gunter scale.

slope function A term sometimes used for the derivative in introducing the methods of analysis by considering the slopes of cartesian graphs.
See gradient.

small *See* large.

small circle A circle on the surface of a sphere which is not a great circle. It is not the circle of intersection of the sphere with any plane that does not pass through its centre.

small sample Any sample whose size is less than 30 taken from a population. This number is chosen empirically as the point in parametric statistical analysis at which 'small sample' techniques must be applied to get consistent results.
See t-test.

smooth function In an interval $a < x < b$ a function is smooth if

(i) it is everywhere continuous
(ii) it is everywhere differentiable
(iii) the differences δ in the values of $f(x)$ between any two consecutive turning values are not large compared with the differences between the values of x at those points.

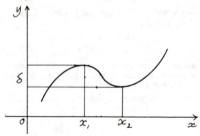

In the diagram $f(x_1)-f(x_2)$ is not large compared with (x_1-x_2). The third criterion is not precisely defined but is adequate in describing physical systems such as damped vibrations. The second condition requires the first.

snakes and ladders The well-known board game is often simplified to a small square with one snake and one ladder, so that a transition probability matrix from state to state can be constructed. In the example squares 4 and 7 cannot be permanently occupied and represent impossible states of the system.

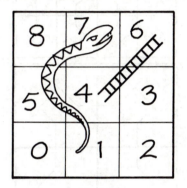

	Position after throw								
	0	1	2	3 · 4		5	6	7	8
0	0	$\frac{1}{6}$	$\frac{1}{6}$	$\frac{1}{6}$	0	$\frac{1}{6}$	$\frac{1}{3}$	0	0
1	0	$\frac{1}{6}$	$\frac{1}{6}$	$\frac{1}{6}$	0	$\frac{1}{6}$	$\frac{1}{3}$	0	0
2	0	$\frac{1}{6}$	0	$\frac{1}{6}$	0	$\frac{1}{6}$	$\frac{1}{3}$	0	$\frac{1}{6}$
3	0	$\frac{1}{6}$	0	0	0	$\frac{1}{6}$	$\frac{1}{3}$	0	$\frac{1}{3}$
5	0	$\frac{1}{6}$	0	0	0	0	$\frac{1}{6}$	0	$\frac{2}{3}$
6	0	$\frac{1}{6}$	0	0	0	0	0	0	$\frac{5}{6}$
8	0	0	0	0	0	0	0	0	1

Initial position

The counter is put initially on zero, an ordinary die is used, and any throw that lands on 8 or beyond is counted as a finishing throw.

snapshot diagram A convenient description of a diagram which shows one phrase or position of a cyclic or moving system, as of a wave motion. The diagram may superimpose several successive positions.

solar day The elapsed time between two successive returns of the leading edge or limb of the sun to a given meridian. It is also called the tropical day, and is about 4 minutes longer than the sidereal day owing to the earth's motion in orbit.

solid angle The solid angle is the cone subtended at the centre of a sphere by any area described on its surface, and is measured as the ratio between that area and the square of the radius of the sphere. The unit is the steradian (sr), where the area equals the square on the radius. It follows that one complete spherical region subtends 4π sr at its centre. A solid angle can be generated by regions of any shape, so that equal solid angles are not isometric.

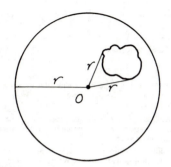

The steradian is a supplementary unit of SI.

solid geometry Term applied to the Euclidean geometry of solids, defined in Euclid Book XI Def. 1 as having length, breadth and depth. The solids discussed by Euclid include spheres, cylinders, cones, and those polyhedra whose faces are discussed in plane geometry.

solid of revolution The three-dimensional region generated by rotating a curve or part of a curve between intercepting lines about a fixed line.

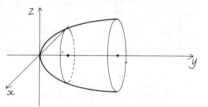

The diagram shows the curve $z^2=y$ between $y=a$ and $y=b$ rotated about the y axis. The volume is given by

$$\pi \int_a^b z^2 \, dy$$

solidus The sign / used to denote fractions, as a/b.

soliton *See* wave motion.

solution Applied to problems generally, but is also specifically used either as a synonym for a root of an equation, or, as with differential equations, to describe a function for which the equation is true.

solution of triangles Any procedure for calculating unknown sides and angles of plane or spherical triangles, given sufficient data to make this possible. For plane triangles this data corresponds to the conditions for congruence. For spherical triangles, which express their sides in terms of angles subtended at the centre of a sphere, triangles cannot in general be congruent; but for any one sphere of a given radius, such as the earth in problems of navigation or surveying, the conditions are the same. Typical procedures are the use of the sine rule, the cosine rule and the Pythagoras theorem. There are corresponding formulae for the solution of triangles in hyperbolic and elliptic geometry.

solution set The set of all roots of a given equation. In all the examples $(x, y \in \mathbb{R})$

solution set is $\{-3, -2\}$

$$\left. \begin{array}{l} 3x+2y=6 \\ 6x+4y=10 \end{array} \right\}$$

solution set is empty

$$\left. \begin{array}{l} 3x+2y=6 \\ 6x+4y=12 \end{array} \right\}$$

solution set is infinite, containing all pairs of the form $x = 2t$, $y = 3(1-t)$ where t is a real parameter.

solution space   A subspace of a vector space whose elements satisfy sets of simultaneous equations, usually taken as linear.

solvability   An important criterion which can often be established in mathematics. Where no solution to a problem is known it may be proved either that no solution is possible, or that it is possible in principle. Thus a polynomial equation of degree five or more is not solvable in radicals, but in principle a solution to any required degree of approximation can always be found.

some   Used in traditional logic for 'some but not all' and denoted by i, as in $SiP =$ some S is P. In mathematics 'at least one' is preferred.

soroban   The Japanese abacus, which represents numbers by using a split base. Numbers are given by beads in columns to base 10, but each column records to base 5, using one five-bead above and four unit-beads below a central 'heaven' bar. This reduces the number of beads that have to be moved at each operation and allows very rapid addition and subtraction.

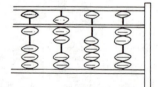

The soroban shown records 1702.

source   1. A point in a fluid at which the fluid is supposed to be flowing in or 'created'.
2. A comparable point in a body, maintained at a higher temperature so that heat flows outwards from it.

space   Any set of elements that has all or some of the analytical or topological properties of the set of points in physical space is called a 'space', and is assigned a whole number n called its dimension which represents the number of coordinates required to specify an element completely. This number is 3 for any point in physical space defined by position. Other examples are vector, phase, sample and function spaces, whose elements are vectors, phase states, and so on.

space filling curve   Any mapping or a unit interval (of dimension 1) into a unit square, which thus contradicts the intuitive impression that only a two-dimension region or the set $\mathbb{R}^2$ could be so mapped. Described and named by Peano. As the pattern is iterated $1, 2, 3 \ldots n$ times, its perimeter line tends to occupy the entire region as $n \to \infty$

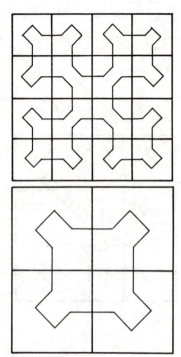

space-time   *See* Minkowski.

span   *See* generator (4).

Spearman's ρ (*rho*)   Also rank order correlation coefficient, introduced by C. Spearman in 1906. Equal sets of bivariate data

$$\{X_1, X_2, X_3 \ldots X_n\} \text{ and } \{Y_1, Y_2, Y_3 \ldots Y_n\}$$

are separately ranked in order 1 to n. The quantity d_i is the difference in rank between each X_i, Y_i in the pairs of results, and the coefficient is defined as

$$\rho = 1 - \frac{6\sum d^2}{n(n^2-1)}$$

It is unreliable for small n. Critical values of ρ for n up to 100 are available.

speed   A scalar corresponding to the vector quantity velocity, and giving its numerical magnitude. If $\mathbf{r}(t)$ is the position vector of a particle at point P at time t with respect to an origin O, the speed of the particle at P is

$$v = \left| \frac{d\,\mathbf{r}(t)}{dt} \right|$$

It is also given by $\dfrac{ds}{dt}$ or $\dot{s}$ if the distance s travelled by a particle from an origin to a point in its path is $s = f(t)$.

speed of light   The natural constant denoted c and given by $2.998 \times 10^8 \, \text{ms}^{-1}$ (to four significant figures).

sphere Euclid (Book XI Def. 14) defines a sphere as formed by the revolution of a semicircle about its diameter, Aristotle as the figure whose extreme points are all equidistant from its centre. Both definitions seem to consider points within a sphere as part of it. A sphere is now taken as a *surface* formed by the set of all points in space equidistant from a fixed point. In $\mathbb{R}^3$, if $P=(x_1, y_1, z_1)$, $(x-x_1)^2+(y-y_1)^2+(z-z_1)^2=k^2$ represents a sphere of centre P, radius k. For the sphere as solid, *see* ball and open ball.

spherical cap *See* cap.

spherical coordinates A three-dimensional form of polar coordinates, which label a point in space relative to a centre or pole O by a distance r and two angles θ, ϕ measured from two planes at right angles to one another, intersecting on a fixed base line which contains O. The angles θ, ϕ correspond to latitude and longitude on the earth, but are measured from 0 to 2π through complete turns.

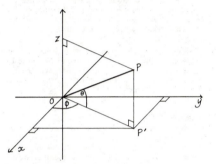

In the diagram xOy corresponds to the equatorial plane, xOz to the Greenwich meridional plane, P is a point in space and P' its projection on xOy. Then in cartesian coordinates

$$x=r\cos\theta\cos\phi$$
$$y=r\cos\theta\sin\phi$$
$$z=r\sin\theta$$

In some older textbooks not using right-handed axes the angles θ, ϕ may be chosen differently so that

$$x=r\cos\theta$$
$$y=r\sin\theta\cos\phi$$
$$z=r\sin\theta\sin\phi$$

spherical degree That part of the surface of a sphere intercepted between four radii, each forming an angle of $1°$ with the two adjacent rays. No longer in use and replaced by the steradian.

spherical excess The angle by which the sum of the angles of a spherical triangle is greater than two right angles.

spherical geometry The geometry of configurations drawn on the surface of a sphere, in which arcs of great circles correspond to straight lines on a plane since both are geodesics. The topological properties of the figures so drawn are the same as those of corresponding plane figures, but the metrical properties are different. In particular the angle sum of a spherical triangle is greater than two but less than or equal to three right angles. Spherical geometry is a special realization of general elliptic geometry.

spherical triangle If three points A, B, C are taken on the surface of a sphere, the spherical triangle ABC is formed by the shorter arcs a, b, c of the three great circles passing through AB, BC, CD. The angles at A, B, C are measured between the tangents to the great circles at these points, the sides a, b, c as the angles subtended at the centre of the sphere. Only one great circle is shown in the diagram.

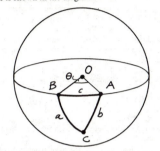

If small circle arcs are taken the distances along them would be greater, corresponding to plane configurations with curved sides.

spherical zone *See* zone.

spheroid *See* oblate spheroid, prolate spheroid.

spin *See* angular momentum.

spiral A plane curve of the form $r=f(\theta)$ in polar coordinates, for which r increases or decreases monotonically as θ increases.

- $r^n=a\theta$
  $r=ae^{b\theta}$

The first gives the Archimedean spiral if $n=1$, the second the logarithmic spiral.

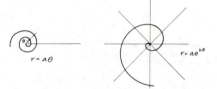

$r=a\theta$ $r=ae^{b\theta}$

spiral similarity The result of combining an enlargement of scale factor a with a rotation about the same centre C through an angle.

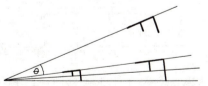

spread *See* dispersion.

spurious correlation Although correlation is taken as evidence of a causal relationship, its calculation often assumes a linear relation and bivariate normal distribution of the population, even if non-parametric rank order methods are used. Correlation between two attributes may also be numerically significant only because both are dependent on a third. Care must be taken in using correlation as evidence for a hypothesis.

square 1. A quadrilateral that is both equilateral and right angled (Euclid Book I Def. 22). There are other equivalent definitions (*see* redundant).
2. A number (or algebraic expression) formed by multiplying a quantity by itself, so called because Euclid measures areas by equivalent squares.
3. (verb) The process of so multiplying numbers or expressions by themselves.

square brackets Their uses include:
1. the writing of associative expressions when parentheses have already been used $a = [b - 2(c + d)]$
2. denoting closed intervals $[a, b]$
3. denoting the greatest integer function $[5] = 2$
4. sometimes denoting matrices $\begin{bmatrix} 1 & 0 \\ 0 & 1 \end{bmatrix}$

Note that (3) often uses the special symbol $\llbracket \; \rrbracket$ and that large parentheses are sometimes used for matrices.

square of opposition Schematic diagram in traditional logic to show the relation between propositions involving the quantifiers *all* (A), *none* (E) *some* (I), *not all* (O).
Thus: *all* (A) is the contrary of *none* (E)
    some (I) is the contradictory of *none* (E)
The other terms are shown on the square.

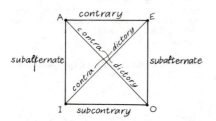

square wave A periodic function so called from the shape of its graph. If a, b, $c \in \mathbb{R}$ $(b, c > 0)$, a square wave function is

$$f(x) = \begin{cases} c \text{ when } (a + 2nb) \leqslant x \leqslant [a + (2n + 1)b] \\ 0 \text{ when } [a + (2n + 1)b] < x < [a + (2n + 2)b] \end{cases}$$

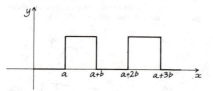

The function describes a train of electrical pulses of constant amplitude and frequency, which is of importance in the design of electronic circuits. It can be approximated to over an interval by a Fourier series.

squaring the circle Not the same as quadrature of the circle, which is any method for obtaining its area. Euclidean geometry defined areas by reducing them to equivalent rectangles or squares, subject to the Platonic restriction on permissible constructions. Geometers were not able to give an exact Euclidean construction for a square equal in area to a given circle, although the problem could be solved to any required degree of approximation using methods of exhaustion. In 1882 Lindemann proved that the ratio was transcendental and hence cannot be constructed by Euclidean methods. Throughout the history of mathematics the problem has attracted claims to an exact geometrical solution, some of them postdating Lindemann's proof of its impossibility. One, in 1887, was promulgated in the USA by a bill of the Indiana State Legislature. *See* quadratrix.

squeezing matrix *See* stretch transformation.

stability A system of equations is stable if small changes in the coefficients of the variables do not lead to large changes in the solutions. It normally corresponds to the physical stability of the system described by the equations. The term is also used of step-by-step methods of solving differential equations, which are stable if the errors that may build up in each step can be kept under control. *See* ill-conditioned equations.

stabilizer The stabilizer of any given element a of a set A in the group G is the subgroup $G(a)$, whose elements leave a unchanged after a given binary operation. That is $G(a) = \{x \in G : x \odot a = a, a \in A\}$, where $\odot$ is the operation.

stack *See* queue.

stagnation point *See* stream line.

standard deviation This is the root mean square (RMS) value of the deviations from the mean for populations, samples, or variates, and is thus the square root of the variance in each case. It is sometimes used in statistical analysis or as a descriptive parameter, but less commonly than the variance. Three symbols are used:

s = standard deviation of a sample
$\hat{\sigma}$ or S = best estimate of the standard deviation of a population
σ = standard deviation of a population

standard form 1. The expression of a number in the form $a \times 10^n$, where $1 < a < 10$ and n is any signed non-negative integer. Also called index or scientific notation.
2. Any commonly used results such as those involving trigonometric functions, derivatives or integrals, which are derived and then listed for reference and use. It is assumed that such forms would not be worked out from first principles each time they occur in a mathematical demonstration.

standardised score *Also* z score. See normal distribution curve.

standardization A statistical procedure whereby disparate sets of scores (such as marks in two examinations) are reduced to a common scale for purposes of comparison, often by means of the standard normal score.

standard normal distribution *See* normal distribution curve.

star polygon The figure formed by joining every rth point or vertex of an n-gon (or n points on the circumference of a circle), where $r > 2$ and n, r are relatively prime. Denoted by $\{n/r\}$ and often called *n*-grams.

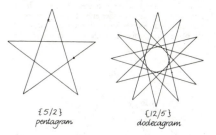

$\{5/2\}$
pentagram

$\{12/5\}$
dodecagram

state 1. As well as its common use (as in solid state) the word now often applies to any distinct set of measurements that characterizes a physical system. 2. Verb, to make an assertion, denoted in propositional logic by $\vdash$ where it asserts a proposition which is about to be proved or taken as true

$$\vdash : p \,\&\, q \to p$$

See also steady state.

statement In mathematics or logic, a declarative sentence which is capable of being judged as true or false, in principle if not in practice.

- $\forall x \in \mathbb{R}, \dfrac{d(x^2)}{dx} = 2x$ is a statement.

'The number of ultimate particles in the universe is prime' is a statement.
$3x^2 = 12$ is not a statement, since its truth depends on the value assigned to x. This is sometimes called an open sentence and corresponds to an equation in mathematics.

statics (From Gk. *statikos*, 'at a standstill). The study of mechanics not involving movement, the ideal of Greek quantitative science. It now includes the study of equilibrium under forces, systems of struts and ties in equilibrium, internal and bending stresses and the position of centres of mass and gravity. Hydrostatics extends the study to the forces exerted by or within fluids at rest such as fluid pressure, buoyancy, capillarity and equilibrium of soap films.

stationary point Any point on a curve where the derivative is zero. That is, if $f'(a)=0$, f has a stationary point at a. Such points may represent maxima, minima or points of inflection. So called because at the point the rate of change of $f(x)$ is zero.

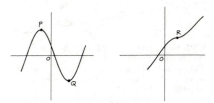

stationary time series A time series in which the autocovariances are independent of t.

stationary value 1. The value of any function at its stationary point.
2. In the calculus of variations, the corresponding value of the integral of a function along a path for which it becomes a maximum or minimum.

statistical control A term used in operational research and production control. A process is 'in statistical control' or simply 'in control' if the deviations (of dimensions, production, number of defects and so on) are within the expected values determined statistically by sampling the process. *See also* control chart.

statistical mechanics The derivation of 'exact' physical laws by considering apparently continuous physical systems as assemblies of very large numbers of discrete entities whose properties are subject to a probability distribution. Thus, the kinetic theory of gases assumes them to be composed of elementary elastic particles. The usual model of a physical law is an exact mathematical function, such as the gas law $pv = k$. This is modified as required when the number of particles or other conditions are such that the probability of residuals in predicted values is high.

statistics Originally the collection of data of value for purposes of state, such as population counts or revenue totals. It now means any study of the distribution of values or of their correlation with one another, involving sampling, counting, estimating or ranking according to criteria. In every case chance variations are involved and exact prediction is logically impossible however much previous information is available. The term 'statistic' is used for any function of sampled data, such as a sample mean or variance. It is also applied to similar parameters drawn from a population, and can then be an exact measure, as average income of an entire group when each individual value is know. Such measures can only be applied to other populations subject to probabilities.

steady state A dynamic system under a system of forces will usually be in a state of change or acceleration. If the rate of change of the system decreases to zero over a time t, then the system reaches dynamic equilibrium. It is then said to be in a steady state, which must be distinguished from static equilibrium.

- A body falling through a viscous medium with acceleration $\mathbf{a} = -kv^2$ acquires a steady terminal velocity since $\mathbf{a} \to 0$.

Steiner, Jakob Swiss mathematician (1796–1863). He gave the first proof that the circle is the figure enclosing the greatest area for the least perimeter, and proved results in geometry by inversion of simpler configurations for which the result was known.

Steiner's Circles A circle Γ_2 is wholly within a circle Γ_1 and a set (or chain) of circles $S_1, S_2 \ldots S_n$ is drawn having common tangents with Γ_1, Γ_2 and with each other, as in the diagram. If the chain is closed (that is if S_n has a common tangent with S_1) any other set of touching circles drawn within Γ_2, Γ_1 will be closed.

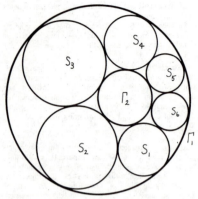

The theorem can be proved by forming the chain S within *concentric* circles, and inverting the configuration with respect to a suitable circle, a circle not passing through any of the centres of the concentric configuration.

stella octangula The eight-pointed star formed by joining the vertices of an octagon so that vertex n_i is joined to n_{i+3}. The star polygon $\{8/3\}$

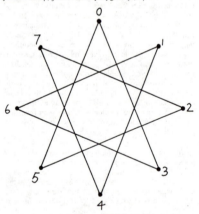

step function Any function whose graph is a sequence of two or more horizontal sections with vertical jumps or discontinuities.

$$f(x) = n \, (n \leqslant x \leqslant n+1; \, n \in \mathbb{N})$$

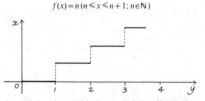

In statistics, the empirical or cumulative distribution is a step function, although it is often drawn as a curve for large n.

See Heaviside step function, Dirac δ function.

steradian *See* solid angle.

stereographic projection A projection of the surface of a sphere from a vertex at one end of a diameter to a tangent plane at the other end. It has the property that any circles on the sphere project into circles on the plane, but the distance scale increases towards the edges of the map.

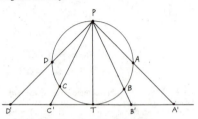

It is rare in maps, but is used in crystallography to plot atoms whose spatial configuration may be inscribed in a sphere. Eight atoms arranged at the vertices of an inscribed cube project as shown.

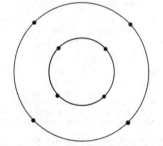

Stevinus, Simon Or Stevin. Flemish mathematician and engineer (1548–1620). He published a work that first described decimal fractions, although his notation was less convenient than the modern point system. It was Stevin, not Galileo, who dropped unequal masses and demonstrated that they reached the ground together.

Stewart's theorem If A, B, C are three collinear points and P is any other point on or not on the line, then, taking account of the sign of the line segments, $PA^2.BC + PB^2.CA + PC^2.AB + BC.CA.AB = 0$.

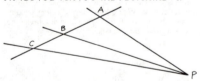

If B is the midpoint of AC this gives the median of a triangle ACP in terms of its sides.

Stirling's formula An expression giving an approximate value to $n!$ where n is large. Given by J. Stirling (1692–1770) as

$$n! \approx n^n (2\pi n)^{1/2} e^{-n}$$

it was, in fact, first determined by Demoivre.

stochastic Describes any process or sequence of

events subject to random effects rather than strict causal laws, so that any event occurs with a probability less than unity. Examples of stochastic sequences or processes are:

1. Independent, in which the probability of the nth event, although not constant, is independent of the outcome of the previous $(n-1)$ events.
2. A Bernoulli process, in which the probability of each outcome is constant, but independent of the occurrence of the event at a previous trial.
3. A Markov chain process in which the probability of an event depends on the outcome of the previous event (but of no others).

The word stochastic is from Greek *stochastē*, a mark set up for archery practice.

stochastic matrix An $n \times n$ matrix whose rows and columns represent the n states of the event space, and whose elements are the probabilities of passing from one event to the next.
See transition matrix.

Stokes, Sir George Cambridge mathematician (1819–1903) who contributed to hydrodynamics and the electromagnetic theory of light. Stokes' theorem, which applies for example to the velocity or vector field representing the steady flow of an incompressible fluid, shows how to calculate the circulation round a loop.

stop point Also terminus point. A finite point on a curve at which a function has a discontinuity, so that its plot on coordinate axes terminates.

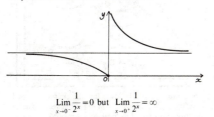

$$\text{Lim}_{x \to 0^-} \frac{1}{2^x} = 0 \text{ but } \text{Lim}_{x \to 0^+} \frac{1}{2^x} = \infty$$

and the graph has a stop point at $(0,0)$ (note that $2^{1/x}$ is not defined at $x=0$).

straight line Any attempted definition of a straight line tends to draw on the intuitive concept. It is usually expressed in mathematics as a set of points satisfying a suitable equation. For example, if A is a point with position vector **a** with respect to an origin O, the straight line through A with direction **b** is the set of points with position vector **r** given by

$$r = \mathbf{a} + t\mathbf{b} \quad (t \in \mathbb{R})$$

See line.

strain A measure of the dimensional deformation of a solid under stress. For a long wire it is defined as

$$\frac{l - l_0}{l_0}$$

Where l is the stretched length and l_0 the length before applying the stress. For an elastic solid in general the deformation will vary from point to point and in the region of any one point will have different components along the x, y, z axes.

stream line If a fluid is in motion each element of its volume has a directed velocity at any given point which is tangential to a curve called the stream line. Normally stream lines vary with time and can only be plotted for any one instant, but for steady flow they remain constant and coincide with the actual paths of the elements.

Since a particle cannot move in two directions at once stream lines cannot coincide or cross except at stagnation points (P) where the velocity is zero. Such points represent discontinuities in the stream line functions.

stress The measure of the force producing a strain in an elastic solid. For a long thin wire under tension it is the ratio between the applied force and the cross-sectional area. For an elastic solid in general the internal stresses will vary from point to point and will have different components along the x, y, z axes at any point, and can be represented as force per unit area acting over any small element of area orientated within the solid, in equilibrium with all surrounding forces.

stretch transformation This is of the type given by a matrix transformation such as

$$\begin{pmatrix} a & 0 \\ 0 & 1 \end{pmatrix} \begin{pmatrix} x \\ y \end{pmatrix} = \begin{pmatrix} x' \\ y' \end{pmatrix}$$

where $a \neq 1$. In the example the configuration of points (x, y) is stretched along the x axis. If $a < 1$ the corresponding transformation is a squeeze.

strictly decreasing Also called monotonic decreasing. A function f for which $f(b) < f(a)$ for all points $a < b$ in its domain.

● $f(x) = -x$

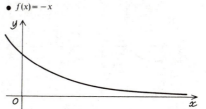

A strictly increasing function is similarly defined with $f(a) > f(b)$ for all $b > a$.

string A term used in computer programming or in discussing the foundations of mathematics. It is any sequence of mathematical or numerical symbols whatsoever. Since the use of symbols is governed by axioms or rules of procedure, there should be three kinds of string in mathematics:

1. Well-formed strings which represent possible operations or true statements, as $3 + 2 = 5$.
2. Well-formed strings which represent false statements, as $(a+b)^2 = a^2 + b^2$.
3. Ill-formed strings, as $+(-=0X)$ which have no meaning or use in mathematics.

See Gödel's theorem.

strip pattern A pattern in which a motif wholly contained within a rectangular region is translated repeatedly along a line in the direction of one side of the rectangle. The translations are integral multiples of the length of one side. The motif could be on a printing roller through which a strip of paper is fed. The motif itself can be generated from an asymmetric unit by various operations of rotational and reflective symmetry. The possible ways of generating the motif can be analysed into seven types which serve to classify the strip patterns.

See also wallpaper patterns.

stroke function *See* Sheffer stroke function.

strong *See* weak.

strong law of large numbers *See* weak law of large numbers. The strong law (Cantelli 1917) makes a more precise formulation, that the probability of large deviations of the occurrence ratio r from the probability p is small if $n > N$ where N is a finite number which can in principle be determined in each case.

strophoid The curve given in cartesians by $y^2(a-x) = x^2(a+x)$ $a > 0$.

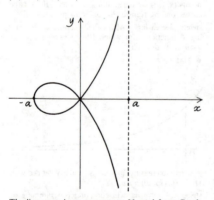

The line $x = a$ is an asymptote. Named from Greek *strophē*, a turning.
See also folium of Descartes.

'Student' Pen name of statistician W. S. Gossett (1876–1937), used because his employers, brewers of a well-known brand of stout, did not permit publication of research carried out by staff. He devised the *t*-tests of significance, based on the distribution that bears his name.

'Student's' *t*-distribution A random variable x is said to have this distribution, with n degrees of freedom, if for some integer $n > 0$

$$f(x) = \frac{\Gamma\dfrac{n+1}{2}}{\sqrt{n\pi}\,\Gamma\!\left(\dfrac{n}{2}\right)\left(1+\dfrac{x^2}{n}\right)^{n+1/2}} \quad (-\infty < x < \infty)$$

'Student' devised this distribution giving $f(x)$ in terms of gamma functions to overcome the inaccuracy of the normal distribution for small samples with $n \leqslant 30$. Tables give values of y for values of n, α such that

$$P(x \leqslant y) = \int_{-\infty}^{y} f(x)\,\mathrm{d}x = \alpha$$

The distribution is symmetrical and its graph resembles that of the normal distribution.
See also *t*-test.

suan pan The Chinese form of the abacus. It uses a split base on each column of beads.

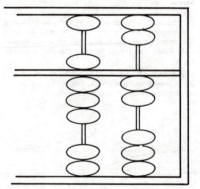

There are five unit beads below the central bar, and two five-beads above it. When five beads are in position they are removed and replaced with one five-bead. When the two five-beads are down, they are removed and replaced with a bead on the next column. Although still made in this form in large numbers, in use only four unit-beads and one five-bead are actually moved, exactly as in the Japanese *soroban*, to which the device is then equivalent.

sub- Prefix applied to any mathematical structure such as set, group, module, ring, field, space etc. A substructure is part of or contained within the structure, and has its properties. It is usual for the set of all substructures to include the structure itself: if not it is called a proper substructure, which is thus any substructure that excludes at least one member of the structure.

subfield If F is a field and S a subset of F, it is also a subfield if it satisfies all the criteria for a field using the additive and multiplicative operations of F. $\mathbb{Q}$ and $\mathbb{N}$ can be considered as subsets of the field $\mathbb{R}$. $\mathbb{Q}$ is a subfield but $\mathbb{N}$ is not.

submultiple If ka is a product with k an integer and a either real or complex, then λa is a submultiple of ka if λ is a rational factor of k.

● $2k\pi$ is a submultiple of $6k\pi$.

subnormal ' Let P be any point on the graph of $y = f(x)$, and let the tangent and normal to the graph at P meet the x axis at T and N

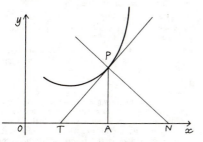

If A is the foot of the perpendicular from P to the x axis, then AN, the projection of PN on the axis, is the subnormal, TA the projection of TP, is the subtangent.

subring Any subset of a ring R which is a ring with respect to the additive and multiplicative operations defining R.

subscript Any subsidiary symbol written below another, usually as a means of identifying sets of entities of the same type, as a_1, a_2, $a_3 \ldots$ A similar symbol written above is a superscript, $f'(x)$, $f''(x) \ldots$ Printers use the words 'inferior' and 'superior' to describe such symbols.

subset A set R is called a subset of S if every member of R is also a member of S. R can be formed by taking all, some or none of the elements of S, and hence the set of all subsets of S, sometimes written $P(S)$, includes both S and the empty set.
$$S = \{1, 2, 3\}$$
$$P(S) = [\{1, 2, 3\}, \{1, 2\}, \{2, 3\}, \{1, 3\}, \{1\}, \{2\}, \{3\}, \emptyset]$$
See also proper subset.

substitution The replacing of any element in an expression by another to yield a different expression. Thus the substitution of $\frac{1}{x}$ for x in $\frac{x-1}{x}$ gives $1 - x$.

substitution formula A method for determining integrals by a substitution of one variable for another to yield an expression readily integrated. The formula can be written in three forms:

1. $\int f(u)\,du = \int f(u)\frac{du}{dx}dx \quad u = g(x)$

2. $\int f(u)\,du = \int f[g(x)]\,g'(x)\,dx \quad u = g(x)$

3. $\int_{g(a)}^{g(b)} f(u)\,du = \int_a^b f[g(x)]\,g'(x)dx \quad u = g(x)$

For example $I = \int_a^b \sin^3 x \cos x\,dx$

has the required form if the substitution $u = \sin x$ is made, so that $f(u) = u^3$, $g(x) = \sin x$, $g'(x) = \cos x$.

substitution operator From the definition of the Kronecker delta δ_{ij} and the two index summation

convention it follows that
$$\delta_{ij} a_j = \sum_{j=1}^{n} \delta_{ij} a_i$$
$$= 0 + \ldots + a_i + 0 + \ldots + 0$$
$$= a_i$$
Hence the operator substitutes a_j by a_i in any expression.

subtangent See subnormal

subtraction In the arithmetic of natural numbers subtraction is the operation of counting back from a given number through its predecessors (see Peano's axioms) the required number of steps as given by the subtrahend.

- $9 - 3 = \{(9 - 1) - 1\} - 1 = 6$

For single-digit numbers the results have to be tabulated or learnt by heart; for multidigit numbers many different algorithms are available. Subtraction is defined formally as the inverse operation to addition. If an operation $+$ is defined on a set A so that for each x, $y \in A$ there is a $z \in A$ such that $z = z + y$, then, if for a, b, $c \in A$
$$b = a + c$$
we write $c = b - a$. The operation $-$ is then called subtraction. If $\{A, +\}$ is a group and the inverse element of $a \in A$ is (^-a) then $b - a$ is defined as $b + (^-a)$.

Subtraction can be represented on a line AB by marking off the interval BP along the line in the direction from B to A. AP then represents $AB - BP$ as the difference between two measures. The operation is not associative or commutative.

subtrahend From Lat. *subtrahendus*, that which is to be subtracted. A term once common in older arithmetic books.

successor See Peano's axioms, in which the concept of succession is taken as the usual non-mathematical use of the word. The successor of any number n is defined by the symbol $n + 1$, the successor of $n + 1$ is $(n + 1) + 1$ and so on. The axioms, given a suitable starting value such as zero, generate a sequence of successors $(0 + 1)$, $(0 + 1) + 1$, ... which have the properties of the natural numbers.

success ratio The same as occurrence ratio, counting a specified occurrence as a 'success'.

sufficient See necessary and sufficient.

sufficiently large 1. An imprecise term in mathematics, given to a quantity which is large enough for the required result to be obtained or a given criterion to be met.
2. Formally, if a sequence S_n converges towards a limit, then for a sufficiently large value of n, it will differ from the limit L by less than a quantity $\varepsilon > 0$, where
$$|L - S_n| < \varepsilon \quad \forall n > n(\varepsilon)$$
Here 'sufficiently large n' is any $n > n(\varepsilon)$ where $n(\varepsilon)$ depends on the chosen specified non-zero ε value, however small.

suffix Or subscript. An indexing symbol placed below and after another symbol, as X_1, X_j, X_{ij}. The last example is a double suffix.

summation 1. The process of adding two or more

elements. If the elements are numbers $a_1, a_2 \ldots a_n$ the summation $a_1 + a_2 + \ldots + a_n$ is denoted by

$$\sum_{i=1}^{i=n} a_i$$

The symbols are an instruction to begin with $i = 1$, adding each subsequent a_i where $i = 2, 3 \ldots$ to the sum of the predecessors until $i = n$ is reached. The notation is sometimes contracted to

$$\sum_{i=1}^{n} a_i$$

The summation can begin with any value of i other than one

If $a_i = i^2$

$$\sum_{i=4}^{i=7} a_i = 4^2 + 5^2 + 6^2 + 7^2$$
$$= 126$$

2. A summation convention used in physics and introduced by Einstein to avoid the sigma notation, regards an expression such as

$$x_i a^i (i = 1, 2, 3)$$

in which an index occurs *twice*, as equivalent to

$$\sum_{i=1}^{i=3} x_i a^i$$

That is $x_i a^i = x_1 a^1 + x_2 a^2 + x_3 a^3$

The convention is used when there are multiple index symbols as in $\delta_{ij} a_j$.
See substitution operator.

sum of four squares   Diophantus (3 A.D.) assumed that every whole number (positive integer) was the sum of four squares. The conjecture was proved by Lagrange in 1722.

● $54 = 4 + 9 + 16 + 25$

Fermat generalized the conjecture to all polygonal numbers.

sum to infinity   An earlier expression that has retained informal use in mathematics. It is not a sum at all, but the limit of a finite sum. It is often written S_α to correspond to the finite sum S_n, but S is a better notation

● $S_n = a + ar + ar^2 + \ldots + ar^n$

$$= \frac{a(1 - r^n)}{1 - r}$$

Then $S = \lim_{n \to \infty} S_n$

This limit exists if $|r| < 1$ and the result is given by

$$S = \frac{a}{1 - r}$$

See also convergent series.

superior limit   Synonym for upper limit. *See* limit.

superposition   A method of proof in geometry commonly used by Euclid, which consists in

imagining one configuration superimposed on another, usually to demonstrate congruence. Its use is equivalent to the axiom that configurations are invariant under translation.

superscript   *See* subscript.

supremum   Synonym for least upper bound, written sup.

surds   From Lat. *surdus*, deaf and hence not open to reason. A former name for irrational numbers in the form of roots, as $\sqrt{2}$, $\sqrt{5}$.

surface   1. The word is used in its ordinary sense in phrases like 'surface area of a cube'.
2. The set of all points whose coordinates satisfy an implicit relation of the form $f(x, y, z) = 0$. The corresponding parametric equations are of the form $x = f(u, v)$, $y = g(u, v)$, $z = h(u, v)$ where u, v take real values in some domain D. The functions f, g, h are usually required to be continuous.

surface integral   A surface S in three dimensions is divided into small regions δS. If a function $f(x, y, z)$ is defined at each point of S one can form the sum $\Sigma f(x, y, z) \delta S$. The surface integral, written $\iint f\, dS$ is the limit of this sum as δS tends to zero, given that this limit exists. It has many applications in physics, as in finding the total charge on a surface when the local charge density is known. Surface integrals can also be expressed in terms of vectors.

surface of revolution   Any surface generated by rotating a line or curve about an axis. Rotation of a circle about a diameter produces a sphere.

surjection   A mapping from set S to S' whose range is the whole of S'. (Lat. *surjacto*, throw on). Also called an onto mapping.

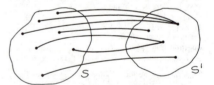

See also into mapping, injective, bijection.

swamping   A function representing an oscillation, signal or periodic change, is swamped when a function of much greater amplitude is superimposed, so that Fourier analysis or a corresponding physical process cannot easily recover the original signal function.

switching algebra   Synonym for Boolean algebra, from its application by C. E. Shannon (1938) to the description of electrical circuits containing on-off switches, relays or equivalent electronic devices.

syllogism   The analysis of an argument into three parts, the major premise, the minor premise and the conclusion.

● The opposite angles of cyclic quadrilaterals are supplementary—major premise.
  ABCD is cyclic—minor premise.
  Therefore $A + C = 180°$—conclusion.

The various figures and moods of the syllogism, whose study made up most of traditional logic, arose from the different arrangements of the parts and the actual or implied presence of the 'quantifying' words *all*, *some*, *not all*, *not*.

Sylow's theorem If m is p^n where p is prime and $n = 1, 2, 3 \ldots$ then any group whose order is divisible by m has a subgroup of that order. Thus the icosahedral group of order 60 has at least a subgroup of order 4 since $4 = 2^2$.

Sylvester's Law of Inertia Any quadratic function over the field of real numbers can be reduced by non-singular transformation of the variables to the form $z_1^2 + \ldots + z_p^2 - z_{p+1}^2 - \ldots - z_r^2$.
The number p of positive terms is an invariant of the given function, in the sense that p depends only on the function and not on the method used to reduce it.

symbol Any letter, numeral, mark or sign used to denote some mathematical quantity, object or operation. A word is not taken as a symbol in mathematics, but any statement not containing words is regarded as a string of symbols. It is convenient to standardize symbols as far as possible: a list of some forms adopted in this book is given in Appendix 2.

symbolic logic Evolved from traditional logic by the use of symbols to indicate propositions and the relations between them, but now taken as a formal axiomatic system whose elements p, q, $r \ldots$ are statements and whose operational symbols $\vee$ (or), $\sim$ (not) and so on are defined by rules of combination to yield compound statements which are true (T), false (F) or otherwise categorized. *See* truth table, Boolean algebra, connective.

symmedian The symmetric of the median of a triangle with respect to the internal bisector from the same vertex.

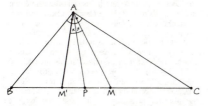

If AM is a median of triangle ABC and AP is the bisector of angle BAC, then AM' is the symmedian if angle MAP' = angle PAM'. The symmedians of a triangle are concurrent at the Lemoine point.

symmetric difference The set function denoted $A \Delta B$ and given by $(A \backslash B) \cup (B \backslash A)$ or $(A \cup B) \backslash (A \cup B)$. It corresponds to the shaded area in the diagram, and is so called because it is commutative.

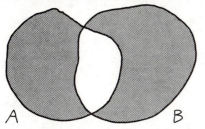

symmetric equation An equation which expresses a symmetric relation, as $x^2 + y^2 + z^2 + 3xyz = 0$, which remains unchanged if the variables are interchanged in pairs.

symmetric function 1. The graph of a function is symmetric about a vertical axis if $f(x) = f(-x)$, and has point symmetry about the origin if $f(x) = -f(-x)$.

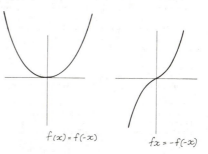

$f(x) = f(-x)$ $fx = -f(-x)$

2. Any function of two or more variables which remains unchanged after the interchange of two of its variables, as symmetric functions of the roots α, β, γ of a cubic as given by

$$(\alpha + \beta + \gamma), (\beta + \gamma)(\gamma + \alpha)(\alpha + \beta)$$

These are usually written, for any polynomial equation

$$\Sigma\alpha, \Sigma(\alpha + \beta), \Sigma\alpha\beta, \Sigma\alpha^2\beta, \ldots$$

symmetric group Also called permutation group. A group generated by compounding the total permutations of n numbers $\{1, 2, 3 \ldots n\}$ taken n at a time, denoted $S(n)$ or S_n, such as the group of order 6 whose elements are a_0, a_1, a_2, a_3, a_4, a_5, given by (123), (231), (312), (132), (321), (213). This has the operation table

	a_0	a_1	a_2	a_3	a_4	a_5
a_0	a_0	a_1	a_2	a_3	a_4	a_5
a_1	a_1	a_2	a_0	a_4	a_5	a_3
a_2	a_2	a_0	a_1	a_5	a_3	a_4
a_3	a_3	a_4	a_5	a_0	a_2	a_1
a_4	a_4	a_5	a_3	a_1	a_0	a_2
a_5	a_5	a_3	a_4	a_2	a_1	a_0

The group is realized geometrically by the total symmetries of an equilateral triangle ABC.

Here the subset $\{a_0, a_1, a_2\}$ forms a cyclic subgroup C_3 of S_n.
See Cayley's theorem.

symmetric relation Any relation R between elements a, b, $c \ldots$ such that $aRb \Rightarrow bRa$. That is, the relation is unaltered by the interchange of the variables in pairs

● Joan is sitting next to Jack
$xy + yz + zx = 0$
AB is parallel to CD

symmetric roots Roots of an equation that are symmetrical with respect to zero.
● $x^2 - 4 = 0$ has roots $x = +2$ and -2.

symmetry Gk. *summetria* originally meant of harmonious proportions, but the term now applies to any configuration of points or set of elements in which one corresponds in position to another relative to a point, line or plane, in such a way that corresponding pairs may be interchanged without altering the form of the configuration or the structure of the set.
See bilateral symmetry, point of symmetry, central symmetry, rotational symmetry, central inversion.

synthetic division A method for dividing a polynomial $f(x)$ by $(x - a)$ using detached coefficients. It is described in detail in books of elementary algebra but is easily seen from an example with $a = 2$

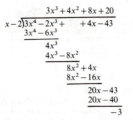

This gives, using detached coefficients

3	−2	0	4	−43
	6	8	16	40
3	4	8	20	−3

The result is $3x^3 + 4x^2 + 8x + 20$ Rem $- 3$
The second line of coefficients is always added to the coefficients of the polynomial, so that the sign of each coefficient needs to be changed if, as here, the coefficient of x^0 in the divisor is negative.

synthetic geometry A name given to geometry by Euclidean methods after Descartes had introduced algebraic methods and laid the foundations for analytical or coordinate geometry.

synthetic proposition A synthetic proposition (true or false) is one which gives empirical information not implicitly contained in the subject of the proposition; e.g., some swans are black. It can be argued that there are no synthetic propositions in mathematics, since the truth of any statement is deducible within the system.
See analytic proposition.

systematic error Any error in measurement, experiment or trial that is recurrent and influences all observations. It may be due to faulty calibration of apparatus, erroneous initial or operational assumptions or a personal factor which depends on the observer.

system of equations Also called set of simultaneous equations. A set of equations having the same variables so that the nature of the solution set and methods for finding it can be discussed. Common systems are linear equations such as

$$\left. \begin{array}{l} 3x + 2y + 4z = 2 \\ 5x + 3y \quad\ = 4 \\ 2x \qquad\ = 1 \end{array} \right\}$$

and differential equations such as

$$\left. \begin{array}{l} \dfrac{dx}{dt} - \dfrac{dy}{dt} = t^2 \\[2ex] \dfrac{dx}{dt} + \dfrac{dy}{dt} = -2t \end{array} \right\}$$

systems analysis A method of approach to the problems of business and industrial organizations by analysing them in terms of subproblems and their interconnections. This is usually done as a preliminary to devising a computer program that will handle the routine operations of the business. The problem to be solved must be exactly defined, and all relevant data examined and analysed, often in the light of a current procedure which is proving inefficient. It is then analysed in terms of programmable operations. The analyst is often responsible for preparing, testing and modifying the program and supervising its documentation and maintenance.

T

tableau In any set of simultaneous equations in x_1, $x_2 \ldots$ the x_i are variables which carry the coefficients whose values give the solutions. A tableau, often used in linear programming involving a large number of equations, merely records the coefficients. The x can be used as column headings. Thus

$$2x + 3y = 2$$
$$4x - y = 3$$

could be written as a tableau

x	y	1
2	3	2
4	-1	3

The method would normally only be used for more than two or three equations. Further columns can be added for slack variables if needed, and can be extended downwards as solution proceeds.

tabulation The setting down of data or results in rows and/or columns either for presentation or as a preliminary processing of data prior to computation. Most forms of statistical analysis depend heavily on a systematic tabulation of the data to be analysed.

tachnode From Gk. *tachē*, rapid. A name used for a node or cusp P, as on a roulette, which is approached and left very rapidly as the generating curve rolls.

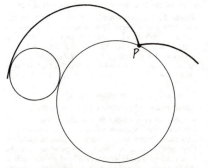

Tait, Peter Guthrie Scottish mathematician (1831–1902). Remembered for his work on particle dynamics, quaternions and knots.
See also Hamilton.

tally Verb or noun. Applied to any system of counting which does not use the sequence of numerals. Originally a stick (Lat. *talea*) cut with notches to correspond to items, and split down the middle as a record or receipt. It is convenient to use tally marks of five when counting events, adding the strokes one at a time. In China and Japan a five-stroke character is used in the same way.

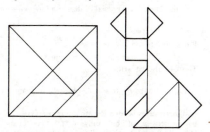

tangent *See* circular functions.

tangent curve Also called an envelope. A curve which touches every member of a system of lines, which are therefore tangents to the curve.

● The set of lines $ty = x + t^2$, as t takes all real values, touch the parabola $y^2 = 4ax$, which is their envelope curve.

tangential component If the coordinates of a point P on a curve are given in terms of a parameter θ, if $\hat{\mathbf{t}}$ is a unit vector along the tangent to the curve at P in the direction of increasing θ and if $\mathbf{F}(x, y)$ is a vector function, then the tangential component of $\mathbf{F}$ is defined as $\mathbf{F}.\hat{\mathbf{t}}$. Informally, it is the component of $\mathbf{F}$ at P in the direction of the tangent.
See also normal component.

tangent plane A plane which touches a surface at a point, thus containing all the lines tangent to a surface at the point.

tangram A traditional Chinese dissection of a square into seven pieces, which can be assembled to represent objects and persons.

tanh *See* hyperbolic functions.

tapered sawtooth A sawtooth function whose amplitude is steadily decreasing, so that each peak is lower than its predecessor. The period remains constant.

Tartaglia Nickname of Nicolo Fontana Brescia (1500–1557). He wrote an early work on commercial arithmetic, but is remembered for discovering the general solution to a cubic equation, which was afterwards fraudulently published by Cardano.

tautochrone A curve along which a mass sliding without friction under gravity will arrive at any given point after the same elapsed time, whatever its starting point along the curve. For a small arc it approximates to a circle, but is in general a cycloid (Huygens 1673). A pendulum bob constrained to move in a cycloidal arc has a period independent of its amplitude.
Since the evolute of a cycloid is a similar cycloid this can be done by swinging the pendulum between cycloidal check-pieces at its point of suspension.
See also brachystochrone.

tautology Any compound proposition that has the value 'true' for all values of its constituent propositions, as in $[(p \Rightarrow q) \wedge (q \Rightarrow r)] \Rightarrow (p \Rightarrow r)$. Such a tautology can allow the simplest form of an expression to be chosen, or can reduce the number of symbols to be defined.

An important form of tautology is given by logically equivalent propositions. These have the same truth table and are thus interchangeable.

p	q	$(p \vee q)$	p'	q'	$(p' \wedge q')$	$(p' \wedge q')'$
T	T	T	F	F	F	T
T	F	T	F	T	F	T
F	T	T	T	F	F	T
F	F	F	T	T	T	F

Hence $(p \vee q)$, $(p' \wedge q')'$ are equivalent.
See De Morgan's laws, Sheffer stroke function.

Taylor polynomial An approximating polynomial that gives the value of any other function either exactly or to a required degree of accuracy provided it and its first n derivates are continuous in the interval $[a, b]$. If the value of $f(a) = a_0$, if the first and higher derivatives $f^{(1)}(a)$, $f^{(2)}(a)$, ... $f^{(n)}(a)$ all exist, and the coefficients $a_1, a_2, \ldots a_n$ are formed by taking

$$a_k = \frac{f^{(k)}(a)}{k!} \quad (1 \leqslant k \leqslant n)$$

then the Taylor polynomial of degree n for $x = a + h$ in $[a, b]$ is

$$P_n(x) = a_0 + a_1 h + a_2 h^2 + \ldots + a_n h^n$$

If $a = 0$ the polynomial becomes

$$P_n(x) = a_0 + a_1 x + a_2 x^2 + \ldots + a_n x^n$$

This can also be written

$$P_n(x) = f(0) + x f^{(1)}(0) + \frac{x^2}{2!} f^{(2)}(0) + \ldots + \frac{x^n}{n!} f^{(n)}(0)$$

If all derivatives beyond the nth are zero $P_n(x) = f(x)$ but otherwise, if but only if $f^{(n+1)}(x)$ exists, $f(x) = P_n(x) + R_n(x)$ where $R_n(x)$ is the remainder term. This term $R_n(x)$ can be given in several ways

1. $R_n(x) = \dfrac{f^{(n+1)}(t)}{(n+1)!}(x - a)^{n+1}$

where t lies between x and a. This is the Lagrange form.

2. $R_n(x) = \dfrac{1}{n!}\int_a^x (x - t)^n f^{(n+1)}(t)\, dt$

This is the integral form.

3. $R_n(x) = \dfrac{f^{(n+1)}(t)}{n}(x - t)^n (x - a)$.

This is the Cauchy form.
See also mean value theorem.

Taylor's series The name given to Taylor's polynomial with remainder term, by which any function is given as the series

$$f(x) = P_n(x) + R_n(x)$$

Provided that $R_n(x) \to 0$ as $n \to \infty$, $P_n(x)$ then becomes

an infinite series converging to the value $f(x)$. Taylor's series requires the existence of derivatives of every order and x must lie in some neighbourhood of a. Thus we get $\sin x = x - \dfrac{x^3}{3!} - \dfrac{x^5}{5!} - \ldots$. In such an example the remainder term $R_n(x)$ merely expands to give further terms, as

$$e^x = 1 + x + \frac{x^2}{2!} + \ldots + \frac{x^n}{n!} + \int_0^x \frac{e^t}{n!}(x - t)^n\, dt$$

$$= 1 + x + \frac{x^2}{2!} + \ldots + \frac{x^n}{n!} + \frac{x^{n+1}}{(n+1)!} + \ldots$$

Taylor's theorem This gives the general form of the remainder term in Taylor's series, which may be expressed in any of the three ways given above under Taylor polynomial.

Tchebychev, P. L. Russian mathematician (1821–1894) whose work on probability and algebra has proved of value in statistics and numerical methods.

Tchebychev's inequality If X is taken from any random population of mean μ and variance σ^2, then for any positive ε

$$P(|X - \mu|) \leqslant \frac{\sigma^2}{\varepsilon^2}$$

This can be used to prove the law of large numbers, expressing the probable convergence of the sample mean to the true mean as the sample size increases.

Tchebychev's polynomials Since trigonometric identities can express functions such as $\cos n\theta$ in terms of powers of $\cos \theta$, they can be written as polynomials if $x = \cos \theta$. They can be denoted as $\cos n\theta = T_n(x)$ so that $T_0(x) = 1$, $T_2(x) = 2x^2 - 1$ and so on. Since $-1 \leqslant \cos n\theta \leqslant 1$ it follows that Tchebychev's polynomials always lie between these limits, if $|x| \leqslant 1$.
See min-max approximation.

t-distribution *See* 'Student's' t-distribution.

temperature A measure specifying one of the physical manifestations of heat. Heat energy will only pass from a body having a higher temperature into one having a lower. Temperature can be measured on a scale having two fixed points, such as the freezing and boiling points of a liquid, suitably divided, by a thermodynamic scale based on the properties of a gas as its heat content changes, or by the wave length of radiation emitted by a hot body. *See* Appendix 1.

tensor A mathematical entity most conveniently discussed from a physical example.

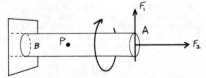

Consider a rod of elastic material fixed at B which is stretched, bent and twisted simultaneously by forces applied at A. Then the stresses in any given direction will vary from point to point within the solid, and the stresses at any one point P will vary with direction. The face of any small element of the solid at P, orientated in any direction (given by three coordinates), is in equilibrium under forces in three directions; the stress at P is thus given uniquely by nine components. These are said to form a tensor of order two and can be represented by a 3×3 matrix. Since the laws governing the distribution of stresses through the body will be independent of the coordinate system chosen, the elements of the tensor must transform from one system to another by suitable transformation procedures to leave these laws invariant. A tensor can be defined as a system of components that obeys such a transformation. The physical example suggests that a vector, having three components, can be regarded as a tensor of the first order. General relativity is developed using tensors in x, y, z, t.

tensor analysis The study of tensors and tensor functions, applied particularly to the geometry of spaces with intrinsic curvature.
See also Riemann integration, Riemann sum.

term Any numerical or algebraic quantity appearing as a single element or compound entity in a sequence or in a sum or series of sums, as in the expression 'nth term.'

● $1 + 2 + 3 + 4 + 5$
4 is the fourth term.

$2a + 3b^2$

$3b^2$ is the second term.
a, $(a + b)$, $(a + 2b)$, $(a + 3b)$
$(a + 2b)$ is the third term.

terminating decimal *See* recurring decimal.
terminus point *See* stop point.

ternary Relating to the number three. A ternary notation is to base three and a ternary operation is between three elements each of which must be specified, as in 'carry a digit from the tens column to the hundreds column'.

tessellation (Lat. *tesserae*, dice. Originally small marked cubes used in gambling, and then similar pieces of stone or tile used in mosaic decorations.) Tessellation is now any complete covering of a surface with plane geometric shapes. Triangles, squares and hexagons are the only regular polygons which can tessellate, since the sum of the angles at each point where the vertices meet must be $360°$. Tessellating motifs can be constructed using the points of parallel grids.
Covering using two or more regular shapes, such as octagons and squares, can be reduced to a tessellation with one irregular shape by joining in pairs.

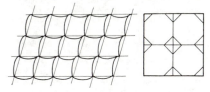

tesseract Or hypercube. On the analogy of a cube formed by six square plane faces assembled in three dimensions, the tesseract is a (non-realizable)

configuration whose 'faces' are eight cubes assembled in four dimensions.
See also polytope.

tetragon *See* polygon. A rarely used alternative name for a quadrilateral, from Gk. *tetragonon*.

tetrahedron *See* polyhedron.

tetromino *See* polyomino.

Thales Greek philosopher, born at Miletus c. 600 B.C. Later tradition credited him with the formulation of several results in geometry, including the base angle theorem for an isosceles triangle and the 'angle-side-angle' criterion for congruent triangles. He is said to have measured heights by shadows and the distance of ships when off shore.

theorem In any sequence of mathematical deductions which purport to follow logically from initial axioms, postulates, definitions or hypotheses, a theorem is a deduction considered to be of special significance. Theorems, when established, are used as starting points for further deduction. Some accounts of mathematics consider any derivable statement such as the number facts in arithmetic as a theorem, but the term is usually applied to conclusions not intuitively obvious from the postulates, and requiring a chain of reasoning.
See also corollary, lemma.

theory The word is used differently in mathematics from in science. A scientific theory sets out to explain and unify a set of agreed facts; but in pure mathematics a theory (group theory, set theory) aims to develop a consistent set of theorems from an axiomatic starting point which may or may not be realized in physical applications.

there is Also 'there exists'. A phrase, symbolized by $\exists$ meaning 'there is at least one', as in $(\exists x)x^2 = x$ which reads 'There is at least one x for which $x^2 = x$.' The statement may be true for more than one x, but need not be.

three dimensional A space is three dimensional if it requires three linearly independent measures of distance relative to an origin to determine a point uniquely, as in cartesian coordinates. Spherical coordinates (r, θ, ϕ) fix a point with one measure of distance r and two angles relative to a fixed direction, but are equivalent to three distances since for any r the angle may be replaced with arcs.

three term logic Originally introduced by J. S. Mill, who stated that propositions could be true, false or meaningless, e.g. prime numbers are yellow. A better term is 'not properly formulated'. A properly formulated proposition can only use the terms appropriate to its subject,
p = prime numbers are always even (false)
q = He eats too much (true or false)
r = He has stopped eating too much (properly formulated if, but only if, q is or was true).
Other middle terms such as 'undecidable' (*see* Gödel's theorem) or 'undecided' are also possible. If p = 'Goldbach's conjecture is true', p is neither true nor false, but undecided. Ramsay (1925), objecting to the 'neither', argued that the correct formulation should be 'p is either true or false but we do not know which'.
See excluded middle.

time series   A set of variates $\{X_t\}$ indexed by time t, that is, any set of sequential values which are dependent on time. If plotted graphically the horizontal axis normally represents the units of time. *See also* trend line.

time series analysis   Statistical analysis of time series in order to establish trends, patterns of seasonal variation, probable interpolated or extrapolated values and so on. Of importance in economic or business management.

time t   In applied mathematics generally time t is regarded as an independent continuous variable which can in principle be measured absolutely and can tend to zero. This agrees with our intuitive concept of time, but this independence is not logically necessary. *See* relativity.

tolerance   To be distinguished from error. Tolerances are the upper and lower limits of error permissible in any measure or dimension, and are usually expressed as plus/minus values around the nominal required measure.

topological equivalence   1. Used of topological spaces between which there is 1:1 mapping or bijection.
2. If two geometrical configurations are topologically equivalent, one can be transformed continuously into the other.

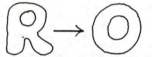

topological invariant   Any property of a configuration, such as continuity or connectedness, that is preserved under a topological mapping. The connectedness of net A is preserved under transformation to net B, but its metrical properties are not invariant.

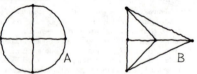

topological space   *See* topology.

topology   1. Informally, the study of those properties of geometrical configurations that are preserved under continuous transformation. Thus connectivity is a topological property, metric relations are not.
2. If A is any set which is partitioned into a system of subsets T, such that (i) $\emptyset$. $A \in T$ and (ii) the intersection or the union of any subsets of T is also a subset of T, then T is called a topology.
It is usual to call the subsets of T the open sets of A, so that the intersection and union of the open sets is an open set.
A *topological space* (A, T) defined on A is the set A together with T. This definition includes under topology any set or configuration that has a mathematical structure.

torque   *See* couple.

Torricelli's theorem   The area of one complete arch

208

of a cycloid is three times the area of the generating circle.
Torricelli (1608–1647) is better known for his work on the mercury barometer.

torus   Originally a semicircular moulding surrounding a column, the word is used in mathematics for a solid or surface in the shape of an anchor ring, traced by a circle whose centre moves on a circular path always at right angles to the plane of the circle.

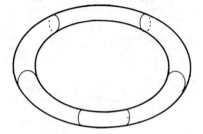

total derivative   If $z = f(x, y)$ but y is also a function of x, the total derivative $\dfrac{dz}{dx}$ is given by

$$\frac{dz}{dx} = \frac{\partial z}{\partial x} + \frac{\partial z}{\partial y} \cdot \frac{dy}{dx}$$

The expression can be extended to n variables giving

$$\frac{dF}{dx} = \sum_{j=1}^{n} \frac{\partial F}{\partial u_j} \cdot \frac{du_j}{dx}$$

total differential   *See* differential. The relation $dy = f'(x)\,dx$ between actual differentials can be extended to two or more variables. If $z = f(x, y)$ and x, y can vary indepently, then

$$dz = \frac{\partial f(x, y)}{\partial x} dx + \frac{\partial f(x, y)}{\partial y} dy$$

If in the above the differentials are replaced by finite δx, δy, δz the expression gives an approximation to δz as long as the increments are small.

totally ordered set   A set S ordered by a binary ordering relation that exists between all possible pairs of its elements, that is, aRb or bRa for all a, $b \in S$. It can be represented by points arranged uniquely on a line.

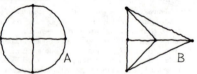

Here R could be 'to the left of'. The points as labelled could also be totally ordered alphabetically or in terms of distance from an origin. Any well-ordered set is totally ordered.

total matrix algebra   The results of the operations of addition, matrix and scalar multiplication, on the set of all $n \times n$ matrices whose elements belong to a field F. The algebra may be denoted $M_n(F)$. Thus $M_4(\mathbb{Q})$ is the sub-algebra of the set of 4×4 matrices with rational elements.

total probability law   If the events $\{H_1, H_2, H_3 \ldots\}$ form a partition of a sample space, then the probability of an event E is given by

$$p(E) = \sum_i p(E|H_i)\, p(H_i)$$

See conditional probability.

totient function Denoted by $\phi(n)$ and due to Euler (1760). The number of positive integers less than n and having no factor in common with n (but including unity). Thus $\phi(9) = 6$, which is the number of integers in the set $\{1, 2, 4, 5, 7, 8\}$. (From Lat. *totiens*, as many as.)
See also primitive roots.

touching Used of curves which have a common tangent. A curve which touches an axis has that axis as a tangent.

trace 1. See locus.
2. The sum of the terms in the leading diagonal of a square matrix.
3. The point at which a line when produced meets another gives the trace of the first on the second.

tractrix The involute of a catenary $y = \cosh x/c$ described from a point at the vertex of the curve.

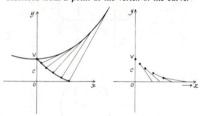

If x, y is a horizontal cartesian plane, and if a string of length $VO = c$ has a mass m attached at V and the point O is then moved slowly along Ox, the locus of m, if the cartesian plane is taken to be rough, is the involute: hence the name (Lat. *tractum*, drawn). The intrinsic equation of the tractrix is $s = c\, \log\dfrac{c}{y}$, corresponding to $s = c \tan\psi$ for the generating catenary. The surface of rotation formed by rotating the tractrix about Ox has constant negative curvature and is thus a pseudosphere.

trajectory The path of a particle travelling under impressed forces, as in gravitational fields.

trammel Any mechanical device, which, by constraining the motion of a rod or other solid, causes a fixed point on it to generate a given curve.

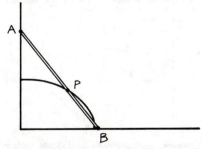

As rod AB slides in the grooves OY, OX the point P describes the arc of an ellipse. A straight edge and

compasses are in fact trammels, although constructions involving circles and straight lines were not regarded by the Greeks as empirical.

transcendental function Any function that is not algebraic and cannot therefore be expressed as a polynomial, as the exponential and associated trigonometric or hyperbolic functions. From the phrase '*quod algebrae vires transcendit*'.

transcendental irrationals. See irrational number.

transcendental number Defined as any number which is not algebraic, and thus cannot satisfy a polynomial of the form

$$\sum_{r=0}^{n} a_r x^r = 0 \ (a_r \in \mathbb{Z})$$

It follows that a transcendental number is irrational since it will not satisfy the defining equation for a rational

$$a_0 + a_1 x = 0 (a_r \in \mathbb{Z})$$

In addition it will not satisfy an equation such as $x^2 - 2 = 0$ which gives the irrational solution $x = \sqrt{2}$. Many transcendental numbers can be expressed as the limits of infinite series, but since this is true of any number it is difficult to prove the transcendence of any number such as π since there is no positive criterion for this property.
See squaring the circle, Euler's constant. Transcendental numbers form a non-denumerably infinite set.

transfinite cardinal The definition of cardinal does not require the operational process of one-to-one correspondence to terminate (although in finite counting procedures it does). If the terms of an infinite set can be arranged unambiguously in order (say of magnitude) then the correspondence with the set $\mathbb{N}$ (taken as representing the cardinals $\hat{\mathbb{N}}$) can be continued indefinitely.
The set of primes gives

2	3	5	7	11	13	...
1	2	3	4	5	6	...

This does not terminate since there is no greatest prime. The set is said to be denumerably infinite and to have cardinality $\aleph_0$ (aleph null). $\aleph_0$ is then said to be transfinite. The same process applies to all denumerably infinite sets, which therefore have the same cardinality $\aleph_0$. The set of reals $\mathbb{R}$ is non-denumerable since it cannot be put into an unambiguous order, and is said to have the cardinality of the continuum, denoted c. This is again a transfinite number, and presumably $c > \aleph_0$.

transfinite numbers Cantor, Kamke and others developed an arithmetic using transfinite cardinals as a starting point, applying arithmetical operations to postulate actually infinite quantities. The validity and even the meaning of such results as

$$\aleph_0 + \aleph_0 = \aleph_0{}^2 = \aleph_0$$

have been queried by Brouwer and others.

transfinite ordinal The ordinal equivalent of the transfinite cardinal aleph null, usually called ω, omega. Thus if the cardinals are arranged in order of increasing magnitude 1, 2, 3... the cardinal $\aleph_0$ occupies the ωth position. As with transfinite numbers generally, there is controversy over the possible meaning of expressions such as ordinal $\omega + 1$.

transform (noun) The image of any set of elements that has undergone transformation. *See also* Laplace transform, Fourier transform.

transformation 1. Any operation which transforms one expression or configuration into another.
2. An operation which maps all points in $\mathbb{R}$ (or $\mathbb{R}^2$ or $\mathbb{R}^3$) into itself. The word is commonly used for reflections, rotations, enlargements and shears in the plane, which can be described by a transformation matrix.
3. In general, let a pair of functions $u(x, y)$, $v(x, y)$ be continuous and differentiable at each point of some domain S in a plane P of which x, y are cartesian coordinates. Let the equations $u = u(x, y)$, $v = v(x, y)$ set up a correspondence between the points of S and the points of S', in the u, v plane P'. Then S' is a map of S, and any configuration in the plane P is transformed into a configuration in P'.

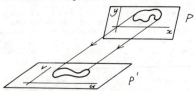

transformation geometry The application of certain transformations to plane or spatial configurations, and the determination of which properties remain invariant under the transformation and which are modified. Elementary geometry usually considers five main types

(i) reflection
(ii) rotation
(iii) translation
(iv) enlargement
(v) shear

The first three transformations produce an image having the same dimensions as the original or source configuration and are known as isometries. The fourth changes the sizes only and is taken to include reduction. The fifth changes both size and shape.

transformation group A group whose elements consist of transformations. Thus the matrix transformation

$$\begin{pmatrix} a & b \\ c & d \end{pmatrix} \begin{pmatrix} x \\ y \end{pmatrix} = \begin{pmatrix} x' \\ y' \end{pmatrix}$$

forms an infinite group for all a, b, c, d with the identity

$$\begin{pmatrix} 1 & 0 \\ 0 & 1 \end{pmatrix}$$

transformation matrix The matrix describing any transformation, usually expressed as a matrix operation on a vector quantity.

$$\begin{pmatrix} \cos\theta & -\sin\theta \\ \sin\theta & \cos\theta \end{pmatrix} \begin{pmatrix} x \\ y \end{pmatrix} = \begin{pmatrix} x' \\ y' \end{pmatrix}$$

This 2×2 matrix rotates the line OP where $P = (x, y)$, through an angle θ about the origin O, so that $P \rightarrow P' = (x', y')$. The other geometric transformations

such as reflection, dilatation and shear can all be specified by suitable matrices acting on points expressed as cartesian coordinates.

transient In applied mathematics a transient is any force or effect whose duration is vanishingly small, as the impulse of a projectile stopped by a solid or the reaction of an electrical circuit to the closing of a switch. If the system considered is governed by differential equations the effects of transients can be modelled by using unit step functions.

transition The movement from one specified state to another. Transition time is that taken for the movement to be completed, or is the interval between one transition and the next.

transition matrix A square matrix whose elements are probabilities. The ijth entry is the probability that a system will change from state i to state j. It follows that the sum of the entries in each row is unity. Thus, if for three states A, B, C subject to change, the probabilities of A, B, C at the next stage are given by

	A	B	C
A	$\frac{1}{2}$	$\frac{1}{4}$	$\frac{1}{4}$
B	$\frac{1}{4}$	$\frac{1}{2}$	$\frac{1}{4}$
C	$\frac{1}{4}$	$\frac{1}{4}$	$\frac{1}{2}$

then the transition matrix T is

$$T = \begin{pmatrix} \frac{1}{2} & \frac{1}{4} & \frac{1}{4} \\ \frac{1}{4} & \frac{1}{2} & \frac{1}{4} \\ \frac{1}{4} & \frac{1}{4} & \frac{1}{2} \end{pmatrix}$$

The powers T^2, T^3... of T give the probabilities of state i being followed by state j after 2, 3 ... stages. *See* Markov chain.

transition probability *See* Markov chain.

transitive relation A binary relation R between members of a set $\{a, b, c ...\}$ such that aRb and $bRc \Rightarrow aRc$, as the relation $<$ on the set $\mathbb{N}$. It has also been called an 'ancestral' relation, since it describes 'is an ancestor of'.

translation The transformation of any configuration Q to an isometry Q' so that the lines joining points in Q to the corresponding points in Q' are parallel. That is, it is equivalent to transformation by a constant vector of all points in the configuration, and the position but not the size, shape or orientation of Q is transformed.

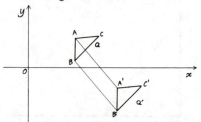

transpose Also transposition. To change any term from one side of an equation to another, or to change the subject of a formula

- $x^2 + 5x - 6 = 0 \Rightarrow x^2 + 5x = 6$

$$v^2 = u^2 + 2as \Rightarrow s = \frac{v^2 - u^2}{2a}$$

The transpose of a matrix A is the matrix A' or A^{T} whose rows are the columns of A and whose columns are the rows of A

$$A = \begin{pmatrix} 1 & 2 & 1 \\ 3 & 0 & 3 \end{pmatrix} \quad A' = \begin{pmatrix} 1 & 3 \\ 2 & 0 \\ 1 & 3 \end{pmatrix}$$

transverse axis This is defined relative to a given configuration across which it runs. Thus the transverse axis of a hyperbola cuts both branches as shown.

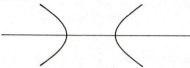

transverse Mercator A Mercator projection whose base line corresponds not with the equator but a meridian. The current Ordnance Survey maps of Great Britain use a transverse Mercator projection on a meridian 2°W, near which distortion is vanishingly small. This produces the least distortion for the land area as a whole.

trapezoidal rule Once used in numerical integration, and operated by regarding the strips into which a region is divided as trapezia.

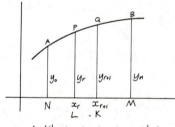

$$A \approx h(\tfrac{1}{2}y_0 + y_1 + y_2 + \ldots + y_{n-1} + \tfrac{1}{2}y_n)$$

See also Simpson's rule, mid-ordinate rule.

traverse Any base line b surveyed across a site or plot of ground, relative to which other points are fixed by offset distances d_i at right angles.

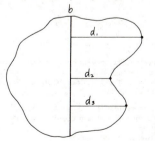

As a verb, to take a path through a network or tree.

tree diagram A branching network without loops. A method of representing the possible outcomes of a sequence of events, each possibility being regarded as a branch of the tree. It is commonly used for generating the elements of a probability space, by assigning numerical weightings or probabilities to each branch or node. Any connected path or traverse through the network specifies a possible outcome and its probability.

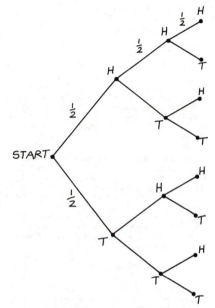

Results of repeatedly spinning a coin. Event HTH occurs with probability $\tfrac{1}{2} \times \tfrac{1}{2} \times \tfrac{1}{2} = \tfrac{1}{8}$

See also random walk, Markov chain.

trend line A line of best fit calculated for a set of values in a time series. Trend lines are often extrapolated beyond the data as a means of forecasting future situations.

trial In statistics or the experimental investigation of probabilities, a trial is any repetition of the relevant action, such as the taking of a sample or the spinning of a coin. Each trial is an element of the event or sample space being considered.

triangle inequality If the distance between the elements x, y of any set is given by $d(x, y)$, then for any three elements x, y, z

$$d(x, z) \leqslant d(x, y) + d(y, z)$$

This is generalization of the corresponding distances between three points on a Euclidean plane, which are collinear under equality.

triangle of forces A special case of the sum of two vectors as represented on a vector polygon.

211

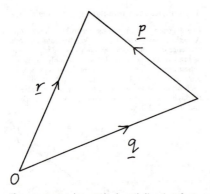

If **q**, **p** represent, in magnitude and direction, forces acting through O, then their resultant is given by **r**. Alternatively, if **r** is in the opposite sense from that shown, the forces **p**, **q**, **r** are in equilibrium. Also applicable to velocities, displacements, accelerations or any physical quantities specified by magnitude and direction.
See also parallelogram of forces.

triangle of reference   Gives a non-metric equivalent of plane cartesian axes using homogeneous coordinates. Any triangle is taken with coordinates (X_r, Y_r, Z_r), $(r=1, 2, 3)$ in a cartesian plane. Usually the vertices are taken as $A=(1, 0, 0)$, $B=(0, 1, 0)$ and $C=(0, 0, 1)$. The sides BC, CA, AB then become $X=0, Y=0$ and $Z=0$. Choose any point I not on the sides of the triangle whose homogeneous coordinates are (α, β, γ) referred to any system A, Y, Z and make the transformation

$$X' = \frac{X}{\alpha}, \ Y' = \frac{Y}{\beta}, \ Z' = \frac{Z}{\gamma}$$

We now have a system of coordinates $X' \ Y' \ Z'$ in which the point $I=(1, 1, 1)$ and the original triangle is unchanged, with $X'=0$, $Y'=0$, $Z'=0$. It is now possible to refer any points or lines of the projective plane to this system, uniquely determined by the original choice of the triangle of reference and the unit point.

triangular matrix   A square matrix whose elements on one side of the leading diagonal are zero

$$\begin{pmatrix} 4 & 2 & 3 \\ 0 & 6 & 7 \\ 0 & 0 & 1 \end{pmatrix} \quad \begin{pmatrix} 9 & 0 & 0 \\ 1 & 2 & 0 \\ 3 & 5 & 6 \end{pmatrix}$$

upper triangular   lower triangular

triangular numbers   Integers represented by a growing pattern of dots in a triangular array, so that each row has one more than its predecessor:

1   3   6   10

The nth triangular number is $\frac{1}{2}n(n+1)$.
See polygonal numbers, gnomon.

triangulation   A method of surveying in which visible landmarks are fixed by taking angular bearings from a fixed base line or known length. The first observation enables triangles to be constructed to scale having the base line as one side. Subsequent observations use these sides as secondary base lines, thus extending the survey as required. It is usual to complete the survey by returning to the base line, which should then correspond to the closing line of the last triangle. In practice triangulation has been largely replaced by radar ranging and aerial photogrammetry.

trichotomy law   Any law or rule that logically requires a set to be divided into three mutually exclusive and uniquely determined subsets.

● Given $x \in \mathbb{R}$ and any number $a \in \mathbb{R}$
$x > a$
$x = a$
$x < a$

trigonometric functions   *See* circular functions.

trigonometry   That branch of elementary mathematics that deals with the solution of triangles; that is, the determination of sides and angles not given, using the trigonometric ratios. It also covers the application of such calculations to practical problems in surveying, navigation and so on, but usually excludes analytic processes involving the circular (or trigonometric) functions.

trihedral   The angle formed by the intersection of three planes.

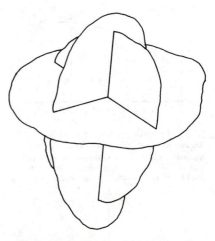

trilateral   The configuration formed by three lines passing through three non-collinear points taken in pairs. It is the Euclidean triangle with its sides produced indefinitely.

trilinear coordinates   A more general and non-metric form of cartesian coordinates in two dimensions.
See triangle of reference.

trillion In England a trillion is $10^{18} = (10^6 \times 10^6 \times 10^6)$ and in the USA and France is $10^{12} = (10^6 \times 10^3 \times 10^3)$. The index notation should be used in any mathematical context.

trinomial Any expression which is the sum of three terms, as $ax^2 + bx + c$ or any function of this, as $(ax^2 + bx + c)^4$.
See also binomial.

triple integral *See* multiple integral.

triple product *See* vector triple product.

trisection Cutting or dividing an angle, line or region into three equal parts. The problem of trisecting an angle using only a straight edge and compasses was handed down from the Greeks as one of the Delian problems. Many approximate constructions are suggested, but an exact trisection by these methods was proved impossible in 1845. The problem is solvable by the method of verging.

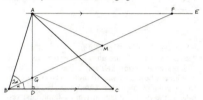

Consider $\triangle ABC$. Drop perpendicular AD to BC and draw AE parallel to BC. Construct the verging line FB through B which has intercept FG on AD and AE, so that FG = 2AB. By joining A to the midpoint of FG it can easily be shown that $\angle ABG = 2\angle GBC$, so that BF is the trisector.
Also the point G lies on a conchoid with B as origin and $a = BD$, $k = 2AB$, and can therefore be constructed. Other curves such as the limaçon, the quadratrix and the spiral of Archimedes also provide a solution.

trisectrix A special case of the type two limaçon given by $r = a(1 + 2\cos\theta)$.

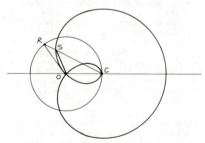

With the generating circle at pole O and centre C draw another circle centre O and radius O. With R any point on this circle draw radius RO and chord RC, cutting the limaçon at S. Then SO trisects angle ROC.
See also conchoid.

triskelion (Gk. having three legs). The configuration formed by three legs meeting a centre, found as a decoration on the bosses of Greek shields. The diagrammatic version is commonly used to illustrate a configuration that has rotational symmetry of order three but no other symmetries.

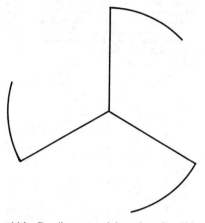

trivial Describes any result in mathematics which, though true, is obvious and sheds no light on the process or theorem investigated.

- The differential equation

$$a\frac{d^2x}{dt^2} + b\frac{dx}{dt} + cx = 0$$

has the trivial solution $x = 0$, but this does not help to find the general solution if it exists.

trochoid Generic name for the curtate and prolate cycloids.

true bearing A bearing, measured from 000° to 359°, or 001° to 360° clockwise from zero at true North. True North and South at any point on the earth's surface is given by the meridian through the point.
See magnetic bearing.

truncated 1. Applied to any numerical quantity from which one or more of the last significant digits are deleted.

$$12479 \rightarrow 12400$$

2. Used of any configuration having a solid apex, as a cone or pyramid, when this is cut off by a plane, which may or may not be parallel to the base.
3. A truncated series is one in which terms beyond a given term are ignored, as in series used for computing logarithms to a given accuracy.

truncation error 1. The error introduced by taking a finite approximation to an infinite series. Also called the error or remainder term. Truncation error or remainder terms occur in Taylor and Fourier series, Chebychev polynomials and other expressions.
2. Also used for the error in taking n terms from a terminating series of m terms ($n < m$).
3. The error made by ignoring all digits beyond the nth in a decimal fraction.

truth In mathematics a proposition is true if it follows logically from preliminary axioms and conditions, and does not at the same time yield contradictions. A statement is empirically true if it corresponds to the facts as agreed. Truth also emerges as a concept from the coherence of sets of statements into more general systems: the more consistent the systems the firmer is the guarantee of truth for any one set. Thus astrology does not cohere with general astronomy and physics and its statements have a lower probability of truth.

truth set   For a compound proposition P such as $(p \lor q) \& r$ the truth set of truth values assigned to the elements of P is the set of those sets of values for which P is true. Using the example

p	q	r	$(p \lor q) \& r$
T	T	T	T
T	T	F	F
T	F	T	T
T	F	F	F
F	T	T	T
F	T	F	F
F	F	T	F
F	F	F	F

Here the truth set is {TTT, TFT, FTT}.

truth table   Devised by Wittgenstein (1918) as a means of listing the 'truth possibilities' of elementary and compound propositions and defining their logical connectives, using T, F for true and false:

'And' (&) is defined as

p	q	$p \& q$
T	T	T
T	F	F
F	T	F
F	F	F

Truth tables are now generalized for the elements oᵢ a Boolean algebra, using 1, 0 for T, F, and may be extended to multi-term logic in the same way by defining additional truth values.

truth value   In two term logic the values TRUE or FALSE (or the corresponding numerical values 1, 0) which may be assigned to any proposition. Any other values such as UNDETERMINED or UNDECIDABLE can be added for multi-term logic and denoted as fractional values. In switching algebra the truth values correspond to ON–OFF, HIGH–LOW potential difference, or similar binary states.

t-test   A test which assumes that the test statistic is distributed as 'Student's' t under the null hypothesis H_0. An example is the one-sample test for reliability of a hypothetical mean μ_0 of a population, assumed to be normally distributed as $N(\mu, \sigma^2)$, but with μ and σ^2 unknown. The sample $\{X_1, X_2 \ldots X_n\}$ $(n \leqslant 30)$ is used to test $H_0 : \mu = \mu_0$ taking the sample mean $\bar{X}$ and sample variance S^2. The value of t is derived from

$$t = \frac{(\bar{X} - \mu_0)(\sqrt{n-1})}{S}$$

with $n-1$ degrees of freedom.

Tucker circle   If a triangle DEF is contained within and homothetic to a triangle ABC with respect to the Lemoine point L where the symmedians intersect, then its sides, if produced, meet those of ABC in six concyclic points lying on the Tucker circle.

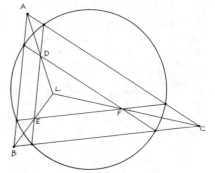

turbulence   *See* laminar flow.

Turing, A. M.   Cambridge mathematician (1912–1953), who described (1936) a theoretical 'Turing Machine' whose abstract structure must be common to all possible numerical computers. He also considered the question 'Can machines think' and proposed a critical test for comparing human thought with mechanical results.

Turing test   Name now given to the intelligence game proposed by Turing (1950). A man (A) and a woman (B) are in a room equipped with a teleprinter which is the only link with an investigator C in another room, who knows them only by labels X, Y but does not know whether X = A or X = B. C can address any questions whatsoever individually to X or Y who must reply to them, but in any form whatever, true or false. After each reply the person not addressed can make any comment whatever, true or false. The object of the game is for C to determine whether X = A or Y = A. For A it is to lead C to a false identification, and for B it is to assist C in a correct identification. The game is repeated, perhaps with different subjects as A or B until a significant ratio of correct to incorrect identifications is established. The human subject C is now replaced by a programmed computer C' and the experiment is re-run. If the number of correct identifications does not fall significantly, C' is held to be simulating the human intelligence of C. To date this has not been achieved.

turning point   A local maximum or minimum point on a curve, at which the ordinates cease increasing and begin decreasing or vice versa. For a continuous curve f at such a point the derivative $f' = 0$ and the second derivative $f'' \neq 0$. If the derivates do not exist the turning point can often be found by considering right and left derivatives

● $f : x \mapsto \sin x$ has a turning point at $\pi/2$
   since $f'(\pi/2) = 0$
   $f''(\pi/2) = 0$
   $|x|$ has a turning point at $x = 0$ at which point the right and left derivatives change sign.

To be distinguished from point of inflexion.

twelve coin problem The coins are identical in appearance but one is either heavier or lighter than the rest. What is the minimum number of weighing operations that will always identify the coin, given a balance without weights or calibrations?

twisted curve Any curve described in space of three dimensions and not lying in a plane. Thus a curve with parametric equations

$$x = at$$
$$y = at^2$$
$$z = at^3$$

is a twisted cubic, whose orthogonal projection on the xy plane is a parabola.

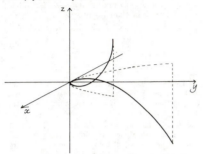

two-dimensional Used of anything that can be completely specified by sets of coordinate pairs.
- The phase space of a gas at constant temperature as given by $PV = $ constant.
The points in a plane specified by cartesian coordinates (x, y).

Any surface, such as that of a sphere, is intrinsically two-dimensional, and points on it can be specified by, say, latitude and longitude. The metric of such a surface gives an intrinsic non-Euclidean geometry. For the sphere this does of course correspond to a three-dimensional Euclidean geometry of the space in which it is imbedded, but completely non-Euclidean two-dimensional manifolds may be constructed.

two parameter function *See* parameter.

two point equation 1. The cartesian equation for a straight line passing through two given points $P = (x_1, y_1)$ $Q = (x_2, y_2)$ given by

$$y - y_1 = \frac{y_1 - y_2}{x_1 - x_2} (x - x_1)$$

2. A differential equation with boundary conditions specified at two points, such as the wave equation for a vibrating string whose two ends are fixed points (or nodes).

two tailed test *See* one-sided test.

two term logic The traditional logic in which propositions can take one and only one of two and only two truth values, true (T) or false (F). *See* three term logic.

type I error The rejection, as a result of a significance test, of a null hypothesis H_0 when H_0 is in fact true.
See also significance level.

type II error The result of a significance test failing to reject the null hypothesis H_0, when H_0 is in fact false.

U

unary operation An operation performed on one element only, as complementation, extracting a square root, cubing (but not exponentiation in general which requires a second specified element).

unbiased (*or* **unbiassed**) An adjective usually applied to estimators, when their expected values are equal to the quantities being estimated. Thus $\bar{X}$, the sample mean, is an unbiased estimator of the population mean μ, since $E(\bar{X}) = \mu$ if $\bar{X} = \frac{1}{n} \sum_{i=1}^{n} X_i$. Applied to hypothesis testing, it implies that the probability of rejecting the null hypothesis H_0 is never less when H_0 is untrue than when it is true.

unbiased estimate If $\hat{\theta}$ is an estimate of a quantity θ then, if the expected value of $\hat{\theta}$ is θ, that is $E(\hat{\theta}) = \theta$, we say that $\hat{\theta}$ is an unbiased estimator of θ. Thus a sample of size n can be taken from a population of mean μ and variance σ^2. The sample mean and variance are $\bar{X}$, s^2. Then $E(\bar{X}) = \mu$ so that $\bar{X}$ is an unbiased estimate of μ, but

$$E(s^2) = \frac{n-1}{n} \sigma^2$$

showing that s is a biased estimator of σ.

unbounded region The intuitive concept can be given a formal definition. An unbounded plane region (or region in $\mathbb{R}^2$) is one that cannot all be included in a circle $|z| = k$ ($z \in \mathbb{C}$) or $x^2 + y^2 = k^2$, however large a value is assigned to k. An example is the infinite strip between the lines $y = 0$ and $y = 1$.

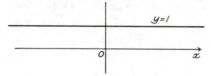

Similarly in $\mathbb{R}^3$ the region is defined relative to a sphere $x^2 + y^2 + z^2 = k^2$.

uncorrelated data Any sets of data for which the correlation is not significantly different from zero when taken in pairs, or for which there is no auto-correlation within the set.

undecidable Used of any proposition to which, in two term logic, a truth value cannot be assigned. This may be merely empirically undecidable, as at present with Goldbach's conjecture, or, more importantly, undecidable in principle, as shown by Gödel's theorem.

undefined terms Because it is not possible to define concepts such as point or line in terms of simpler concepts which are themselves defined, the ultimate objects of some branches of mathematics, particularly geometry, are now considered to be undefined. They are given the properties required of them and have relationships consistent with the axioms that state these properties.
See point, line, axiom.

undetermined coefficients By assuming that an expression to be found is of a form $At_1 + Bt_2 + Ct_3 + \ldots$ where t_1, t_2, t_3 are terms involving variables or functions and derivatives of variables, sets of simultaneous equations can be constructed for suitable t, and hence the expression is determined when the coefficients are found.

undetermined forms A term formerly used to describe such combinations of symbols as $0/0$, ∞/∞, $0°$, $0 \times \infty$ and so on. The modern treatment is to leave such expressions *undefined*. Thus a rational number is defined as a/b ($b \neq 0$), so that $0/b = 0$ but $0/0$ is not a member of the set $\mathbb{Q}$, and is undefined. Any functions which would take such undefined values are themselves undefined at such points or are assigned values only as a result of a limiting process.

● $f(x) = \dfrac{1}{x}$ if $x = 0$

$\dfrac{f(x+h) - f(x)}{h}$ if $h = 0$

undirected distance The numerical or scalar value of the distance between two points without reference to direction or bearing, the magnitude p of the position vector **p**.

undistributed middle *See* distribution. The name given in traditional logic to a fallacious argument in two term logic when the middle term is not distributed in at least one of the premises. Thus

$$\begin{array}{l} p \text{ is } q \\ r \text{ is } q \\ \hline p \text{ is } r \end{array}$$

hence

We are not told whether some q is not p and hence the middle term q is not distributed. The argument is not valid.

unfavourable game Any game of chance in which the rules are such that one player is always at a disadvantage.

unicursal network Also unicursive. A network which can be traced completely by going over each arc once and once only without lifting the tracing point from the configuration. The criterion for such a network is that there should be not more than two odd nodes. The tracing must either start or finish at any odd node that is present: if there are two it must start at one and finish at the other, since any intermediate node must have a path out corresponding to any path in and thus be of even order.

uniform circular motion That of a particle moving in a circle with constant angular velocity ω, or with uniform speed v around the circumference of a circle. Since the particle is changing direction constantly, it has an acceleration, given by $r\omega^2$ or v^2/r towards the centre.
See centrifugal force.

uniform convergence *See* Cauchy sequence. A sequence of functions defined on an interval I of the real numbers such that $x \in I$ converges uniformly on this interval (with respect to x) to a limiting function f if, for each arbitrarily small $\epsilon > 0$ there is an integer $N(\epsilon)$ which depends on ϵ but is independent of x. This integer $N(\epsilon)$ is such that for all $n \geqslant N(\epsilon)$ $|f_n(x) - f(x)| < \epsilon$

- Let $x \in \mathbb{R}$ and $f_n(x) = \dfrac{1}{n}\sin(nx + n)$ $n \in \mathbb{N}$

  Then, if $f(x) = 0$ and $N(\epsilon) = 1/\epsilon$

$$\left| \frac{1}{n}\sin(nx + n) - 0 \right| < \epsilon$$

If $f_n(x) = \dfrac{x}{n}$ and $f(x) = 0$, then $f_n(x) \to 0$ for all x as $n \to \infty$, but the criterion does not hold since $N(\epsilon)$ is dependent on x. One can always choose $x > n$ for all n. Hence $f_n(x)$ converges to zero but not uniformly.

uniform distribution 1. A continuous distribution over a finite range with constant density over that range. It follows that the probability of an observation falling in a specified interval lying within the range is proportional to the length of the interval. Also called rectangular distribution because its graphical representation is a rectangle.

- A measure of length x recorded to the nearest metre has a true value x_0 which will lie, with uniform probability 0.01 within any one centimetre of the interval $x \pm 0.5$ m.

2. A discrete distribution with a constant probability, such as the scores 1 to 6 from the throw of a die which occur with uniform probability 1/6.

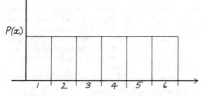

$P(x)$

unimodal Having a single mode or local maximum. Applies to probability density and distribution functions, histograms, frequency polygons and so on.

union The union A of two sets P, Q is the set containing those and only those elements which are contained in either P or Q or both. It is written $A = P \cup Q$ and can be represented by a Venn diagram.

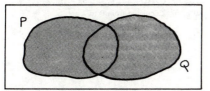

The concept can be extended to n sets $P, Q, R \dots$ and written $A = P \cup Q \cup R \cup \dots$
Also $P \cup Q \cup R \cup \dots = \{x : x \in P \vee x \in Q \vee x \in R \vee \dots\}$
See also intersection.

unique The word is always used literally in mathematics, never metaphorically.

- Each member of A has a unique image in B.
- The resolution of n into prime factors is unique.

unique factorization *See* prime factors.

uniqueness theorem A theorem that occurs, for example, in considering sets of equations, stating that if certain conditions are met there is a unique set of solutions. It is sometimes accompanied by an existence theorem that proves that solutions exist. Neither theorem need actually give solutions to the equations.

unit Any quantity or measure which models (or is arbitrarily given) the properties of unity. For Euclid a unit of length was any line interval used to express the measure of another line interval numerically as a multiple of this unit. See Appendix 1 for a discussion of units now used to measure physical quantities. There are many specific uses of the word. Thus a unit square is one of side unity, a unit matrix I is defined so that multiplication of a square matrix by I is equivalent to scalar multiplication by unity.

- $\begin{pmatrix} a & b \\ c & d \end{pmatrix} \begin{pmatrix} 1 & 0 \\ 0 & 1 \end{pmatrix} = \begin{pmatrix} a & b \\ c & d \end{pmatrix}$

The units of an integral domain are the divisors of its unit element.

- $1/(3 \pm \sqrt{2}) = 3 \mp \sqrt{2}$
  Thus $3 \pm \sqrt{2}$ are units of the domain $a + b\sqrt{2}$, $a, b \in \mathbb{Z}$

unitary group The group U_n, formed by the set of unitary $n \times n$ matrices under the operation matrix multiplication. The special unitary group SU_n is a subgroup of U_n consisting of those unitary matrices whose determinant is $+1$. The group SU_3 is of interest in that its properties seem to model the behaviour of certain subatomic particles.

unitary matrix A generalization, made by admitting complex elements, of the $n \times n$ orthogonal matrix A, for which $|A| = \pm 1$ and $A \times A^T = A^T \times A = I$. Then a matrix U is unitary if $U \times \bar{U}^T = \bar{U}^T \times U = I$ where $\bar{U}$ is the complex conjugate of U and $\bar{U}^T$ its transpose. The product of any two unitary matrices is a unitary matrix and, as with real orthogonal matrices, $|U| = \pm 1$.

- $\left| \begin{array}{cc} \dfrac{-1}{2}(2 + i) & \\ \dfrac{2 - i}{10} & 1 \end{array} \right| = -\dfrac{1}{2} - \dfrac{5}{10} = -1$

and the corresponding matrix is unitary.

unit ball The solid sphere corresponding to the unit spherical surface $x^2 + y^2 + z^2 = 1$. The ball $x^2 + y^2 + z^2 < 1$ is said to be open, the ball $x^2 + y^2 + z^2 \leqslant 1$ is closed.

unit circle A circle of radius unity, usually taken with its centre at the origin.

unit class A class or set containing only one element, also called a singleton.

unit disc The disc $x^2 + y^2 \leqslant 1$ having radius unity. It is open if $x^2 + y^2 < 1$, otherwise closed.
See also unit circle.

217

unit element Any member of a set which has the formal properties abstracted from the behaviour of unity in arithmetic. If A is a set and $*$ a binary operation, and if for all $x \in A$ there is an element $e \in A$ such that

$$x * e = e * x = x$$

then e is the unit element. For any one set the operation must be specified. The number 1 is a unit element of $\mathbb{N}$ only if $*$ is multiplication: the unit element for addition is zero.
See also element, annihilator.

unit sphere The surface represented in cartesian coordinates by $x^2 + y^2 + z^2 = 1$. It should be distinguished from the unit ball.

unit step function *See* Heaviside step function.

unit vector A vector of magnitude unity, that is, if $\mathbf{a} = (x, y)$, $x^2 + y^2 = 1$. The unit vector in the direction of $\mathbf{a}$ is sometimes written $\hat{\mathbf{a}}$. The unit vectors along the x, y, z axes are written $\mathbf{i}$, $\mathbf{j}$, $\mathbf{k}$ and can act as a basis for any vector of dimension 3. Then $\mathbf{i} = (1, 0, 0)$ $\mathbf{j} = (0, 1, 0)$ $\mathbf{k} = (0, 0, 1)$.

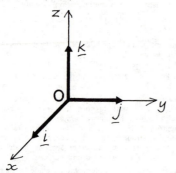

unity 1. Often synonymous with *unit element*, especially in USA.
2. The number 'one', in mathematics the real or complex number corresponding to cardinal one (the cardinal of a singleton set), often taken to be the number of elements in the set of all null sets (which cannot exist plurally since they would not be distinguishable).

The cube roots of unity are the values of x satisfying $x^3 = 1$ ($x \in \mathbb{C}$).

universal affirmative In traditional logic, the affirmation in the statement 'all p is q' as distinct from the particular affirmative 'some p is q'. The two affirmations are denoted by A, I, the first two vowels in Lat. *affirmo*, affirm.

$p \, A \, q$ or $P \, a \, Q$—all p is q.
$p \, I \, q$ or $P \, i \, Q$—some p is q.
See universal negative.

universal negative The negation in the statement 'no p is q' as distinct from the particular negative of 'some p is not q'. The subject p in the first case is said to be distributed, in the second undistributed. The two negations are denoted by E and O in traditional logic, from the vowels of 'nEgO', I deny.

$p \, E \, q$ or $p \, e \, q$—no p is q.
$p \, O \, q$ or $p \, o \, q$—some p is not q.

universal set Also universe of discourse. The totality of entities or elements actually under consideration, the union of all sets which satisfy a particular defining criterion.

● Sets of isosceles triangles form subsets of the universal set of all triangles if defined as triangles but of the universal set of polygons if defined as polygons.

unweighted index Also called simple index.
See weighted index.

upper bound A number which may be assigned to any sequence, whether or not it is convergent. It is any number B with the property that any number $n > B$ is greater than all (or all but a finite number) of the terms of the sequence. Lower bound is similarly defined.

$$\text{For } 1, \tfrac{1}{2}, \tfrac{1}{3}, \tfrac{1}{4} \ldots \tfrac{1}{n} \text{ any number } B \geqslant 1$$

is an upper bound.
See also least upper bound.

upper limit *See* limit, limits of integration.

upper Riemann sum *See* Riemann sum.

urn model A traditional and very convenient model for discussing discrete probabilities. An urn contains balls of various colours in known or unknown proportions, and it is required to determine, for example, the probability of selecting a ball of any one colour, or the probability that the colours are present in a given ratio.
The reference is to the 'urn of fate' as in Horace III, i
omne capax movet urna nomen
The capacious urn keeps all names in motion.
This in turn is a reference to Athenian elections conducted by putting black or white beans in urns.

useful limits Many mathematical models involve integrals taken with limits at infinity. In practice results to the required number of significant figures can be obtained from smaller numerical limits. The areas under the normal curve, for example are usually only calculated from 0 to 4.

V

valid Used of a proposition or proof that is sound, defensible and well grounded on axioms, accepted laws or initial suppositions.

vanish A variable or other quantity is said to vanish when it becomes equal to zero. This is usually a criterion for some required property, and must be distinguished from 'tend to zero'.

● Two vector are at right angles if their scalar product vanishes.

vanishing point The convergent point of 'vanishing' lines. A convention of perspective drawing developed during the Renaissance for representing parallel lines running away from an observer. The drawing then reproduces the angles subtended at the eye by solid objects in the field of view.

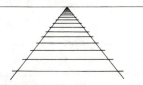

Ruskin demonstrated that the convention was not optically exact.

variable A general purpose term in mathematics for an entity which can take various values in any particular context. The domain of the variable may be limited to a particular set of numbers or algebraic entities. In the same context a constant is a quantity which is restricted to a single value in any one expression. Thus in the real equation $ax + b = 0$, a and b are given as constants and x, the variable, is any number from the set $\mathbb{R}$ which in the context makes the statement true. If one variable is expressed in terms of another, as in $y = x^2$, the one whose values may be assigned at will is the independent variable, the other is dependent.

variable of integration The variable (or variables) occurring in an integral, the quantities that take on all the values in the domain of the integration.

● x in $\displaystyle\int_0^1 \frac{dx}{\sqrt{(1 - x^2)}}$

r, θ in $\displaystyle\int_{\theta=0}^{2\pi} \int_{r=0}^{a} r e^{-r^2}\, dr\, d\theta$

In an indefinite integral such as $\int x^n\, dx$ the symbol x is not a true but a dummy variable, used for convenience in specifying the rule for integration of powers irrespective of the domain.

variance For a population $x_1, x_2 \ldots x_n$ of size N, the variance is the mean square of the deviations of x_i from the population mean μ and is denoted by σ^2. For any random variable, or equivalently for its probability distribution, the variance is defined as the expectation of $(x - \mu)^2$, where μ is the expected value $E(x)$ of x. It is denoted σ^2, where

$$\sigma^2 = E[(X - \mu)^2]$$

This corresponds to the first definition for a discrete population.
See also sample variance.

variate A term frequently used for a random variable or a quantity subject to random influences, and therefore playing the same part in statistics or probability theory as the word variable in algebra or analysis.
See also bivariate distribution.

variation 1. *See* Lagrange notation.
2. The difference of direction between true and magnetic north at any point on the earth's surface at a given date. Also called declination.
See also deviation.

vector 1. Originally introduced as a directed line segment to represent displacement.

For example, the displacement of a force moving from O to P would be represented by $\overrightarrow{OP}$. That is, the operation 'carries' the force from O to P, and hence $\overrightarrow{OP}$ was called a vector (Lat. *carrier*) by Hamilton (1853). $\overrightarrow{OP}$ represents the displacement of the force in magnitude and direction, but its actual position in space is not specified, so that all vector representations parallel to and equal to $\overrightarrow{OP}$ are equivalent. Vectors can be multiplied by scalars and combined by the parallelogram law.
2. The term applied to physical quantities such as force, velocity, momentum, or spin that have a magnitude associated with a direction, all of which are called vector quantities.
3. A local or bound vector is one beginning or ending at a fixed point in space, for example in describing a force acting at that point.
4. Formal definition. An ordered set of elements $\mathbf{u} = (x_1, x_2, x_3, \ldots x_n)$ which obeys the laws of vector algebra. The n-value is called the dimension of the vector, and the sum of two vectors only exists if they have the same dimensions.
For $n = 2$ or $n = 3$ vectors may be represented by directed line segments, denoted $\overrightarrow{OP}$, $\underline{OP}$, $\mathbf{OP}$, $\bar{r}$ or $\underline{r}$, but for vectors in general most texts now use bold roman in lower case or sometimes upper case, $\mathbf{v}$ or $\mathbf{V}$.

vector addition *See* vector algebra.

vector algebra A set of rules by which vectors may be combined and operated on, chosen so that the parallelogram rule for vectors of dimension 2 or 3 holds good, as required for applications in physics, but which are otherwise quite general. There are two defined operations:
1. Vector addition. If $\mathbf{A} = (a_1, a_2, a_3, \ldots)$ and $\mathbf{B} = (b_1, b_2, b_3, \ldots)$

$$\mathbf{A} + \mathbf{B} = (a_1 + b_1), (a_2 + b_3) \ldots$$

2. Scalar multiplication. If $\mathbf{A} = (a_1, a_2, a_3, \ldots)$ and λ is a real scalar

$$\lambda\mathbf{A} = (\lambda a_1, \lambda a_2, \lambda a_3, \ldots)$$

The processes are accordingly commutative and associative, while scalar multiplication distributes over addition. Since the set of vectors contains the zero vector $\mathbf{O} = (0, 0, 0 \ldots)$ and since $\mathbf{A} + \lambda\mathbf{A} = \mathbf{A} + (-\mathbf{A}) = 0$ if $\lambda = -1$, the set under these operations is seen to be a commutative additive group (or module) with multiplication by a scalar. Note that multiplication

and division of vectors are not generally defined, but various forms of products can be constructed under specific conditions.
See also scalar product, triple product, vector product, quaternions.

vector analysis The application of the methods of analysis to vectors using limiting values, derivatives, integrals, rates of change and so on in ways suitably formulated to handle vector variables. The term is often loosely used for vector algebra or the study of vectors generally.

vector difference If two vectors **u**, **v** are given by their components as

$$\mathbf{u} = (a_1, a_2, a_3 \ldots)$$
$$\mathbf{v} = (b_1, b_2, b_3 \ldots)$$

then their difference is defined as $\mathbf{u} + (-\mathbf{v})$ where $-\mathbf{v} = (-b_1, -b_2, -b_3 \ldots)$ so that $\mathbf{u} - \mathbf{v} = (a_1 - b_1)$, $(a_2 - b_2)$, $(a_3 - b_3) \ldots$ If vectors in two dimensions are represented by $\mathbf{u} = OA$, $\mathbf{v} = OB$ their difference is given by the parallelogram law for addition, as $\mathbf{u} - \mathbf{v} = OA + OB'$ where $OB' = -OB$. This difference is equal in magnitude to the vector closing the triangle AOB and in the direction from B to A. The operation is not associative for more than two vectors.

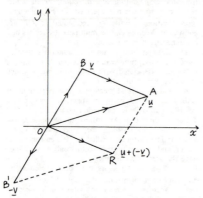

vector field A region of space at every point of which a vector is defined; for example, the wind velocity at each point in the atmosphere or the magnetic field strength over any region. It is associated with a scalar field that gives the magnitudes of the quantities concerned at each point. A directional field arising from a differential equation is a vector field.

vector geometry The geometric properties of configurations, normally in Euclidean metric geometry, established by vector methods. These are less appropriate for plane geometry, but for configurations in three dimensions they offer elegant and compact treatment.

vectorial angle The angle made by a radius vector with its base line. In the theory of alternating currents or other systems in simple harmonic motions it is equivalent to the phase angle.

vector methods The treatment of any topic in pure or applied mathematics using vector algebra or vector analysis as the theoretical tool. The power of the

method lies in the fact that a single vector symbol **a** of dimension n contains n independent variables. For many practical applications $n = 2$ or 3, but the algebra and analysis is valid for all n.

vector operator *See* del.

vector polygon A closed polygon whose sides represent a set of two dimensional vectors whose sum is zero. In particular the polygon of forces represents a system of forces in equilibrium.

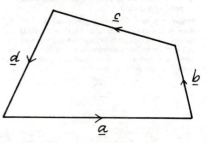

vector product A function of two vectors in two or three dimensions, defined specifically to extend vector methods to physical concepts such as the moment of a force. Also called the cross product, although this term is ambiguous out of context. For vectors **a**, **b** the vector product $\mathbf{a} \times \mathbf{b} = ab \sin\theta \,\hat{\mathbf{n}}$ where a, b are the scalar magnitudes, θ is the angle between them, and $\hat{\mathbf{n}}$ is a unit vector at right angles to the plane of **a**, **b**, in the direction of motion of a right-handed screw turning from direction **a** to direction **b**. It follows at once that $\mathbf{a} \times \mathbf{b} = -\mathbf{b} \times \mathbf{a}$ and the process is neither commutative nor associative.
The results for the base vectors **i**, **j**, **k** are important
$$\mathbf{i} \times \mathbf{i} = \mathbf{j} \times \mathbf{j} = \mathbf{k} \times \mathbf{k} = 0$$
$$\mathbf{i} \times \mathbf{j} = -\mathbf{j} \times \mathbf{i} = \mathbf{k}, \mathbf{j} \times \mathbf{k} = -\mathbf{k} \times \mathbf{j} = \mathbf{i}, \mathbf{k} \times \mathbf{i} = -\mathbf{i} \times \mathbf{k} = \mathbf{j}$$
For vectors expressed in cartesian form as $\mathbf{a} = (a_1, a_2, a_3)$ $\mathbf{b} = (b_1, b_2, b_3)$ a vector product can also be written

$$\mathbf{a} \times \mathbf{b} = \begin{vmatrix} \mathbf{i} & \mathbf{j} & \mathbf{k} \\ a_1 & a_2 & a_3 \\ b_1 & b_2 & b_3 \end{vmatrix}$$

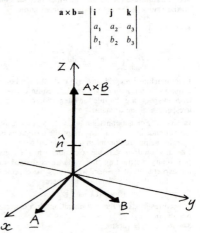

vector space Any set of elements whatsoever which may be operated on by the two rules of vector algebra, given that the set is closed to the operations. It is a very general concept derived from the properties of sets of vectors, and allows new elements of the space to be generated as linear combinations of the elements in a subset of the space chosen as a base vector. The formal definition of a vector space generalizes the rules for vector algebra, replacing vector addition by any additive process, and the set of real scalars by any field $F = [\{a, b, \ldots\}, +, .]$.

Then a set $V = \{u, v, w \ldots\}$ over the field F is a vector space if F is an abelian additive group $(V, +)$ and for all a, $b \in F$ and all u, $v \in V$, the following five laws hold

(i) $au \in V$
(ii) $a(u + v) = au + av$
(iii) $(a + b)u = au + bu$
(iv) $(ab)u = a(bu)$
(v) $1u = u$

Note that the symbol $+$ is any additive process in (ii) but scalar addition in (iii). The elements $u, v, w \ldots$ are called vectors, but now the space includes polynomials, matrices of the same order and many other mathematical entities.

vector triple product This is the product $a \times (b \times c)$ in this order and by definition associated as shown by the brackets, using one of the definitions given for vector product twice. The expressions reduce to $a \times (b \times c) = (a.c)b - (a.b)c$, where the dot represents formation of scalar product. The product is neither commutative nor associative with more than three vectors. It represents a vector in the same plane as b and c.

vel Latin. The inclusive disjunction, for which the English 'or' is ambiguous, although the symbol is usually read this way. For statements p, q it is denoted by $p \vee q$ and means *either p or both*. If the word OR is used it is equivalent to *vel*, not *aut*, which is then denoted by XOR. OR can be defined by the truth table

p	q	$p \vee q$
T	T	T
T	F	T
F	T	T
F	F	F

See aut.

velocity Uniform velocity is the ratio between distance travelled in a given direction and time taken, the rate at which total distance increases per unit of time. For non-uniform linear motion where $s = f(t)$ velocity is given by $f'(t)$ or $\dfrac{ds}{dt}$, often written as $\dot{s}$. For general motion in a plane, if the displacement vector is $r = f(t)$, $g(t)$ where f and g are functions of time, the velocity at time t is given by $\dot{r} = f'(t)$, $g'(t)$. A similar expression describes movement in three dimensions. In ordinary use the word velocity is not necessarily associated with a direction, and is then equivalent to *speed*, the corresponding scalar.

velocity polygon A special case of the vector polygon where the vectors represent velocities. Also triangle of velocities.

Venn diagram Introduced by the logician John Venn (1834–1883) to illustrate universal propositions by modified Euler's circles. The diagram consists of two empty intersecting circles, one of which contains the subject S of the proposition, the other the predicate P. Venn then shaded out the region which does not apply.

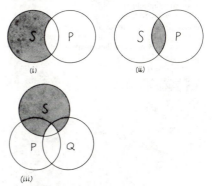

(i)   (ii)

(iii)

Thus (i) represents All S is P; (ii) represents No S is P; (iii) represents All S is P and Q. The shaded parts are ignored in reading the diagrams. The diagrams have been adapted (usually without reference to their original form) to illustrate set relationships. Here the circles are taken to enclose the sets and need not intersect. Any intersecting arcs do in fact partition the sets. The shading is then used to draw attention to the subsets involved.

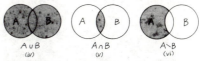

$A \cup B$ $A \cap B$ $A \setminus B$
(iv)   (v)   (vi)

Note particularly the difference between the set diagram (v) and the true Venn diagram (ii).

verging Translates the Gk. *neuseis*, a type of geometric problem discussed by Apollonius and later by Archimedes, in which a line AP, on which two other fixed lines intercept a given length BC = d, has to be constructed so that if produced it passes through a given point P.

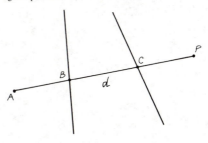

The construction is not possible by straight edge and compasses.
See trisection and conchoid.

versine   The function $(1 - \cos\theta)$. *See* haversine.

vertical   Usually with reference to the figure of the earth, assumed spherical, and derived from Lat. *vertex*, the pole of the heavens. A direction normal to the tangent plane (plane of the horizon) at any point, and hence leading from the earth's centre towards the zenith. In ordinary speech the word is synonymous with upright.
See perpendicular.

vicious circle   A term for any argument whose conclusion is assumed to be true when formulating the premises. It is claimed that many traditional arguments are in fact circular.

> All men are mortal.
> Socrates was a man.
> Therefore Socrates was mortal.

Here it can be argued that the truth of the major premise depends on the fact that Socrates *was* mortal: had he proved immortal the premise would be false.

virtual force   One which appears as the reaction to an actual force, defined as that which accelerates a moving body along or away from the path it would naturally follow. Centrifugal and Coriolis forces are examples of virtual forces. These appear as the reactions to forces pulling a body in towards a centre or keeping it on a path that requires a change of angular momentum. Gravity is an actual force postulated by Newton, but a virtual force as formulated in General Relativity.

volume   A measure of the three-dimensional space occupied by a geometrical configuration or a material body. The unit of volume is the unit cube, so that its dimensions are L^3.

volume of revolution   *See* solid of revolution.

W

Wallis' formula   An early precalculus example of non-rigorous integration. In modern notation Wallis evaluated

$$I = \int_0^1 (x - x^2)^n \, dx$$

for several positive integral values of n and concluded (using incomplete induction from his set of determined values) that

$$I = \frac{(n!)^2}{(2n+1)!}$$

He then assumed that his formula held good for fractional values of n, and hence obtained the area of a quadrant of the circle $x^2 + y^2 = 1$, given by

$$\frac{\pi}{4} = \int_0^1 (1 - x^2)^{1/2} \, dx$$

as

$$\frac{\pi}{4} = \frac{(\frac{1}{2}!)^2}{2!}$$

From this, by trial interpolations between $n=0$ and $n=1$, he arrived at the Wallis product for π. It is interesting to note that the formula gives $\frac{1}{2}! = \sqrt{\pi}/2$, which agrees with the gamma function value.

Wallis' product   The formula

$$\frac{\pi}{2} = \frac{2.2.4.4.6.6.\dots}{1.1.3.3.5.5.7.7.\dots}$$

derived by Wallis in his early attempt to achieve the quadrature of the circle $x^2 + y^2 = 1$, made before the binomial theorem had established an expansion for $(1 - x^2)^{1/2}$. The value of π can now be established by evaluating

$$\int_0^{\pi/2} \sin^n x \, dx$$

but it was obtained by Wallis by algebraic manipulation and inductive assumptions.

wallpaper patterns   The discussion of strip patterns extended to those which can cover a plane as on wallpaper, in which the translations can take place in two non-parallel directions until the plane surface is covered in a grid or lattice of parallelograms. When for example the parallelogram is a rhombus with one angle $60°$ the lattice has six-fold or hexagonal symmetry about each lattice point. Within each lattice region a motif may be constructed whose symmetries cannot go beyond those of the lattice. There are seventeen possibilities.

Waring's problem   The theorem, proposed conjecturally by Waring (1734–1798) that any integer can be expressed as the sum of not more than nine cubes.

Watt, James   Scottish engineer (1736–1789), originally a repairer of mathematical instruments. He invented the external condenser for steam engines, but the device of greatest interest to mathematics was his centrifugal governor which gave one of the first uses of negative feedback. He also, albeit vainly, advocated the adoption of the metric system in an attempt to standardize engineering measurements.

wave equation   The differential equation describing motion in which a displacement from an equilibrium position is subject to a restoring force proportional to the displacement, or any other change of physical state subject to a similar law. The solution of this equation shows that the displacement or other physical change of state is given by a periodic function in the general form of a sine curve. For a displacement e occurring at a distance x from an origin at time t (as in a long stretched string plucked at a given point) the equation is

$$\frac{\partial^2 e}{\partial x^2} = \frac{1}{c^2} \frac{\partial^2 e}{\partial t^2}$$

In this equation c is the velocity with which the disturbance passes through the system. It corresponds to the speed of sound in air or of electromagnetic waves in space. In general, the wave equation enables the state of a system subject to wave motion to be described at any required position or time.

wave mechanics   A branch of applied mathematics in atomic and nuclear physics which uses a wave equation in a quantity ψ to discuss the position and motion of electrons and other sub-atomic particles. The quantity ψ is taken as a probability distribution and is not a variable taking definite values as in ordinary particle mechanics.

wave motion   For a wave on the surface of water the physical displacement of any small element of fluid approximates to simple harmonic motion. By analogy, any periodic changes of state propagated through a system as a function of time are referred to as 'waves'. The function describing them is either sinusoidal or can be compounded of sinusoidal expressions. A non-periodic pulse or 'soliton' is also regarded as a wave. Typical wave representations are shown in the diagrams.

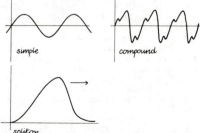

simple   *compound*

soliton

See Fourier series, harmonic analysis.

weak As descriptions of theorems 'weak' and 'strong' have become standard terms. A weak theorem is usually the form most easily proved, but allows anomalous results or indeterminate examples. The corresponding strong theorem will include conditions that do not permit such results.
See strong law of large numbers, weak law of large numbers.

weak law of large numbers This states that the occurrence ratio r of any given event in a large number n of events, is not likely to differ from the probability p of that event. This does not exclude the possibility that large deviations may in fact occur.
See strong law of large numbers.

Weierstrass, K. W. T. German mathematician (1815–1897). Noted in his day as an inspiring teacher at university levels. He developed a theory of complex functions using power series.

weight Although properly defined as the apparent force acting on a massive body in a gravitational field, such as that of the earth or moon, the word is commonly used as a synonym for mass. This use will certainly persist, but should be avoided in the context of quantitative science.

weighted index A simple aggregate index number (as in average price index) does not take into account the relative importance of the component items chosen to make up the index, or the different quantities purchased over each period. When these are taken into account the index is said to be weighted.

weighted mean If there are n numerical quantities $\{a, \dots a_n\}$ each associated with n weightings $\{w, \dots w_n\}$ the weighted mean is given by

$$\frac{\sum_{i=1}^{n} (w_i\, a_i)}{\sum_{i=1}^{n} (a_i)}$$

The arithmetic mean is the special case where all weightings are equal and non-zero. Elements having greater weightings have a greater influence on the mean. The weightings may be arbitrarily assigned, but usually depend on related quantities such as relative frequency or cost price.

well ordered Describes an ordered set in which every possible subset contains a least element. The natural numbers ordered by the relation 'less than' are well ordered, e.g., the subset P given by $1 < P < 10$ has the least element 2. The rational numbers ordered by magnitude are not, since the set $1 < Q < 2$ has no least member.

well ordering theorem The theorem that every set can be given an ordering relation in which it is well ordered. For rational numbers a suitable ordering is given by the Farey sequence.

Wessel, Caspar Norwegian mathematician (1745–1818) whose work, published by the Danish Royal Academy in 1798, gave the first account of complex numbers as directed line segments in a plane. The account was not noticed until it appeared in a later French translation.
See also Argand, Gauss.

Whitehead, A. N. English logician and philosopher (1861–1947) associated with Bertrand Russell in the production of *Principia Mathematica*.

whole number Usually taken as synonymous either with natural numbers or with positive integers. There is no general agreement on the inclusion of zero as a whole number.

width Not a defined term in mathematics. It is taken to be the length of the shorter of the two pairs of sides that define a rectangle, and hence is used for the corresponding dimension of any irregular figure that could be enclosed within a rectangle.

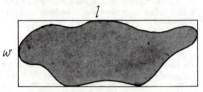

The other dimension is called the length. Width is also used interchangeably with length in discussing intervals on the real number line: one can speak of an interval of length Δx or width Δx.

Wilcoxon rank sum test An earlier (1945) version of the Mann–Whitney test. also called the Wilcoxon matched pairs signed ranks test, since it tests median differences from matched pairs of results from independent trials.

Wilson's theorem For any prime P the continued product $1.2.3\dots (p-1) \equiv -1 \pmod p$.

winding number If a closed loop is formed in a plane having a discontinuity or disconnection the term describes the number of times the loop goes round the discontinuity. Loops of different winding numbers cannot be homotopic.

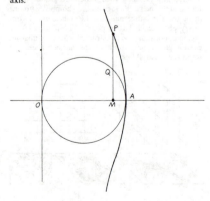

witch of Agnesi Discussed by Agnesi but known much earlier and probably discovered by Fermat. The curve $xy^2 = 4a^2(2a - x)$. It can be constructed by drawing ordinates PQM cutting the semicircle OA on the x axis at Q. The curve is the locus of P if $PQ/QM = OA/OM$ and is symmetric about the x axis.

Wittgenstein, L. Austrian born but naturalized British philosopher (1889–1951), who studied and was influenced by Frege and *Principia Mathematica*. In *Remarks on the Foundation of Mathematics* (1937–1944) he discussed the relation between mathematics and knowledge generally. His wider interests lay outside mathematics and have greatly influenced modern thought.

work 1. If a constant force P in a direction OA acts on a particle and causes it to move a distance d in a direction OB, then the work done is defined as

$$W = Pd\cos\alpha$$

where $AOB = \alpha$.

2. If a constant force $\mathbf{p}$ moves a particle through a distance $\mathbf{d}$, the work done is the scalar product $\mathbf{p}.\mathbf{d}$.

3. If a variable force $P(x)$ acts through an interval $b - a$ along the axis of OX, the work done is defined as

$$W = \int_a^b P(x)\,dx$$

4. If the point of application of the force does not move in a straight line, the expression becomes

$$W = \int_C \mathbf{P}.d\mathbf{r}$$

This is the work done by a force field P on a particle whose position vector is $\mathbf{r}$ as it moves along a specified curve C. The definitions are equivalent within their contexts.

world vector A term sometimes used for a four-dimensional vector giving space and time coordinates, constructed on the analogy of a three-dimensional vector and used in discussing the propagation of light. The set $\mathbf{i}$, $\mathbf{j}$, $\mathbf{k}$ is generalized by writing $\mathbf{i}_1$, $\mathbf{i}_2$, $\mathbf{i}_3$, $\mathbf{i}_4$ the coordinates x, y, z, t by writing x_1, x_2, x_3, x_4. The vector then becomes

$$\mathbf{W} = (x_1\mathbf{i}_1 + x_2\mathbf{i}_2 + x_3\mathbf{i}_3 + x_4\mathbf{i}_4)$$

wrench A system of forces, to which any other system can be reduced, consisting of a couple and a force along or parallel to the axis of the couple. The ratio of the moment of the couple and the magnitude of the force is called the pitch of the wrench. A screw exerts a wrench when rotated.

Wronskian A matrix whose elements are functions and their derivatives. Thus if three functions of x are u, v, w the Wronskian is:

$$W = \begin{vmatrix} u & v & w \\ \dfrac{du}{dx} & \dfrac{dv}{dx} & \dfrac{dw}{dx} \\ \dfrac{d^2u}{dx^2} & \dfrac{d^2v}{dx^2} & \dfrac{d^2w}{dx^2} \end{vmatrix}$$

If the determinant $|W| = 0$ the functions u, v, w are linearly dependent, that is, there are constants l, m, n not all zero such that $lu + mv + nw = 0$.

Yates' correction This is a correction for continuity when using the χ^2 test for a 2×2 contingency table which then has only one degree of freedom. It modifies the test statistic to

$$\chi^2 = \sum_{i=1}^{2} \frac{(|O_i - E_i| - \frac{1}{2})^2}{E_i}$$

Without this correction the chi-square value would be higher and lead to incorrect rejection of the null hypothesis.

Young's modulus *See* elasticity.

Z

Zeeman machine A simple device due to Zeeman to illustrate 'catastrophe' effects. A rigid disc D otherwise free to rotate is constrained by an elastic cord PQ, the other end R of which can be moved freely over the region S in the plane of the disc.

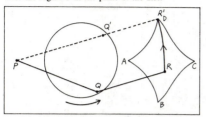

As R is moved it will be seen that there is a region (approximately shown by $ABCD$) that defines a sudden change from one configuration to another. Thus if R is moved along the arc shown the point Q moves in the direction shown by the arrow, but when R is at R' on the catastrophe boundary AD, Q jumps to a position near Q. The actual movement (like most effects described by the catastrophe curves and surfaces) is of course continuous, but there is a good approximate correspondence.
See catastrophe.

zenith A direction or notional point immediately overhead (heavily corrupted from the Arabic phrase *samt-ar-rās*, way of the head). It is defined for any point on the earth's surface by producing the line from the centre of the earth passing through that point. The nadir is the reciprocal direction, and is towards a point immediately below. The line defining zenith and nadir is normal to the horizon plane.
See also vertical.

Zeno Greek philosopher (fl. 500 B.C.). He propounded a number of paradoxes. The most famous of these, 'Achilles and the Tortoise', demonstrated that a fast runner could not overtake a slower ahead of him, because having reached the point where the tortoise was when the race began, Achilles had still to run the finite distance by which the slower had advanced, and so on indefinitely. A second, the 'Arrow', argued that at any one instant the tip of the arrow occupies a point in space, but since a multiplicity of instants is still only one instant, the arrow is not moving. Since the reasoning contradicts experience it is clearly fallacious, but it is not easy to explain, by verbal discussion, how this arises. Refer Aristotle, *Physics, Book VI* for a full account.

zero 1. The cardinal number of the empty or null set, denoted 0.

2. The placeholder 0 in column notation, indicating an empty column, and represented as on a bead abacus by leaving the wire empty.
3. The additive identity I such that $a+I=I+a=a$ where a is a number. Early mathematics had no symbol corresponding to zero. It was introduced into Europe by the Arabs from Indian sources, originally as a place holder (Arabic *sifr*, empty, hence 'cipher'). Recognition of zero as a number was a major step in the development of mathematics, but since it cannot be the denominator of a rational number or function it is often necessary to exclude or delete it from $\mathbb{N}$ and $\mathbb{Z}$.

zero element *See* annihilator.

zero matrix *See* null matrix.

zeros of a function The values of the domain of a function which are mapped on to zero or, less formally, the points at which the value of a function is zero.

Zeros of $f:x \mapsto x^2+5x+6$ are $-2, -3$
Zeros of $f:x \mapsto \sin x$ are $n\pi$ $(n=0, \pm 1, \pm 2 \ldots)$

zero vector The zero vector of order n has all elements zero, and is denoted **0**.

$$\mathbf{0} = (0, 0, 0, \ldots)$$

Also called null vector. The zero vector must be expanded formally to the required order to enable it to be added to other vectors.

zeta function Due to Riemann, and given by

$$\zeta(x) = \frac{1}{1^x} + \frac{1}{2^x} + \frac{1}{3^x} + \cdots$$

The series converges if $x > 1$. It holds good for complex exponents, and can be related to the gamma function $\Gamma(x)$.

zone That part of a sphere enclosed between two parallel planes which cut its surface, and by analogy a similar region on any surface closed between the planes.

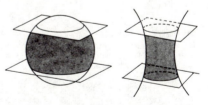

z score *See* standard normal distribution, normal deviation.

Appendix 1 Système International d'Unités (SI)

The compilers of this dictionary take the view that, apart from the nautical mile which directly relates distances on the earth's surface to differences in latitude and longitude, and a few special physical units such as the charge of an electron, no units of measure should be introduced into mathematics courses apart from the present International System agreed at a conference of nations in 1960. The history of measure and the many attempts to standardize units is of great interest, but the difficulties of transition still met in Great Britain are, we think, best furthered by resolute adherence to the policy now firmly established in schools and among examination boards.

The fundamental units

The agreed system is based on seven fundamental units, which are here given informally.

1. Metre. The unit of length or distance, defined in terms of the wave length of radiation emitted by the krypton-86 atom.
2. Kilogram(me). The unit of mass, given by the international platinum-iridium prototype deposited at Sèvres. Likely to be redefined as an atom count.
3. Second. The unit of time, defined in terms of the period of radiation emitted by the caesium-133 atom.
4. Ampere (no *grave* accent). The unit of electric current, defined in terms of the force between two parallel conductors carrying the current.
4. Kelvin. The unit of temperature, given as a fraction, actually 1/273.16 of the interval between absolute zero and the triple point of water (at which water, water vapour and ice are in equilibrium).
5. Candela. The unit of light intensity, defined in terms of the light emitted by molten platinum at its solidification point.
6. Mole. The unit of substance, given in terms of a count of elementary particles — atoms, molecules, etc., as specified — compared with the atoms in 0.012 Kg of carbon-12.

The symbols

The agreed names and symbols for the units are not contractions. They are written without full stops or indications of plurality such as -s.

metre	m
kilogramme	kg
second	s
ampere	A
kelvin	K (not °K)
candela	cd
mole	mol

The supplementary and customary units

The system adds the supplementary units of plane angle, the radian (rad), and solid angle, the steradian (sr), as given in the dictionary entries. It also admits the 'customary' units of days, hours, weeks, etc., the Celsius thermometer scale (°C) which takes the triple point of water as 0°C, and the litre (*l*) as a measure of capacity.

The prefixes

The agreed prefixes with their symbols for fractions or multiples of the units are as follows:

10^{-1}	(deci)	(d)
10^{-2}	(centi)	(c)
10^{-3}	milli	m
10^{-6}	micro	μ
10^{-9}	nano	n
10^{-12}	pico	p
10^{-15}	femato	f
10^{-18}	atto	a
10	(deka)	(da)
10^{2}	(hecto)	(h)
10^{3}	kilo	k
10^{6}	mega	M
10^{9}	giga	G
10^{12}	tera	T

The kilogram(me) now replaces the original metric gram(me) as the fundamental unit. The four prefixes in brackets are 'customary' and used for convenience only.

The derived units

All other units of measure are derived by compounding the fundamental units to form a coherent system; one, that is, without numerical factors. The list of prefixes is also applied to the derived units, many of which have agreed names and symbols. Units which may appear in mathematics courses are

area	metre squared	m^2
volume	metre cubed	m^3
density	kilogram per metre cubed	$kg\,m^{-3}$
velocity	metre per second	ms^{-1}
acceleration	metre per second squared	ms^{-2}
force	newton (N)	$kg\,ms^{-2}$
momentum	kilogram metre per second	$kg\,ms^{-1}$
energy	joule (J)	$kg\,m^2\,s^{-2}$
power	watt (W)	Js^{-1}
frequency	hertz (Hz)	s^{-1}
pressure/tension	pascal (Pa)	Nm^{-2}
impulse	newton second	Ns
angular velocity	radian per second	$rad\,s^{-1}$
action	joule second	Js

Forms such as m/s² instead of ms⁻² are often used but are not recommended. Older names are also found, such as micron for micrometre, metric tonne for megagramme, Ångstrom (Å) or 'tenth metre' for 10^{-10} m. Many of these, together with the hectare (ha) for $10\,000\,m^2$, are convenient and will continue in general use.

SI and dimensions

The use of dimensional analysis (*see* entry for dimension) is now exactly equivalent to writing derived units in full, the symbols **M**, **L**, **T** now corresponding to the symbols kg, m and s of SI. Thus power is analysed dimensionally as LM^2T^{-2} and the agreed unit is the watt defined in full as $kg\,m^2\,s^{-2}$. This equivalence is perfectly general and may be applied to all derived units of the system.

Appendix 2   The Symbols of Mathematics

A symbol in mathematics can stand for a single word, a phrase, a sentence or a sequence of sentences describing an operation or an algorithm. Any properly formed string of symbols reads as grammatical prose, containing words whose meanings are taken to be known in the context. Thus

$$\int_0^\pi \sin\theta\,d\theta = 2$$

reads 'the integral of sine *theta* with respect to *theta*, taken between the limits *pi* and zero, is numerically equal to two'; but apart from the five words 'of, the, to, is, and' the words and phrases are terms in mathematics.

In this dictionary the symbols are given with the entries describing the mathematical terms. They are not defined here but are listed with one or two entry words that will explain them in context. The symbols are grouped where it is convenient to do so, but no attempt is made to order them.

Symbol	See under
$a, b, c, \ldots$	coefficient, abstract
$x, y, z, \ldots$	variable
$\mathbb{N}, \mathbb{Z}, \mathbb{Q}, \mathbb{R}, \mathbb{C}$	number system
$\forall, \exists, v$	quantifier
$A, B, C, \ldots$	matrix, set
$|x|, |A|$	absolute, determinant
$A \times B$	cartesian product, cross product
$(ABCD)$	cross ratio, permutation
$a_{ij}, |a_{ij}|$	array, determinant
$|(A^{(i)}|$	Cramer's rule
A^{T}, A'	transpose, complement
$\mathbf{L, M, T, I}$	dimensions
$^+a, ^-a$	directed numbers
x^1, x^2, x^3	contravariant
x_1, x_2, x_3	covariant
a^{-1}, A^{-1}	inverse, inverse matrix
$n!, \underline{|n}$	factorial
$\bar{a}, \bar{l}$	bar
$\mathbf{i, j, k}$	i, j, k, complex number
sin, cos, tan, cosec, csc, sec, cot, $\sin^{-1}$, etc., arc-sin, etc.	circular functions
sinh, cosh, tanh, etc. $\sinh^{-1}$, arsinh, etc.	hyberbolic functions
$f, f(x), f(a), f : x$	function
sn x	elliptic function
$\Gamma(x)$	gamma function
$B(s, t)$	beta function
$J_0(x)$	Bessel function
$S^\perp$	orthogonal complement
$f'(x), Df(x), \dfrac{df(x)}{dx}$	derivative
$Df, D^n f, f^{(n)}(x)$	derivative
$D(x, y)$	distance
$\ddot{x}, \ddot{y}$	dot notation
$e, \exp(x)$	exponential constant
$dx, d_a f$	differential
$\dfrac{\delta y}{\delta x}, f_1(x), D_1 f$	partial differentiation
log, ln	logarithm
$\bar{0}, \bar{1}, \bar{2}$	cardinal
$\int, \iint$	integral, repeated integral
$\displaystyle\int_a^b f(x)\,dx$	definite integral
$=, \equiv$	equality, equation
$\neq, <, \leqslant, >, \geqslant$	inequality
$[a, b]$	closed interval
(a, b)	open interval
$[\![x]\!]$	greatest integer
$\lim, x \to$	limit
$\in$	*estis*, convergence
S_n	series
U_n, SU_n	unitary group
$R\,|\,N, G\,|\,H$	difference ring, quotient set
π	pi
ω	angular velocity, *n*th root of unity
γ	Euler's constant
$\phi(n)$	primitive roots
$\emptyset$	empty set
δ, Δ	difference operator, discriminant
$\delta x, \Delta x$	increment
δ, δ_{ij}	Dirac function, Krönecker delta
∇	differential operator
λ, μ, ν	direction cosines
$\cup, \cap, \backslash$	union, intersection, complement
$\subset, \subseteq, \Delta$	proper subset, symmetric difference
$o(g), O(g)$	order of magnitude
$\aleph_0$	transfinite cardinal
∞	infinity
$\|\ \|$	Banach space
$\approx$	approximation
$N(0, 1)$	standard normal distribution
χ^2	*chi* squared
$p(A)$	probability
$p(A\,|\,B)$	conditional probability
$\sigma^2, \sigma, \hat{\sigma}^2, s$	variance, standard deviation
$*, \circ$	abstract, composite function
$\dbinom{n}{r}, \,^nC_r$	combination
$\mathbf{a.b}, \langle \mathbf{a}, \mathbf{b} \rangle$	scalar product
$[\mathbf{a}, \mathbf{b}, \mathbf{c}]$	scalar triple product
$\mathbf{a} \times \mathbf{b}, \mathbf{a} \vee \mathbf{b}$	vector product
$+$	addition, Boolean algebra
$-, \sim$	subtraction, difference
$\times, .$	multiplication
Σ	summation
Π	infinite product
$\{\}$	set, sequence
$\vdash$	assertion
$\longleftrightarrow, \Leftrightarrow, \sim, \&, \vee, \underline{v}, \mapsto$	connectives

229

∧ , ∩, ,, →, ⇒, ,
° , " '''

√

connectives
angular measure, duo—
decimals
radical

The letters of the Greek alphabet, developed from Phoenicean originals and still retaining their semitic names, are used widely in mathematics

alpha	A	α		nu	N	ν
beta	B	β		ksi	Ξ	ξ
gamma	Γ	γ		omicron	O	o
delta	Δ	δ		pi	Π	π
epsilon	E	ε		rho	P	ρ
zeta	Z	ζ		sigma	Σ	σ
eta	H	η		tau	T	τ
theta	Θ	θ		upsilon	U	υ
iota	I	ι		phi	Φ	φ
kappa	K	κ		chi	X	χ

lambda	Λ	λ		psi	Ψ	ψ
mu	M	μ		omega	Ω	ω

The ancient Greeks did not use the 'small' letters, which only arose during the 7th century A.D. or later for speed in writing. To show their relative sizes and positions when written they are here printed in a line.

α β γ δ ε ζ η θ ι κ λ μ ν ξ o π ρ σ τ υ φ χ ψ ω

The form ς for final sigma is not used in mathematics.

Symbols for vectors are usually printed in bold roman type, those for sets and matrices can be roman or bold roman capitals, or italic capitals. In general, italic is used in printing mathematics to avoid confusion when symbols are in a prose context. This dictionary uses roman capitals for labelling geometrical figures.